# Medical Spanish

A Conversational Approach

# Medical Spanish

## A Conversational Approach

*Second Edition*

**Thomas P. Kearon, M.A., M.S.**

**Maria Antonia DiLorenzo-Kearon, Ph.D.**

HEINLE
CENGAGE Learning

Australia • Brazil • Japan • Korea • Mexico • Singapore • Spain • United Kingdom • United States

**HEINLE**
CENGAGE Learning™

**Medical Spanish: A Conversational Approach, Second Edition**

Thomas P. Kearon, Maria Antonia DiLorenzo-Kearon, Ph.D.

Publisher: Phyllis Dobbins

Acquisitions Editor: Jeff Gilbreath

Market Strategist: Kenneth S. Kassee

Project Editor: Mary K. Coman

Project Editor: Jon Davies

Art Director: Michelle Krabill

Production Manager: Angela Williams Urquhart

Cover images: (from top) © Jeff Kaufman/FPG International; Michael Krasowitz/FPG International; Art Montes de Oca/FPG International

For product information and technology assistance, contact us at **Cengage Learning Customer & Sales Support, 1-800-354-9706**

For permission to use material from this text or product, submit all requests online at **cengage.com/permissions**
Further permissions questions can be e-mailed to **permissionrequest@cengage.com**

Library of Congress Catalog Card Number: 99-60180

ISBN-13: 978-0-03-031106-2

ISBN-10: 0-03-031106-3

**Heinle**
25 Thomson Place
Boston, MA 02210
USA

Cengage Learning is a leading provider of customized learning solutions with office locations around the globe, including Singapore, the United Kingdom, Australia, Mexico, Brazil, and Japan. Locate your local office at: **international.cengage.com/region**

Cengage Learning products are represented in Canada by Nelson Education, Ltd.

For your course and learning solutions, visit **academic.cengage.com**

Purchase any of our products at your local college store or at our preferred online store **www.ichapters.com**

Printed in the United States of America
11 12 13 09

# Preface

Since the first edition of *Medical Spanish: A Conversational Approach* was published in 1981, the demand for instructional materials for health professionals has increased tremendously. Hispanic Americans continue to be the fastest growing ethnic minority in the United States, and health-care providers in all major areas of the country are ever more cognizant of the need for a basic conversational knowledge of Spanish. At the same time, professionals in all health fields find themselves with increasing demands on their time. Therefore, they can truly benefit from a course that is specifically tailored to their needs.

This edition has been significantly updated both in terms of content and methodology. Important changes have occurred in the field of health care and disease in the past twenty years. With this in mind, we have added material on drug abuse, communicable diseases, and sexually transmitted diseases, with special attention focused on HIV and AIDS. Perhaps more importantly, the focus of the book has moved farther away from grammar presented in isolation and has taken on a more conversational character. Structure, grammar, and syntax are presented in context. Most of the translation and yes-no drills have been replaced with more creative activities such as role-playing and progressive substitution drills. Also included are ample activities that can be practiced with a partner.

The organization of the text, however, remains basically unchanged. The medical topics are also similar to those in the first edition. The conversations in each chapter are used as springboards for the introduction of medical terminology and language patterns. These are subsequently explained in short notes, then expanded through drills and practices.

Each chapter also contains a **Nota cultural,** which provides some basic information about cultural points of interest to the health professional. These cultural notes are not intended to offer a complete study of culture, but rather to provide a fundamental understanding of cultural differences and to generate some interest and motivation for students to learn more. At the end of each chapter, there is a short summary that includes additional grammar and/or vocabulary pertinent to that lesson.

We have also decided to include a basic discussion and practice of the subjunctive toward the end of the book. It is presented in a simplified fashion, always in context, and relevant to the needs of the health professional. We feel that some use of the subjunctive is essential to effective communication. It can be easily omitted, however, by the instructor who feels that it is outside the scope of his or her curriculum.

We are also pleased that this edition contains a substantially greater quantity of graphics than the first, with additional line drawings throughout the text as well as photographs and realia items. All of these features not only enhance the visual quality of the text but also can be used as vehicles for discussion and conversation.

The audio CD included with the textbook follows the scope and sequence of the text. Some of the material, such as the vocabulary lists, is taken directly from the text, but much of the material is unique to the CD and expands on the practice that is provided in the textbook. The audio icon located in various places throughout the textbook indicates that additional material can be found on the audio CD. The audio portion can be used in conjunction with the text or it can stand alone.

The workbook that accompanies this edition of *Medical Spanish* also follows the organization of the textbook but contains expanded drills for written practice and reinforcement of the material in the text.

## Acknowledgments

We would like to take this opportunity to express our appreciation to our colleagues who reviewed this manuscript:

Amalía S. Tio, *Cornell University*

Margaret Lyman, *Bakersfield College*

José A. Carmona, *Daytona Beach Community College*

Tom Manzo, *Jamestown College*

Humberto Delgado-Jenkins, *DeKalb College*

We would also like to thank our editorial consultant, Professor June K. Laval of Kennesaw State University and the accuracy reviewers that reviewed the final stages of the text to ensure medical accuracy and proper Spanish usage: Jim Stapleton, University of New Mexico Medical School; Carol Heald, University of New Mexico Continuing Education; and June K. Laval, Kennesaw State University. Holt, Rinehart and Winston gave us the editorial guidance needed to complete this edition, and we would like to thank the team members: Phyllis Dobbins, publisher; Jeff Gilbreath, acquisitions editor; Mary K. Mayo, developmental editor; Jon Davies, project editor; Michelle Krabill, art director; and Angela Urquhart, production manager.

Thomas P. Kearon

Maria Antonia DiLorenzo-Kearon

# Student Listening CD Script

[Directions to the actors or the person recording are in brackets and should not be heard. The directions in **_bold italics_** are to the student and should be read aloud.]

*Medical Spanish: A Conversational Approach,* Second Edition, by Thomas Kearon and Maria DiLorenzo Kearon.

## CAPÍTULO PRELIMINAR

*(The following exercises can be found printed in the front matter of your textbook.)*

## LA PRONUNCIACIÓN

### Las vocales

***Let's practice pronunciation by repeating the sounds of Spanish. Pay special attention to the sounds of the vowels in these words.***

***Repita:***

[Pause between each word for the student to repeat.]

| a | e | i | o | u |
|------|------|------|------|------|
| ma | me | mi | mo | mu |
| tapa | nene | vida | todo | pudo |
| pata | mate | mide | codo | mudo |
| cama | mesa | cine | palo | sube |

[Pause to indicate new exercise.]

### Las consonantes

***Now let's practice the consonants.***

***Repita:***

[Pause between each word for the student to repeat.]

| casa | ocho | habla | señor | roto |
|------|------|------|------|------|
| como | gato | hombre | riñón | carro |
| acción | agua | jota | queso | avión |
| cine | gota | jitano | quijada | vidrio |
| ceja | gente | llama | cara | zapato |
| chiste | gitano | mejilla | brazo | feliz |

*Kihada*

[Pause to indicate new exercise.]

***Listen to these sentences and repeat them. Try to be aware of which syllable receives the greatest stress.***

***Repita:***

[Pause between each sentence for the student to repeat.]

La mamá habla con el médico.
[Pause.]
El brazo está fracturado.
[Pause.]
El hombre usa los músculos para trabajar.
[Pause.]
El médico pone el libro sobre la mesa.
[Pause.]
Usted tiene una úlcera.

[Pause to indicate new exercise.]

***Listen and repeat the following examples. Notice how the final vowel of one word will often join with the initial unstressed vowel of the next word.***

***Repita:***

[Pause between each sentence for the student to repeat.]

Tomé esta medicina.
Mira hacia arriba.
Como ahora.
Llego a las dos.
Como en la cafetería.

[Pause to indicate new section.]

## SALUDOS Y CORTESÍAS

### Expresiones básicas

***Repeat the following basic vocabulary and expressions.***

***Repita:***

[Pause only after the Spanish sentences for the student to repeat. The student will hear the English translations, but there should be no pause after them. English will generally come first, followed by the Spanish translation.

The Spanish translation should be repeated as indicated.]

Good morning
Buenos días. [Pause.] Buenos días.

What is your name?
¿Cómo se llama usted? [Pause.] ¿Cómo se llama usted?

Pleased to meet you.
Mucho gusto. [Pause.] Mucho gusto.

The pleasure is mine.
El gusto es mío. [Pause.] El gusto es mío.

Good afternoon.
Buenas tardes. [Pause.] Buenas tardes.

How are you?
¿Cómo está usted? [Pause.] ¿Cómo está usted?

Fine, thanks.
Bien, gracias. [Pause.] Bien, gracias.

And yourself?
¿Y usted? [Pause.] ¿Y usted?

I am sick.
Estoy enfermo. [Pause.] Estoy enfermo.

What's wrong?
¿Qué le pasa? [Pause.] ¿Qué le pasa?

I'm in pain.
Tengo dolor. [Pause.] Tengo dolor.

Excuse me.
Perdón. [Pause.] Perdón.

How can I help you?
¿En qué puedo servirle? [Pause.] ¿En qué puedo servirle?

Where is the bathroom?
¿Dónde está el baño? [Pause.] ¿Dónde está el baño?

It's on the right.
Está a la derecha. [Pause.] Está a la derecha.

It's on the left.
Está a la izquierda. [Pause.] Está a la izquierda.

Please.
Por favor. [Pause.] Por favor.

Thank you.
Gracias. [Pause.] Gracias.

You're welcome.
De nada. [Pause.] De nada.

[Pause to indicate new exercise.]

*Play the role of the health care provider in the conversation by supplying the lines (in Spanish) in the pauses provided.*

[Two actors—male doctor, male patient; do not record speaker designations—only spoken dialogue and directions.]

**Patient:** Buenos días, doctor.

*Say:*
Good morning, sir. What's your name?
[Pause for the student to give the answer, then the second actor gives the correct answer.]
**Doctor:** Buenos días señor. ¿Cómo se llama? [This is the answer that the student should give. The second actor says it after the pause so that the student can compare his answer with the correct response.]
**Patient:** Me llamo Francisco Rivera.

*Say:*
Pleased to meet you.
[Pause.]
**Doctor:** Mucho gusto.
**Patient:** El gusto es mío.

*Say:*
How can I help you?
[Pause.]
**Doctor:** ¿En qué puedo servirle?
**Patient:** Tengo dolor.

[Pause to indicate new exercise.]

*Listen to the following dates and translate them into Spanish during the pauses provided.*

Friday, January fourteenth [Pause.]
viernes, el catorce de enero

Monday, the fifth of November [Pause.]
lunes, el cinco de noviembre

Wednesday, the twenty-first of August [Pause.]
miércoles, el veintiuno de agosto

Thursday, the tenth of September [Pause.]
jueves, el diez de septiembre

[Pause to indicate new chapter.]

# CAPÍTULO UNO
## ¿DÓNDE TIENE UD. DOLOR?

*(The following exercises can be found printed in the front matter of your textbook.)*

*Escuche la conversación. Listen to the conversation.*

[Two actors—male doctor, male patient; do not record speaker designations—only spoken dialogue.]

**Doctor:** Buenos días, señor Vega. ¿Cómo está Ud. hoy?
**Patient:** Estoy muy mal, doctor Rivera. Tengo escalofríos.

**Doctor:** ¿Tiene Ud. dolor de cabeza?
**Patient:** Sí, tengo un dolor de cabeza muy fuerte.
**Doctor:** ¿Tiene Ud. dolor de estómago?
**Patient:** Sí, también tengo dolor de estómago.
**Doctor:** ¿Tiene Ud. diarrea?
**Patient:** No, no tengo diarrea.
**Doctor:** ¿Tiene Ud. la garganta irritada?
**Patient:** Sí, y además tengo mucha flema.
**Doctor:** ¿Desde cuándo tiene Ud. estos síntomas?
**Patient:** Desde ayer.

[Pause to indicate new exercise.]

*Repita el vocabulario:*

to have diarrhea
tener diarrea [Pause.] tener diarrea

to have a headache
tener dolor de cabeza [Pause.] tener dolor de cabeza

to have a stomachache
tener dolor de estómago [Pause.] tener dolor de
  estómago

to have chills
tener escalofríos [Pause.] tener escalofríos

to have a sore throat
tener la garganta irritada [Pause.] tener la garganta
  irritada

to have a lot of phlegm
tener mucha flema [Pause.] tener mucha flema

to have symptoms
tener síntomas [Pause.] tener síntomas

[Pause to indicate new exercise.]

*Let's combine these expressions with some other vocabulary that you already know to form new sentences. In Spanish, say the new sentence aloud in the pause provided.*

*Say:*
I have chills.
[Pause after the English sentence, then give the Spanish
  translation.]
Yo tengo escalofríos.

*Say:*
The patient has chills.
[Pause.]
El paciente tiene escalofríos.

*Say:*
The patient has a headache.
[Pause.]
El paciente tiene dolor de cabeza.

*Say:*
Mrs. García has a headache.

[Pause.]
La señora García tiene dolor de cabeza.

*Say:*
We have a sore throat.
[Pause.]
Nosotros tenemos la garganta irritada.

*Say:*
They have a sore throat.
[Pause.]
Ellos tienen la garganta irritada.

*Say:*
They have many symptoms.
[Pause.]
Ellos tienen muchos síntomas.

[Pause to indicate new chapter.]

# CAPÍTULO DOS
# ¿CÓMO ESTÁ UD.?

*(The following exercises can be found printed in the front matter of your textbook.)*

*Escuche la conversación:*

[Two actors—male nurse, female patient; do not record speaker designations—only spoken dialogue.]

**Nurse:** ¿Cómo está Ud. hoy, señora Moreno?
**Patient:** No estoy bien. Estoy inquieta y nerviosa.
  Tengo miedo.
**Nurse:** Favor de hablar más despacio. ¿Por qué tiene
  Ud. miedo, señora?
**Patient:** Mi familia no está aquí. Tengo miedo del
  procedimiento que van a hacer mañana.
**Nurse:** ¿Dónde está su familia?
**Patient:** Mi familia está en El Salvador.
**Nurse:** No se preocupe, señora. Todo está bien. No hay
  problema. ¿Está Ud. cansada?
**Patient:** Sí, estoy cansada, y además estoy muy
  preocupada.
**Nurse:** ¿Por qué no toma Ud. un vaso de agua?
**Patient:** Muchas gracias, señor. Ahora estoy tranquila.

[Pause to indicate new exercise.]

*Repita el vocabulario:*

[Say the English first, but do not pause.]

bored
aburrido, aburrida [Pause.] aburrido, aburrida

upset
agitado, agitada [Pause.] agitado, agitada

exhausted
agotado, agotada [Pause.] agotado, agotada

anxious
ansioso, ansiosa [Pause.] ansioso, ansiosa

drunk
borracho, borracha [Pause.] borracho, borracha

confused
confundido, confundida [Pause.] confundido, confundida

content
contento, contenta [Pause.] contento, contenta

depressed
deprimido, deprimida [Pause.] deprimido, deprimida

awake
despierto, despierta [Pause.] despierto, despierta

asleep
dormido, dormida [Pause.] dormido, dormida

sick
enfermo, enferma [Pause.] enfermo, enferma

angry
enojado, enojada [Pause.] enojado, enojada

sober
sobrio, sobria [Pause.] sobrio, sobria

[Pause to indicate new exercise.]

*Escuche la conversacion:*

[Use the same actors as in the previous conversation; do not record speaker designations—only spoken dialogue.]

**Nurse:** Buenos días, señora Moreno. Ud. tiene la operación el miércoles. ¿Dónde está su esposo?
**Patient:** Mi esposo está en El Salvador.
**Nurse:** ¿Cuántos hijos tiene Ud.?
**Patient:** Tengo dos hijos y una hija.
**Nurse:** ¿Dónde están sus hijos?
**Patient:** Mis hijos no están aquí. Mi hija está en la sala de espera.
**Nurse:** ¿Tiene Ud. otros parientes aquí?
**Patient:** Sí, mi hermano está en la oficina de ingresos.

*Now answer the following questions in English in the pauses provided.*

When is the patient having an operation?
[Pause for the student to give the answer, then say:]
On Wednesday.

Where is her husband?
[Pause.]
In El Salvador.

How many children does she have?
[Pause.]
Two sons and one daughter.

Where is her daughter?
[Pause.]
In the waiting room.

Who is in the Admissions Office?
[Pause.]
Her brother.

[Pause to indicate new chapter.]

# Capítulo tres
## El cuerpo

*(The following exercises can be found printed in the front matter of your textbook.)*

*Play the role of the health care provider in the conversation by supplying the lines (in Spanish) in the pauses provided.*

[Two actors—female doctor, male patient; do not record speaker designations—only spoken dialogue and directions.]

Patient: Buenas tardes, doctora.

*Say:*
Good afternoon, sir. Do you speak English?
[Pause for the student to give the answer, then the second actor gives the correct answer.]
**Doctor:** Buenas tardes, señor. ¿Habla Ud. inglés?
**Patient:** No, no hablo inglés, solamente hablo español.

*Ask:*
Where does it hurt?
[Pause.]
**Doctor:** ¿Dónde tiene dolor?
**Patient:** Tengo dolor de estómago.

*Ask:*
Are you nauseous?
[Pause.]
**Doctor:** ¿Tiene Ud. náuseas?
**Patient:** Sí, tengo náuseas.

*Ask:*
Do you have an appetite?
[Pause.]
**Doctor:** ¿Tiene Ud. apetito?
**Patient:** No, doctora, no tengo apetito.

*Ask:*
For how long have you had the pain?
[Pause.]
**Doctor:** ¿Desde cuándo tiene Ud. dolor?
**Patient:** Desde hace una semana.

*Ask:*
Are you taking some medicine for the pain?
[Pause.]

**Doctor:** ¿Toma Ud. alguna medicina para el dolor?
**Patient:** No, doctora, no tomo nada.

*Say:*
You need a medical examination.
[Pause.]
**Doctor:** Ud. necesita un examen médico.
**Patient:** Muy bien, doctora.

[Pause to indicate new exercise.]

*Repita el vocabulario:*

the head
la cabeza [Pause.] la cabeza

the eyes
los ojos [Pause.] los ojos

the ears
las orejas [Pause.] las orejas

the mouth
la boca [Pause.] la boca

the nose
la nariz [Pause.] la nariz

the hair
el cabello [Pause.] el cabello

the throat
la garganta [Pause.] la garganta

the face
la cara [Pause.] la cara

the neck
el cuello [Pause.] el cuello

the back
la espalda [Pause.] la espalda

the chest
el pecho [Pause.] el pecho

the arm
el brazo [Pause.] el brazo

the shoulder
el hombro [Pause.] el hombro

the hand
la mano [Pause.] la mano

the fingers
los dedos [Pause.] los dedos

the stomach
el estómago [Pause.] el estómago

the leg
la pierna [Pause.] la pierna

the foot
el pie [Pause.] el pie

the toes
los dedos del pie [Pause.] los dedos del pie

[Pause to indicate new exercise.]

*Now, listen to the conversation and answer the questions that follow.*

[Two actors—female doctor, female patient; do not record speaker designations—only spoken dialogue.]

**Patient:** ¿Qué me va a hacer, doctora?
**Doctor:** Le voy a dar un examen médico.
**Patient:** ¿Me va a doler?
**Doctor:** No. Le voy a auscultar, y le voy a tomar la presión. Muy bien. Su presión está en ciento treinta sobre ochenta y dos.
**Patient:** ¿Me va a hacer otras pruebas?
**Doctor:** Sí, vamos a tomar una muestra de sangre.
**Patient:** ¿Cuándo voy a saber los resultados?
**Doctor:** Vamos a saber los resultados dentro de dos o tres días.

*Now answer these questions in English in the pauses provided.*

How is the patient's blood pressure?
[Pause.]
Good.

What other test is the doctor going to do?
[Pause.]
The doctor will draw some blood.

[Pause to indicate new chapter.]

# CAPÍTULO CUATRO
## LAS COMIDAS Y LA NUTRICIÓN

*(The following exercises can be found printed in the front matter of your textbook.)*

*Escuche la conversación:*

[Two actors—female doctor, male patient; do not record speaker designations—only spoken dialogue.]

**Patient:** Doctora, me duele el estómago.
**Doctor:** ¿Cuándo le duele más?
**Patient:** Me duele más por la mañana y antes de comer.
**Doctor:** ¿Cómo es el dolor?
**Patient:** Es como un ardor.
**Doctor:** Creo que Ud. tiene gastritis. Vamos a hacerle algunas pruebas. Pero Ud. tiene que seguir una dieta especial.
**Patient:** ¿Qué dieta debo seguir, doctora?
**Doctor:** Ud. debe evitar las comidas fritas, picantes y grasientas. Ud. debe evitar también el alcohol, el café y los cigarrillos. Ud. debe comer las comidas blandas,

el pan blanco, las sopas calientes y las carnes asadas sin especias.

**Patient:** Es una dieta muy estricta. ¿Por cuánto tiempo debo seguirla?

**Doctor:** Ud. debe seguir la dieta por seis semanas.

**Patient:** ¿Puede Ud. recetarme algo?

**Doctor:** Ud. debe tomar un antiácido, pero para eso no se necesita una receta. Se puede comprar en cualquier farmacia.

[Pause to indicate new exercise.]

*Repita las frases. Repeat these sentences using the new vocabulary.*

Ud. debe evitar las comidas fritas.
[Pause.]
Ud. debe evitar las comidas picantes.
[Pause.]
Ud. debe evitar el café.
[Pause.]
Ud. debe comer mucha fruta.
[Pause.]
Ud. debe comer muchos vegetales.
[Pause.]
Ud. debe comer mucho pescado.
[Pause.]
Ud. debe usar pocas especias.
[Pause.]
Ud. debe tomar un antiácido.
[Pause.]
Ud. no debe tomar cerveza.
[Pause.]
Ud. debe beber mucha agua.
[Pause.]
Ud. debe seguir una dieta equilibrada.
[Pause.]
Ud. debe seguir una dieta blanda.
[Pause.]
Ud. debe seguir un régimen estricto.
[Pause.]

[Pause to indicate new exercise.]

*Answer the following questions according to the cues provided.*

¿Cuál prefiere Ud., el té o el café?                    el té
[Pause for the student to give the answer, then give the correct answer.]
Yo prefiero el té.

¿Cuál prefieren Uds., el pescado o la carne?        la carne
[Pause.]
Nosotros preferimos la carne.

¿Cuál prefieres tú, la pera o la manzana?        la manzana
[Pause.]
Yo prefiero la manzana.

¿Cuál prefiere la doctora, el pan blanco o el pan de trigo?                    el pan blanco
[Pause.]
La doctora prefiere el pan blanco.

[Pause to indicate new section.]

## LECTURA

*Listen to the following passage, then answer the questions that follow in Spanish.*

La nutrición es muy importante para la salud de cualquier individuo. Para evitar las enfermedades, es necesario seguir una dieta equilibrada. Se debe de comer comidas ricas en proteína como la carne, la leche, los cereales, el queso y los huevos. También se debe comer vegetales ricos en vitaminas como la lechuga, la espinaca, los guisantes, el maíz y el apio.

Cuando un individuo sufre de una enfermedad específica, debe seguir una dieta especial. Por ejemplo, la persona que sufre de una enfermedad gastrointestinal debe seguir una dieta blanda. Para el paciente que sufre de la alta presión, se recomienda una dieta de sal reducida. El médico o el dietista es responsable de recomendarle al paciente la dieta más beneficiosa para su salud y bienestar.

*Answer the following questions in Spanish.*

¿Es importante la nutrición?
[Pause.]
Si, la nutrición es importante.

¿Cuáles son las comidas ricas en proteína?
[Pause.]
Las comidas ricas en proteína son esas como la carne, la leche, los cereales, el queso y los huevos.

¿Cuáles son algunos vegetales?
[Pause.]
Algunos vegetales son el maíz, el apio, los guisantes y la lechuga.

[Pause to indicate new chapter.]

# CAPÍTULO CINCO
## ¿QUÉ HORA ES?

*(The following exercises can be found printed in the front matter of your textbook.)*

*Escuche la conversación:*

[Three actors—young woman receptionist, male patient, female doctor; do not record speaker designations—only spoken dialogue.]

**Patient:** Buenos días, señorita.

**Receptionist:** Buenos días, señor. ¿En qué puedo servirle?
**Patient:** Tengo una cita con la doctora Méndez.
**Receptionist:** ¿A qué hora es su cita?
**Patient:** Es a las once.
**Receptionist:** Muy bien, señor. La doctora va a llegar a las once y media. Favor de llenar este formulario. Puede sentarse.
**Patient:** Gracias, señorita.

[Pause.]

**Patient:** Buenos días, doctora.
**Doctor:** Buenos días, señor Reyes. ¿Cómo se siente Ud. hoy?
**Patient:** No me siento bien, doctora. Me duele toda la cabeza. Me duelen los ojos, la nariz y los oídos.
**Doctor:** ¿Desde cuándo se siente así?
**Patient:** Desde hace un par de semanas.
**Doctor:** Ud. tiene un caso de sinusitis. Tiene la nariz tapada y los oídos tapados también. Además, Ud. tiene la presión un poco alta, y tiene un poco de temperatura.
**Patient:** ¿Qué debo hacer, doctora?
**Doctor:** Yo le receto un antibiótico que Ud. debe tomar cada seis horas. También, debe tomar muchos líquidos y descansar mucho.
**Patient:** Muchas gracias, doctora.
**Doctor:** De nada, señor. Adiós.

[Pause to indicate new exercise.]

*Repita el vocabulario:*

the head
la cabeza [Pause.] la cabeza

the eyes
los ojos [Pause.] los ojos

the nose
la nariz [Pause.] la nariz

the ears
las orejas [Pause.] las orejas

the ears
los oídos [Pause.] los oídos

the mouth
la boca [Pause.] la boca

the scalp
el cuero cabelludo [Pause.] el cuero cabelludo

the hair
el pelo [Pause.] el pelo

the forehead
la frente [Pause.] la frente

the eyebrows
las cejas [Pause.] las cejas

the temple
la sien [Pause.] la sien

the cheek
la mejilla [Pause.] la mejilla

the nostrils
las fosas nasales [Pause.] las fosas nasales

the jaw
la quijada [Pause.] la quijada

the jaw
la mandíbula [Pause.] la mandíbula

the neck
el cuello [Pause.] el cuello

the Adam's apple
la nuez de Adán [Pause.] la nuez de Adán

[Pause to indicate new exercise.]

*Say the following sentences in Spanish.*

The doctor is going to arrive at eleven thirty.
[Pause for the student to give the answer, then give the correct answer.]
La doctora va a llegar a las once y media.

The doctor is going to leave at two thirty.
[Pause.]
La doctora va a salir a las dos y media.

The patient is going to arrive at three.
[Pause.]
El paciente va a llegar a las tres.

The patients are going to leave at four ten.
[Pause.]
Los pacientes van a salir a las cuatro y diez.

[Pause to indicate new exercise.]

*Play the role of the health care provider in this conversation. After the English is said, translate the sentence into Spanish in the pause provided.*

[Two actors—male doctor, female patient; do not record speaker designations—only spoken dialogue and directions.]

*Ask:*
Do you sleep enough?
[Pause for the student to give the answer, then the first actor gives the correct answer.]
**Doctor:** ¿Duerme Ud. bastante?
[The second actor responds.]
**Patient:** No, no duermo mucho.

*Ask:*
How many hours do you sleep every night?
[Pause.]
**Doctor:** ¿Cuántas horas duerme Ud. cada noche?

**Patient:** Duermo solamente cinco o seis horas cada noche.

*Ask:*

What time do you go to bed?

[Pause.]

**Doctor:** ¿A qué hora se acuesta?

**Patient:** Me acuesto a las once de la noche.

*Ask:*

What time do you wake up?

[Pause.]

**Doctor:** ¿A qué hora se despierta Ud.?

**Patient:** Me despierto a las cinco de la madrugada para ir a trabajar muy temprano.

*Ask:*

Do you fall asleep right away?

[Pause.]

**Doctor:** ¿Se duerme Ud. en seguida?

**Patient:** No. Muchas veces no me duermo en seguida.

*Ask:*

Why?

[Pause.]

**Doctor:** ¿Por qué?

**Patient:** Porque estoy muy nerviosa.

[Pause to indicate new chapter.]

# CAPÍTULO SEIS
# LAS ENFERMEDADES CONTAGIOSAS Y LA HISTORIA CLÍNICA

*(The following exercises can be found printed in the front matter of your textbook.)*

*Escuche la conversación:*

[Two actors—male doctor, male patient; do not record speaker designations—only spoken dialogue.]

**Doctor:** Antes de examinarle a Ud., tengo que hacerle algunas preguntas.

**Patient:** Está bien, doctor.

**Doctor:** ¿Toma Ud. alguna medicina?

**Patient:** No, doctor, no tomo nada.

**Doctor:** ¿Ha tenido Ud. alguna vez una operación?

**Patient:** Sí, doctor, tuve una operación del apéndice.

**Doctor:** ¿Cuándo tuvo la operación?

**Patient:** Tuve la operación hace dos años.

**Doctor:** ¿Ha tenido el sarampión, la varicela o la rubéola?

**Patient:** Sí, doctor, he tenido todas esas enfermedades.

**Doctor:** ¿Ha tenido Ud. una prueba de la tuberculina?

**Patient:** Sí, doctor, hace un año, con resultados negativos.

**Doctor:** ¿Ha tenido Ud. las paperas, la viruela o la tos ferina?

**Patient:** No, doctor, nunca he tenido esas enfermedades.

[Pause to indicate new section.]

## LAS ENFERMEDADES Y LAS DOLENCIAS

*Repitan el vocabulario:*

tonsillitis
la amigdalitis [Pause.] la amigdalitis

bronchitis
la bronquitis [Pause.] la bronquitis

cataracts
las cataratas [Pause.] las cataratas

diarrhea
la diarrea [Pause.] la diarrea

diphtheria
la difteria [Pause.] la difteria

dysentery
la disentería [Pause.] la disentería

phlegm
la flema [Pause.] la flema

gastritis
la gastritis [Pause.] la gastritis

glaucoma
el glaucoma [Pause.] el glaucoma

flu
la gripe [Pause.] la gripe

hemorrhoids
los hemorroides [Pause.] los hemorroides

hepatitis
la hepatitis [Pause.] la hepatitis

laryngitis
la laringitis [Pause.] la laringitis

meningitis
la meningitis [Pause.] la meningitis

pneumonia
la pulmonía [Pause.] la pulmonía

a cold
un resfriado [Pause.] un resfriado

typhoid
la tifoidea [Pause.] la tifoidea

tuberculosis
la tuberculosis [Pause.] la tuberculosis

vaccines
las vacunas [Pause.] las vacunas

[Pause to indicate new exercise.]

*In the pause provided, ask the patient the following questions in Spanish.*

Have you had problems with your hearing?
[Pause for the student to give the answer, then give the correct answer:]
¿Ha tenido problemas del oído?

Have you suffered from problems with your eyes?
[Pause.]
¿Ha sufrido de problemas con los ojos?

Have you ever had pneumonia?
[Pause.]
¿Ha tenido alguna vez la pulmonía?

Have you had the mumps?
[Pause.]
¿Ha tenido paperas?

Have you had measles?
[Pause.]
¿Ha tenido sarampión?

Have you had German measles?
[Pause.]
¿Ha tenido rubéola?

Have you had chicken pox?
[Pause.]
¿Ha tenido varicela?

[Pause to indicate new section.]

## EL EXAMEN MÉDICO

*Repitan las frases:*

Open your mouth.
Abra la boca. [Pause.] Abra la boca.

Lie down.
Acuéstese. [Pause.] Acuéstese.

Close your mouth.
Cierre la boca. [Pause.] Cierre la boca.

Say, "ah."
Diga, «ah». [Pause.] Diga, «ah».

Get up.
Levántese. [Pause.] Levántese.

Take off your clothing.
Quítese la ropa. [Pause.] Quítese la ropa.

Breathe deeply.
Respire profundamente. [Pause.] Respire profundamente.

Stick out your tongue.
Saque la lengua. [Pause.] Saque la lengua.

Sit down.
Siéntese. [Pause.] Siéntese.

[Pause to indicate new exercise.]

*Play the role of the health care provider in the following conversation and supply the lines in the pauses provided.*

[Two actors—female doctor, male patient; do not record speaker designations—only spoken dialogue and directions.]

*Say:*
Take off your shirt and lie down, please.
[Pause for the student to give the answer, then the first actor gives the correct answer.]
**Doctor:** Quítese la camisa y acuéstese, por favor.
[The second actor responds.]
**Patient:** Muy bien, doctora.

*Say:*
Bend your right knee, please. Does it hurt now?
[Pause.]
**Doctor:** Doble la rodilla derecha, por favor. ¿Le duele ahora?
**Patient:** Sí, doctora, y me duele la espalda también.

*Say:*
Lie face down. Does it hurt here?
[Pause.]
**Doctor:** Acuéstese boca abajo. ¿Le duele aquí?
**Patient:** No, doctora.

*Say:*
Raise your arms. Does it hurt now?
[Pause.]
**Doctor:** Levante los brazos. ¿Le duele ahora?
**Patient:** Sí, doctora.

*Say:*
Get up and put on your shirt.
[Pause.]
**Doctor:** Levántese y póngase la camisa.

[Pause to indicate new chapter.]

# CAPÍTULO SIETE
# EN EL HOSPITAL; LOS ÓRGANOS

*(The following exercises can be found printed in the front matter of your textbook.)*

*Escuche la conversación:*

[Two actresses—female doctor, female patient; do not record speaker designations—only spoken dialogue.]

**Doctor:** Buenos días, señora Martínez. ¿Cómo se siente Ud. hoy?
**Patient:** No muy bien, doctora.
**Doctor:** ¿Qué le pasa? ¿Por qué está tan nerviosa?

**Patient:** Hace seis meses que tengo un bulto en el seno. Es grande y muy duro pero no tengo dolor. ¿Puede ser un quiste o un tumor?
**Doctor:** Trate de calmarse. Vamos a ver lo que tiene. Voy a examinarle el seno.
**Patient:** Estoy muy preocupada, doctora. Si es maligno, no quiero una mastectomía.
**Doctor:** Puedo sentir algo en el seno izquierdo. Puede ser un fibroma, pero no puedo hacer un diagnóstico ahora. Tenemos que hacer una mamografía.
**Patient:** ¿Qué es una mamografía?
**Doctor:** Es una radiografía del seno.
**Patient:** ¿Es necesario hacer la mamografía?
**Doctor:** Sí, y cuanto antes. Si es algo grave, es mejor descubrirlo inmediatamente.

[Pause to indicate new exercise.]

*Repita el vocabulario:*

the heart
el corazón [Pause.] el corazón

the lungs
los pulmones [Pause.] los pulmones

the stomach
el estómago [Pause.] el estómago

the liver
el hígado [Pause.] el hígado

the kidneys
los riñones [Pause.] los riñones

the intestines
los intestinos [Pause.] los intestinos

the pancreas
el páncreas [Pause.] el páncreas

the spleen
el bazo [Pause.] el bazo

the brain
el cerebro [Pause.] el cerebro

the colon
el colon [Pause.] el colon

the bladder
la vejiga [Pause.] la vejiga

the gallbladder
la vesícula biliar [Pause.] la vesícula biliar

the tonsils
las amígdalas [Pause.] las amígdalas

the nerves
los nervios [Pause.] los nervios

the bones
los huesos [Pause.] los huesos

[Pause to indicate new exercise.]

*You are interviewing a patient who has chest pains. Ask the following questions in Spanish.*

*Ask:*
Does it hurt all the time?
[Pause.]
¿Le duele todo el tiempo?

*Ask:*
How long has he/she had the pain?
[Pause.]
¿Cuánto tiempo hace que le duele?

*Ask:*
What kind of pain is it?
[Pause.]
¿Cómo es el dolor?

*Ask:*
Where does it hurt?
[Pause.]
¿Dónde le duele?

*Ask:*
Are there other symptoms?
[Pause.]
¿Hay otros síntomas?

[Pause to indicate new chapter.]

# CAPÍTULO OCHO
# EN LA SALA DE EMERGENCIAS

*(The following exercises can be found printed in the front matter of your textbook.)*

*Escuche la conversación:*

[Two actors—female patient, female doctor; do not record speaker designations—only spoken dialogue]

**Doctor:** Buenas tardes, señora. ¿Qué le pasó a su hijo?
**Patient:** Mi hijo se cortó el dedo y no deja de sangrar.
**Doctor:** ¿Cómo se llama Ud., señora?
**Patient:** Yo soy la señora Hernández, y mi hijo se llama Felipe.
**Doctor:** ¿Cuántos años tiene Felipe?
**Patient:** Tiene ocho años.
**Doctor:** ¿Cuándo se cortó?
**Patient:** Hace una hora que se cortó.
**Doctor:** ¿Cómo lo hizo?
**Patient:** Se cortó con un cuchillo.
**Doctor:** Voy a limpiarle la herida a su hijo y aplicarle una solución desinfectante. ¿Ha tenido Felipe una inyección para el tétano recientemente?
**Patient:** No, doctora.

[Pause to indicate new exercise.]

*Play the part of the health care professional in the following conversation. Say the sentences and questions in Spanish in the pauses provided.*

[Use the same actors as in the previous conversation; do not record speaker designations—only spoken dialogue and directions.]

*Say:*

Good morning, ma'am. What happened to your son?
[Pause for the student to give the answer, then the first actor gives the correct answer.]
**Doctor:** Buenos días, señora. ¿Qué le pasó a su hijo?
[The second actor responds.]
**Patient:** Mi hijo se cortó el dedo.

*Ask:*

What is your name?
[Pause.]
**Doctor:** ¿Cómo se llama?
**Patient:** Me llamo la señora Hernández.

*Ask:*

What is your son's name?
[Pause.]
**Doctor:** ¿Cómo se llama su hijo?
**Patient:** Mi hijo se llama Felipe.

*Ask:*

How old is Felipe?
[Pause.]
**Doctor:** ¿Cuántos años tiene Felipe?
**Patient:** Tiene ocho años.

*Ask:*

When did he cut himself?
[Pause.]
**Doctor:** ¿Cuándo se cortó?
**Patient:** Se cortó hace una hora.

*Ask:*

How did he cut himself?
[Pause.]
**Doctor:** ¿Cómo se cortó?
**Patient:** Se cortó con un cuchillo.

[Pause to indicate new chapter.]

# CAPÍTULO NUEVE
# LAS DROGAS Y EL ALCOHOLISMO

*(The following exercises can be found printed in the front matter of your textbook.)*

*Escuche la conversación:*

[Two actors—female doctor, female patient; do not record speaker designations—only spoken dialogue.]

**Patient:** Perdone, doctora, ¿puedo hablar con Ud.?

**Doctor:** Sí, por supuesto. ¿Cuál es su problema, señora?
**Patient:** Creo que mi hijo toma drogas.
**Doctor:** ¿Por qué cree Ud. eso?
**Patient:** Pues, anoche volvió a casa muy tarde, hablaba tonterías, y no sabía donde estaba.
**Doctor:** Posiblemente estaba borracho.
**Patient:** No, a veces mi marido viene a casa borracho y no es lo mismo.
**Doctor:** ¿Cuántos años tiene su hijo?
**Patient:** Tiene solamente catorce años.
**Doctor:** ¿Sabe Ud. qué drogas toma?
**Patient:** Creo que fuma la marihuana. Quizás toma cocaína o crack también, pero espero que no.
**Doctor:** ¿Ha encontrado alguna vez píldoras en el dormitorio de su hijo?
**Patient:** No. ¿Por qué?
**Doctor:** Porque las píldoras como los barbitúricos, las anfetaminas y otras son muy dañinas. Ud. debe traer a su hijo aquí para un examen médico.
**Patient:** Sí, creo que Ud. tiene razón, doctora. Muchas gracias por su ayuda.

[Pause to indicate new exercise.]

*Repita el vocabulario:*

the addict
el adicto [Pause.] el adicto

the hypodermic needle
la aguja hipodérmica [Pause.] la aguja hipodérmica

the alcohol
el alcohol [Pause.] el alcohol

the alcoholic
el alcohólico [Pause.] el alcohólico

the alcoholism
el alcoholismo [Pause.] el alcoholismo

the amphetamines
las anfetaminas [Pause.] las anfetaminas

the barbiturates
los barbitúricos [Pause.] los barbitúricos

the cocaine
la cocaína [Pause.] la cocaína

the codeine
la codeína [Pause.] la codeína

the crack
el crack [Pause.] el crack

the detoxification
la desintoxicación [Pause.] la desintoxicación

the overdose
la dosis excesiva [Pause.] la dosis excesiva

the addiction to drugs
la drogadicción [Pause.] la drogadicción

the heroin
la heroína [Pause.] la heroína

the injection
la inyección [Pause.] la inyección

the teenager
el jovencito, la jovencita [Pause.] el jovencito,
    la jovencita

the marijuana
la marihuana [Pause.] la marihuana

the methadone
la metadona [Pause.] la metadona

the narcotics addict
el narcómano, la narcómana [Pause.] el narcómano,
    la narcómana

the narcotics
los narcóticos [Pause.] los narcóticos

the overdose
la sobredosis [Pause.] la sobredosis

the withdrawal
la suspensión del uso [Pause.] la suspensión del uso

to drink
beber [Pause.] beber

to take; to drink (alcohol)
tomar [Pause.] tomar

to take drugs
usar drogas [Pause.] usar drogas

drunk
borracho, borracha [Pause.] borracho, borracha

[Pause to indicate new exercise.]

***Listen to each sentence and answer the question that fol-
lows in the pause provided.***

El adicto se envenenó ayer con una aguja sucia.
¿Quién se envenenó?
[Pause for the student to give the answer, then give the
    correct answer.]
El adicto se envenenó.

¿Cómo se envenenó?
[Pause.]
Se envenenó con una aguja sucia.

¿Cuándo se envenenó?
[Pause.]
Se envenenó ayer.

El hombre sufrió una sobredosis de heroína y murió
    anoche.

¿Quién sufrió una sobredosis?
[Pause.]
El hombre sufrió una sobredosis de heroína.

¿Qué le pasó al hombre?
[Pause.]
El hombre murió.

¿Cuándo se murió el hombre?
[Pause.]
El hombre murió anoche.

El paciente tenía huellas de aguja hipodérmica en ambos
    brazos.
¿Quién tenía huellas?
[Pause.]
El paciente tenía huellas.

¿Qué tenía el paciente?
[Pause.]
El paciente tenía huellas de aguja hipodérmica.

¿En qué parte del cuerpo tenía las huellas?
[Pause.]
Tenía huellas en ambos brazos.

[Pause to indicate new chapter.]

# CAPÍTULO DIEZ
# LA MATERNIDAD

***(The following exercises can be found printed in the
front matter of your textbook.)***

***Escuche la conversación:***

[Two actors—female doctor, female patient; do not
record speaker designations—only spoken dialogue]

**Doctor:** Los resultados del laboratorio indican que Ud.
    está encinta.
**Patient:** ¡No es posible! No puedo cuidar a un niño.
**Doctor:** ¿Cuántos años tiene Ud.?
**Patient:** Tengo solamente dieciocho años y no tengo
    dinero.
**Doctor:** ¿Tiene Ud. marido?
**Patient:** No, doctora. Tengo un novio, pero él no tiene
    trabajo.
**Doctor:** ¿Entonces, vive Ud. con sus padres?
**Patient:** Sí, pero no me van a ayudar porque no quieren
    problemas en su casa.
**Doctor:** Pues, si Ud. quiere, el niño o la niña puede ser
    adoptado fácilmente.
**Patient:** No, doctora. La verdad es que no quiero
    seguir con el embarazo. ¿Puede recomendarme la
    mejor clínica para tener un aborto?
**Doctor:** Por supuesto. Pero también le voy a dar
    información sobre algunos servicios sociales que le

pueden ayudar con el cuidado del niño, si Ud. decide no tener el aborto.

**Patient:** Muchas gracias por toda su ayuda, doctora.
**Doctor:** De nada, señorita.

[Pause to indicate new exercise.]

*Repita el vocabulario:*

the baby, the infant
el bebé [Pause.] el bebé

the bag of waters
la bolsa de aguas [Pause.] la bolsa de aguas

the cramps
los calambres [Pause.] los calambres

the midwife
la partera; la comadrona [Pause.] la partera;
   la comadrona

the contractions
las contracciones [Pause.] las contracciones

the umbilical cord
el cordón umbilical [Pause.] el cordón umbilical

the cervix
el cuello uterino [Pause.] el cuello uterino

the dilation
la dilatación [Pause.] la dilatación

the fetus
el feto [Pause.] el feto

the maternity
la maternidad [Pause.] la maternidad

the obstetrician
el obstétrico, la obstétrica [Pause.] el obstétrico,
   la obstétrica

the childbirth
el parto [Pause.] el parto

the delivery room
la sala de partos [Pause.] la sala de partos

to push
empujar [Pause.] empujar

to be pregnant
estar embarazada [Pause.] estar embarazada

to be pregnant
estar encinta [Pause.] estar encinta

to be born
nacer [Pause.] nacer

to weigh
pesar [Pause.] pesar

[Pause to indicate new exercise.]

*Take part in the following conversation by providing the questions as indicated. In the pauses provided ask the following questions in Spanish.*

[Two actors—female doctor, female patient; do not record speaker designations—only spoken dialogue and directions.]

*Ask:*
Is this your first pregnancy?
[Pause for the student to give the answer, then the first
   actor gives the correct answer.]
**Doctor:** ¿Es éste su primer embarazo?
[The second actor responds.]
**Patient:** No, es mi segundo.

*Ask:*
Have you ever had an abortion?
[Pause.]
**Doctor:** ¿Ha tenido Ud. alguna vez un aborto?
**Patient:** No, no he tenido nunca un aborto.

*Ask:*
Did you have problems with your first pregnancy?
[Pause.]
**Doctor:** ¿Tuvo Ud. problemas con su primer embarazo?
**Patient:** Sí, fue necesario hacer una operación cesárea.

[Pause to indicate new chapter.]

# CAPÍTULO ONCE
# EL CUIDADO POSTNATAL
# Y LA PEDIATRÍA

*(The following exercises can be found printed in the front matter of your textbook.)*

*Escuche la conversación:*

[Two actors—female patient, male doctor; do not record speaker designations—only spoken dialogue.]

**Patient:** Estoy muy preocupada, doctor.
**Doctor:** ¿Qué pasa?
**Patient:** Hace dos días que mi bebé llora todito el
   tiempo, y además creo que tiene fiebre.
**Doctor:** ¿Cuántos años tiene la criatura?
**Patient:** Tiene dieciséis meses de edad.
**Doctor:** ¿Tose mucho el niño?
**Patient:** Sí, tiene tos y tiene la garganta irritada
   también.
**Doctor:** ¿Tiene diarrea?
**Patient:** No, no tiene diarrea pero no quiere comer
   nada.
**Doctor:** Voy a examinarle al niño ahora.

[Pause to indicate a passage of time.]

**Doctor:** Acabo de examinar a su bebé, señora.
**Patient:** ¿Y qué le pasa?
**Doctor:** Tiene la temperatura en cien grados, y tiene una infección de la garganta que le ha llegado hasta los oídos.
**Patient:** ¿Es esto muy grave, doctor?
**Doctor:** Es bastante común en la niñez, pero si se deja sin tratar puede ser peligroso para el niño.
**Patient:** ¿Estará bien mi hijo?
**Doctor:** Sí, señora, no se preocupe. Le voy a dar un antibiótico para la infección y algo para aliviar el dolor de oído que sufre.
**Patient:** Muchas gracias, doctor.

[Pause to indicate new exercise.]

*In the pauses provided, say the following in Spanish.*

What's wrong?
[Pause.]
¿Qué le pasa?

How old is your baby?
[Pause.]
¿Cuántos años tiene su bebé?

Does the child cough much?
[Pause.]
¿Tose mucho el niño?

Does the child have diarrhea?
[Pause.]
¿Tiene el niño diarrea?

Does the child have an appetite?
[Pause.]
¿Tiene el niño apetito?

The child has a temperature of a hundred and two.
[Pause.]
El niño tiene la temperatura en ciento dos grados.

He has a throat infection.
[Pause.]
Tiene una infección de la garganta.

I am going to give him an antibiotic.
[Pause.]
Voy a darle un antibiótico.

The child should get a lot of rest.
[Pause.]
El niño debe descansar mucho.

[Pause to indicate new chapter.]

# Capítulo doce
# Las enfermedades crónicas y degenerativas—el cáncer, el SIDA

*(The following exercises can be found printed in the front matter of your textbook.)*

*Escuche la conversación:*

[Two actors—male doctor, male patient; do not record speaker designations—only spoken dialogue.]

**Doctor:** Buenos días, señor. ¿Qué tiene Ud.?
**Patient:** Doctor, tengo mucha tos.
**Doctor:** ¿Desde cuándo tiene tos?
**Patient:** Hace tres meses. Y es una tos muy dolorosa.
**Doctor:** ¿Fuma Ud.?
**Patient:** Sí, doctor, fumo como un paquete diario.
**Doctor:** ¿Desde cuándo fuma Ud.?
**Patient:** Desde los dieciocho años de edad. Ya hace tiempo que mi esposa me pide que deje el hábito, pero no lo he podido hacer.
**Doctor:** ¿Cuántos años tiene Ud.?
**Patient:** Tengo cincuenta y cuatro años.
**Doctor:** ¿Hay otros síntomas además de la tos?
**Patient:** A veces escupo sangre. ¿Qué puede ser, doctor?
**Doctor:** Bueno, primero es necesario hacer algunas pruebas para saber qué le pasa.

[Pause to indicate new exercise.]

*In the pauses provided, ask the following in Spanish.*

*Ask:*
What's wrong with you?
[Pause.]
¿Qué tiene Ud.?

*Ask:*
How long have you had a cough?
[Pause.]
¿Desde cuándo tiene tos?

*Ask:*
Do you smoke?
[Pause.]
¿Fuma Ud.?

*Ask:*
How old are you?
[Pause.]
¿Cuántos años tiene Ud.?

*Ask:*
Do you have any other symptoms?
[Pause.]
¿Hay otros síntomas?

*Ask:*
I have to do some tests.
[Pause.]
Tengo que hacerle algunas pruebas.

[Pause to indicate new section.]

## EL SIDA Y LAS ENFERMEDADES PASADAS SEXUALMENTE

*Repita el vocabulario:*

the causes
las causas [Pause.] las causas

the condom
el condón [Pause.] el condón

the casual contact
el contacto casual [Pause.] el contacto casual

the sexual contact
el contacto sexual [Pause.] el contacto sexual

the venereal diseases
las enfermedades venéreas [Pause.] las enfermedades
venéreas

the gonorrhea
la gonorrea [Pause.] la gonorrea

the genital herpes
el herpes genital [Pause.] el herpes genital

the opportunistic infection
la infección oportunística [Pause.] la infección
oportunística

the antiviral medication
el medicamento antiviral; antivirósico [Pause.]
el medicamento antiviral; antivirósico

the danger
el peligro [Pause.] el peligro

the pneumonia
la pulmonía [Pause.] la pulmonía

the immune system
el sistema inmunológico [Pause.] el sistema
inmunológico

the sexual transmission
la transmisión sexual [Pause.] la transmisión sexual

to share needles
compartir agujas hipodérmicas [Pause.] compartir
agujas hipodérmicas

infected
infectado, infectada [Pause.] infectado, infectada

[Pause to indicate new chapter.]

## CAPÍTULO TRECE
## PRUEBAS Y PROCEDIMIENTOS

*(The following exercises can be found printed in the front matter of your textbook.)*

*Escuche la conversación:*

[Two actors—male doctor, female patient; do not record speaker designations—only spoken dialogue.]

**Doctor:** ¿Sufre Ud. de asma?
**Patient:** No, no sufro de asma.
**Doctor:** ¿Sufre Ud. de fiebre de heno o de alergias?
**Patient:** No, no sufro de ninguna alergia.
**Doctor:** ¿Ha tenido Ud. problemas del corazón, de los pulmones o de los riñones?
**Patient:** Creo que no.
**Doctor:** ¿Ha tenido alguna vez Ud. alta presión?
**Patient:** No, doctor.
**Doctor:** ¿Tiene Ud. catarro o dolor de garganta?
**Patient:** No, no tengo catarro y no me duele la garganta.
**Doctor:** ¿Tiene Ud. tos?
**Patient:** Tengo un poco de tos ahora pero creo que es a causa de los nervios.
**Doctor:** Entonces, eso es todo. Le vamos a poner una inyección mañana y Ud. se va a dormir. Después de la prueba le vamos a llevar a la sala de recuperación, donde Ud. va a descansar. Hasta mañana, señora.
**Patient:** Hasta mañana, doctor.

[Pause to indicate new exercise.]

*In the pauses provided, ask the following questions in Spanish .*

*Ask:*
How do you feel?
[Pause.]
¿Cómo se siente Ud.?

*Ask:*
Do you suffer from hay fever?
[Pause.]
¿Sufre Ud. de fiebre de heno?

*Ask:*
Do you have allergies?
[Pause.]
¿Tiene alergias?

*Ask:*
Do you have heart trouble?
[Pause.]
¿Tiene problemas del corazón?

*Ask:*
Do you have problems breathing?
[Pause.]

¿Tiene Ud. problemas de la respiración?

*Ask:*
Is your throat irritated?
[Pause.]
¿Tiene la garganta irritada?

*Ask:*
Do you have a cough?
[Pause.]
¿Tiene Ud. tos?

[Pause to indicate new exercise.]

*Listen to the conversation then answer the question, What kind of test is the patient having?*

*Escuche la conversación:*

[Two actors—male doctor, male patient; do not record speaker designations—only spoken dialogue.]

**Doctor:** Le voy a hacer una radiografía del pecho.
**Patient:** ¿Para qué se necesita la radiografía?
**Doctor:** Para saber si Ud. tiene alguna enfermedad de los pulmones.
**Patient:** ¿Qué tengo que hacer?
**Doctor:** Tiene que quitarse la camisa y pararse enfrente de este aparato.
**Patient:** ¿Va a durar mucho tiempo?
**Doctor:** No. Sólo va a durar quince minutos.
**Patient:** ¿Me va a doler?
**Doctor:** No. Ud. no va a sentir ningún dolor en absoluto.
**Patient:** ¿Cuándo voy a saber los resultados?
**Doctor:** Después de la prueba el médico discutirá los resultados con Ud.

[Pause.]

What kind of test is the patient having?
[Pause for the student to give the answer, then give the correct answer.]
The patient is having a chest X ray.

[Pause to indicate new chapter.]

# Capítulo catorce
## El dentista, el terapeuta físico y el optometrista

*(The following exercises can be found printed in the front matter of your textbook.)*

*Escuche la conversación:*

[Two actors—female patient, female doctor; do not record speaker designations—only spoken dialogue.]

**Patient:** ¿Va a examinarme los ojos ahora?
**Doctor:** Sí, pase por favor. Mire esta carta y dígame lo que ve. Ahora lea la segunda línea, por favor.
**Patient:** La segunda línea dice, O, F, D, P, R.
**Doctor:** Lea la tercera línea, por favor.
**Patient:** E, C, U, B, F.
**Doctor:** Y ahora la cuarta línea.
**Patient:** No puedo ver bien la cuarta línea. Está muy borrosa.
**Doctor:** ¿No puede ver ninguna letra en la cuarta línea?
**Patient:** No, todo se vuelve borroso después de la tercera línea. ¿Necesito usar lentes?
**Doctor:** Sí, señorita. Le voy a preparar una receta ahora.
**Patient:** ¿Cuándo estarán listos los lentes?
**Doctor:** Estarán listos dentro de una hora.

[Pause to indicate new exercise.]

*Tell the patient whom he or she should visit depending on the cues and the symptoms.*

Me duele una muela.
dentista
[Pause for student to give the answer, then give the correct answer.]
Ud. tiene que visitar al dentista.

Necesito una dentadura.
dentista
[Pause.]
Ud. tiene que visitar al dentista.

No puedo ver bien.
optometrista
[Pause.]
Ud. tiene que visitar a la optometrista.

Me duele la muñeca.
terapeuta físico
[Pause.]
Ud. tiene que visitar al terapeuta físico.

Tengo una muela impactada.
dentista
[Pause.]
Ud. tiene que visitar a la dentista.

No puedo hacer un puño.
terapeuta física
[Pause.]
Ud. tiene que visitar a la terapeuta física.

Tengo la vista borrosa.
optometrista
[Pause.]
Ud. tiene que visitar al optometrista.

# Contents

# Medical Spanish

A Conversational Approach

# Capítulo preliminar

# LA PRONUNCIACIÓN

Spanish pronunciation is relatively easy for speakers of English. The following simplified pronunciation guide is provided so that you can begin speaking right away. For the finer points and for an explanation of dialectical variations, see the Appendix.

##  LAS VOCALES

As in English, the vowels are **a, e, i, o,** and **u.** The letter **y** is a vowel when it appears as the final letter in a word, as in **soy** *(I am).*

**a** is similar to the *a* in *father.*

Here are some examples to practice with:

| | | | |
|---|---|---|---|
| 1. pa | 4. ba | 7. bata | 10. pata |
| 2. ca | 5. ta | 8. lata | 11. mata |
| 3. ma | 6. tapa | 9. papa | 12. cama |

**e** is similar to the *a* in *cake,* but shorter. The vowels are not lengthened as they are in English.

| | | | |
|---|---|---|---|
| 1. pe | 4. se | 7. bebé | 10. mate |
| 2. le | 5. be | 8. vete | 11. mesa |
| 3. me | 6. nene | 9. pepe | 12. pesa |

**i** is similar to the *ee* in *see.* Again, it is shorter than the sound in English.

| | | | |
|---|---|---|---|
| 1. li | 4. si | 7. vida | 10. cine |
| 2. ti | 5. fi | 8. mide | 11. casi |
| 3. mi | 6. pita | 9. pide | 12. mima |

*d between* *i : A* *i : e* *(vowels) sound like "th"*

**o** is similar to the *o* in *go.* Maintain a clear and open sound.

| | | | |
|---|---|---|---|
| 1. to | 4. so | 7. moto | 10. codo |
| 2. mo | 5. co | 8. voto | 11. pelo |
| 3. fo | 6. todo | 9. moco | 12. palo |

**u** is similar to the *oo* in *boot.*

| | | | |
|---|---|---|---|
| 1. mu | 4. su | 7. cura | 10. supo |
| 2. tu | 5. bu | 8. mudo | 11. tubo |
| 3. lu | 6. pudo | 9. usa | 12. sube |

## Para practicar

Repeat after your instructor or use the above guide to practice pronouncing the following words.

*Sounds like (hugo)*

| | | | |
|---|---|---|---|
| 1. cama | 4. mesa | 7. torso | 10. jugo |
| 2. palabra | 5. dinero | 8. dormido | 11. mocoso |
| 3. Pedro | 6. cocina | 9. muslo | 12. poderoso |

*K  S*

## LAS CONSONANTES

Many of the consonants are identical or very similar in English and Spanish. However, it is important to be aware of the following points.

| Letter | Sounds Like | Where | Examples |
|--------|-------------|-------|----------|
| c | *c* in *cat* | before **a, o, u** and all consonants | casa, como, acción |
| c | *c* in *cinema* | before **e** and **i** | cine, ceja |
| ch | *ch* in *chocolate* | everywhere | chiste, ocho |
| g | *g* in *good* | before **a, o, u** | gato, agua, gota |
| g | *h* in *hat* | before **e, i** | gente, gitano |
| h | silent | everywhere | habla, hombre |
| j | *h* in *heavy* | everywhere | jota, jugo |
| ll | *y* in *yes* | everywhere | llama, mejilla |
| ñ | *ni* in *onion* | everywhere | señor, riñón |
| q | *k* in *kite* | everywhere; always followed by **u**, which is silent | queso, quijada |
| r | *r* in *ready* | everywhere, except at the beginning of a word | cara, puro |
| rr | trill or multiple flap | **rr** everywhere and **r** at the beginning; no equivalent sound in English | roto, carro |
| v | *b* in *observe* | everywhere | avión, vidrio |
| z | *s* in *soap*; never like *z* in *zebra* | everywhere | zapato, feliz |

 ## ACENTOS Y ÉNFASIS

The rules for stress in Spanish are very easy and come quite naturally with a little practice. If a word ends in a vowel, **n,** or **s,** the stress is on the next to last syllable (**vaso, ha**blan, **pe**sos). When a word ends in a consonant other than **n** or **s,** then the stress is on the last syllable (**comer, ca**nal). Any deviation from these rules is indicated by an accent mark (pa**pá,** in**glés**). Always stress the syllable that carries an accent mark.

## Para practicar

Practice saying these sentences aloud. Be especially careful where you place the stress on each word.

1. La mamá habla con el médico.
2. Pedro pela la papa.
3. El brazo está fracturado.
4. La enfermera hace la cama.
5. La cocina está arriba.
6. El hombre usa los músculos para trabajar.
7. No me gusta el jugo.
8. Todos van al hospital.
9. El médico pone el libro sobre la mesa.
10. Usted tiene una úlcera.

## ENLACE (LINKING)

In normal speech, the final vowel of one word will often join with the initial unstressed vowel of the next word. Look at the following examples:

Tome_esta medicina.    Como_ahora.    Como_en la cafetería

Mira_hacia_arriba.    Llego_a las dos.

## Para practicar

Pronounce the following sentences keeping in mind the linking of vowels.

1. Me duele el_estómago hoy. = my stomach hurts me
2. Sigo una dieta estricta. = follow
3. La enfermera trabaja en el cuarto. = The nurse works in the room
4. El médico examina al paciente. = The Dr. exams the patient
5. Me_está recetando unas píldoras.
6. Mi padre está en_el hospital.
7. La puerta está_abierta. = The door is open
8. La_asistenta hace el trabajo.
9. El_hombre está escribiendo una carta. The man is writing a letter
10. Mi madre está bien. My mom is well

## EL ALFABETO

The following are the letters of the Spanish alphabet. The letters **ch** and **ll** used to be (but are no longer) considered separate letters; they are only listed separately in dictionaries published before 1994. The **w** and **k** are only used in words of foreign origin.

Try to say the alphabet with correct pronunciation.

La "E" simboliza ejercicio

American Heart Association

| Letter | Name | Letter | Name |
|--------|------|--------|------|
| a | a | ñ | eñe |
| b | be | o | o |
| c | ce | p | pe |
| d | de | q | cu |
| e | e | r | ere |
| f | efe | rr | erre |
| g | ge | s | ese |
| h | hache | t | te |
| i | i | u | u |
| j | jota | v | ve |
| k | ka | w | doble v, doble u |
| l | ele | x | equis |
| m | eme | y | i griega |
| n | ene | z | zeta |

## 🔊 SALUDOS Y CORTESÍAS

## Conversaciones

You are the doctor (**el médico**) and you meet your patient, Francisco Rivera, for the first time.

| | |
|---|---|
| Médico: | Buenos días. |
| Paciente: | Buenos días, doctor. |
| Médico: | ¿Cómo se llama usted? |
| Paciente: | Me llamo Francisco Rivera. |
| Médico: | Yo soy el doctor Smith. |
| Paciente: | Mucho gusto, doctor. |
| Médico: | El gusto es mío, señor Rivera. |

You are the doctor (**la doctora**), and in addition to greeting your patient, you also want to know how she feels.

| | |
|---|---|
| Doctora: | Buenas tardes, señora. |
| Paciente: | Buenas tardes, doctora. ¿Cómo está usted? |
| Doctora: | Bien, gracias. ¿Y usted? |
| Paciente: | Estoy enferma. |
| Doctora: | ¿Qué le pasa? |
| Paciente: | Tengo dolor. |

Note that a male doctor is **el médico,** and a female doctor is **la doctora.** However, when addressing a doctor, an individual would call you **doctor** (male) or **doctora** (female).

You have asked the patient to give a urine sample. He asks you where the bathroom is.

| | |
|---|---|
| Paciente: | Perdón, doctora. |
| Doctora: | Sí, señor. ¿En qué puedo servirle? |
| Paciente: | ¿Dónde está el baño, por favor? |
| Doctora: | Está a la derecha. |
| Paciente: | Gracias, doctora. |
| Doctora: | De nada, señor. |

As you can see from the preceding conversations, in written Spanish, an upside down question mark ¿ is placed at the beginning of a question, with a regular question mark at the end. The same is done with exclamation points.

Notice also that there are two words for *is* in Spanish. **Es** is used to talk about permanent characteristics of a person or thing, while **está** is used to refer to a person's condition or the location of a person or thing. See Chapter 2 for more on these two verbs.

## Vocabulario

| | |
|---|---|
| Buenos días. | *Good morning.* |
| ¿Cómo se llama usted? | *What is your name?* |
| Me llamo ... | *My name is…* |
| Yo soy... | *I am…* |
| Mucho gusto. | *Pleased to meet you.* |
| El gusto es mío. | *The pleasure is mine.* |
| Buenas tardes. | *Good afternoon.* |
| ¿Cómo está usted? | *How are you?* |
| Bien, gracias. | *Fine, thanks.* |
| ¿Y usted? | *And yourself?* |
| enfermo, enferma | *sick* |
| ¿Qué le pasa? | *What's wrong?* |
| Tengo dolor. | *I'm in pain.* |
| Perdón. | *Excuse me.* |
| ¿En qué puedo servirle? | *How can I help you?* |
| ¿Dónde está el baño? | *Where is the bathroom?* |
| Está a la derecha. | *It's on the right.* |
| Por favor. | *Please.* |
| Gracias. | *Thank you.* |
| De nada. | *You're welcome.* |

## Más vocabulario

| | |
|---|---|
| sí | *yes* |
| no | *no, not* |
| señor | *Mr., sir* |
| señora | *Mrs., ma'am* |
| señorita | *Miss* |
| Buenas noches. | *Good night.* |
| Adiós. | *Good-bye.* |
| Hasta luego. | *See you later.* |
| Hasta mañana. | *See you tomorrow.* |
| Regular. | *So-so.* |
| Muy mal. | *Not well.* |
| Está a la izquierda. | *It's on the left.* |
| Está a la derecha. | *It's on the right.* |

### Para practicar

Take turns asking and answering questions with your classmate using the cued responses.

| MODELO | ¿Cómo se llama usted? | *Miguel* |
|---|---|---|
| | **Me llamo Miguel.** | |

1. ¿Cómo está usted?     *Fine, thanks.*     B
2. ¿Qué le pasa?     *I'm in pain.*     Tengo dolor

3. ¿Dónde está el baño?          *It's on the right.*  Está a la derecha
4. ¿Dónde está el teléfono?      *It's on the left.*   Está a la izquierda
5. Mucho gusto.                  *The pleasure's mine.*
6. Buenas tardes, doctor.        *Good afternoon. How can I help you?*
7. Gracias, doctora.             *You're welcome.*  De nada

el = for men
la = for women

## Sustituciones

Ask where the following items or persons are located.

**MODELO**     **¿Dónde está <u>el hospital</u>?**

1.

¿Dónde está el teléfono?

3.

¿Dónde está la Paciente?

2.

¿Dónde está la Doctora? (or Medica)

4.
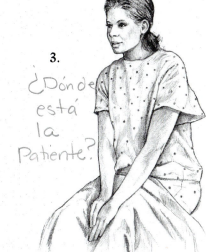
¿Dónde está el medico?

## Para practicar

A Spanish-speaking patient comes to the hospital. How would you say the following?

1. How are you? — *Cómo está*
2. What is your name? — *Cómo se llama*
3. How can I help you? — *En qué le puedo ayudar*
4. What's wrong? ⟶ *Qué le pasa*
   *(Qué tiene)*
5. I am Doctor…(your name). *Yo Soy Dr. Smith*

---

| **NOTA CULTURAL** | **WAYS OF SAYING "EXCUSE ME"** |
|---|---|

As a general rule, Spanish is a somewhat more polite language than English. "Please," "thank you," and "you're welcome" are probably heard more frequently in Spanish than they are in English. Also, as you will see later on, the structure of the language itself provides an individual with several options for softening requests or speaking diplomatically if he or she so chooses. You can start getting used to it now. Practice using these different ways of saying "excuse me."

Perdón.    Perdóneme.    Con su permiso.
Perdone.   Permiso.    *discúlpeme*

---

## LOS NÚMEROS

The numbers for zero through fifteen are as follows:

| | | | | | | | |
|---|---|---|---|---|---|---|---|
| 0 | cero | 4 | cuatro | 8 | ocho | 12 | doce |
| 1 | uno | 5 | cinco | 9 | nueve | 13 | trece |
| 2 | dos | 6 | seis | 10 | diez | 14 | catorce |
| 3 | tres | 7 | siete | 11 | once | 15 | quince |

The numbers fifteen through nineteen combine the word for *ten* (**diez**), the word for *and* (**y**), and the words for *six* through *nine*.

16    diez y seis (*alternate spelling:* dieciséis)
17    diez y siete (diecisiete)
18    diez y ocho (dieciocho)
19    diez y nueve (diecinueve)
20    veinte

The numbers twenty-one through twenty-nine combine **veinte** and **y** plus the words for *one* through *nine*.

21    veinte y uno (*alternate spelling:* veintiuno)
22    veinte y dos (veintidós)
23    veinte y tres (veintitrés)

24    veinte y cuatro (veinticuatro)
25    veinte y cinco (veinticinco)
26    veinte y seis (veintiséis)
27    veinte y siete (veintisiete)
28    veinte y ocho (veintiocho)
29    veinte y nueve (veintinueve)

*nu e v a*

Do the same for thirty-one through thirty-nine, forty-one through forty-nine, and so on.

30    treinta
31    treinta y uno *(no alternate spellings)*
32    treinta y dos...
40    cuarenta
50    cincuenta
60    sesenta
70    setenta
80    ochenta
90    noventa
100   ciento, cien

*(used in front of a noun)*

*used (in front of another #)*

Use **cien** before nouns (**cien pacientes**) and before **mil** and **millones.**

101        ciento uno
102        ciento dos
150        ciento cincuenta
174        ciento setenta y cuatro
200        doscientos
300        trescientos
400        cuatrocientos
500        quinientos
600        seiscientos
700        setecientos
800        ochocientos
900        novecientos
1.000      mil
2.000      dos mil
100.000    cien mil
1.000.000  un millón
2.000.000  dos millones

In Spanish, a period is used instead of a comma in whole numbers.

## LOS NÚMEROS ORDINALES

In Spanish, ordinal numbers are generally used only up to *tenth*. Beyond *tenth*, cardinal numbers are used.

| | |
|---|---|
| primer, primero, primera | *first* |
| segundo, segunda | *second* |
| tercer, tercero, tercera | *third* |

| cuarto, cuarta | *fourth* |
| quinto, quinta | *fifth* |
| sexto, sexta | *sixth* |
| séptimo, séptima | *seventh* |
| octavo, octava | *eighth* |
| noveno, novena | *ninth* |
| décimo, décima | *tenth* |

Notice that the forms **primero** and **tercero** drop the final **-o** when they precede masculine singular nouns (**el** *primer* **libro, el** *tercer* **hospital**). All of the ordinal numbers have a feminine form which ends in **-a**. It is used when the number precedes a feminine noun. (We will see more about the gender of nouns later on.)

## PARA PREGUNTAR CUÁNTOS AÑOS TIENE ALGUIEN (ASKING HOW OLD SOMEONE IS)

To ask someone for their age, say **¿Cuántos años tiene usted?** The response is **Tengo —— años.** For example:

*[handwritten: → another way to say this is "¿Cuál es suedad?"]*

| ¿Cuántos años tiene usted? *[handwritten: How many years do you have]* | How old are you? |
| Tengo treinta años. | *I am thirty years old.* |
| ¿Cuántos años tiene el médico? | *How old is the doctor?* |
| El médico tiene cuarenta y dos años. | *The doctor is forty-two years old.* |

## Para practicar

Ask your partner about each person's age. Your partner responds using the cues provided.

**MODELO**    A:    **¿Cuántos años tiene la doctora?**    50
          B:    **La doctora tiene cincuenta años.**

1. ¿Cuántos años tiene el médico?          42    *[handwritten: Cuarenta y dos]*
2. ¿Cuántos años tiene el paciente?        14    *[handwritten: Catorce]*
3. ¿Cuántos años tiene usted?              77    *[handwritten: Setenta y siete]*
4. ¿Cuántos años tiene el señor Pérez?     55    *[handwritten: Cincuenta y cinco]*
5. ¿Cuántos años tiene la señora García?   27    *[handwritten: Veinte y siete]*

## PARA DAR NÚMEROS DE TELÉFONO (GIVING PHONE NUMBERS)

Often, when Spanish speakers give groups of numbers, they will break them up into blocks of two at a time. For example, the telephone number *432-6173* would be given as **cuatro - treinta y dos - sesenta y uno - setenta y tres.**

## Para practicar

Say aloud the following phone numbers in Spanish.

**MODELO**    435-7981
          **Cuatro - treinta y cinco - setenta y nueve - ochenta y uno**

1. 367-9821   *Tres - sesenta y siete - noventa y ocho veinte y uno*
2. 786-7342   *Siete - ochenta y seis - setenta y tres cuarenta y dos*
3. 879-5498   *Ocho - setenta y nueve — cincuenta y cuatro - noventa y ocho*
4. 675-7834
5. 213-4563

*Seis setenta y cinco - setenta y ocho treinta y cuatro*

## Conversación

| | |
|---|---|
| Doctora: | Buenos días, señor. ¿Cuántos años tiene usted? |
| Paciente: | Tengo cuarenta y dos años. |
| Doctora: | ¿Cuántos años tiene su hijo? |
| Paciente: | Él tiene dieciocho años.    *18 — diez y ocho or dieciocho* |
| Doctora: | ¿Cuál es su número de teléfono? |
| Paciente: | Mi número de teléfono es 435-8930    *(quatro treinta cinco ochenta nueve treinta)* |
| Doctora: | ¿Cuál es su dirección? |
| Paciente: | Yo vivo en el 4320 de la Avenida B. |
| Doctora: | ¿Cuál es su número de seguro social? |
| Paciente: | Mi número de seguro social es 478-90-8723 |

*Dos trece - cuarenta y cinco - sesenta y tres*

## Vocabulario

| | |
|---|---|
| **su hijo** | *your son* |
| **hija** | *daughter* |
| **él** | *he* |
| **ella** | *she* |
| el **número de teléfono** | *telephone number* |
| **mi** | *my* |
| la **dirección** | *address* |
| **Yo vivo en...** | *I live at...* |
| el **número de seguro social** | *Social Security number* |

*el without the accent means "the"*

## Notas

*el domicilio = another name for address (domisile)*

### ¿Cuál? and ¿Qué?

**¿Cuál?** is a pronoun that means *which?* or *what?* It is used to ask for specific information among many choices and is usually followed by **es** *(is)*.

| | |
|---|---|
| ¿Cuál es su dirección? | *What (which) is your address?* |
| ¿Cuál es su antibiótico? | *Which is your antibiotic?* |

**¿Qué?** means *what* when asking for a definition of something or when followed by a noun.

| | |
|---|---|
| ¿Qué es un antibiótico? | *What is an antibiotic?* |
| ¿Qué medicina toma usted? | *What medicine are you taking?* |

## Para practicar

Take turns practicing the following with your partner or classmate. Use the given cues for your answers.

| MODELO | ¿Cuántos años tiene el doctor Irizarry?    54 |
|---|---|
| | **El doctor Irizarry tiene cincuenta y cuatro años.** |

1. ¿Cuántos años tiene el paciente?          23
2. ¿Cuántos años tiene la doctora?           56
3. ¿Cuántos años tiene el señor Ramos?       32
4. ¿Cuántos años tiene usted?                Tengo... *(Say your age.)*
5. ¿Cuál es su número de teléfono?           *(Say your phone number.)*
6. ¿Cuál es su número de seguro social?      *(Give your number.)*

## Los días de la semana

| ¿Qué día es hoy? | *What day is today?* |
|---|---|
| Hoy es... | *Today is...* |
| lunes | *Monday* |
| martes | *Tuesday* |
| miércoles | *Wednesday* |
| jueves | *Thursday* |
| viernes | *Friday* |
| sábado | *Saturday* |
| domingo | *Sunday* |

Notice that the days of the week are not capitalized in Spanish.

anything

## Para practicar

Answer the questions according to the cued responses.

1. ¿Qué día es hoy?              *(Say the day.)*
2. ¿Qué día es mañana?          *(Tomorrow.)*
3. ¿Qué día es pasado mañana?   *(Day after tomorrow.)*

hoy es martes
hoy es miércoles
hoy es jueves

## Los meses del año

In Spanish, to ask about the month, one says literally, "In what month are we?" The answer is "We are in the month of..." Notice that this is different from the way one asks about the day of the week.

¿En qué mes estamos?    *What month is it?*
Estamos en...           *It is...*

( Don't Capitalize)

| enero | abril | julio | octubre |
|---|---|---|---|
| febrero | mayo | agosto | noviembre |
| marzo | junio | septiembre | diciembre |

Notice that the months of the year are not capitalized in Spanish.

To ask the date, say: **¿Cuál es la fecha de hoy?**

Hoy es el seis de octubre.　　　　　　　　*Today is October 6.*

Or

Hoy es el diecisiete de febrero.　　　　　　*Today is February 17.*

But, for the first of the month, use **primero** *(first)*:

Hoy es el primero de junio.　　　　　　　*Today is June 1.*

_[handwritten: 1st]_

An example of how a full date is expressed in Spanish is:

Hoy es lunes, el veinte de octubre de　　　*Today is Monday, October 20, 1999.*
　mil novecientos noventa y nueve.

## Para practicar

Answer each question using the cued responses.

1. ¿Cuál es la fecha de hoy?　　　　　*(Give today's date.)*　_[handwritten: Hoy es el veinte de abril.]_
2. ¿Cuál es la fecha de mañana?　　　*(Give tomorrow's date.)*
3. ¿Cuál es la fecha de su cumpleaños?　*(Give your birthday.)*　_[handwritten: Hoy es el veinte uno de abril.]_
4. ¿Cuál es la fecha de la cita *(appointment)*?　*December 14*

_[handwritten: el Catorce de Diciembre.]_　_[handwritten: el Catorce de Septiembre.]_

## EL TIEMPO _[handwritten: (weather)]_

To ask how the weather is one says, **¿Qué tiempo hace?** One can answer with any of the following:

Hace buen tiempo.　_[handwritten: what is the weather]_　*The weather is nice.*　_[handwritten: Hace = cool fresco]_　_[handwritten: It is cool]_
Hace mal tiempo.　　　　　　　　　　*The weather is bad.*
Hace sol.　　　　　　　　　　　　　　*It's sunny.*
Está nublado.　　　　　　　　　　　　*It's cloudy.*
Está lloviendo.　　　　　　　　　　　*It's raining.*
Está nevando.　　　　　　　　　　　　*It's snowing.*

_[handwritten: Hace Viento　　　It's windy]_

The following two expressions can refer either to the weather outdoors or to the temperature inside:

Hace calor.　_[handwritten: Calor = warm]_ _[handwritten: mu]_　*It's hot.*　_[handwritten: food taste　Caliente = hot for temp. of food]_
Hace frío.　　　　　　　　　　　　　*It's cold.*

You can also add the word **mucho** to express degree:

Hace mucho calor.　　　　　　　　　　*It's very hot.*　_[handwritten: Picante = spicy hot]_
Hace mucho frío.　　　　　　　　　　　*It's very cold.*

*Hace =*
*vs*
*Esta= Use infront of a verb*

## Para practicar

Practice asking and answering these questions about the weather using the cued responses.

> **MODELO**    ¿Qué tiempo hace?    *It's sunny.*
> **Hace sol.**

1. ¿Qué tiempo hace?                    *It's raining.*  — *Esta lloviendo*
2. ¿Qué tiempo hace ahora?              *It's nice weather.* — *Hace buen tiempo*
3. ¿Qué tiempo hace en el verano?       *It's hot.* — *Hace calor*
4. ¿Qué tiempo hace en el invierno?     *It's cold.* — *Hace frío*
5. ¿Qué tiempo hace en México?          *It's very hot.* — *Hace mucho calor*

## Para practicar más

**Create a conversation.** How would you express the following in Spanish?

1. Good morning.    *Buenos días*
2. How can I help you?  — *En que puedo servirle*
3. I am Doctor…    — *Yo soy la Doctora*
4. What is your name?
5. How are you?    *¿Como se llama usted?*
6. How old are you?
7. What is your address?
8. What's wrong?    *¿Como esta usted?*

*¿Que le pasa?*

*Cuántos años tiene usted*
*or Cual es suedad*

## RESUMEN Y REPASO

## Vocabulario

*Cuál es su direccion*

| **Saludos** | **Greetings** |
|---|---|
| Buenos días. | *Good morning.* |
| Buenas tardes. | *Good afternoon.* |
| Buenas noches. | *Good night.* |
| ¡Hola! / *que tal* | *Hi!* / *Hi what's new* |
| ¿Cómo está usted? | *How are you?* |

| **Para decir adiós** | **Ways to Say Good-Bye** |
|---|---|
| Adiós. | *Good-bye.* |
| Hasta mañana. | *See you tomorrow.* |
| Hasta luego. | *See you later.* |
| Hasta la vista. | *See you later.* |

| **Para pedir información** | **To Find Out Information** |
|---|---|
| ¿Cómo está usted? | *How are you?* |
| ¿Cómo se llama usted? | *What's your name?* |
| ¿Cuántos años tiene usted? | *How old are you?* |
| ¿Cuál es su número de teléfono? | *What is your telephone number?* |
| ¿Cuál es su número de seguro social? | *What is your social security number?* |

| | |
|---|---|
| ¿Cuál es su dirección? | *What is your address?* |
| ¿En qué puedo servirle? | *How can I help you?* |
| ¿Dónde está el baño? | *Where is the bathroom?* |
| ¿Dónde está el hospital? | *Where is the hospital?* |
| ¿Dónde está la sala de espera? | *Where is the waiting room?* |

**Expresiones de cortesía** — ***Expressions of Courtesy***

| | |
|---|---|
| Mucho gusto. | *Pleased to meet you.* |
| El gusto es mío. | *The pleasure is mine.* |
| Por favor. | *Please.* |
| Gracias. | *Thank you.* |
| De nada. / Por nada | *You're welcome.* |
| Perdón. | *Pardon me.* |

**Los días de la semana** — ***Days of the Week***

| | |
|---|---|
| lunes | *Monday* |
| martes | *Tuesday* |
| miércoles | *Wednesday* |
| jueves | *Thursday* |
| viernes | *Friday* |
| sábado | *Saturday* |
| domingo | *Sunday* |

**Los meses del año** — ***Months of the Year***

| | |
|---|---|
| enero | *January* |
| febrero | *February* |
| marzo | *March* |
| abril | *April* |
| mayo | *May* |
| junio | *June* |
| julio | *July* |
| agosto | *August* |
| septiembre | *September* |
| octubre | *October* |
| noviembre | *November* |
| diciembre | *December* |

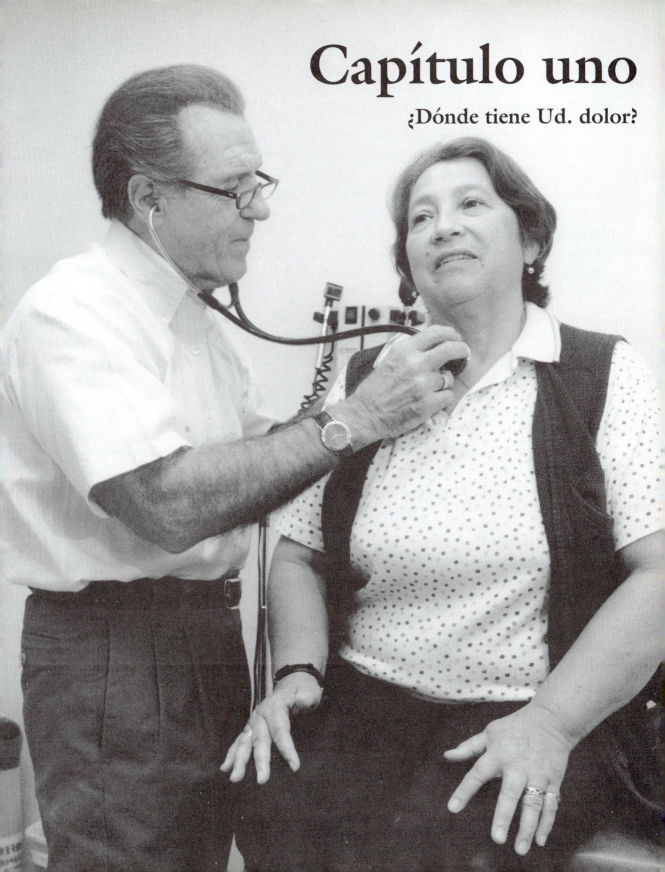

# Capítulo uno

¿Dónde tiene Ud. dolor?

##  Conversación

| | |
|---|---|
| Médico: | Buenos días, señor Vega. ¿Cómo está Ud. hoy? |
| Paciente: | Estoy muy mal, doctor Rivera. Tengo escalofríos. |
| Médico: | ¿Tiene Ud. dolor de cabeza? |
| Paciente: | Sí, tengo un dolor de cabeza muy fuerte. |
| Médico: | ¿Tiene Ud. dolor de estómago? |
| Paciente: | Sí, también tengo dolor de estómago. |
| Médico: | ¿Tiene Ud. diarrea? |
| Paciente: | No, no tengo diarrea. |
| Médico: | ¿Tiene Ud. la garganta irritada? |
| Paciente: | Sí, y además tengo mucha flema. |
| Médico: | ¿Desde cuándo tiene Ud. estos síntomas? |
| Paciente: | Desde ayer. |

*[Handwritten annotations: "Good morning", "Chills", "not well", "Strong", "furthermore", "Since / when have you had the symptoms", "yesterday"]*

## Notas

### Usted and Accent Marks

**Usted** is a subject pronoun and it means *you*. It is used when addressing adults or strangers in formal situations. It is usually abbreviated **Ud.** although it is still pronounced **usted.** For the remainder of this text it will be shown in abbreviated form.

Accent marks may be and often are omitted from capital letters. However, this text will use them everywhere so that you may have a greater opportunity to become accustomed to their use.

##  Vocabulario

| | | | |
|---|---|---|---|
| **tener diarrea** | *to have diarrhea* | **tener escalofríos** | *to have chills* |
| **tener dolor de cabeza** | *to have a headache* | **tener la garganta irritada** | *to have a sore throat* |
| **tener dolor de estómago** | *to have a stomachache* | **tener mucha flema** | *to have a lot of phlegm* |
| | | **tener síntomas** | *to have symptoms* |

## Preguntas

1. ¿Cómo está el paciente?
2. ¿Dónde tiene dolor el paciente?
3. ¿Tiene el paciente la garganta irritada?
4. ¿Desde cuándo tiene los síntomas el paciente?

## Nota

### Word Order in Sentences

When asking a question in Spanish, the verb comes first, followed by the subject. For example:

¿Tiene el paciente diarrea?    *Does the patient have diarrhea?*

*[Handwritten: "Wrong" / "¿Tiene diarrea el Paciente? (This is Correct)"]*

There are no auxiliary or helping verbs as in English.

In a declarative sentence the word order is much the same as in English, with the subject first, followed by the verb, and ending with any objects. For example:

El paciente tiene diarrea.                    *The patient has diarrhea.*

## Vocabulario

¿Dónde tiene dolor?                  *Where does it hurt?*
¿Qué tiene Ud.?                      *What's wrong with you?*
Tengo dolor de cabeza.               *I have a headache.*
¿Desde cuándo tiene dolor?           *Since when have you had the pain?*
¿Qué toma para el dolor?             *What are you taking for the pain?*

**El cuerpo (*The body*)**

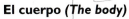
*[handwritten: I take]*

*[handwritten right margin: Tome]*

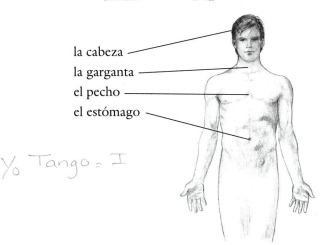

la cabeza
la garganta
el pecho
el estómago

la espalda

*[handwritten: Yo Tango = I]*

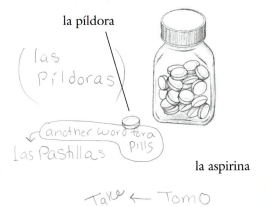

la píldora

*[handwritten: (las Píldoras)]*

*[handwritten: ←another word for pills]*
*[handwritten: las Pastillas]*

el antibiótico

el antibiótico

las gotas
*[handwritten: (Drops) USA]*

las gotas

la aspirina

la aspirina

*[handwritten: Take ← Tomo laspirina]*

el jarabe

*[handwritten: Para la tos. (Cough Syrup)]*

el jarabe

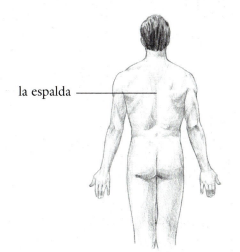

## Para practicar

Ask your partner the following questions using the cues provided. Your partner answers affirmatively to each question.

**MODELO**    ¿Tiene el paciente...?    *diarrhea*
A:    **¿Tiene el paciente diarrea?**
B:    **Sí, el paciente tiene diarrea.**

1. ¿Tiene el paciente...?    *sore throat*
2. ¿Tiene la paciente...?    *stomach ache*
3. ¿Tiene Ud....?    *headache*
4. ¿Tiene el señor Pérez...?    *chills*
5. ¿Tiene la señora García...?    *backache*

*• Tiene el paciente (la garganta irritada)*
*• Tiene la paciente (dolor de estómago)*
*• Tiene usted dolor de cabeza.*
*• Tiene el señor Pérez (escalofríos.)*
*• Tiene la señora García (dolor de espalda)*

## Para practicar más

Take turns playing doctor and patient.

**MODELO**    **¿Dónde tiene Ud. dolor?**
**Tengo dolor de cabeza.**

**MODELO**    **¿Qué tiene Ud.?**
**Tengo dolor de cabeza.**

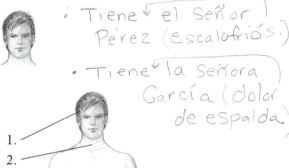

1.
2.
3.
4.

**MODELO**    **¿Desde cuándo tiene dolor?**    *For how long have you had the pain?*
Desde ayer    *Since yesterday*
**Tengo dolor desde ayer.**    *I have the pain since yesterday.*

1. Desde anoche = *Since last night*
2. Desde el martes = *Since tuesday*
3. Desde la semana pasada = *since last week*
4. Desde el mes pasado = *Since last month*
5. Desde la mañana = *Since the morning*
*Desde un año = Since 1 year*

# Para comunicarse

Create a dialogue between doctor and patient. Include the following:

> Greetings
>
> Ask the patient how long he/she has had pain.
>
> Ask the patient what he/she is taking for the pain.

# Nota

### Subject Pronouns

The following are the subject pronouns in Spanish:

| | | | |
|---|---|---|---|
| yo | *I* | nosotros/nosotras | *we* |
| tú | *you* | | |
| él | *he* | ellos/ellas | *they* |
| ella | *she* | | |
| usted (Ud.) | *you* | ustedes (Uds.) | *you* (pl.) |

**Nosotros** is used for masculine or masculine and feminine combined. **Nosotras** is reserved for feminine only. Therefore, **nosotros** is the form that you will be using most of the time. The same holds true for the forms **ellos** and **ellas.**

There are two ways of saying *you* in the singular: **tú** and **usted (Ud.).** Usted is used in formal address and is the form that you will be using most of the time. **Tú** is used only when speaking to children or people with whom you are familiar. **Ustedes (Uds.)** is the form for *you* in the plural *(all of you)* and is used for both familiar and formal address.

Subject pronouns in Spanish are often omitted and reserved for emphasis or clarification:

| (Yo) Tengo dolor. | *I have pain.* |
|---|---|
| (Nosotros) Tenemos seguro. | *We have insurance.* |

Notice that **él** (with the accent mark) means *he,* while **el** (no accent mark) means *the.*

# Para practicar

Tell which subject pronouns you would use when talking *about* the following people:

1. the patient (male)   él paciente
2. yourself   yo
3. yourself and another doctor   nosotros / nosotras
4. Mr. and Mrs. Moreno   ellos
5. two female patients   ellas

Tell which subject pronouns you would use when talking *to* the following people:

1. a child   tú
2. your best friend   tú
3. your new patient   usted
4. a group of nurses   ustdos

## Nota

### The Verb <u>Tener</u>—to Have

In Spanish, the form of the verb changes according to the subject. Here are the subject pronouns in Spanish and the forms of the verb **tener** that accompany them:

| | | | | | |
|---|---|---|---|---|---|
| yo | **tengo** | *I have* | nosotros/nosotras | **tenemos** | *we have* |
| tú | **tienes** | *you* (familiar) *have* | | | |
| él/ella | **tiene** | *he/she has* | ellos/ellas | **tienen** | *they have* |
| usted (Ud.) | **tiene** | *you* (formal) *have* | ustedes (Uds.) | **tienen** | *you* (plural) *have* |

## Tengo malas noticias...

Las enfermedades del corazón siguen siendo la causa principal de muerte en los Estados Unidos. Unas 1.000.000 de personas sufren cada año de ataques al corazón. En el Estado de Nueva York 200 personas mueren diariamente de enfermedades cardíacas.

## Para practicar

Ask your partner the following questions, then reverse roles.

(escupe = Spit)

| MODELO | tos |
|---|---|
| | A: **¿Qué tiene Ud.? ¿Tiene tos?** |
| | B: **Sí, tengo tos.** |
| | *or* |
| | **No, no tengo tos.** |

1. flema
2. dolor de estómago
3. dolor de cabeza   *Tengo dolor de Cabeza*
4. catarro → *head Cold*
5. escalofríos

## Para practicar más

Now do the same exercise over again, only this time use the **tú** form.

> **MODELO**    tos
> A:   **¿Qué tienes tú? ¿Tienes tos?**
> B:   **Sí, tengo tos.**
>      *or*
>      **No, no tengo tos.**

## Nota

### Other Expressions with Tener

The verb **tener** is also used in many expressions in which *to be* is used in English. For example:

El paciente tiene calor.                    *The patient is warm.*

Here are several more for you to use:

| | |
|---|---|
| tener frío | *to be cold* |
| tener hambre | *to be hungry* |
| tener sed | *to be thirsty* |
| tener miedo | *to be afraid* |
| tener prisa | *to be in a hurry* |
| tener razón | *to be right* |
| tener sueño | *to be sleepy* |

## Para practicar

Answer the questions using the cued responses.

> **MODELO**    ¿Quién tiene calor? *(Who is hot?)*    la señora García
>               **La señora García tiene calor.**

1. ¿Quién tiene frío?      los pacientes *tiene frío*
2. ¿Quién tiene hambre?    el señor Martínez
3. ¿Quién tiene sed?       la mujer *tiene Sed*
4. ¿Quién tiene miedo?     el niño *tiene miedo*
5. ¿Quién tiene sueño?     yo *tiene Sueño*

## Vocabulario

| Enfermedades comunes con tener | Common Ailments with Tener |
|---|---|
| tener ansiedad | *to have anxiety* |
| tener calentura | *to have a temperature* |
| tener catarro | *to have a cold* |
| tener resfriado | *to have a cold* |
| tener convulsiones | *to have convulsions* = *another word* *ataquas* |
| tener escalofríos | *to have chills* |

| | |
|---|---|
| tener fiebre | *to have a fever* |
| tener gripe *or gripa* | *to have the flu* |
| tener insomnia | *to have insomnia* |
| tener mareos | *to be dizzy* |
| tener palpitaciones | *to have palpitations* |
| tener vómitos | *to be vomiting* |

## Para practicar

Answer the following questions using the cues.

> **MODELO**    ¿Quién tiene catarro?    la señora García
> **La señora García tiene catarro.**

1. ¿Quién tiene resfriado?     el señor Gómez
2. ¿Quién tiene gripe?     la paciente
3. ¿Quién tiene escalofríos?     el paciente en el cuarto 223
4. ¿Quién tiene fiebre?     el paciente
5. ¿Quién tiene calentura?     el niño

## Conversación

Doctora:    Buenas tardes, señor.

Paciente:    Buenas tardes, doctora.

Doctora:    ¿Cómo está Ud.?

Paciente:    No estoy bien. *I am not well*

Doctora:    ¿Cuál es el problema? *What is the problem*

Paciente:    Tengo un dolor de estómago muy fuerte. *I have strong stomach pain*

Doctora:    ¿Desde cuándo tiene dolor de estómago? *how long have you had stomach pain*

Paciente:    Desde esta mañana. *= Since this morning*

Doctora:    ¿Tiene otros síntomas? *= any other symptoms*

Paciente:    Sí, doctora, tengo escalofríos. *yes doctor, chills*

Doctora:    Necesito hacer un examen médico. *I have the*

## Vocabulario

*(hacer le) — le means to do the test for / con a person, any procedure*

| | | | |
|---|---|---|---|
| fuerte | *strong, severe* | **Necesito...** | *I need* |
| esta mañana | *this morning* | **hacer** *= to take a test* | *to do, to make* |
| los síntomas | *symptoms* | un **examen médico** | *medical examination* |

## Preguntas

1. ¿Dónde tiene dolor el paciente?
2. ¿Desde cuándo tiene dolor el paciente?
3. ¿Qué otros síntomas tiene el paciente?
4. ¿Qué necesita hacer la doctora?

## Nota

### Making a Negative Sentence

In Spanish, one can make a sentence negative by placing the word **no** directly before the verb. It serves the same purpose as the words *not, don't, won't,* and *doesn't* in English.

El paciente no tiene dolor.                    *The patient doesn't have pain.*

Since the word **no** also answers a question negatively, a sentence might often contain the word **no** twice. For example:

¿Tiene cita el paciente?                    *Does the patient have an appointment?*
No, no tiene cita.                    *No, he doesn't have an appointment.*

## Para practicar

You are the health professional. Use the cued word or words to ask the patient if she has the following ailments. Your partner plays the role of the patient and answers your questions in the negative.

**MODELO**    escalofríos
        A:    **¿Tiene Ud. escalofríos?**
        B:    **No, no tengo escalofríos.**

1. dolor de cabeza    *No, no tengo dolor de cabeza*
2. fiebre    *No, no tengo fiebre*
3. dolor de espalda    *No, no tengo dolor de espalda*
4. dolor de estómago    *No, no tengo dolor de estómago*
5. catarro
6. frío
7. calor

## Conversación

Paciente:    Buenas tardes, doctor.    *Good dây doctor (afternoon)*
Médico:    Buenas tardes. ¿Habla Ud. inglés?    *Good day. Do you speak english*
Paciente:    No, no hablo inglés.    *no I don't speak english*
Médico:    ¿Qué tiene Ud.?    *what is going on with you.*
Paciente:    Tengo un dolor de cabeza muy fuerte.    *I have a very strong headache*
Médico:    ¿Qué toma Ud. para el dolor de cabeza?
Paciente:    No tomo nada.    *Taking nothing*
Médico:    Ud. sufre de los nervios. Tiene que tomar las pastillas que receto (para Ud.) y descansar mucho.    *Suffering from nerves (you are)   take pills that I am Prescribing   and rest   Le*
Paciente:    Muchas gracias, doctor.
Médico:    De nada. Ud. tiene que regresar en una semana.    *return   in next week*
Paciente:    Muy bien, doctor. Adiós.

## Vocabulario

| | |
|---|---|
| ¿Habla Ud....? | *Do you speak . . . ?* |
| No hablo... | *I don't speak . . .* |
| el inglés | *English* |
| muy | *very* |
| para = purpose | *for* |
| tomar | *to take* |
| nada | *nothing* |
| sufrir de | *to suffer from* |
| la pastilla | *pill* |
| recetar | *to prescribe* |
| descansar | *to rest* |
| regresar | *to return* |

## Preguntas

1. ¿Habla el paciente inglés?
2. ¿Qué tiene el paciente?
3. ¿Qué toma el paciente para el dolor?
4. ¿De qué sufre el paciente?
5. ¿Qué tiene que tomar el paciente?
6. ¿Qué más tiene que hacer el paciente?
7. ¿Cuándo tiene que regresar el paciente?

## Nota

**Tener que... *(To have to...)***

To say that one has to do something in Spanish, one uses a form of the verb **tener,** followed by **que,** followed by the infinitive form of another verb. The infinitive form is what you will find in the dictionary. It always ends in **-r** and means *"to" do something.* For example:

| | |
|---|---|
| Tengo que descansar. | *I have to rest.* |
| Ud. tiene que regresar en una semana. | *You have to return in one week.* |

## Sustituciones

Substitute the underlined words with the cued items. Be sure to make any other necessary changes.

**MODELO**    Ud. tiene que regresar en <u>una</u> semana.    dos
**Ud. tiene que regresar en <u>dos</u> semanas.**

1. <u>Ud.</u> tiene que regresar en dos semanas.    tú    · Tu tienes que
2. <u>Ud.</u> tiene que regresar en dos semanas.    ella    · ella tiene
3. <u>Ud.</u> tiene que regresar en <u>dos</u> semanas.    la paciente, tres    la paciente tiene
4. Ud. tiene que regresar en dos <u>semanas</u>. ←días
5. Ud. tiene que regresar en dos <u>semanas</u>. ←meses

## Para practicar

Tell the patient that he or she has to do the following things.

> **MODELO**   descansar *(to rest)*
> **Ud. tiene que descansar.**

1. tomar la medicina *(take the medicine)*  *Usted tiene que tomar la medicina*
2. tomar el antibiótico *(take the antibiotic)*  *Usted tiene que tomar el antibiót...*
3. descansar mucho *(get a lot of rest)*  *Usted tiene que descansar much...*
4. beber muchos líquidos *(drink plenty of fluids)*
5. ir al hospital *(go to the hospital)*
6. regresar en una semana *(return in one week)*
7. dar una muestra de la orina *(give a urine specimen)*  *Usted tiene que*

## Para practicar más

Ask your partner the questions using the cues provided.

> **MODELO**   el paciente / tomar las pastillas
> A:   **¿Tiene que tomar las pastillas el paciente?**
> B:   **Sí, el paciente tiene que tomar las pastillas.**
>      *or*
>      **No, el paciente no tiene que tomar las pastillas.**

1. la señora Acevedo / beber mucha agua *(water)*
2. el señor Molina / regresar en dos semanas
3. los pacientes / ir a la oficina   *tienen*
4. la doctora / recetar el antibiótico
5. el paciente / tomar las pastillas

## Nota

### Gender of Nouns and Articles  ★ ON TEST

In Spanish all nouns are either masculine or feminine. Generally, nouns ending in **-o** or referring to male beings are masculine. Nouns ending in **-a** or referring to female beings are feminine. This is important because in Spanish the definite article *(the)*, the indefinite article *(a, an)*, and adjectives (as you will see later on) all must agree with the noun to which they refer.

The definite article used before a masculine singular noun is **el** *(the)*; before a feminine singular noun use **la.** The indefinite article for a masculine noun is **un** *(a, an)*; before a feminine singular noun it is **una.** For example:

| | |
|---|---|
| el médico | *the doctor (male)* |
| la doctora | *the doctor (female)* |
| el antibiótico | *the antibiotic* |
| la pastilla | *the pill* |

Unfortunately, not all nouns end in -o or -a, so it is important to learn each noun along with its appropriate definite article. However, there are some general rules to go by. Usually, nouns ending in **-ador, -al, -ente, -ma,** and **-or** are masculine. Nouns ending in **-ción, -sión, -dad, -tad,** and **-ud** are usually feminine. Some nouns referring to people and professions ending in **-a** can be either masculine or feminine. Their gender is indicated by the use of the definite article. For example: **el terapeuta** or **la terapeuta; el especialista** or **la especialista.**

Of course, there are the exceptions to the basic rule, as some nouns can end in **-o** and be feminine (**la mano,** *hand*), while some nouns will end in **-a** and be masculine (**el día,** *day*).

*Tango las manos frío.*

## Para practicar

Tell the gender of these nouns by placing **el** or **la** before each one.

1. medicina = *la medicina*
2. biología = *la biología*
3. dinero = *el dinero*
4. casa = *la casa* → *(el hogar)* — *another word for home*
5. niño = *el niño*
6. idi<u>oma</u> = *el idioma*
7. prob<u>lema</u> = *el problema.* → *Cuál es el problema.*
8. lec<u>ción</u> = *la lección*
9. comuni<u>dad</u> = *la comunidad*
10. deci<u>sión</u> = *la decisión*
11. /hospi<u>tal</u> = *el hospital*
12. paciente *(masc.)* = *el paciente*
13. paciente *(fem.)* = *la paciente*
14. dolor = *el dolor*

## Nota

### Pluralization of Nouns

The rules for pluralization of nouns in Spanish are quite simple and not unlike English. Nouns that end in a vowel form the plural by adding **-s.** Nouns ending in a consonant form the plural by adding **-es.** The definite articles **el** and **la** become **los** and **las** respectively when they accompany plural nouns. The indefinite articles **un** and **una** become **unos** and **unas** (meaning *some* or *a few*). For example:

| | |
|---|---|
| el médico | los médicos |
| la pastilla | las pastillas |
| un paciente | unos pacientes |
| una doctora | unas doctoras |

## Para practicar

Change these nouns and their articles to the plural.

**MODELO**    la medicina
**las medicinas**

1. la semana — las semanas
2. el paciente — los pacientes
3. el dolor — los dolores
4. el líquido — los líquidos
5. el hospital — los hospitales
6. la doctora — las doctoras
7. la píldora — las píldoras
8. la paciente — las pacientes
9. el síntoma — los síntomas
10. la medicina — las medicinas
11. el laboratorio — los laboratorios

## Para practicar más

Now do the same thing with the underlined nouns in context.

**MODELO**    Hablo con el médico.          *I'm speaking with the doctor.*
**Hablo con los médicos.**    *I'm speaking with the doctors.*

1. Trabajo en la clínica. *(I work in the clinic.)* — las clínicas
2. Consultan con el especialista. *(They are consulting with the specialist.)* — los especialistas
3. Necesito la receta. *(I need the prescription.)* — las recetas
4. Hablo con el terapeuta. *(I am speaking with the therapist.)* — (terapista)
5. Hablo con la doctora. *(I am speaking with the doctor.)* — las doctoras

 los terapista

## Recuerde *(Remember)*

Think back to the conversation at the beginning of the chapter. Can you answer the following questions in Spanish?

1. Who is Mr. Vega's doctor?
2. What are Mr. Vega's symptoms?
3. Since when has he been sick?

## NOTA CULTURAL | THE SPANISH LANGUAGE

The word **Castellano** *(Castilian)* has been used in the past to refer to the Spanish language, so named after the central province of Spain, **Castilla.** The Spanish language has spread far and wide since then with an estimated 17 million speakers in the United States. Although there are many variations in pronunciation, vocabulary, and usage throughout the Spanish-speaking world, speakers of Spanish can all understand each other perfectly well. In this text you will learn standard Spanish pronunciation and usage. Just follow each lesson carefully and you will be able to communicate with any native speaker of Spanish, regardless of their country of origin.

**España**

**Las Américas**

**Las naciones**

1) Cuba
2) Rep blica Dominicana
3) Puerto Rico
4) M xico
5) Guatemala
6) El Salvador
7) Honduras
8) Nicaragua
9) Costa Rica
10) Panam
11) Colombia
12) Venezuela
13) Ecuador
14) Per
15) Bolivia
16) Chile
17) Argentina
18) Paraguay
19) Uruguay

**Regiones/Autonomías**

1) Galicia
2) Asturias
3) Cantabria
4) País Vasco
5) Navarra
6) La Rioja
7) Aragón
8) Cataluña
9) Valencia
10) Murcia
11) Andalucía
12) Extremadura
13) Castilla-La Mancha
14) Madrid
15) Castilla-León
16) Canarias

## RESUMEN Y REPASO

# Vocabulario

**El cuerpo** — *The Body*

la **cabeza** — *head*

la **espalda** — *back*

el **estómago** — *stomach*

la **garganta** — *throat*

el **pecho** — *chest*

| **Los síntomas** | **Symptoms** |
|---|---|
| la **ansiedad** | *anxiety* |
| las **convulsiones** | *convulsions* |
| la **diarrea** | *diarrhea* |
| el **dolor** | *pain* |
| los **escalofríos** | *chills* |
| la **fiebre** → or Calentura | *fever* |
| la **flema** | *phlegm* |
| la **garganta irritada** | *sore throat* |
| los **mareos** | *dizziness* |
| las **náuseas** | *nausea* |
| las **palpitaciones** | *palpitations* |
| la **tos** | *cough* |
| los **vómitos** | *vomiting* |

| **Las medicinas** | **Medicines** |
|---|---|
| el **antibiótico** | *antibiotic* ✓ |
| la **aspirina** | *aspirin* |
| las **gotas** | *drops* |
| el **jarabe** | *syrup* |
| las **píldoras** | *pills* |

| **Las enfermedades** | **Diseases** |
|---|---|
| el **catarro** | *cold* |
| la **gripe** → or la gripa | *flu* |
| el **resfriado** | *cold* |

| **Las condiciones** | **Conditions** |
|---|---|
| tener **calor** | ~~*to be hot*~~ warm |
| tener **frío** | *to be cold* |
| tener **miedo** | *to be afraid* |
| tener **sed** | *to be thirsty* |
| tener **sueño** | *to be sleepy* |

hot is mucho Calor

| **Las palabras interrogativas** | **Interrogatives** |
|---|---|
| ¿**Quién**? | *Who?* |
| ¿**Qué**? | *What?* |
| ¿**Cuál**? | *What?; which?* |
| ¿**Dónde**? | *Where?* |
| ¿**Desde cuándo**? | *Since when?* , also "how long" |
| ¿**Cómo**? | *How?* |

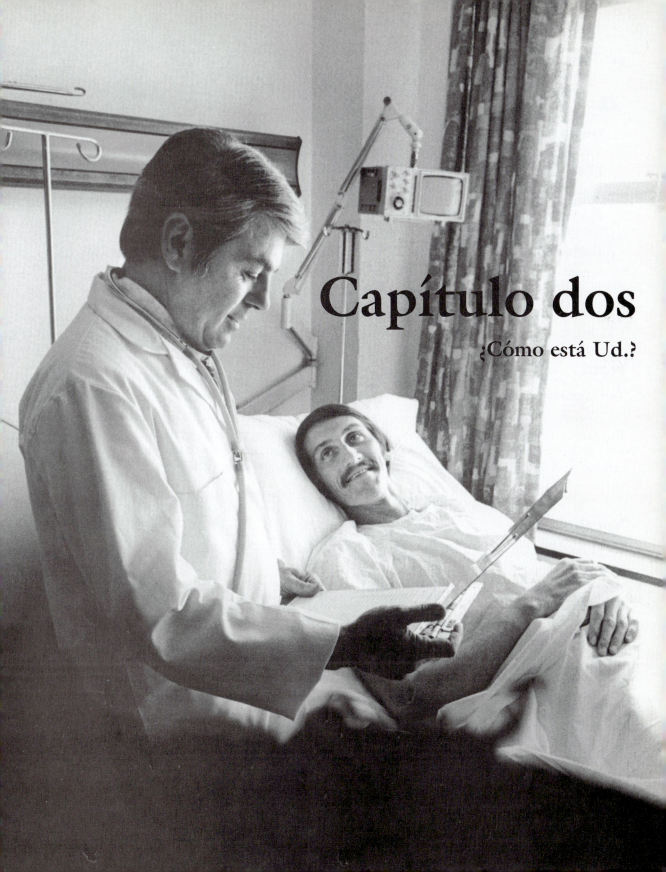

# Capítulo dos

¿Cómo está Ud.?

## Conversación

| | |
|---|---|
| Enfermero: | ¿Cómo está Ud. hoy, señora Moreno? |
| Señora: | No estoy bien. Estoy inquieta y nerviosa. Tengo miedo. |
| Enfermero: | Favor de hablar más despacio. ¿Por qué tiene Ud. miedo, señora? |
| Señora: | Mi familia no está aquí. Tengo miedo del procedimiento que van a hacer mañana. |
| Enfermero: | ¿Dónde está su familia? |
| Señora: | Mi familia está en El Salvador. |
| Enfermero: | No se preocupe, señora. Todo está bien. No hay problema. ¿Está Ud. cansada? |
| Señora: | Sí, estoy cansada, y además estoy muy preocupada. |
| Enfermero: | ¿Por qué no toma Ud. un vaso de agua? |
| Señora: | Muchas gracias, señor. Ahora estoy tranquila. |

## Nota

### Two Important Expressions

Two important expressions to remember are **Favor de hablar más despacio** *(Please speak more slowly)* and **Repita por favor** *(Please repeat)*. In normal speech, especially in hurried or trying circumstances, the Spanish speaker may not enunciate every word clearly, resulting in sentences that sound very fast. Ask them to speak more slowly or simply to repeat. They will be glad to oblige you.

## Vocabulario

| | |
|---|---|
| ¿Cómo está Ud.? | *How are you?* |
| hoy | *today* |
| estoy | *I am* |
| inquieto, -a | *restless, uneasy* |
| nervioso, -a | *nervous* |
| ¿Por qué? | *Why?* |
| mi familia | *my family* |
| el procedimiento | *procedure* |
| No se preocupe. | *Don't worry.* |
| todo | *everything* |
| No hay problema. | *There's no problem.* |
| cansado, -a | *tired* |
| además | *besides, in addition* |
| muy | *very* |
| preocupado, -a | *worried* |
| un vaso de agua | *glass of water* |
| ahora | *now* |
| tranquilo, -a | *calm, tranquil* |

# Nota

### Describing How Someone Feels

Use **está** *(is)* to describe a person's condition—how they feel. For example:

La paciente está nerviosa.                    *The patient is nervous.*

When talking about more than one person, use **están.** For example:

Las pacientes están nerviosas.                *The patients are nervous.*

When you ask a person how they feel, they will respond with **estoy** *(I am)*. For example:

Estoy muy nerviosa.                           *I am very nervous.*

The adjective can end in either **-o** (masculine) or **-a** (feminine). For example: **El señor Castillo está nervioso.** But: **La señora está nerviosa.**

Adjectives must agree with the nouns that they modify. If the noun is masculine, the adjective usually ends in **-o.** If it is feminine, then the adjective usually ends in **-a.** Notice that adjectives in Spanish usually follow the verb that they modify.

# Para practicar

With your partner, take turns naming the person's condition, using the given cues. Be sure to use the correct ending on the adjective (**-o** or **-a**).

> **MODELO**    ¿Cómo está el paciente?    *nervous*
> **El paciente está nervioso.**

1. ¿Cómo está el paciente?    *calm*        El paciente está
2. ¿Cómo está la señorita?    *restless*
3. ¿Cómo está el señor?       *tired*
4. ¿Cómo está la familia?     *worried*
5. ¿Cómo está Ud.?            *???*

# Más vocabulario

| | | | |
|---|---|---|---|
| **aburrido, -a** | *bored* | **deprimido, -a** | *depressed* |
| **agitado, -a** | *upset* | **despierto, -a** | *awake* |
| **agotado, -a** | *exhausted* | **dormido, -a** | *asleep* |
| **ansioso, -a** | *anxious* | **enfermo, -a** | *sick* |
| **borracho, -a** | *drunk* | **enojado, -a** | *angry* |
| **confundido, -a** | *confused* | **sobrio, -a** | *sober* |
| **contento, -a** | *happy* | | |

# Nota

### Pluralizing Adjectives of Condition

In order to form the plural of the adjective, add an -**s.** For example:

El paciente está **enfermo.**     Los pacientes están **enfermos.**

Some adjectives do not end in -**o** or -**a.** In this case just add plural endings when necessary.

El médico es inteligente.                    *The doctor is intelligent.*
Los médicos son inteligentes.               *The doctors are intelligent.*

## Para practicar

Answer the questions by forming the correct plural forms of the cued adjectives.

> **MODELO**   ¿Cómo están las pacientes?     enfermo
> **Las pacientes están enfermas.**

1. ¿Cómo están las mujeres?          ansioso     *Las mujeres están ansiosas.*
2. ¿Cómo están los enfermeros?       contento    *Los enfermeros está Contentos.*
3. ¿Cómo están los médicos?          agotado     *Los médicos está agotados.*
4. ¿Cómo están los hombres?          deprimido   *deprimidos*
5. ¿Cómo están los pacientes?        enojado     *enojados*
6. ¿Cómo están las doctoras?         cansado     *Cansadas*

# Nota

### Telling Where Someone or Something Is Located

Use **está** to indicate location of a person, place or thing; use **están** for the plural. For example:

La señora **está** en el hospital.             *The lady is in the hospital.*
Las señoras **están** en el hospital.          *The ladies are in the hospital.*

## Para practicar

Answer according to the cues.

> **MODELO**   ¿Dónde está el enfermero?     en el hospital
> **El enfermero está en el hospital.**

1. ¿Dónde está el médico?            en la oficina
2. ¿Dónde están los pacientes?       en la sala de espera
3. ¿Dónde están las señoras?         en el hospital
4. ¿Dónde está la enfermera?         en la sala de operaciones
5. ¿Dónde está el señor Gómez?       en el baño
6. ¿Dónde está la familia?           en el cuarto
7. ¿Dónde están los pacientes?       en la sala de emergencias

## Vocabulario

| **Lugares en el hospital** ————————→ | *Places in the Hospital* |
|---|---|
| el **ascensor**  *or* elvador | *elevator* |
| la **cafetería** | *cafeteria* |
| la **clínica** | *clinic* |
| el **cuarto** | *room* |
| el **departamento de servicios sociales** | *Social Services Department* |
| la **farmacia** | *pharmacy* |
| el **hospital** | *hospital* |
| el **laboratorio** | *laboratory* |
| el **pasillo** | *hallway* |
| la **oficina de ingresos** | *admissions office* |
| la **sala de emergencias** | *emergency room* |
| la **sala de espera** | *waiting room* |
| la **sala de operaciones** | *operating room* |
| los **servicios públicos** | *public restrooms* |
| los **teléfonos públicos** | *public telephones* |
| la **tienda de regalos** | *gift shop* |
| la **unidad de cuidados intensivos** | *intensive care unit* |

Sala

## Más vocabulario

| **allí** | *there* |
|---|---|
| **aquí** | *here* |
| **a la derecha** | *on the right* |
| **a la izquierda** | *on the left* |
| **derecho** | *straight* |
| la **planta baja** | *ground floor* |
| el **primer piso** | *first floor* |
| el **sótano** | *basement* |

Note that **la planta baja** *(the ground floor)* is actually the first floor. Therefore, **el primer piso** is typically called the second floor in English.

## Para practicar

Ask your partner where the following are located.

**MODELO**    el departamento de servicios sociales
A:  **¿Dónde está el departamento de servicios sociales?**
el primer piso
B:  **Está en el primer piso.**

1. la oficina de ingresos
   la planta baja   están en
2. la sala de emergencias
   el sótano   están en

3rd floor

3. la sala de operaciones
   el (tercer piso)   esta enel tercer piso
4. los servicios públicos
   a la izquierda   estan
5. los teléfonos públicos
   a la derecha   estan
6. la sala de espera
   derecho   esta

(straignt ahead)

## Conversación

Mrs.

Enfermera:    Señora Moreno, ¿dónde está su (esposo?) husband

Paciente:     Mi esposo está en El Salvador. my husband is in el Salvador

Enfermera:    ¿Tiene Ud. hijos? do have any Children

Paciente:     Sí, tengo un hijo y una hija. yes I have one boy and one girl

Enfermera:    ¿Dónde está su hijo?

Paciente:     Mi hijo está en El Salvador con mi esposo.

Enfermera:    ¿Y su hija? and your daugnter

Paciente:     Mi hija está en la sala de espera.

## Vocabulario

| **La familia** | **The Family** |
| --- | --- |
| el **padre** | father |
| la **madre** | mother |
| los **padres** | parents |
| el **hijo** | son |
| la **hija** | daughter |
| los **hijos** | children |
| el **hermano** | brother |
| la **hermana** | sister |
| los **hermanos** | brothers and sisters |
| el **abuelo** | grandfather |
| la **abuela** | grandmother |
| los **abuelos** | grandparents |
| el **tío** | uncle |
| la **tía** | aunt |
| los **tíos** | aunts and uncles |
| el **primo** | cousin (masc.) |
| la **prima** | cousin (fem.) |
| los **primos** | cousins |
| el **nieto** | grandson |
| la **nieta** | granddaughter |
| los **nietos** | grandchildren |
| el **esposo**, el **marido** | husband |
| la **esposa**, la **señora** | wife |

# ¿QUÉ NIVEL ES PELIGROSO?

La mayoría de las personas adultas deberían procurar mantener el *nivel total de su colesterol* por menos de 200. Los niveles actualmente indicados por los Institutos Nacionales de Salud son los siguientes:

Nivel deseable de colesterol en la sangre: . . . . . . Por menos de 200
Nivel que bordea niveles elevados: . . . . . . . . . . . de 200 a 239
Nivel elevado de colesterol: . . . . . . . . . . . . . . . de 240 para arriba.

# ¿QUÉ ES LO QUE CAUSA EL COLESTEROL ELEVADO?

El colesterol tiende a subir con la edad. Los hombres generalmente tienen niveles de colesterol más elevados que las mujeres. La cantidad de ejercicio físico que usted hace, los alimentos que consume y el hábito de fumar pueden afectar sus niveles de colesterol. Además, en algunas familias puede haber propensión al colesterol elevado. Algunas personas tienen trastornos poco comunes que son la causa de niveles de colesterol muy elevados. Y no hay que olvidar que los niveles de colesterol pueden variar de un análisis a otro.

# ¿CÓMO SE PUEDE BAJAR EL COLESTEROL?

La mayoría de las personas pueden reducir el riesgo de las enfermedades del corazón haciendo cambios en su estilo de vida. Por lo general, con sólo cambiar lo que se come se pueden reducir los niveles de colesterol. Sin embargo, a las personas que corren un grave peligro de sufrir enfermedades del corazón, los médicos a veces les recetan una dieta combinada con medicamentos para controlar el colesterol.

# ¿QUÉ DEBO COMER?

**Coma menos colesterol.** El colesterol sólo está en la carne, los mariscos, los huevos y los productos lácteos. Los alimentos vegetales (cereales, frutas, hortalizas, legumbres y aceites vegetales) no contienen colesterol. La Asociación Americana del Corazón dice que el adulto medio no debería comer más de 300 miligramos de colesterol al día.

**Consuma menos grasa.** Solamente un porcentaje no mayor del 30% del total de las calorías que usted consume debería provenir de la grasa. Controlar la cantidad y la clase de grasas que usted come es más importante aún que medir el colesterol. La clase de grasas que hay en la carne, en la mayoría de los productos lácteos y en algunos aceites (como el aceite de palma y de coco) es la peor para el corazón. Es mejor no consumir grasas que puedan elevar su colesterol.

Para bajar su colesterol, disminuya la cantidad de grasa que come y reemplace por otros los alimentos que son malos para el corazón. Eso no quiere decir que usted tiene que renunciar a comer alimentos agradables—simplemente coma sensatamente.

## Sustituciones

Substitute the underlined words with the cued items. Be sure to make any other necessary changes.

| **MODELO** | Mi <u>hija</u> está en la sala de espera.    hijo |
| --- | --- |
| | **Mi <u>hijo</u> está en la sala de espera.** |

1. Mi <u>hija</u> está en <u>la sala de espera</u>.    esposa, el hospital
2. <u>Mi hija</u> está en la sala de espera.    La doctora, operaciones
3. Mi <u>hija</u> está <u>en la sala de espera</u>.    padre, en casa
4. Mi <u>hija</u> está en <u>la sala de espera</u>.    mamá, la clínica
5. <u>Mi hija</u> está en <u>la sala de espera</u>.    El médico, la oficina

| **N O T A   C U L T U R A L** | **T H E   F A M I L Y** |
| --- | --- |

The family is very important for Spanish-speaking people. Often the immediate family is considered to include extended family members, such as grandparents, cousins, aunts, uncles, and other relatives. Also, the **padrinos**, or *godparents*, are important members of the family, and often take part in family decisions and other personal matters.

## Nota

### Mi, mis, su, sus

The possessive adjective *my* in Spanish is **mi** for singular nouns and **mis** for plural nouns. For example:

**mi** hermano    *my brother*             **mis** hermanos    *my brothers*

To say *your*, use **tu** if the noun is singular and **tus** if it is plural. For example:

**tu** hermano    *your brother*             **tus** hermanos    *your brothers*

**Tu** and **tus** are familiar forms. Notice that **tú** (with an accent mark) means *you*, while **tu** (no accent mark) means *your*.

The formal possessive pronouns are **su** and **sus**. They also mean *your*, but are used in the same situations where you would use **Ud.** or **Uds.**

**Su** and **sus** can also mean *his, her,* or *their.* For example, **su hermano** can mean *his brother, her brother, their brother,* or *your brother.* To avoid confusion, a prepositional phrase can be used to clarify meaning. For example:

el hermano de él       *his brother (the brother of him)*
el hermano de Ud.     *your brother (the brother of you)*

There are four forms for *our;* **nuestro, nuestra, nuestros, nuestras.** These four forms are used for masculine and feminine, singular and plural. They must agree with the noun that follows. For example:

**nuestro** hermano      *our brother*         **nuestra** hermana      *our sister*
**nuestros** hermanos    *our brothers*        **nuestras** hermanas    *our sisters*

## Para practicar

Answer using the cues.

| MODELO | ¿Dónde está su marido?    El Salvador |
|---|---|
| | **Mi marido está en El Salvador.** |

1. ¿Dónde está su hijo?          la sala de emergencias
2. ¿Dónde está su hermano?    la tienda de regalos
3. ¿Dónde está su esposo?      la sala de operaciones
4. ¿Dónde está su abuela?      el departamento de servicios sociales
5. ¿Dónde está su padre?       la unidad de cuidados intensivos

*[handwritten annotations: husband; gift shop; father; grandmother; (intensive care unit); Mi hijo está en la sala...; Mi hermano está en; Mi esposo está en la sala; Mi abuela está en dep; Mi padre está]*

## Para practicar más

Change each sentence by using a prepositional phrase instead of a possessive adjective.

| MODELO | ¿Dónde está su hermano?    ella |
|---|---|
| | **¿Dónde está el hermano de ella?** |

1. ¿Dónde está su padre?      Ud.
2. ¿Dónde está su abuela?     él
3. ¿Dónde está su mamá?       ella
4. ¿Dónde está su hijo?       ellos
5. ¿Dónde está su hermana?    Uds.

## Para practicar más

Change the following sentences by substituting **nuestro, nuestros, nuestra,** or **nuestras** for **mi** or **mis.**

| MODELO | Mi hermano está en el hospital. |
|---|---|
| | **Nuestro hermano está en el hospital.** |

1. Mi hija está en la sala de emergencias.
2. Mis padres están en la clínica.
3. Mi abuelo está en su casa.
4. Mis hijas están en el hospital.
5. Mi mamá está en la sala de espera.

*[handwritten annotations: Nuestra hija; Nuestros padres están en la clínica; Nuestro abuelo está en su casa; Nuestras hijas están en el hospital; Nuestra mamá está en la sala de espera; a big room]*

## Nota

### Conjugation of the Verb Estar—to Be

The following are the forms of the verb **estar:**

| yo | estoy | *I am* | nosotros/nosotras | estamos | *we are* |
|---|---|---|---|---|---|
| tú | estás | *you* (fam.) *are* | | | |
| él/ella | está | *he/she is* | ellos/ellas | están | *they are* |
| Ud. | está | *you* (form.) *are* | Uds. | están | *you* (pl.) *are* |

## Para practicar

Tell which form of **estar** you would use:

1. to talk to a patient — *está (usted)*
2. to talk about yourself — *estoy (Yo)*
3. to talk about several patients — *están (ellos)*
4. to talk to several people — *están (ustedes)*

## Conversación

| | |
|---|---|
| Anestesiólogo: | Buenos días, señora Moreno. |
| Paciente: | Buenos días. ¿Quién es Ud.? *who are you?* |
| Anestesiólogo: | Soy el doctor Rodríguez. *I am* |
| Paciente: | Pero ya tengo un médico, el doctor López. *but I already have a doctor, doctor lópez* |
| Anestesiólogo: | Señora Moreno, el doctor López es el cirujano que le va a hacer el procedimiento. Yo soy el anestesiólogo. *surgeon* |
| Paciente: | ¿Por qué está Ud. aquí? *why are you here?* |
| Anestesiólogo: | Necesito información. ¿Cómo está Ud., señora? |
| Paciente: | Estoy bien, gracias. |

## Vocabulario

| **Los especialistas** | **The** *Specialists* |
|---|---|
| el **anestesiólogo**, la **anestesióloga** | *anesthesiologist* |
| el **cirujano**, la **cirujana** | *surgeon* |
| el **enfermero**, la **enfermera** | *nurse* |
| el **farmacéutico**, la **farmacéutica** | *pharmacist* |
| el **fisioterapeuta**, la **fisioterapeuta** | *physiotherapist* |
| el **ginecólogo**, la **ginecóloga** | *gynecologist* |
| el **neurólogo**, la **neuróloga** | *neurologist* |
| el **obstétrico**, la **obstétrica** | *obstetrician* |
| el **ortopedista**, la **ortopedista** | *orthopedist* |
| el **pediatra**, la **pediatra** | *pediatrician* |
| el **psiquiatra**, la **psiquiatra** | *psychiatrist* |
| el **radiólogo**, la **radióloga** | *radiologist* |
| el **técnico**, la **técnica** *word (Does not exist)* | *technician* |
| el **terapeuta**, la **terapeuta** | *therapist* |
| el **urólogo**, la **uróloga** | *urologist* |

## Nota

### Soy with "Who Are You?"

To ask *"Who are you?"* in Spanish, say «**¿Quién es Ud.?**» The answer is «**(Yo) soy...**» (*"I am..."*).

## Para practicar

Ask your partner the following questions using the cues.

> **MODELO**   el anestesiólogo
> A: **¿Quién es Ud.?**
> B: **Soy el anestesiólogo.**

1. el cirujano ~~Soy el~~ *Surgeon (Cirujana)*
2. la técnica ———————— , Δto técnico
3. el urólogo (uróloga)
4. la neuróloga
5. el pediatra
6. el doctor López
7. la doctora Molina

## Nota

### Soy with «¿Cómo es?»

To ask what someone is like in Spanish, say «¿Cómo es?» Be careful of this expression, as it is a bit different from English. Since there are two words for *is* in Spanish, **es** and **está,** two different ideas can be expressed with the same type of construction. **¿Cómo está el médico?** means *How is the doctor's condition?* or *How is the doctor? ¿Cómo es el médico?* is asking for a description or for his personal characteristics. In English, you would say, *What is the doctor like?* rather than *How is the doctor?* For example:

¿Cómo es el técnico?                    *What is the technician like?*
El técnico es simpático.                *The technician is nice.*

## Vocabulario

| | |
|---|---|
| competente | *competent* |
| diligente | *diligent* |
| impaciente | *impatient* |
| paciente | *patient* |
| simpático, -a | *nice; charming* |

## Para practicar

Answer the questions using the cued responses.

> **MODELO**   **¿Cómo es la doctora?**          *What is the doctor like?*
> **La doctora es inteligente.**          *The doctor is intelligent.*

1. ¿Cómo es la pediatra?        *patient*
2. ¿Cómo es la enfermera?       *impatient*
3. ¿Cómo es el radiólogo?       *nice* ⟶ simpático
4. ¿Cómo es el psiquiatra?      *competent*
5. ¿Cómo es la ginecóloga?      *diligent*

## Más vocabulario

**Las descripciones físicas** *(Physical descriptions)*

alto

baja

flaca

gordo

## Para practicar

Supply the adjective according to the cues.

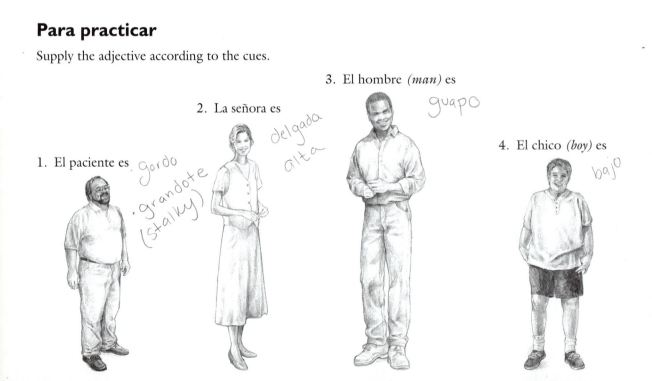

3. El hombre *(man)* es

guapo

2. La señora es

delgada

alta

1. El paciente es

gordo

grandote

(stalky)

4. El chico *(boy)* es

bajo

## Nota

### ¿De dónde es?

To ask where someone is from, use «**¿De dónde es...?**» Notice that in Spanish you may not end a sentence or a clause with a preposition. For example:

¿De dónde es el médico?                    *Where is the doctor from?*
El médico es de Nueva York.                *The doctor is from New York.*

## Para practicar

Answer the question **¿De dónde es...?** according to the cues.

> **MODELO**    ¿De dónde es Ud.?    la República Dominicana
> **Soy de la República Dominicana.**

1. ¿De dónde es el paciente?        Cuba        S
2. ¿De dónde es el médico?          Puerto Rico
3. ¿De dónde es la cirujana?        México
4. ¿De dónde es la pediatra?        El Salvador
5. ¿De dónde es la señora García?   Guatemala
6. ¿De dónde es el psiquiatra?      Colombia
7. ¿De dónde es el ginecólogo?      Los Estados Unidos
8. ¿De dónde es Ud.?                ???

## Nota

### Nationalities

The letter **x** in **México** and **mexicano** *(Mexican)* is pronounced like the letter *h* in *heavy*. Notice also that nationalities are *not* capitalized in Spanish.

## Vocabulario     *= on test*

| Las nacionalidades | Nationalities |
| --- | --- |
| argentino, -a | *Argentinian* |
| colombiano, -a | *Colombian* |
| cubano, -a | *Cuban* |
| dominicano, -a | *Dominican* |
| ecuatoriano, -a | *Ecuadoran* |
| español, española | *Spanish* |
| guatemalteco, -a ✓ | *Guatemalan* |
| hondureño, -a | *Honduran* |
| panameño, -a | *Panamanian* |
| peruano, -a | *Peruvian* |
| puertorriqueño, -a | *Puerto Rican* |
| salvadoreño, -a | *Salvadoran* |
| venezolano, -a ✓ | *Venezuelan* |

## Nota

### The Verb <u>Ser</u>—to Be

The following are the forms of the verb **ser:**

| | | | | | |
|---|---|---|---|---|---|
| yo | **soy** | *I am* | nosotros/nosotras | **somos** | *we are* |
| tú | **eres** | *you* (fam.) *are* | | | |
| el/ella | **es** | *he/she is* | ellos/ellas | **son** | *they are* |
| Ud. | **es** | *you* (form.) *are* | Uds. | **son** | *you* (pl.) *are* |

## Para practicar

Tell each person's nationality.

| MODELO | El paciente es de México. |
|---|---|
| | **Es mexicano.** |

1. El médico es de Cuba.  *es Cubano*
2. La doctora es de España.  *es Española*
3. Los pacientes son de Puerto Rico.  *son puertorriquenos*
4. La enfermera es de Venezuela.  *es venezolana*
5. La señora es de Guatemala.  *es Guatemalteca*
6. Las especialistas son de México.  *son méxicanas*

## RESUMEN Y REPASO

## Vocabulario

**Frases útiles**
Está bien.
Favor de hablar más despacio.
No hay problema.
No se preocupe.

**Useful Phrases**
*It's fine.*
*Please speak more slowly.*
*There's no problem.*
*Don't worry.*

**Para hacer una pregunta**
¿Dónde?
¿De dónde?
¿Cómo?
¿Quién?
¿Por qué?

**To Ask a Question**
*Where?*
*From where?*
*How?*
*Who?*
*Why?*

**Más miembros de la familia**
el cuñado
la cuñada
el suegro
la suegra
el sobrino

**More Family Members**
*brother-in-law*
*sister-in-law*
*father-in-law*
*mother-in-law*
*nephew*

| | |
|---|---|
| la sobrina | *niece* |
| el padrino | *godfather* |
| la madrina | *godmother* |
| el ahijado | *godson* |
| la ahijada | *goddaughter* |

**Más adjetivos**     **More Adjectives**

| | |
|---|---|
| ocupado, -a | *busy* |
| pálido, -a | *pale* |
| vacío, -a | *empty* |
| lleno, -a | *full* |
| cerrado, -a | *closed* |
| abierto, -a | *open* |
| triste | *sad* |
| alegre | *happy* |
| listo, -a | *ready; clever* |
| caliente | *hot* |
| frío, -a | *cold* |
| sentado, -a | *seated* |
| parado, -a | *standing* |
| limpio, -a | *clean* |
| sucio, -a | *dirty* |

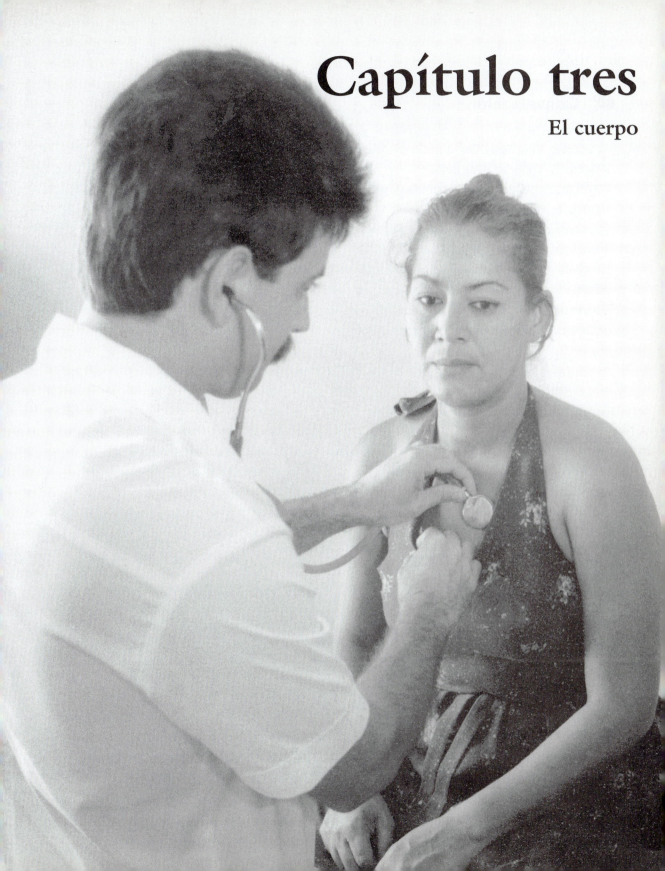

# Capítulo tres

## El cuerpo

## 👁 Conversación

*[handwritten: Good afternoon sir. Do you speak english]*

Doctora: Buenas tardes, señor. ¿Habla Ud. inglés?

Paciente: Buenas tardes, doctora. No, no hablo inglés, solamente hablo español.

*[handwritten: I only speak spanish]*

Doctora: ¿Dónde tiene dolor?

Paciente: Tengo dolor de estómago, y tengo náuseas.

Doctora: ¿Tiene apetito?

Paciente: No, doctora, no tengo apetito.

*[handwritten: ascas = another]*

Doctora: ¿Desde cuándo tiene dolor?

Paciente: Desde hace una semana.

*[handwritten: since one week]*

Doctora: ¿Toma Ud. alguna medicina para el dolor?

*[handwritten: are you takeing some medicine for the pain]*

Paciente: No, doctora, no tomo nada.

*[handwritten: no, I don't take anything]*

Doctora: Ud. necesita un examen médico.

*[handwritten: You need]*

## Vocabulario

| | |
|---|---|
| **Hablo...** | *I speak.* |
| el **español** | *Spanish* |
| **solamente** | *only* |
| el **apetito** | *appetite* |
| **¿Toma Ud....?** | *Do you take?* |
| **alguna** | *some, any* |
| la **medicina** | *medicine* |
| **para** | *for* |
| **No tomo nada.** | *I don't take anything.* |
| **Ud. necesita...** | *You need…* |
| un **examen médico** | *physical examination* |

*[handwritten: ¿Toma Usted? Do you drink]*

*[handwritten: físico = physical]*

## Recuerde

**Usted** (abbreviated **Ud.**) is the formal form of *you* (singular). Use it when addressing adults, especially if you are not on a familiar basis with them. However, if you are a health-care professional who deals mainly with children, you should become accustomed to using the **tú** or familiar form of *you*, which is used when addressing children and other individuals with whom you are familiar. In Latin America, there is only one form for *you* (plural), regardless of whether it is formal or familiar, and that is **ustedes** (abbreviated **Uds.**). (Remember, **vosotros** is used in Spain.)

## Más vocabulario

**El cuerpo humano (*The human body*)**

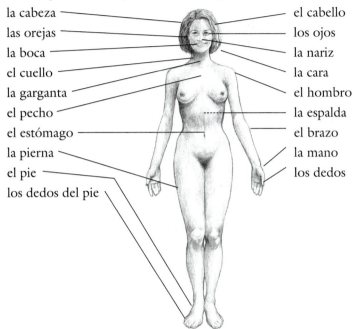

la cabeza — el cabello
las orejas — los ojos
la boca — la nariz
el cuello — la cara
la garganta — el hombro
el pecho — la espalda
el estómago — el brazo
la pierna — la mano
el pie — los dedos
los dedos del pie

## ⁶ Para comunicarse

Complete the conversations by following the model.

> **MODELO**  Médico:     **¿Dónde tiene dolor?**
> Paciente:   cabeza
>             **Tengo dolor de cabeza.**
> Médico:     aspirina
>             **Ud. necesita aspirina.**

1. Médico:    _____
   Paciente:  estómago
   Médico:    un antibiótico

2. Médico:    _____
   Paciente:  los ojos   *Tengo dolor en los ojos. (Pain in the eyes)*
   Médico:    gotas *(drops)*

3. Médico:    _____
   Paciente:  garganta
   Médico:    jarabe para la tos
                    *Syrup for the Cough*

4. Médico: _____
   Paciente:  la espalda
   Médico:    aspirina

5. Médico: _____
   Paciente:  el pecho
   Médico:    un electrocardiograma

6. Médico: _____
   Paciente:  cabeza
   Médico:    un examen médico

## Para practicar

**¿Con quién habla Ud.?** *(With whom are you speaking?).* Answer the questions using the cues provided.

> **MODELO**    ¿Con quién habla Ud.?    la doctora
> **Hablo con la doctora.**

1. ¿Con quién habla Ud.?              el enfermero        *hablo con el enfermero.*
2. ¿Con quién habla Ud.?              mi familia          *hablo con mi familia.*
3. ¿Con quién habla el paciente?      el especialista     *El paciente habla con el especi...*
4. ¿Con quién habla la señora?        el médico           *La Señora habla con el médico...*
5. ¿Con quién habla el señor García?  la recepcionista    *El Señor García habla con la recepci...*
6. ¿Con quién habla la enfermera?     la doctora Sánchez  *La Enfermera habla con la doctora Sánchez.*

## Nota

### Titles and Direct Address

When speaking to a person directly, use the title without the definite article (**el** or **la**). For example: **¿Cómo está Ud., doctora Sanchez?**

However, when speaking about a person, the title must be preceded by the appropriate article: **La doctora Sanchez está en el hospital.**

Other titles include:

| el **señor** | *Mr., sir* | el **profesor** | *Professor* |
| la **señora** | *Mrs., madam* | la **profesora** | *Professor* (fem.) |
| la **señorita** | *Miss* | | |

## Para practicar

Say each sentence supplying **el** or **la** when needed.

1. ¿Cómo está Ud., _____ doctor?

2. _El_ doctor está en el hospital.

3. _El_ señor García está muy enfermo.

4. _La_ señora tiene dolor de cabeza.

5. Ud. necesita un antibiótico, _____ señor.

## Para practicar más

Arrange the words and phrases below to tell some facts about your patient.

1. el paciente / toma / medicina / dolor   *el paciente toma  .medicina .*
2. la paciente / medicina / necesita      *Para dolor.*
3. el señor / inglés / no / habla      *El Señor no habla inglés*
4. la señora / un examen médico / no / necesita

*→ la paciente necesita medicina.*

## Para practicar más

How would you ask your patient the following questions?

1. Do you speak English?   *habla ^usted inglés?*
2. What's wrong?   *Que tiene?*
3. Where does it hurt?   *donde esta dolor?*
4. Since when have you had the pain?   *Desde quando tiene dolor.*
5. What do you take for the pain?   *Que toma para el dolor*

## Nota

### Hablar and -ar Verbs.

Many verbs in Spanish are called regular verbs because they follow a similar pattern. Knowing these patterns makes it easier to remember the different forms (or conjugations). One class of verbs, **-ar** verbs, ends in **-ar** in the infinitive form.

All regular verbs follow the same pattern as the sample verb, **hablar,** below.

**hablar**   *to speak*   *hablar,   fracturar*

| | | | | | |
|---|---|---|---|---|---|
| yo | **hablo** | *I speak* | nosotros/nosotras | **hablamos** | *we speak* |
| tú | **hablas** | *you* (fam.) *speak* | | | |
| él/ella | **habla** | *he/she speaks* | ellos/ellas | **hablan** | *they speak* |
| Ud. | **habla** | *you* (form.) *speak* | Uds. | **hablan** | *you* (pl.) *speak* |

These simple present tense forms are used to express all actions in the present. Therefore, **yo hablo** can mean *I speak, I do speak,* or *I am speaking.*

# Recuerde

**Nosotras** and **ellas** are used for feminine subjects *only*. For masculine only or masculine and feminine combined, or if the gender of the persons is unknown, use the masculine forms (**nosotros** and **ellos**).

Remember that the subject can be and often is omitted in normal conversation. However, this text will use them whenever a verb pattern is given.

If the subject is a noun, rather than a pronoun, it must also agree with the correct verb form (third person singular or plural). For example:

**Él** habla español.          **Carlos** habla español.
**Ellos** hablan español.    **Los pacientes** hablan español.

The following are some regular **-ar** verbs. They follow the same pattern as the verb **hablar.**

| | | | |
|---|---|---|---|
| ayudar | *to help* | operar | *to operate* |
| consultar | *to consult* | orinar | *to urinate* |
| descansar | *to rest* | pasar | *to pass; to enter* |
| entrar (en) | *to enter* | preparar | *to prepare* |
| escuchar | *to listen* +o | sacar | *to remove; to take out* , to draw blood, |
| esperar | *to wait* for | señalar | *to point to*   to stick out |
| explicar | *to explain* | tapar | *to cover*   to pull |
| fumar | *to smoke* | tocar | *to touch*   teeth |
| llamar | *to call* | tratar | *to try; to treat* |
| mirar | *to look; to watch* | | |

# ¡Deje de fumar!

Los fumadores tienen un 300% más de probabilidades de sufrir enfermedades coronarias. (Además, el cigarrillo es el causante del 85% de todos los casos de cáncer del pulmón.) Según investigaciones realizadas en este campo, los ex fumadores pueden reparar en un corto período el daño que han sufrido sus corazones.

# Para practicar

Answer the questions using the cues provided.

> **MODELO**   ¿Quién entra en la oficina?   el paciente
> **El paciente entra en la oficina.**

*[handwritten: Changed by teacher to: "apunta" or "escribe"]*

1. ¿Quién consulta con la doctora?   el señor Vega   *[handwritten: el señor Vega]*
2. ¿Quién prepara la receta?   el médico
3. ¿Quién ayuda a la paciente?   el enfermero
4. ¿Quién descansa?   los niños *(the children)*
5. ¿Quién espera los resultados?   yo
6. ¿Quién llama?   nosotros
7. ¿Quién explica la operación?   la doctora Gómez

*[handwritten: llamamos    espero    descansan]*

# Sustituciones

Substitute the underlined words with the cued items. Be sure to make any other necessary changes.

> **MODELO**   Ud. necesita un examen médico.   el paciente
> **El paciente necesita un examen médico.**

*[handwritten: necesitan]*

1. <u>Ud.</u> necesita <u>un examen médico</u>.   el paciente, un antibiótico
2. <u>Ud.</u> necesita <u>un examen médico</u>.   Uds., una receta
3. <u>Ud.</u> necesita <u>un examen médico</u>.   yo, una cita
4. <u>Ud.</u> necesita <u>un examen médico</u>.   la paciente, una operación
5. <u>Ud.</u> necesita <u>un examen médico</u>.   tú, medicina

*[handwritten: necesito    necesitas]*

# Nota

### The Personal <u>a</u>

Whenever a person is the <u>direct object</u> of a sentence, the direct object is always preceded by the preposition **a:**

El médico ~~prepara~~ la receta.   *[handwritten: no person is the direct object; apunta]*   *The doctor prepares the prescription.*

*BUT:*

El médico prepara **a** <u>la paciente</u> para la operación.   *The doctor prepares the patient for the operation.*

*[handwritten: yes, a person is the direct object]*

Notice that when **a** comes before **el,** one combines them into one word: **al.** Also, while **¿quién?** means *who?*, **¿a quién?** means *(to) whom?*

## Para practicar

Answer the questions according to the cues, using **a** or **al** when necessary.

> **MODELO**   ¿Qué espera el paciente?      los resultados
> **El paciente espera los resultados.**
> ¿A quién llama la doctora?      el paciente
> **La doctora llama al paciente.**

1. ¿A quién ayuda la enfermera?     el niño       *al* — *La enfermera ayuda al niño.*
2. ¿Qué saca el cirujano?     el apéndice     *El cirujano saca el apéndice.*
3. ¿Qué mira el paciente?     la televisión     *El paciente mira la televisión.*
4. ¿A quién opera el cirujano?     el señor Vega     *El cirujano opera al señor Vega.*
5. ¿Dónde espera la madre?     en la sala de espera     *La madre espera en la sala de espera.*
6. ¿Qué señala la paciente?     la cicatriz *(scar)*   *(Point out)*   *La paciente señala la cicatriz.*

## Para practicar más

Communicate the following to a patient.

1. Ask the patient if she speaks English.     *usted — ¿Habla inglés?*
2. Tell the patient that you speak Spanish.     *Yo hablo español.*
3. Ask the patient if he smokes.     *¿Fuma usted?*
4. Ask the patient if she is taking any medicines.     *¿Toma medicina?*  *(está tomando medicina?)*
5. Tell the patient that his mother (**su mamá**) is waiting in the waiting room.     *Su mamá espera en la sala de espera?*
6. Tell the patient that you are preparing a prescription.     *Yo preparo la receta. (una)*

## Conversación

Paciente:   ¿Qué me va a hacer, doctora?   *What are going to to me doctor?*

Doctora:   Le voy a dar un examen médico.   *I am going to give you a physical examination*

Paciente:   ¿Me va a doler mucho?   *will it hurt me much?*

Doctora:   No, no le va a doler. Primero le voy a auscultar, le voy a tomar la presión, y le voy a examinar los ojos, la boca y los oídos.   *first going listen with a stethoscope, I am going to take blood pressure   eyes mouth ears*

Paciente:   ¿Me va a hacer otras pruebas?   *are going to take other tests*

Doctora:   Sí, vamos a tomar una muestra de sangre.   *we are going to take a blood sample*

Paciente:   ¿Ud. me va a tomar la muestra?

Doctora:   No, la enfermera le va a tomar la muestra. Después vamos a mandar la muestra al laboratorio y vamos a saber los resultados en dos o tres días.

Paciente:   ¿Hay algo más, doctora?   *Is there anything else doctora?*

Doctora:   Sí, también le vamos a tomar una muestra de la orina y hacer unas radiografías.

## Nota     *Hacer* [handwritten]

### Hay

A very useful word to remember is **hay** (pronounced like the word *hi*, but with the *h* silent). It means *there is* or *there are*, or as an interrogative, *Is there?* or *Are there?* For example:

¿Hay algo más?                                    *Is there anything else?*
No hay nada.                                       *There is nothing.*

Use the expression **¿Qué hay de nuevo?** to ask *What's new?*

## Vocabulario

| | |
|---|---|
| hacer | *to do; to make* |
| dar | *to give* |
| le voy a dar | *I am going to give (to) you* |
| me | *(to) me* |
| auscultar | *to listen with a stethoscope* |
| tomar la presión | *to take the (blood) pressure* |
| otras pruebas | *other tests* |
| una **muestra de sangre** | *blood sample* |
| mandar | *to send* (also means to order) [handwritten] |
| el laboratorio | *laboratory* |
| vamos a | *we are going to* |
| saber | *to know; to find out* |
| una **muestra de la orina** | *urine sample* |
| las **radiografías** | *X rays* |

*(rayos - x)* [handwritten]

## Para practicar

Your patient asks you what you are going to do (**¿Qué va a hacer?**).

Tell him/her what you are going to do. Use the indirect object pronoun **le** (*to* or *for* him or her) before the verb.

**MODELO**     ¿Qué va a hacer?     examinar
               **Le voy a examinar.**

1. ¿Qué va a hacer?     auscultar
2. ¿Qué va a hacer?     tomar la presión
3. ¿Qué va a hacer?     tomar una muestra de la orina
4. ¿Qué va a hacer?     tomar una muestra de sangre
5. ¿Qué va a hacer?     hacer radiografías

[handwritten:]
Le voy a uscultar.
Le voy a tomar la presión.
Le voy a tom

tomar radiografías
sacar radiografías

## Más vocabulario

| **Pruebas y procedimientos** | **Tests and Procedures** |
| --- | --- |
| la colonoscopia | *colonoscopy* |
| la histerectomía | *hysterectomy* |
| la imagen por resonancia magnética | *MRI* |
| la mamografía | *mammography* |
| el sonograma | *sonogram* |
| la tomografía computada (T/C) | *C/T scan* |
| la vasectomía | *vasectomy* |
| poner una inyección | *to give an injection* |
| tomar el pulso | *to take the pulse* |
| tomar la temperatura | *to take the temperature* |

*(handwritten annotation above "poner": invasive)*

## Para practicar

**El diagnóstico** *(The diagnosis)*. The patient tells you about his/her symptoms. Tell him/her what you are going to do.

> **MODELO**   Paciente:   Tengo mucho calor.
> Doctora:   **Le voy a tomar la temperatura.**

1. Tengo dolor cuando orino. *(handwritten: when↓)* *(handwritten: Le voy a tomar una muestra de orina.)*
2. Tengo dolor de estómago y diarrea con sangre *(blood)*. *(handwritten: Le voy a to)*
3. Tengo dolor de garganta, y tengo tos *(cough)*. *(handwritten: Le voy a auscultar.)*
4. Tengo dolor de cabeza cada día *(every day)*. *(handwritten: Le voy a la tomografía computada. tomar)*

---

## NOTA CULTURAL   LOS COGNADOS (COGNATES)

A cognate is a word whose meaning one can easily guess because of its similarity to the same word in one's own language. As you surely have noticed by now, there are many cognates in Spanish. In the field of medicine the number of cognates is even greater. This is because many of these words are derived from either Greek or Latin, and these languages form a common root between English and Spanish.

Many of these cognates are direct and very obvious. For example:

| | | | |
| --- | --- | --- | --- |
| el aborto | la anemia | el hospital | examinar |
| el accidente | el antibiótico | las náuseas | nervioso, -a |
| la ambulancia | el apetito | el páncreas | |

There are many other cognates that fall into specific categories. For example, words that end in **-itis** are often identical and are usually feminine nouns in Spanish:

| | | |
| --- | --- | --- |
| la apendicitis | la hepatitis | la meningitis |
| la bronquitis | la laringitis | la sinusitis |
| la gastritis | | |

Words that in Spanish have one form for masculine and feminine, and often refer to professions, end in *-ist* in English:

el dentista, la dentista
el especialista, la especialista
el terapeuta, la terapeuta

Words that end in **-tad** and **-dad** in Spanish often end in *-ty* in English. These words are usually feminine in Spanish.

| la comunidad | la generalidad |
|---|---|
| la dificultad | la maternidad |

Words that end in **-ción** or **-sión** in Spanish often end in *-tion* in English. These are usually feminine words.

| la comunicación | la inyección — | *Vascunas (other word for injection)* |
|---|---|---|
| la convulsión | la irritación | |
| la inmunización | la operación | |
| la institución | la palpitación | |
| la instrucción | la respiración | |

Words that end in **-ía** in Spanish and *-y* in English:

| la mamografía | la radiografía |
|---|---|
| la mastectomía | la vasectomía |

Words that end in **-ma** in Spanish are usually of Greek origin and are masculine even though they end in **-a.** In English these words usually end in *-m.*

el diafragma    el problema    el síntoma

There are many words that one can easily figure out with a little bit of detective work and intelligent guessing. Even though Spanish and English are derived from different roots (Spanish comes from Latin, while English comes from Anglo-Saxon), there are many words in English that also come from Latin. These words can be used to figure out the meanings of many words in Spanish, and can also help when trying to memorize new vocabulary. For example, *hand* in Spanish is **la mano.** Nothing similar there, right? But think of the word *manual,* meaning *to do something by hand* and you have found a cognate. Some other examples include:

| el **agua** | *water* | ***aquatic*** |
|---|---|---|
| el **año** | *year* | ***annual*** |
| el **pecho** | *chest* | ***pectoral*** |
| el **sol** | *the sun* | ***solar*** |
| **débil** | *weak* | ***debilitated*** |

Be careful of some false cognates!

| la **red** | *the net* |
|---|---|
| la **sopa** | *soup* |
| **hay** | *there is; there are* |

# Nota

### The Verb <u>Ir</u>—to Go

**Ir** is an irregular verb. This means that its conjugations do not follow a set pattern and that you must remember its forms by themselves. Many very commonly used verbs are irregular, and you must memorize them carefully. Here are the present tense forms of **ir:**

| yo | **voy** | *I go, am going* | nosotros/nosotras | **vamos** | *we go, are going* |
|----|---------|------------------|-------------------|-----------|--------------------|
| tú | **vas** | *you* (fam.) *go, are going* | | | |
| él/ella | **va** | *he/she goes, is going* | ellos/ellas | **van** | *they go, are going* |
| Ud. | **va** | *you* (form.) *go, are going* | Uds. | **van** | *you* (pl.) *go, are going* |

This verb is usually followed by the preposition **a,** which means *to:*

Voy al hospital.                                      *I am going to the hospital.*

As in English, it is also used to say *going to do* something. Use the verb, followed by **a** and the infinitive of another verb. For example:

El cirujano va a operar.                              *The surgeon is going to operate.*

The form, **vamos** by itself, can also mean *let's go.*

Vamos al hospital.                                    *We're going to the hospital.*
                                                      or *Let's go to the hospital.*

# Para practicar

Tell which form of <u>ir</u> you would use to:

1. Say the patient is going to the hospital. *Va al hospital*
2. Say you are going to the hospital. *Yo Voy al hospital*
3. Say the nurses are going to the hospital. *los enfermeros Van al hospital*
4. Say you and the nurses are going to the hospital. *Vamos al hospital Yo y enfermeras*
5. Ask the patient if he is going to the hospital. *Va usted al hospital? (usted - formal you)*

# Para practicar más

Find out from your partner where he/she is going.

*Concerns movement.*

 **MODELO**    **¿Adónde va Ud.?**    al hospital.
                   **Voy al hospital.**

*(voy en casa) when you are*

1. a casa (*home*) *Voy a casa.*
2. a la sala de operaciones *Voy a la sala de operaciones.*
3. a la sala de espera *Voy a la sala de espera.*
4. a la oficina *Voy a la oficina.*
5. a la farmacia *Voy a la farmacia.*
6. a la clínica *Voy a la clínica.*
7. al laboratorio *Voy al laboratorio.*

## Nota

### Indirect Object Pronouns

In Spanish we use indirect pronouns in many cases where they are not used in English. You will need to recognize them and use them in communicative circumstances.

| | |
|---|---|
| me | *(to/for) me* (may) |
| te | *(to/for) you* (tay) |
| nos | *(to/for) us* |
| le | *(to/for) him, her, you* (lay) |
| les | *(to/for) them, you* (pl.) (lays) |

Let's look at some examples:

| | |
|---|---|
| **¿Dónde le duele?** | *Where does it hurt (you)?* |
| **Me duele la pierna.** | *My leg hurts (me).* |
| **¿Qué me va a hacer?** | *What are you going to do (to me)?* |
| **Le voy a examinar.** | *I am going to examine you.* |
| **Le voy a tomar la presión.** | *I am going to take your (blood) pressure.* |
| **¿Qué le pasa?** ¿Qué tiene? | *What's happening (to you)? What's wrong?* |

## Para practicar

Practice with a partner by answering according to the pictures.

**MODELO**   A:  **¿Le duele el estómago?**
                B:  **Sí, me duele el estómago.**
                    *or*
                    **No, no me duele el estómago.**

1.
2.
3.
4.
5.
6.
7.

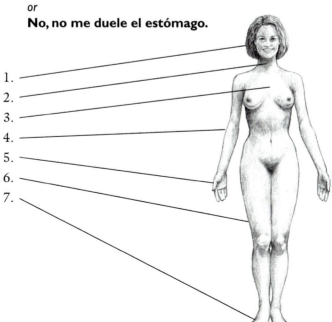

# RESUMEN Y REPASO

## Para practicar

1. Name two ways to ask where it hurts.
2. Name five diagnostic tests.
3. Name three locations in a hospital.
4. Name four patient complaints.

## Vocabulario

| **El cuerpo** | **The Body** |
|---|---|
| la **boca** | *mouth* |
| el **brazo** | *arm* |
| el **cabello** | *hair* |
| la **cabeza** | *head* |
| la **cara** | *face* |
| el **cuello** | *neck* |
| el **dedo** | *finger* |
| el **dedo del pie** | *toe* |
| la **espalda** | *back* |
| el **estómago** | *stomach* |
| la **garganta** | *throat* |
| la **mano** | *hand* |
| la **nariz** | *nose* |
| los **ojos** | *eyes* |
| la **oreja** | *ear* |
| el **pecho** | *chest* |
| el **pie** | *foot* |
| la **pierna** | *leg* |

| **Pruebas y procedimientos** | **Tests and Procedures** |
|---|---|
| la **colonoscopia** | *colonoscopy* |
| el **examen médico** | *physical exam* |
| la **histerectomía** | *hysterectomy* |
| la **imagen por resonancia magnética** | *MRI* |
| la **mamografía** | *mammogram* |
| la **muestra de sangre** | *blood sample* |
| la **presión (sanguínea)** | *blood pressure* |
| el **pulso** | *pulse* |
| las **radiografías** | *x-rays* |
| el **sonograma** | *sonogram* |
| la **temperatura** | *temperature* |
| **auscultar** | *to listen with a stethoscope* |
| **poner una inyección** | *to give an injection* |
| **tomar una muestra de la orina** | *to take a urine sample* |

| | |
|---|---|
| **Para hacer preguntas** | **To Ask Questions** |
| ¿Dónde? | *Where?* |
| ¿Qué? | *What?* |
| ¿Quién? | *Who?* |
| ¿A quién? | *(To) Whom?* |

*A Dónde*

| | |
|---|---|
| **En el hospital** | **In the Hospital** |
| la farmacia | *pharmacy* |
| el laboratorio | *laboratory* |
| la oficina | *office* |
| la sala de espera | *waiting room* |
| la sala de operaciones | *operating room* |

| | |
|---|---|
| **Los verbos** | **Verbs** |
| ayudar | *to help* |
| consultar | *to consult* |
| defecar | *to defecate* |
| entrar (en) | *to enter* |
| escuchar | *to listen to* |
| esperar — | *to wait* for |
| explicar | *to explain* |
| fumar | *to smoke* |
| llamar | *to call* |
| mirar | *to look (at); to watch* |
| operar | *to operate* |
| orinar | *to urinate* |
| pasar | *to pass* |
| preparar | *to prepare* |
| sacar | *to remove,* to draw blood, pull teeth |
| señalar | *to point to* (these are other meanings) |
| tapar | *to cover* |
| tocar | *to touch* |
| tratar | *to treat; to try* |

↓

de tratar

(to try to do something)

# Capítulo cuatro

Las comidas y la nutrición

## 💿 Conversación

**Paciente:**   Doctora, me duele el estómago.

**Doctora:**   ¿Cuándo le duele más?

**Paciente:**   Me duele más por la mañana y antes de comer.

**Doctora:**   ¿Cómo es el dolor?

**Paciente:**   Es como un ardor.

**Doctora:**   Creo que Ud. tiene gastritis. Vamos a hacerle algunas pruebas. Pero Ud. tiene que seguir una dieta especial.

**Paciente:**   ¿Qué dieta debo seguir, doctora?

**Doctora:**   Ud. debe evitar las comidas fritas, picantes y grasientas. Ud. debe evitar también el alcohol, el café y los cigarrillos. Ud. debe comer las comidas blandas, el pan blanco, las sopas calientes y las carnes asadas sin especias.

**Paciente:**   Es una dieta muy estricta. ¿Por cuánto tiempo debo seguirla?

**Doctora:**   Ud. debe seguir la dieta por seis semanas.

**Paciente:**   ¿Puede Ud. recetarme algo?

**Doctora:**   Ud. debe tomar un antiácido, pero para eso no se necesita una receta. Se puede comprar en cualquier farmacia.

## 💿 Vocabulario

| | | | |
|---|---|---|---|
| más | more, most | el **pan** | bread |
| por la **mañana** | in the morning | **blanco, -a** | white |
| **antes de** | before | la **sopa** | soup |
| un **ardor** | burning | **caliente** | hot |
| **creer** | to think | la **carne asada** | broiled meat |
| la **gastritis** | gastritis | **sin** | without |
| **seguir** | to follow | la **especia** | spices |
| una **dieta** | diet | **estricto, -a** | strict |
| **evitar** | to avoid | **algo** | something |
| **frito, -a** | fried | un **antiácido** | antacid |
| **picante** | spicy | **pero** | but |
| **grasiento, -a** | greasy, fatty | **eso** | that |
| el **alcohol** | alcohol | **necesitar** | to need |
| el **café** | coffee | **poder** | to be able, can |
| los **cigarrillos** | cigarettes | **comprar** | to buy |
| **comer** | to eat | **cualquier** | any |
| **blando, -a** | bland | la **farmacia** | pharmacy, drug store |

## Nota

### Use of the Impersonal **Se**

The word **se** is often used in Spanish to show that there is no specific person as the subject of the verb. It is equivalent in English to *you* or *one*, as in **se debe** *(one should)*, or in cases where the passive voice is used in English:

Aquí se habla español.                              *Spanish is spoken here.*

## Preguntas

Answer these questions based on the conversation above.

1. ¿Dónde tiene dolor el paciente? *el estómago*
2. ¿Cuándo le duele más? *Duele más por la mañana y antes de comer*
3. ¿Cómo es el dolor?
4. ¿Qué comidas debe evitar el paciente?
5. ¿Por cuánto tiempo debe seguir la dieta el paciente?

## Sustituciones

Substitute the underlined words with the cued items. Be sure to make any other necessary changes.

**MODELO**    Ud. debe tomar <u>un antiácido.</u>    un antibiótico
             **Ud. debe tomar <u>un antibiótico.</u>**

1. Ud. debe tomar <u>un antiácido</u>.      dos aspirinas
2. <u>Ud.</u> debe tomar <u>un antiácido</u>.      ella, la medicina
3. <u>Ud.</u> debe <u>tomar un antiácido</u>.      la paciente, seguir una dieta blanda
4. <u>Ud.</u> debe <u>tomar un antiácido</u>.      ellos, evitar las comidas fritas
5. <u>Ud.</u> debe <u>tomar un antiácido</u>.      Uds., evitar el café

## Para practicar

Answer the questions according to the cues.

**MODELO**    ¿Qué se debe comer? *(What should one eat?)*    la carne
             **Se debe comer la carne.**

1. ¿Qué se debe comer?      el pan      *Se debe comer el pan.*
2. ¿Qué no se debe comer?      la comida frita      *No se debe comer la comida frita.*
3. ¿Qué se debe comer?      la sopa      *Se debe comer la sopa.*

4. ¿Qué no se debe comer?    la comida grasienta    *No se debe comer la comida grasienta grasosa.*
5. ¿Qué se debe beber *(drink)*?    la leche *(milk)*    *Se debe beber la leche.*
6. ¿Qué no se debe beber?    el café    *No se debe beber el café.*
7. ¿Qué no se debe hacer?    fumar    *No se debe fumar.*
8. ¿Qué se debe hacer?    hacer ejercicio *(exercise)*

*Se debe hacer ejercicio.*
*(ejercicios)*

## Recuerde

**¿Cómo es?** means *What is he/she/it like?*

## Para practicar

Answer using the cues.

> **MODELO**    ¿Cómo es la doctora?    inteligente
> **La doctora es inteligente.**

1. ¿Cómo es el médico?    alto    *El médico es alto*
2. ¿Cómo es el dolor?    fuerte    *El dolor es fuerte.*
3. ¿Cómo es la dieta?    estricta    *La dieta es estricta.*
4. ¿Cómo es la sopa?    deliciosa    *La sopa es deliciosa.*
5. ¿Cómo es la dieta?    equilibrada    *La dieta equilibrada.*

*or rica*

## Conversación

A:    ¿Qué debo hacer, doctor? Estoy muy débil.    *What Should I do doctor? I am very weak*

B:    Ud. debe seguir una dieta equilibrada.    *You should follow a balanced diet.*

A:    ¿Qué debo comer?    *What should I eat?*

B:    Es necesario comer comidas ricas en proteína y vitaminas.    *rich It is necessary to eat food rich in Protein & Vitamins.*

A:    Muchas veces no tengo tiempo para comer bien.    *Often I have no time to eat well.*

B:    Entonces, Ud. debe tomar vitaminas.    *Then You should take vitamins.*

A:    ¿Necesito una receta para comprar vitaminas?    *Is it necessary to have a Rx to buy vitamins*

B:    No, se puede comprar vitaminas en cualquier farmacia o supermercado.
    *no You can buy the Vitamins at any pharmacy or Super market.*

## Vocabulario

| | |
|---|---|
| **débil** | *weak* |
| el **tiempo** | *time* |
| **muchas veces** | *often* |
| **se puede** | *you can, one can* |

## Para practicar

In the following dialogue, play the role of the health care provider and give the Spanish sentences according to the cues.

Paciente: Tengo mucho dolor.

Ud.: *Where does it hurt?*  donde de duele.

Paciente: Me duele el estómago.

Ud.: *Since when does it hurt?*  desde cuando tiene dolor. le duele

Paciente: Desde hace una semana.

Ud.: *What are you taking for the pain?*  Que toma para dolor.

*Que esta tomando.*

Paciente: Tomo un antiácido.

Ud.: *I am going to give you a prescription.*  Le voy a dar una recita.

Paciente: Muchas gracias.

Ud.: *You're welcome.*  de nada

## Vocabulario

### Las comidas y la nutrición *(Foods and nutrition)*

| **El desayuno** | **Breakfast** |
|---|---|
| el **café** | *coffee* |
| el **jugo de naranja** | *orange juice* — also = jugo de arándano (Cranberry Juice) |
| el **té** | *tea* |
| el **cereal** | *cereal* |
| la **fruta** | *fruit* |
| la **mantequilla** | *butter* |
| la **margarina** | *margarine*  Manteca = lard |
| el **pan tostado** | *toast* |
| el **huevo** | *egg* |
| el **tocino** | *bacon* |

| **El almuerzo** | **Lunch** |
|---|---|
| el **agua** | *water* |
| la **leche** | *milk* |
| la **soda** | *soda* — also  refrescos  gaseosa (Carbonated) Soda |
| el **atún** | *tuna* |
| las **galletas** | *crackers; cookies* |
| la **hamburguesa** | *hamburger* |
| el **jamón** | *ham* |
| la **manzana** | *apple* |
| el **pan blanco** | *white bread* |
| el **pan de trigo** | *whole wheat bread* |
| las **papas fritas** | *french fries* — also  Crujientes (Crisp) de papa (french fries)  Crujiente ↑ (Crisp) |
| el **queso** | *cheese* |
| el **sándwich** | torta  also  *sandwich*  also  el requesón (Cottage Cheese) |
| la **sopa** | *soup* |

| **La cena** | **Dinner** |
|---|---|
| la **cerveza** | *beer* |
| el **vino** | *wine* |
| el **aceite de oliva** | *olive oil* |
| el **arroz con pollo** | *chicken with rice* |
| el **bistec** | *steak* |
| la **carne** | *meat* |
| la **ensalada** | *salad* |
| los **frijoles** | *beans* |
| las **habichuelas (verdes)** | *(green) beans* |
| las **legumbres** | *vegetables* |
| el **maíz** | *corn* |
| las **papas** | *potatoes* |
| los **pasteles** | *pies* |
| el **pescado** | *fish* |
| la **pimienta** | *pepper* |
| el **puerco** | *pork* |
| la **sal** | *salt* |
| la **salchicha** | *sausage* |
| los **vegetales** | *vegetables* |

*[handwritten annotations: Helado = ice cream; also lamb = Cordero; Pork Chop = puerco chuleta; low Salt = una dieta baja la sal.]*

## Nota

**The Verb <u>Comer</u> and -er Verbs**

You will recall that the first class of verbs that we saw were -**ar** verbs, or verbs that end in -**ar** in the infinitive. Let's look at another category of verbs, -**er** verbs, whose infinitive ends in -**er.** All regular -**er** verbs follow the same pattern as the verb **comer** *(to eat).*

comer   *to eat*

| yo | **como** | *I eat* | nosotros/nosotras | **comemos** | *we eat* |
|---|---|---|---|---|---|
| tú | **comes** | *you* (fam.) *eat* | | | |
| él/ella | **come** | *he/she eats* | ellos/ellas | **comen** | *they eat* |
| Ud. | **come** | *you* (form.) *eat* | Uds. | **comen** | *you* (pl.) *eat* |

Here are some more regular -er verbs.

| aprender | *to learn* | *[handwritten: aprendo a]* |
|---|---|---|
| beber | *to drink* | |
| comprender | *to understand* | |
| correr | *to run* *[handwritten: (physically run)]* | |
| creer (que) | *to think, to believe (that)* | |
| deber | *should, must; to owe* | |
| responder | *to respond* | |

# GUIA HACIA LA BUENA ALIMENTACION

*Todos los días coma una gran variedad de alimentos de los Cuatro Grupos Alimenticios con moderación.*

### Grupo de Leche

Provee muchos nutrientes que incluyen:
- calcio
- proteína
- riboflavina

**2** porciones para adultos

**3** porciones para niños

**4** porciones para adolescentes y mujeres embarazadas o que están lactando

### Grupo de Carne

Provee muchos nutrientes que incluyen:
- proteína
- hierro
- niacina
- tiamina

**2** porciones para todas las edades

**3** porciones para mujeres embarazadas

### Grupo de Fruta y Vegetal

Provee muchos nutrientes que incluyen:
- vitamina A
- vitamina C

**4** porciones para todas las edades

### Grupo de Pan y Cereal

Provee muchos nutrientes que incluyen:
- carbohidratos
- hierro
- tiamina
- niacina

**4** porciones para todas las edades

## Alimentos Combinados

Los Alimentos Combinados están hechos de más de un grupo alimenticio. Por lo tanto, proveen los mismos nutrientes que las comidas que contienen.

## Categoría de "Otros"

Los alimentos en la categoría de "Otros" frecuentemente son altos en calorías y/o bajos en nutrientes. Estos no toman el lugar de alimentos de los Cuatro Grupos Alimenticios en la provisión de nutrientes.

**Condimentos**
Salsa para barbacoa
Salsa dulce de tomate (catsup)
mostaza
Aceitunas, pepinillos encurtidos (pickles)
Sal
Salsa soya

**Frituras (chips) y productos relacionados**
Frituras (chips) de maíz (doritos)
Rosetas o palomitas de maíz
Papitas fritas
Pretzels
Tortillas fritas (tostaditas)

**Grasas y Aceites**
Crema en polvo para café
Crema, crema agria (jocoque)
Salsa o jugo para carne, salsa de crema
Margarina, mantequilla
Mayonesa
Aceite, manteca de puerco/ cerdo, manteca vegetal
Aderezos

**Dulces o golosinas**
Dulces de chocolate (brownies) galletas
Pasteles o bizcochos tortas
Dulces, confites bombones
Jalea, mermelada
Azúcar, miel, sirop
Panecillos dulces, donas

**Alcohol**
Cerveza
Ginebra, vodka
Whiskey, ron
Vino

**Otras bebidas**
Café, té
Refrescos con sabor a frutas
Refrescos carbonatados (gaseosas)

001NS 1 1989, Copyright © 1989, 5th Edition, NATIONAL DAIRY COUNCIL.® Rosemont, IL 60018-4233. All rights reserved. Printed in U.S.A.　　ISBN 1-55647-001-0

## Para practicar

Answer the questions according to the cues.

| MODELO | ¿Qué come el paciente? *to eat* | fruta |
|---|---|---|

**El paciente come fruta.**

1. ¿Qué come la señora Gómez?    pan blanco   come
2. ¿Qué come Carlos?    pescado   come
3. ¿Qué comen los pacientes?    vegetales   comen  ·legumbres (another word for) ·verduras {vegetable}
4. ¿Qué come Ud.? → yo    carne   como
5. ¿Qué come el médico?    pollo   come
6. ¿Qué bebe el paciente?    vino   toma
7. ¿Qué bebe Paquita?    café   bebe
8. ¿Qué bebe el enfermero?    té   bebe
9. ¿Qué bebes tú? → yo    leche   bebo
10. ¿Qué beben Uds.?    cerveza — tomamos
11. ¿Qué beben ellos?    agua   beben

## Más vocabulario

| | |
|---|---|
| el **desayuno** | *breakfast* |
| el **almuerzo** | *lunch* |
| la **cena** | *dinner* |
| **desayunarse** | *to have breakfast* |
| **almorzar** | *to have lunch* |
| **cenar** | *to have dinner* |
| las **calorías** | *calories* |
| la **comida**   *3 meanings* | *meal*, food, groceries |
| la **dieta equilibrada** | *balanced diet* |
| la **grasa** | *fat* |
| los **minerales** | *minerals* |
| la **proteína** | *protein* |
| el **régimen** | *diet* |
| las **vitaminas** | *vitamins* |
| **tomar** | *to take, to drink (alcohol)* |

## Nota

### The Verb <u>Deber</u>—Ought to, Should; to Owe

The verb **deber** is a regular -**er** verb and means *to owe, must, should,* or *ought to.* It is somewhat equivalent to the expression **tener que** *(to have to).* However, it is stronger than the English *should,* as it implies an obligation. It can be softened by following it with the preposition **de.** For example:

| | |
|---|---|
| Ud. debe de pagar la cuenta. | *You must pay the bill.* |
| Ud. debe de comer más frutas. | *You should eat more fruit.* |

*Toronja = grapefruit*

## Para practicar

Change the following sentences using **deber de** instead of **tener que**. Remember to make the verb agree with the subject.

1. Tú tienes que comer mucha carne.    *debes de* — *more meat*
2. Ud. tiene que preparar la comida.    *debe de*
3. Nosotros tenemos que tomar vitaminas.    *debemos de*
4. Yo tengo que beber mucha leche. -    *debo de*
5. Ella tiene que beber mucho jugo. —    *debe de*
6. Ud. no tiene que tomar vino. —
7. Ud. tiene que seguir un régimen. —    *no debe de*
8. Ellos tienen que comer más vegetales. —    *debe de*  — *eat more*
9. Yo tengo que almorzar ahora. — *now*    *deben de*    — *to have lunch*   *debo de*
10. Ud. tiene que desayunarse cada día.    *= (Per day)* = *todo los días*    *debe de*

*You should    breakfast    ·al día    ·diario*

---

### NOTA CULTURAL            LA COMIDA HISPANA

The Spanish-speaking world is very widespread and has an extremely diverse cuisine. Some general observations, however, can be made. People in Mexico, for example, rely on corn (**el maíz**) as their staple food, and many products are made from it. The **tortilla** is a flat corn pancake that is usually filled with meat, beans, or other vegetables. Other foods made from corn are **tacos, enchiladas,** and **burritos.** Mexican food is often spicy (**picante**) compared to American foods. As a result, a Mexican patient in the hospital may very well complain that the food is too bland (**blanda**).

People from the Caribbean (Puerto Rico, The Dominican Republic, Cuba) are accustomed to eating less meat than most Americans. Some popular dishes are **arroz con habichuelas** (*rice and beans*), **arroz con pollo** (*chicken and rice*), and **sopa de pescado** (*fish soup*). They eat a great variety of fresh vegetables and tropical fruits, such as **guayaba** (*guava*) and **plátano** (*plantain,* usually served fried and eaten as a starch, like potatoes). Their foods are generally not as spicy as Mexican foods, and a very common method of food preparation is frying. Again, they will probably find many North American dishes to be rather bland in comparison to their own.

---

## Nota

### Reflexive Pronouns

Reflexive pronouns are used to show that the subject is acting upon himself or herself. The following are the reflexive pronouns.

| | | | |
|---|---|---|---|
| **me** | *myself* | **nos** | *ourselves* |
| **te** | *yourself* — *informal for (tu)* | | |
| **se** | *himself, herself, itself, yourself* (formal) | **se** | *themselves, yourselves* |

Reflexive pronouns precede the verb and can be used with or without the subject pronoun:

Yo me lavo.   *or*   Me lavo.                                    *I wash myself.*

Many verbs are reflexive in Spanish even though the reflexive meaning may not be apparent in English. Such verbs must be learned as reflexive verbs. Note that a reflexive verb in the dictionary will be given with **se** attached to it. In this case, the **se** means *oneself.* Some reflexive verbs are:

| | |
|---|---|
| acostarse | *to go to bed* (irregular verb) , to lie down |
| bañarse | *to bathe* — |
| cansarse | *to tire* |
| desayunarse | *to have breakfast* |
| despertarse | *to wake up* (irregular verb) |
| dormirse | *to fall asleep* (irregular verb) |
| lavarse | *to wash oneself* — |
| levantarse | *to stand up, to get up* |
| llamarse | *to be called* |
| quejarse de | *to complain of* |
| sentarse | *to sit down* (irregular verb)* |

adormecerse → to snooze

# Para practicar

Change the sentences using the cues.

> **MODELO**    El muchacho se baña.    nosotras
> **Nosotras nos bañamos.**

1. Las señoras se cansan.
   yo                el paciente        el médico            las enfermeras

2. Mi padre se lava cada día.
   nosotros          mis padres         mi hijo              tú

3. Miguel se levanta temprano *(early)*.
   el señor Gómez    las pacientes      yo                   nosotros

4. El paciente se baña.
   yo                Ud.                el niño              tú

5. El médico no se desayuna.
   la señora         mi paciente        ella                 yo

---

*For irregular verb conjugations, see the Appendix.

## Nota

**¿De qué se queja?** *(What is he/she complaining about?)*

Notice that in Spanish one cannot end a sentence with a preposition. For example:

¿De qué se queja el hijo?　　　　　　　　　○ *What is the son complaining about?*
El hijo se queja de la comida.　　　　　　　*The son is complaining about the food.*

## Para practicar

Answer the questions using the cues.

> **MODELO**　　　¿De qué se queja la paciente?　　el almuerzo
> **La paciente se queja del almuerzo.**

¿De qué se queja el paciente?　*de*　el desayuno　　*○ el paciente se queja de.*
¿De qué se queja la señora?　*de*　la cena
¿De qué se queja la mujer?　*de*　el pollo
¿De qué se queja Ud.?　*de*　la comida　　*○ yo me quejo de la comida.*
¿De qué se quejan los pacientes?　*de*　el almuerzo　　*○ los pacientes se quejan del almuerzo.*

##  Nota

### The Verb <u>Preferir</u> and -ir Verbs

The verb **preferir** belongs to the class of **-ir** ending verbs. The following is an example of a regular **-ir** verb.

**escribir**　　*to write*

| yo | escribo | *I write* | nosotros/nosotras | **escribimos** | *we write* |
|---|---|---|---|---|---|
| tú | escribes | *you* (fam.) *write* | | | |
| él/ella | escribe | *he/she writes* | ellos/ellas | escriben | *they write* |
| Ud. | escribe | *you* (form.) *write* | Uds. | escriben | *you* (pl.) *write* |

*abrir → abre  (to open)*

**Preferir** is an irregular verb. It has the same endings as a regular **-ir** verb, but the **-e** in the stem, or main part of the verb, changes to **-ie** (except in the **nosotros** form).

**preferir**　　*to prefer*

| yo | prefiero | *I prefer* | nosotros/nosotras | **preferimos** | *we prefer* |
|---|---|---|---|---|---|
| tú | prefieres | *you* (fam.) *prefer* | | | |
| él/ella | prefiere | *he/she prefers* | ellos/ellas | prefieren | *they prefer* |
| Ud. | prefiere | *you* (form.) *prefer* | Uds. | prefieren | *you* (pl.) *prefer* |

# Para practicar

Answer using the cues.

 ¿Cuál prefiere el paciente, el pan o el arroz?
**El paciente prefiere <u>el arroz</u>.**

1. ¿Cuál prefiere el paciente, el té o el café?

   El paciente prefiere el té.

   Café tera (coffee pot)

2. ¿Cuál prefiere Carlos, la leche o el jugo de naranja?

   Carlos prefiere el jugo de naranja.

3. ¿Cuál prefiere la señorita, la margarina o la mantequilla?

   La señorita prefiere la margarina.

4. ¿Cuál prefieren los pacientes, la cerveza o el vino?

   Los pacientes prefieren la cerveza.

5. ¿Cuál prefieren las pacientes, los huevos o el pescado?

*[handwritten annotations: eggs, fish]*

*Las pacientes prefieren los huevos.*

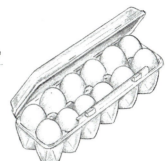

6. ¿Cuál prefiere Ud., el pollo o el bistec?

*[handwritten annotation: Steak]*

*Yo prefiero el pollo.*

7. ¿Cuál prefieres tú, las peras o las manzanas?

*[handwritten annotations: apples, Pears]*

*Yo prefiero las manzanas*

8. ¿Cuál prefiere ella, el atún o el arroz?

*Ella prefiere el atún.*

## Conversación

A:  ¿Qué debo hacer para perder peso, doctora? *what should I do to lose weight doctor?*

B:  Ud. debe seguir una dieta, señor. — *You shold follow a diet Señor.*

A:  ¿Qué debo comer?

B:  Ud. tiene que reducir las calorías y también evitar las comidas grasientas como la mantequilla y el queso. *reduce calories & avoid con grasa fatty foods like butter & cheese*

A:  ¿Qué más? *what else*

B:  Es necesario también comer más vegetales y frutas y evitar los postres y otras comidas ricas. *It is necessary to eat > veggies & fruit, avoid dessert and other rich (fibray) foods*

A:  ¿Qué debo beber? *what should I drink*

B:  Ud. debe beber mucha agua, y además es necesario comer comidas ricas en fibra y vitaminas.

A:  ¿Hay algo más que debo hacer, doctora? *= IS there*

B:  Sí, Ud. debe hacer ejercicio. *yes you should exercise*

## Vocabulario

perder peso                              *to lose weight*
la **fibra**                             *fiber*
hacer ejercicio                          *to exercise*
tres veces a la semana                   *three times a week*

## Para practicar

Give your patient the following instructions in Spanish.

1. You should avoid greasy foods.
2. You should not smoke.
3. You should exercise three times a week.
4. You should eat more vegetables.
5. You should avoid fried foods.
6. You should follow a diet.
7. You should follow the diet for six months *(meses)*.
8. You should avoid alcohol.

## Para practicar más

Ask your patient these questions; he or she answers with the cues. (Try to use full sentences.)

 **MODELO**    Prefiere Ud. el hospital o la clínica?    la clínica
**Prefiero la clínica.**

1. ¿Prefiere Ud. beber el jugo de china o el jugo de tomate?    el jugo de china
2. ¿Qué va a beber Ud., el café o el té?                         el té
3. ¿Va Ud. a comprar el pan blanco o el pan de trigo?           el pan blanco
4. ¿Usa Ud. la sal o la pimienta?                                la pimienta
5. ¿Tiene Ud. que comprar las peras o los plátanos?            las peras
6. ¿Va Ud. a comprar las frutas o los vegetales?               las frutas
7. ¿Prefiere Ud. los huevos o la carne?                         los huevos

Now try to do the same questions using the **tú** form instead of **Ud.** and choose a different answer.

**MODELO**    ¿Prefieres beber el jugo de china o el jugo de tomate?    el jugo de tomate
**Prefiero beber el jugo de tomate.**

 Read the following passage and then try to answer the questions below in Spanish.

## Lectura:   La nutrición y la salud

La nutrición es muy importante para la salud de cualquier individuo. Para evitar las enfermedades, es necesario seguir una dieta equilibrada. Se debe de comer comidas ricas en proteína como la carne, la leche, el queso y los huevos. También se debe comer vegetales ricos en vitaminas como la lechuga, la espinaca, los guisantes, el maíz y el apio.

Cuando un individuo sufre de una enfermedad específica, debe seguir una dieta especial. Por ejemplo, la persona que sufre de una enfermedad gastrointestinal debe seguir una dieta blanda. Para el paciente que sufre de la alta presión, se recomienda una dieta de sal reducida. El médico o el dietista es responsable de recomendarle al paciente la dieta más beneficiosa para su salud y bienestar.

## Preguntas

1. ¿Qué es necesario para evitar las enfermedades?
2. ¿Cuáles son las comidas ricas en proteína?
3. ¿Cuáles son algunos *(some)* vegetales importantes?
4. ¿Qué dieta debe seguir el individuo que sufre de una enfermedad gastrointestinal?
5. ¿Qué dieta se recomienda al paciente que sufre de la alta presión?

## Vocabulario

| | |
|---|---|
| importante | *important* |
| la **salud** | *health* |
| cualquier | *any* |
| el **individuo** | *individual* |
| también | *also* |
| específico, -a | *specific* |
| la **persona** | *person* |
| recomendar | *to recommend* |
| para | *for* |
| su | *his, her, their* |
| el **bienestar** | *well-being* |

## RESUMEN Y REPASO

## Vocabulario

**Las comidas**

| **Las carnes** | **Meats** |
|---|---|
| la **carne de res** | *beef* |
| el **cordero** | *lamb* |
| el **pavo** | *turkey* |
| el **pollo** | *chicken* |
| la **ternera** | *veal* |

| **El pescado y los mariscos** | **Fish and Shellfish** |
|---|---|
| las **almejas** | *clams* |
| los **camarones** | *shrimp* |
| los **cangrejos** | *crabs* |

las **gambas**          *shrimp*
la **langosta**         *lobster*
las **ostras**          *oysters*
el **salmón**           *salmon*
las **sardinas**        *sardines*

**Los vegetales y las verduras**    ***Vegetables and Greens***
el **ajo**              *garlic*
el **apio**             *celery*
el **arroz**            *rice*
el **brócoli**          *broccoli*
la **calabaza**         *squash; pumpkin*
la **cebolla**          *onion*
la **coliflor**         *cauliflower*
el **espárrago**        *asparagus*
la **espinaca**         *spinach*
el **guisante**         *pea*
el **hongo**            *mushroom*
la **lechuga**          *lettuce*
la **papa al horno**    *baked potato*
el **pepino**           *cucumber*
la **remolacha**        *beet*
el **tomate**           *tomato*
la **zanahoria**        *carrot*

**Las frutas**          ***Fruits***
el **albaricoque**      *apricot*
la **cereza**           *cherry*
la **ciruela**          *plum*
la **ciruela pasa**     *prune*
el **coco**             *coconut*
la **fresa**            *strawberry*
la **guayaba**          *guava*
el **guineo**           *banana*
el **limón**            *lemon*
el **melocotón**        *peach*
la **naranja**          *orange*
la **pera**             *pear*
la **piña**             *pineapple*
el **plátano**          *plantain*
la **toronja**          *grapefruit*
la **uva**              *grape*

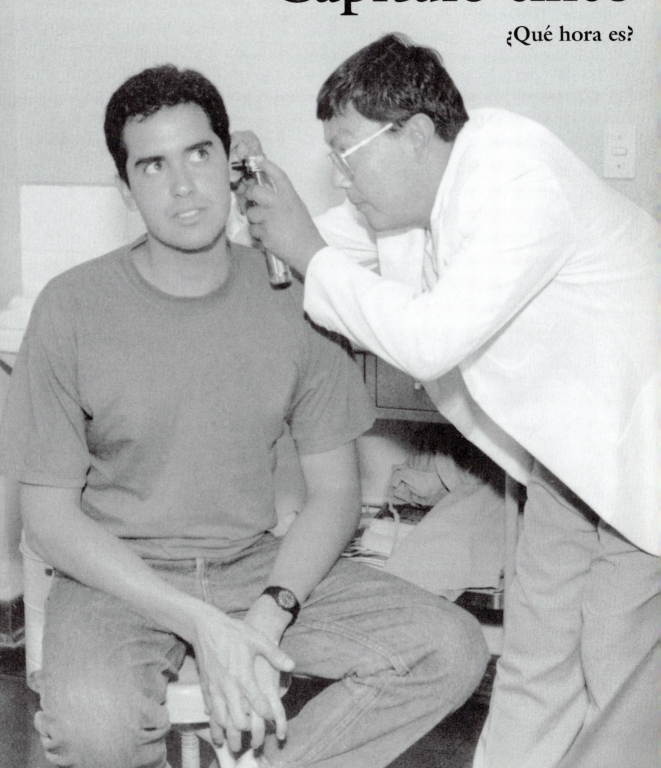

# Capítulo cinco

¿Qué hora es?

**Conversación**

| | |
|---|---|
| El señor Reyes: | Buenos días, señorita. |
| Recepcionista: | Buenos días, señor. ¿En qué puedo servirle? |
| El señor Reyes: | Tengo una cita con la doctora Méndez. |
| Recepcionista: | ¿A qué hora es su cita? |
| El señor Reyes: | Es a las once. |
| Recepcionista: | Muy bien, señor. La doctora va a llegar a las once y media. Favor de llenar este formulario. Puede sentarse. |
| El señor Reyes: | Gracias, señorita. |

**(Llega la doctora.)**

| | |
|---|---|
| El señor Reyes: | Buenos días, doctora. |
| La doctora Méndez: | Buenos días, señor Reyes. ¿Cómo se siente Ud. hoy? |
| El señor Reyes: | No me siento bien, doctora. Me duele toda la cabeza. Me duelen los ojos, la nariz y los oídos. |
| La doctora Méndez: | ¿Desde cuándo se siente así? |
| El señor Reyes: | Desde hace un par de semanas. |

**(La doctora le examina al señor Reyes.)**

| | |
|---|---|
| La doctora Méndez: | Ud. tiene un caso de sinusitis. Tiene la nariz tapada y los oídos tapados también. Además, Ud. tiene la presión un poco alta, y tiene un poco de temperatura. |
| El señor Reyes: | ¿Qué debo hacer, doctora? |
| La doctora Méndez: | Yo le receto un antibiótico que Ud. debe tomar cada seis horas. También debe tomar muchos líquidos y descansar mucho. |
| El señor Reyes: | Muchas gracias, doctora. |
| La doctora Méndez: | De nada señor. Adiós. |

## Vocabulario

| | |
|---|---|
| una **cita** | *appointment* |
| **llegar** | *to arrive* |
| **llenar** | *to fill out* |
| el **formulario** | *form* |
| **sentarse** | *to sit down* |
| **sentirse** | *to feel* |
| **todo, toda** | *all, every* |
| **así** | *so, thus* |
| **un par de** | *a couple of* |
| **semanas** | *weeks* |
| la **sinusitis** | *sinusitis* |
| **tapado, -a** | *stuffed* |
| **cada** | *each, every* |

## ¿SABÍA USTED QUE?

Los derrames cerebrales causan más incapacidad mental y física que cualquier otra enfermedad? Y que unas 150.000 personas mueren cada año a causa de los derrames cerebrales en los Estados Unidos?

## ¡PERO TENEMOS DEFENSA!

En la mayoría de los casos, nuestro cuerpo nos da señales que nos avisan cuando un derrame cerebral puede ocurrir.

## ESTAS SEÑALES SON

Estos síntomas pueden durar, unos cuantos segundos, minutos u horas, pero pueden desaparecer y repetirse más tarde.

## ¿QUÉ DEBEMOS HACER?

Si usted siente uno o más de estos síntomas, llame a su médico o vaya a la clínica inmediatamente y déjele saber al personal médico que usted está sintiendo los síntomas de un derrame cerebral.

## 👁 Más vocabulario

**Partes de la cabeza (*Parts of the head*)**

el cuero cabelludo (*scalp*)

la frente (*forehead*)

la ceja (*eyebrow*)

el ojo (*eye*)

la nariz (*nose*)

la fosa nasal (*nostril*)

la boca (*mouth*)

el cuello (*neck*)

el cabello, el pelo (*hair*)

la sien (*temple*)

la oreja (*outer ear*)

el oído (*inner ear*)

la mejilla, el cachete (*cheek*)

la quijada, la mandíbula (*jaw*)

la barbilla, el mentón (*chin*)

la nuez de Adán (*Adam's apple*)

## Sustituciones

Substitute the underlined word with the cued items. Be sure to make any other necessary changes.

> **MODELO**     La doctora va a llegar <u>a las once y media</u>.     a las doce
> **La doctora va a llegar <u>a las doce</u>.**

1. <u>La doctora</u> va a llegar <u>a las once y media</u>.     el médico, a la una
2. <u>La doctora</u> va a llegar <u>a las once y media</u>.     la paciente, a las dos y cuarto
3. <u>La doctora</u> va a llegar <u>a las once y media</u>.     yo, a las tres y cinco
4. <u>La doctora</u> va a <u>llegar</u> <u>a las once y media</u>.     salir, a las cinco
5. <u>La doctora</u> va a <u>llegar</u> <u>a las once y media</u>.     el médico, salir, a las cinco y media

## Nota

### <u>Hace</u> in Expressions of Time

The verb **hace** (from **hacer:** *to make, to do*) is often used in expressions referring to time. It is roughly equivalent to the word *ago* in English.

¿Desde cuándo se siente así?

*How long have you been feeling this way?*
(*Literally, "Since when are you feeling this way?"*)

Desde hace un par de semanas.

*For a couple of weeks.*
(*Or "Since a couple of weeks ago."*)

## Recuerde

In Spanish, the simple present tense is equivalent to all present tense forms in English. Therefore, **receto** can mean *I prescribe, I do prescribe,* or *I am prescribing.* No additional helping verbs are required. Also, to make a sentence negative, simply put **no** directly before the verb. **No receto** means *I do not prescribe* or *I am not prescribing.*

## Conversaciones

A:  ¿Cómo se siente Ud.?

B:  Me siento mal.

A:  ¿Qué le pasa?

B:  Tengo fiebre.

A:  ¿Desde cuándo se siente mal?

B:  Desde hace una semana.


A:  ¿Cómo se siente su abuela?

B:  Se siente enferma.

A:  ¿Qué le pasa?

B:  Tiene artritis.

A:  ¿Desde cuándo se siente enferma?

B:  Desde hace un año.

## Para practicar

Answer the question **¿Dónde le duele?** using the cued responses.

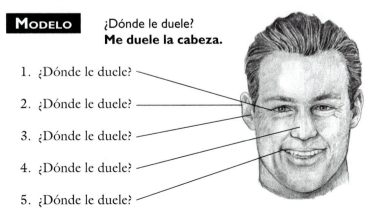

**MODELO**    ¿Dónde le duele?
**Me duele la cabeza.**

1.  ¿Dónde le duele?

2.  ¿Dónde le duele?

3.  ¿Dónde le duele?

4.  ¿Dónde le duele?

5.  ¿Dónde le duele?

## Para practicar más

**¿Como se siente Ud.?** *(How do you feel?)* Answer the questions using the cues provided.

| MODELO | ¿Cómo se siente su mamá?     mal |
|--------|------------------------------------|
| | **Se siente mal.** |
| | ¿Desde cuándo se siente mal?     un mes |
| | **Se siente mal desde hace un mes.** |

1. ¿Cómo se siente su hijo?                    mal
   ¿Desde cuándo se siente mal?               una semana

2. ¿Cómo se siente su padre?                  enfermo
   ¿Desde cuándo se siente enfermo?          dos meses

3. ¿Cómo se siente el paciente?               cansado
   ¿Desde cuándo se siente cansado?          dos semanas

4. ¿Cómo se siente la señora?                 mejor
   ¿Desde cuándo se siente mejor?            un año

5. ¿Cómo se siente su abuelo?                 débil
   ¿Desde cuándo se siente débil?            tres semanas

6 .¿Cómo se siente la paciente?               enferma
   ¿Desde cuándo se siente enferma?          dos días

7. ¿Cómo se siente el niño?                   fuerte
   ¿Desde cuándo se siente fuerte?           dos años

8. ¿Cómo se siente Ud.?                       mareado/mareada *(dizzy)*
   ¿Desde cuándo se siente mareado/mareada?  dos horas

 ## Nota

### Telling Time

To tell time in Spanish, use **son las** with the numbers, except for *one o'clock* where **es la** is used.

*(handwritten: Plural)*

| Es la una. | *It's one o'clock.* | Son las siete. | *It's seven o'clock.* |
|-----------|---------------------|----------------|------------------------|
| Son las dos. | *It's two o'clock.* | Son las ocho. | *It's eight o'clock.* |
| Son las tres. | *It's three o'clock.* | Son las nueve. | *It's nine o'clock.* |
| Son las cuatro. | *It's four o'clock.* | Son las diez. | *It's ten o'clock.* |
| Son las cinco. | *It's five o'clock.* | Son las once. | *It's eleven o'clock.* |
| Son las seis. | *It's six o'clock.* | Son las doce. | *It's twelve o'clock.* |

To give time after the hour, use **y** *(and)*. **Media** means *half* and **cuarto** means *quarter.*

| Son las tres y cinco. | *It's five after three.* | *(handwritten: 3:05)* |
|-----------------------|--------------------------|---|
| Son las cuatro y veinte. | *It's four twenty.* | |
| Son las tres y media. | *It's half past three.* | *(handwritten: Son las tres y trente)* |
| Son las diez y cuarto. | *It's a quarter past ten.* | |

## Más vocabulario

| | | | |
|---|---|---|---|
| ¿A qué hora es...? | *At what time is...?* | tarde | *late* |
| Es a las... | *It is at...* | temprano | *early* |
| una hora | *an hour* | hoy | *today* |
| un cuarto de hora | *a quarter of an hour* | mañana | *tomorrow, morning* |
| una media hora | *a half an hour* | de la madrugada | *AM (early morning hours)* |
| un día | *one day* | de la mañana | *AM* |
| una semana | *one week* | de la tarde | *PM (afternoon and early evening)* |
| un mes | *a month* | | |
| un año | *a year* | de la noche | *PM (late night)* |
| ahora | *now* | mañana por la mañana | *tomorrow morning* |
| ya | *now, already* | | |
| pronto | *soon* | pasado mañana | *day after tomorrow* |

• anteayer = day before yesterday
• en punto = exactly          • a tiempo = on time

## Para practicar

Give the following times.

1. 2:30
2. 4:00
3. 6:52
4. 1:20
5. 7:30
6. 8:15
7. 11:25
8. 9:15
9. 1:47

## Conversaciones

A:  ¿A qué hora llega el médico?

B:  Llega a las dos.

A:  ¿Qué hora es ya?

B:  Es la una y media.


A:  ¿Cuándo sale Ud. del hospital?

B:  Salgo mañana.

A:  ¿A qué hora sale Ud.?

B:  Salgo a las nueve de la mañana.


A:  El médico dice que mi padre no sale del hospital hoy.

B:  ¿Por qué?

A:  Porque no se siente bien.

B:  ¿Cuándo va a salir?

A:  Creo que va a salir en una semana.

## Vocabulario

| | |
|---|---|
| **salir** | *to leave* |
| **salgo** | *I leave* |
| **sale** | *he/she leaves; you leave* |

## Nota

**Hace + que**

You can ask how long an activity has been going on by using the expression **¿Cuánto tiempo hace que...?** To answer, use the verb **hace,** followed by the length of time, plus **que,** and finally the present tense verb for the action that has been taking place. For example:

| | |
|---|---|
| ¿Cuánto tiempo hace que fuma Ud.? | *For how long have you been smoking?* |
| Desde hace cinco años. | *For five years.* |
| Hace cinco años que fumo. | *I have been smoking for five years.* |

## Para practicar

Student A plays the role of the patient and reads the sentences aloud. Student B plays the role of the health professional, who must find out how long the patient has been doing the specified activity. The patient then answers, giving a specific amount of time.

**MODELO**   A:   Estudio español.
   B:   **¿Cuánto tiempo hace que estudia Ud. español?**
   A:   **Hace dos semanas que estudio español.**

1. Tomo la medicina.
2. Tengo dolor de estómago.
3. Vivo en Nueva York.
4. Tomo un antibiótico.
5. Tengo dolor de cabeza.
6. Consulto con un especialista.
7. Tomo las píldoras.
8. Trabajo en la clínica.
9. Sufro de los nervios.
10. Estudio la medicina.

---

### NOTA CULTURAL                    LA HIERBERÍA

**La hierbería** or *herb shop* is often an important health resource for Hispanic individuals, especially those of Mexican background. **Hierberías** offer a variety of dried medicinal plants, and there are often patent mixtures for the most common ailments. Many of these herbs form the basis for modern prescription medicines and over-the-counter remedies. Some examples are: **eucalipto** *(eucaliptus),* used for upper respiratory ailments; **yerba buena** *(peppermint)* for digestion; **acíbar** *(aloe),* used to treat burns and abrasions; and **manzanilla** *(chamomile)* for stomach problems.

## Conversación

Paciente: Doctor, estoy muy cansado. — Doctor I am very tired

Médico: ¿Duerme Ud. bastante? Are you sleeping enough.

Paciente: Para mí es difícil dormir bastante. I have difficulty sleeping enough.

Médico: ¿Por qué? why.

Paciente: Porque tengo que trabajar mucho. I must work much (alot)

Médico: ¿A qué hora se acuesta generalmente? What hour do you go to bed generally

Paciente: Me acuesto a las once de la noche. I go to bed 11 pm

Médico: ¿Y a qué hora se despierta? What do you wake up

Paciente: Me despierto a las cinco de la madrugada para ir a trabajar muy temprano. I wake up 5 am because I have to be @ work early

Médico: ¿Se duerme Ud. en seguida? Do you sleep right away

Paciente: No. Muchas veces no me duermo en seguida porque estoy muy nervioso. No often I don't fall asleep right away nervous

Médico: Voy a recetarle algo para calmarle los nervios y para ayudarle a dormir mejor. Pero Ud. debe tratar de dormir por lo menos ocho horas cada noche. very early

Paciente: Gracias, doctor.

or (le voy a recetar)

## Vocabulario

| | |
|---|---|
| bastante, bastantes | *enough* |
| dormir | *to sleep* |
| acostarse | *to go to bed* |
| despertarse | *to wake up* |
| de la madrugada | *in the (early) morning* |
| dormirse | *to fall asleep* |
| en seguida | *right away,* Stat. |

## Nota

### AM and PM Expressions

Instead of the abbreviations *AM* and *PM*, use the following expressions:

| | |
|---|---|
| de la mañana | *in the morning* |
| de la tarde | *in the afternoon/evening* |
| de la noche | *at night* |
| de la madrugada | *in the (early) morning* |

For example:

Son las once de la noche.                    *It's eleven PM.*

Also:

| | |
|---|---|
| la medianoche | *midnight* |
| el mediodía | *noon* |

## Más vocabulario

| Verbos reflexivos | Reflexive Verbs |
|---|---|
| acostarse | *to go to bed* |
| me acuesto | *I go to bed* |
| se acuesta | *he/she goes to bed; you go to bed* |
| despertarse | *to get up* |
| me despierto | *I get up* |
| se despierta | *he/she gets up; you get up* |
| dormir | *to sleep* |
| duermo | *I sleep* |
| duerme | *he/she sleeps; you sleep* |
| dormirse | *to fall asleep* |
| me duermo | *I fall asleep* |
| se duerme | *he/she falls asleep; you fall asleep* |

## Sustituciones

Substitute the underlined words with the cued items. Be sure to make any other necessary changes.

**MODELO**    Me acuesto <u>a las once</u> de la noche.    a las diez
**Me acuesto <u>a las diez</u> de la noche.**

1. <u>Me</u> acuesto a las diez de la noche.    se
2. Me <u>acuesto</u> a las diez de la <u>noche</u>.    despierto, mañana
3. Me acuesto a las <u>diez</u> de la noche.    nueve y media
4. Me <u>acuesto</u> a las <u>diez de la noche</u>.    despierto, seis de la madrugada
5. Me <u>acuesto</u> a las <u>diez de la noche</u>.    despierto, nueve de la mañana

## Para practicar

Answer the questions by giving the times in Spanish.

**MODELO**    ¿A qué hora se acuesta el paciente?    *8 PM, 5 AM*
**Se acuesta a las ocho de la noche y se despierta a las cinco de la madrugada.**

1. ¿A qué hora se acuesta la señora García?    *8:30 PM, 10 AM*
2. ¿A qué hora se acuesta la paciente?    *9:15 PM, 11:15 AM*
3. ¿A qué hora se acuesta el niño?    *8:30 PM, 6 AM*
4. ¿A qué hora se acuesta su abuelo?    *7:15 PM, 10 AM*
5. ¿A qué hora se acuestan los pacientes?    *10 PM, 5:30 AM*
6. ¿A qué hora se acuestan sus padres?    *11:30 PM, 7 AM*
7. ¿A qué hora se acuesta Ud.?    *???*

## Conversaciones

A:    ¿Duerme bien su marido?
B:    No, no duerme bien.

A:  ¿A qué hora se acuesta generalmente? *what hour does he generally go to sleep*

B:  Se acuesta a las once de la noche y se despierta a las cinco y media de la madrugada. *he goes to ' at 11pm   he wake up 5:30 am*

A:  ¿A qué hora se acuesta Ud.? → *what hour do you go to bed*

B:  Me acuesto a las diez de la noche. *I go to bed at 10pm*

A:  ¿Se duerme en seguida? *Do you sleep right away*

B:  Sí, me duermo en seguida. *yes fall asleep*

A:  ¿A qué hora se despierta Ud.? *what hour do you wake up*

B:  Me despierto a las cuatro y media de la madrugada. *I wake up at 4:30 in the*

A:  ¿Por qué se despierta tan (so) temprano? *why do you wake up so early am.*

B:  Porque tengo que ir a trabajar muy lejos (far away) de aquí. *So early. because I have to leave go to my job is very far away from here.*

## Para practicar

Answer with the cued response.

**MODELO**    ¿A qué hora se acuesta la doctora?    a las diez de la noche
**La doctora se acuesta a las diez de la noche.**

1. ¿A qué hora se acuesta el paciente?    a las nueve y media
2. ¿Se acuesta Ud. tarde o temprano?    tarde
3. ¿A qué hora se despierta su marido?    a las siete
4. ¿Se duerme Ud. en seguida?    no
5. ¿A qué hora se acuesta Ud.?    a las diez y quince

## Conversación

Paciente:  ¿Qué tengo, doctora? *what do I have Dr.*

Doctora:  Ud. tiene una infección. *you have a infection.*

Paciente:  ¿Va a darme Ud. una receta? *Are you going to give me a prescription 4x's a*

Doctora:  Sí, voy a darle una receta para un antibiótico. Ud. debe tomar las píldoras cuatro veces al día, o cada seis horas, por un período de diez días. *yes I am giving you a Rx for an antibiotic. Yes I am going or every six hour for a period of 10 days day*

Paciente:  ¿A qué hora debo tomar las píldoras? *what hour do I take the pills*

Doctora:  Ud. debe tomar una píldora a las seis de la madrugada, una al mediodía, una a las seis de la tarde y una a la medianoche. *You should take 1 @ 6 am, 1 @ noon one at 6 @ night and 1 @ 12*

Paciente:  ¿Debo tomar las píldoras antes o después de comer? *before*

Doctora:  Es mejor tomarlas antes de comer. Pero si le causan problemas del estómago, entonces debe tomarlas después.

Paciente:  ¿Debo dejar de tomar las píldoras si me siento mejor?

Doctora:  No, Ud. tiene que tomarse todas las píldoras, si se siente mejor o no.

## Vocabulario

| | |
|---|---|
| veces al día | *times a day* |
| cada seis horas | *every six hours* |
| cada cuatro horas | *every four hours* |
| cada dos horas | *every two hours* |
| antes de | *before* |
| después de | *after* |
| si | *if* |
| dejar | *to stop (from doing); to leave off* |

## Nota

**Antes de; después de**

The prepositions **antes** *(before)* and **después** *(after)* are used with the preposition **de** before a verb: **antes de comer** *(before eating)*; **después de examinar** *(after examining)*.

## Sustituciones

Substitute the underlined words with the cued items. Be sure to make any other necessary changes.

> **MODELO**     Ud. debe tomar una píldora a las <u>seis</u> de la madrugada.     siete
> **Ud. debe tomar una píldora a las <u>siete</u> de la madrugada.**

1. Ud. debe tomar <u>una</u> píldora a las <u>seis de la madrugada</u>.     dos, nueve de la mañana
2. Ud. debe tomar una <u>píldora</u> <u>a las seis de la madrugada</u>.     pastilla, dos veces al día
3. <u>Ud.</u> debe tomar una píldora a las <u>de la madrugada</u>.     el paciente, de la tarde
4. <u>Ud.</u> debe tomar una píldora a las <u>seis de la madrugada</u>.     los pacientes, nueve de la noche
5. <u>Ud.</u> debe tomar <u>una píldora</u> <u>a las seis de la madrugada</u>.     la señora, el jarabe, antes de acostarse

## Para practicar

Answer the patient's questions using the cued responses.

> **MODELO**     ¿Cuándo debo visitar a la doctora?     *two times a week*
> **Debe visitar a la doctora dos veces a la semana.**

1. ¿Cuántas veces debo tomar las píldoras?                     *four times a day*
2. ¿Cuándo debo tomar el antibiótico?                          *every six hours*
3. ¿Cuántas veces debo tomar el jarabe?                        *twice a day*
4. ¿Cuándo debo hacer ejercicio?                              *before eating*
5. ¿Cuántas veces debo cambiar la venda *(change the bandage)*?  *three times a day*
6. ¿Cuándo debo tomar las cápsulas?                           *every eight hours*
7. ¿Cuándo debo descansar?                                   *after eating*

## Para practicar más

Role-play a conversation between a health professional and a patient using the cued directions.

*donde tiene dolor?*

The patient says she is sick.
She says her stomach hurts. *Yo tengo dolor de estomago*
She says for three weeks. *Tres Semanas*
She asks what you are going to do. *Que va a hacer?*
She asks when she should take the medicine. *Cuando debo tomar la medicina*
She asks for how long.
She asks if she should take it before or after eating.

You ask where it hurts.
You ask for how long. *Desde cuando?*
Tell her you are going to examine her. *Le voy a examinar*
Say that you are going to give her a prescription for some medicine. *Le voy a dar una receta para medicina*
Say she should take it every six hours. *Cara Seis horas*
Answer that she should take it for three weeks.
Answer that she should take it before eating.

## RESUMEN Y REPASO

## Gramática

### Los verbos

**sentirse**   *to feel*

| | | | | | |
|---|---|---|---|---|---|
| yo | **me siento** | *I feel* | nosotros/nosotras | **nos sentimos** | *we feel* |
| tú | **te sientes** | *you* (fam.) *feel* | | | |
| él/ella | **se siente** | *he/she feels* | ellos/ellas | **se sienten** | *they feel* |
| Ud. | **se siente** | *you* (form.) *feel* | Uds. | **se sienten** | *you* (pl.) *feel* |

**sentarse**   *to sit; to sit down*

| | | | | | |
|---|---|---|---|---|---|
| yo | **me siento** | *I sit down* | nosotros/nosotras | **nos sentamos** | *we sit down* |
| tú | **te sientas** | *you* (fam.) *sit down* | | | |
| él/ella | **se sienta** | *he/she sits down* | ellos/ellas | **se sientan** | *they sit down* |
| Ud. | **se sienta** | *you* (form.) *sit down* | Uds. | **se sientan** | *you* (pl.) *sit down* |

**salir**   *to leave*

| | | | | | |
|---|---|---|---|---|---|
| yo | **salgo** | *I leave* | nosotros/nosotras | **salimos** | *we leave* |
| tú | **sales** | *you* (fam.) *leave* | | | |
| él/ella | **sale** | *he/she leaves* | ellos/ellas | **salen** | *they leave* |
| Ud. | **sale** | *you* (form.) *leave* | Uds. | **salen** | *you* (pl.) *leave* |

**acostarse**    *to go to bed*

| yo | **me acuesto** | *I go to bed* | nosotros/nosotras | **nos acostamos** | *we go to bed* |
|---|---|---|---|---|---|
| tú | **te acuestas** | *you* (fam.) *go to bed* | | | |
| él/ella | **se acuesta** | *he/she goes to bed* | ellos/ellas | **se acuestan** | *they go to bed* |
| Ud. | **se acuesta** | *you* (form.) *go to bed* | Uds. | **se acuestan** | *you* (pl.) *go to bed* |

**despertarse**    *to wake up*

| yo | **me despierto** | *I wake up* | nosotros/nosotras | **nos despertamos** | *we wake up* |
|---|---|---|---|---|---|
| tú | **te despiertas** | *you* (fam.) *wake up* | | | |
| él/ella | **se despierta** | *he/she wakes up* | ellos/ellas | **se despiertan** | *they wake up* |
| Ud. | **se despierta** | *you* (form.) *wake up* | Uds. | **se despiertan** | *you* (pl.) *wake up* |

**dormirse**    *to fall asleep*

| yo | **me duermo** | *I fall asleep* | nosotros/nosotras | **nos dormimos** | *we fall asleep* |
|---|---|---|---|---|---|
| tú | **te duermes** | *you* (fam.) *fall asleep* | | | |
| él/ella | **se duerme** | *he/she falls asleep* | ellos/ellas | **se duermen** | *they fall asleep* |
| Ud. | **se duerme** | *you* (form.) *fall asleep* | Uds. | **se duermen** | *they fall asleep* |

Notice that without the reflexive pronouns **dormir** means *to sleep*. For example: **yo duermo** *(I sleep)*, and so on.

# Vocabulario

| **Para decir la hora** | ***Ways to Talk about Time*** |
|---|---|
| ¿Qué hora es? | *What time is it?* |
| antes de | *before* |
| el año | *year* |
| cada | *each, every* |
| un cuarto de hora | *a quarter of an hour* |
| después de | *after* |

| | |
|---|---|
| el **día** | *day* |
| una **hora** | *an hour* |
| la **hora** | *the time (of day), the hour* |
| la **madrugada** | *early morning* |
| la **mañana** | *morning* |
| la **media hora** | *half hour* |
| el **mes** | *month* |
| el **minuto** | *minute* |
| la **noche** | *night* |
| **pronto** | *soon* |
| la **semana** | *week* |
| **tarde** | *late* |
| la **tarde** | *afternoon, evening* |
| **temprano** | *early* |
| una **vez** | *one time, once* |
| dos **veces** | *two times, twice* |

## Para hacer una pregunta

*Ways to Ask a Question*

| | |
|---|---|
| ¿**cómo**? | *how?* |
| ¿**cuál**? ¿**cuáles**? | *which?* |
| ¿**cuándo**? | *when?* |
| ¿**cuánto**? | *how much?* |
| ¿**cuántos**? | *how many?* |
| ¿**dónde**? | *where?* |
| ¿**por qué**? | *why?* |
| ¿**qué**? | *what?* |
| ¿**quién**? ¿**quienes**? | *who?* |

## Para hablar de cómo se siente

*Ways to Talk about How You Feel*

| | |
|---|---|
| **bien** | *well, fine* |
| **cansado, -a** | *tired* |
| **débil** | *weak* |
| **enfermo, -a** | *sick* |
| **fuerte** | *strong* |
| **mal** | *bad, badly, poor, sick* |
| **mareado, -a** | *dizzy* |
| **mejor** | *better* |
| **nervioso, -a** | *nervous* |
| **peor** | *worse* |

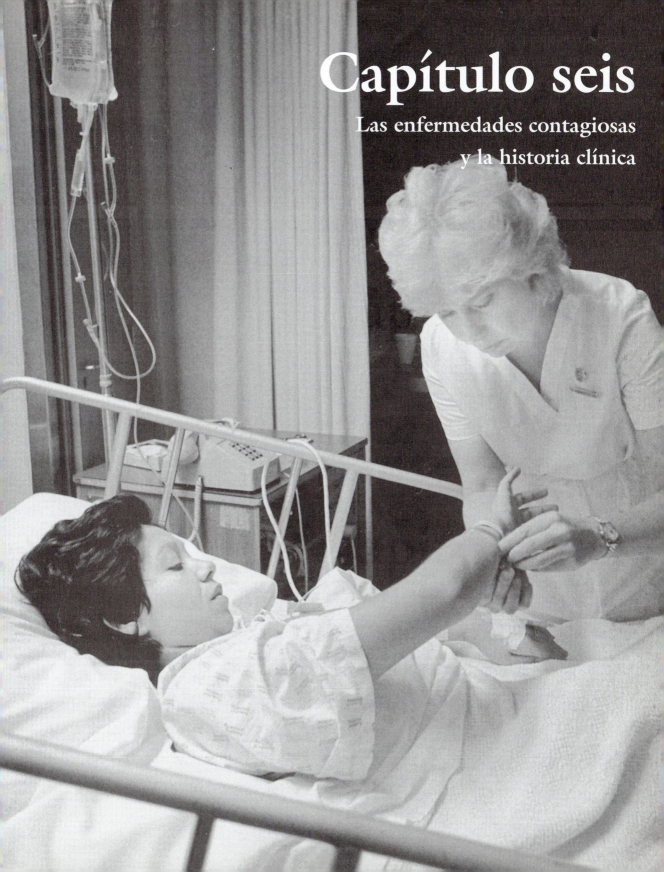

# Capítulo seis

## Las enfermedades contagiosas y la historia clínica

## Conversación

| | |
|---|---|
| Médico: | Antes de examinarle a Ud., tengo que hacerle algunas preguntas. |
| Paciente: | Está bien, doctor. |
| Médico: | ¿Toma Ud. alguna medicina? |
| Paciente: | No, doctor, no tomo nada. |
| Médico: | ¿Ha tenido alguna vez una operación? |
| Paciente: | Sí, doctor, tuve una operación del apéndice. |
| Médico: | ¿Cuándo tuvo la operación? |
| Paciente: | Tuve la operación hace dos años. |
| Médico: | ¿Ha tenido el sarampión, la varicela o la rubéola? |
| Paciente: | Sí, doctor, he tenido todas esas enfermedades. |
| Médico: | ¿Ha tenido Ud. una prueba de la tuberculina? |
| Paciente: | Sí, doctor, hace un año, con resultados negativos. |
| Médico: | ¿Ha tenido Ud. las paperas, la viruela o la tos ferina? |
| Paciente: | No, doctor, nunca he tenido esas enfermedades. |

## Vocabulario

| | |
|---|---|
| **hacer(le) preguntas** | *to ask (one) questions* |
| **algunas** | *some* |
| **nada** | *nothing* |
| **alguna vez** | *some time, any time, ever* |
| **ha tenido** | *he/she has had; you have had* |
| **he tenido** | *I have had* |
| **tuve** | *I had, I received* |
| **tuvo** | *he/she had; you had* |
| el **sarampión** | *measles* |
| la **varicela** | *chicken pox* |
| la **rubéola** | *German measles* |
| **todas esas** | *all of those* |
| **ha recibido** | *has received* |
| **resultados negativos** | *negative results* |
| las **paperas** | *mumps* |
| la **viruela** | *smallpox* |
| la **tos ferina** | *whooping cough* |
| **nunca** | *never, ever* |

 ## Más vocabulario

| **Las enfermedades y las dolencias** | ***Diseases and Ailments*** |
|---|---|
| la **amigdalitis** | *tonsilitis* |
| la **bronquitis** | *bronchitis* |

| | |
|---|---|
| las **cataratas** | *cataracts* |
| un **catarro** | *a cold* |
| la **diarrea** | *diarrhea* |
| la **difteria** | *diphtheria* |
| la **disentería** | *dysentery* |
| la **flema** | *phlegm* |
| la **gastritis** | *gastritis* |
| el **glaucoma** | *glaucoma* |
| la **gripe** | *the flu* |
| los **hemorroides** | *hemorrhoids* |
| la **hepatitis** | *hepatitis* |
| la **laringitis** | *laryngitis* |
| la **meningitis** | *meningitis* |
| la **pulmonía** | *pneumonia* |
| un **resfriado** | *a cold* |
| la **tifoidea** | *typhoid* |
| la **tuberculosis** | *tuberculosis* |
| las **vacunas** | *vaccinations* |

## Sustituciones

Practice pronouncing these words in context by using them to ask the following question.

**MODELO**   ¿Ha tenido Ud. alguna vez <u>una operación</u>?   la tifoidea
**¿Ha tenido Ud. alguna vez <u>la tifoidea</u>?**

1. la pulmonía
2. un resfriado
3. la meningitis
4. el sarampión
5. la rubéola
6. la varicela
7. las paperas
8. la viruela
9. la tos ferina
10. la amigdalitis

## Nota

**Definite Articles: Usage**

In Spanish, one uses the definite articles (**el, la, los, las**) much more than in English. The following are some guidelines that cover many of the most common circumstances.

1. In Spanish the definite articles are used when referring to items in the abstract, whereas in English they would be omitted. For example:

| | |
|---|---|
| Me gusta **la** sopa. | *I like soup.* |
| **La** historia es interesante. | *History is interesting.* |
| **Las** flores son bonitas. | *Flowers are beautiful.* |

2. Definite articles are used with days of the week to mean *on:*

| | |
|---|---|
| Tengo una cita **el** lunes. | *I have an appointment on Monday.* |
| Visito al médico **los** martes. | *I visit the doctor on Tuesdays.* |

3. Definite articles are used for telling time:

| | |
|---|---|
| Es **la** una. | *It's one o'clock.* |
| Son **las** dos. | *It's two o'clock.* |
| Son **las** tres y cinco. | *It's five after three.* |

4. Definite articles, rather than the possessive adjectives, are used with clothing and parts of the body:

| | |
|---|---|
| El paciente se quita **la** camisa. | *The patient takes off his shirt.* |
| Le duele **el** estómago. | *His (her) stomach hurts.* |

5. Definite articles are used with titles, except when speaking directly to the person:

**La** doctora García llega pronto.          *Doctor García will be here soon.*

Other titles:

| | | | | | |
|---|---|---|---|---|---|
| el doctor | *doctor* | la señora | *Mrs.* | el profesor | *Professor* |
| el señor | *Mr.* | la señora | *Miss* | la profesora | *Professor* (fem.) |

## Conversación

A:   ¿Ha tenido Ud. problemas del oído?

B:   Sí, hace muchos años.

A:   ¿Ha sufrido de problemas con los ojos?

B:   No, doctor, nunca he tenido problemas con la visión.

A:   ¿Ha tenido alguna vez la pulmonía?

B:   No, doctor, nunca he tenido la pulmonía.

A:   ¿Ha sufrido de las paperas de niño?

B:   No, nunca he tenido las paperas.

A:   ¿Ha tenido Ud. el sarampión?

B:   Sí, he tenido el sarampión.

A:   ¿Ha sufrido alguna vez de la viruela loca?

B:   No, no he sufrido nunca de la viruela loca.

A:   ¿Ha tenido su hijo convulsiones?

B:   No, doctora, pero sí, ha tenido pulmonía.

A:   ¿Cuándo tuvo pulmonía?

B:   Hace un año que tuvo pulmonía.

A:   ¿Ha sufrido de otras enfermedades graves?

B:   No, doctora, siempre ha tenido buena salud.

# Nota

## Present Perfect Tense and Past Events

Use the following present perfect form to talk about past events:

| | |
|---|---|
| he tenido | *I have had* |
| ha tenido | *he, she, you have/has had* |
| | |
| he sufrido de | *I have suffered from* |
| ha sufrido de | *he, she, you have/has suffered from* |
| | |
| he hablado | *I have spoken* |
| ha hablado | *he, she, you have/has spoken* |
| | |
| he tomado | *I have taken* |
| ha tomado | *he, she, you have/has taken* |
| | |
| he comido | *I have eaten* |
| ha comido | *he, she, you have/has eaten* |
| | |
| he bebido | *I have drunk* |
| ha bebido | *he, she, you have/has drunk* |

# Para comunicarse

Take turns playing the role of health professional (A) and patient (B), using the cues provided.

**MODELO**

A:  la varicela
**¿Ha tenido Ud. la varicela?**
B:  dos años
**Sí, hace dos años.**

1. A:  la rubéola
   B:  quince años

2. A:  las paperas
   B:  diez años

3. A:  la tos ferina
   B:  tres años

4. A:  la bronquitis
   B:  seis meses

5. A:  el tétano
   B:  un año

## Registro individual de vacunas

Nombre y apellidos: _____

Sexo: _____   Fecha de nacimiento: _____

Médico: _____

| VACUNA | FECHA DE VACUNACIÓN | MÉDICO/ CLÍNICA | DOSIS SIGUIENTE FECHA: |
|---|---|---|---|
| Polio (OPV o IPV) | | | |
| Difteria/ Tétano Tos ferina (DTP) | | | |
| Sarampión/ Paperas/ Rubéola (MMR) | | | |
| Hib | | | |
| Tétanos/ Difteria Refuerzo (Td) | | | |
| Gripe | | | |
| Neumococos | | | |
| Otras | | | |

## Si desea más información...

Si usted desea hacer alguna pregunta o necesita otras vacunas, diríjase a su médico o al departmento de salud de su localidad.

Estado de Nueva York, Mario M. Cuomo, Gobernador
Departamento de Salud, David Axelrod, M.D., Comisionado

2317                                                              8/90

## Para practicar

The health professional (A) asks the patient (B) the questions. The patient responds according to the cues.

> **MODELO**    A:   ¿De qué ha sufrido Ud.?      las paperas
>               B:   **He sufrido de las paperas.**

1. ¿Qué ha comido Ud.?                la sopa
2. ¿Qué ha tenido Ud.?                el sarampión y la varicela
3. ¿Qué ha bebido Ud.?                el jugo de naranja
4. ¿Con quién ha hablado Ud.?         con la enfermera
5. ¿Qué ha bebido su padre?           el agua
6. ¿Qué ha tomado su hijo?            la pastilla
7. ¿De qué ha sufrido su mamá?        la tuberculosis
8. ¿Con quién ha hablado su esposo?   la doctora
9. ¿Qué ha tomado Ud.?                dos aspirinas

## Nota

### Negatives

In Spanish, we use the double negative by placing the word **no** before the verb, and another negative word after it. For example:

No he comido nada.                    *I have not eaten anything.*

Some negative words are:

nada      *nothing*
nadie     *no one*
nunca     *never*

## Para practicar

Take the sentences above, and turn student B answers into negative responses.

> **MODELO**    A:   ¿De qué ha sufrido Ud.?
>               B:   **No he sufrido de nada.**

Read the following passage aloud, concentrating on correct pronunciation. Then read it again, and try to answer the Spanish questions below.

## Lectura:   La recuperación

La enfermera entra al cuarto del paciente para saber si se siente mejor. El paciente ha tenido una operación. El cirujano le ha sacado cálculos de los riñones. La operación ha resultado muy bien. La enfermera le toma la temperatura y la presión arterial y le registra el pulso. Todo está normal. El paciente está mucho mejor.

Entra el especialista en el cuarto del paciente. Consulta con la enfermera y deciden que el paciente puede salir del hospital dentro de una semana.

## Vocabulario

| | |
|---|---|
| el **cuarto** | *room* |
| **para** | *for; in order to* |
| **saber** | *to know; to find out* |
| **mejor** | *better* |
| **ha sacado** | *has removed* |
| los **cálculos** | *stones* |
| los **riñones** | *kidneys* |
| **salir** | *to leave; to turn out* |
| **ha salido bien** | *has turned out well* |
| **registrar el pulso** | *to take the pulse* |
| **decidir** | *to decide* |
| **dentro de** | *within* |

## Preguntas

1. ¿Qué quiere saber la enfermera?
2. ¿Qué ha tenido el paciente?
3. ¿Cómo ha salido la operación?
4. ¿Qué hace la enfermera?
5. ¿Cómo está el paciente?
6. ¿Qué deciden la enfermera y el especialista?

## Conversación

Doctora:   ¿Dónde le duele, señor Vargas?

Paciente:   Me duele la garganta.

Doctora:   ¿Desde cuándo le duele?

Paciente:   Me duele desde hace una semana.

Doctora:   Siéntese aquí, por favor, y súbase la manga. Voy a tomarle la presión. ¿Tiene Ud. tos?

Paciente:   Sí, doctora hace tres días que tengo tos. No he podido dormir.

Doctora:   Abra la boca, por favor. Saque la lengua. Cierre la boca. Ahora quítese la camisa, por favor. Le voy a auscultar.

Paciente:   ¿Qué me pasa, doctora?

Doctora:   Ud. tiene una infección viral. Tome una de estas pastillas cada seis horas y tome una cucharada de este jarabe para la tos antes de acostarse. Descanse mucho y tome muchos líquidos.

Paciente:   Muchas gracias, doctora.

Doctora:   De nada, señor Vargas. Que mejore Ud. pronto.

## Vocabulario

| | |
|---|---|
| la **tos** | *cough* |
| **no he podido** | *I have not been able* |
| una **infección viral** | *viral infection* |
| estas **pastillas** | *these pills* |
| una **cucharada** | *tablespoonful* |
| este **jarabe para la tos** | *this cough syrup* |
| **antes de acostarse** | *before going to bed* |
| **Que mejore Ud. pronto.** | *Feel better soon.* |

---

### NOTA CULTURAL | LA MEDICINA FOLKLÓRICA

There are several diseases that have been commonly identified in folk medicinal beliefs of some Hispanic peoples. One of these is called **empacho,** whose symptoms include stomach pain and cramps. It is often thought to be caused by a ball of food stuck to the sides of the stomach or intestines. The treatment usually involves massaging the area along with some spinal manipulation.

---

 ## Vocabulario

**Common Commands for the Examining Room**

| | |
|---|---|
| **abra la boca** | *open your mouth* |
| **acuéstese** | *lie down* |
| **acuéstese boca abajo** | *lie face down* |
| **acuéstese boca arriba** | *lie face up* |
| **bájese de la mesa** | *get down from the table* |
| **cierre la boca** | *close your mouth* |
| **descanse** | *rest* |
| **diga, «ah»** | *say, "ah"* |
| **doble la cabeza a la derecha** | *bend your head to the right* |
| **doble la cabeza a la izquierda** | *bend your head to the left* |
| **doble la cabeza hacia adelante** | *bend your head forward* |
| **doble la cabeza hacia atrás** | *bend your head back* |
| **doble** | *bend* |
| **firme** | *sign* |
| **levántese** | *get up* |
| **llame** | *call* |
| **muévase** | *move* |
| **póngase de lado** | *turn on your side* |
| **póngase de pie** | *stand up* |
| **póngase la camisa** | *put on your shirt* |
| **póngase la ropa** | *put on your clothing* |

| | |
|---|---|
| (que) mejore | *get better* |
| quítese la camisa | *take off your shirt* |
| quítese la ropa | *take off your clothes* |
| respire profundamente | *breathe deeply* |
| saque la lengua | *stick out your tongue* |
| señale | *point* |
| siéntese | *sit down* |
| súbase a la mesa | *get up on the table* |
| súbase la manga | *roll up your sleeve* |
| tome | *take* |

## Recuerde

### Definite Articles versus Possessive Adjectives

In Spanish, use the definite article (**el, la, los, las**) instead of the possessive adjective when referring to one's body parts or clothing. For example:

Quítese la camisa.                                  *Take off your (the) shirt*

## Para practicar

The patient (A) has a complaint. You, the health professional (B), tell him/her what to do.

| A | B |
|---|---|
| 1. Tengo dolor de cabeza. | *Take aspirin.* |
| 2. No me siento bien. | *Get up on the table.* |
| 3. Tengo la garganta irritada. | *Open your mouth.* |
| 4. Me duele el estómago. | *Take off your shirt.* |
| 5. Tengo dolor. | *Point to where it hurts.* |
| 6. ¿Qué debo hacer? | *Take this medicine for ten days.* |
| 7. Tengo mucho calor. | *Roll up your sleeve.* |
| 8. Estoy muy cansado. | *Lie face down.* |

## Nota

### Favor de

An alternative to the direct command form is the expression **favor de,** combined with the infinitive. In addition to being more polite, it is also easier to use. For example: **Quítese la camisa, por favor.** or *Favor de quitarse* **la camisa.**

## Para practicar

Change the direct commands in the above exercise to the polite form with **favor de.**

**MODELO**     Tome aspirina.
                    **Favor de tomar aspirina.**

## Conversaciones

A:    No me siento bien, doctor.

B:    Quítese la camisa y acuéstese boca arriba, por favor. ¿Qué le pasa?

A:    Estoy muy cansado.

B:    Doble la rodilla derecha, por favor. ¿Le duele mucho ahora?

A:    Sí, doctor. Y me duele la espalda también.

B:    Acuéstese boca abajo, ahora. ¿Le duele cuando le toco aquí?

A:    No, doctor.

B:    Levante los brazos. ¿Le duele ahora?

A:    Sí, doctor, mucho.

B:    Bueno. Levántese y póngase la camisa.

A:    Doctora, me duelen el hombro y la espalda.

B:    Quítese la camisa y acuéstese boca abajo. Doble la cabeza hacia la izquierda. Levante el brazo derecho.

A:    Eso duele mucho.

B:    Ahora levante el brazo izquierdo.

A:    Eso no duele. ¿Qué va a hacer?

B:    Voy a hacer unas radiografías.

## Para comunicarse

Now you play the role of the health professional and complete the conversation by replacing the italicized English cues with Spanish.

1. A:    No me siento bien.
   B:    *What's wrong?*
2. A:    No puedo dormir.
   B:    *For how long?*
3. A:    Desde hace un mes.
   B:    *Roll up your sleeve. Do you drink much coffee?*
4. A:    No, doctor, tengo muchos problemas.
   B:    *Take off your shirt and lie down.*
5. A:    ¿Qué va a hacer Ud.?
   B:    *I am going to listen to your heart.*

## Nota

### The Verb <u>Poder</u>—to Be Able

**Poder** means *to be able to* or *can*. It is usually followed by the infinitive of another verb. For example:

Yo puedo hablar español.                    *I can speak Spanish.*

Here are its present tense forms:

| yo | **puedo** | *I can* | nosotros/nosotras | **podemos** | *we can* |
|---|---|---|---|---|---|
| tú | **puedes** | *you* (fam.) *can* | | | |
| él/ella | **puede** | *he/she can* | ellos/ellas | **pueden** | *they can* |
| Ud. | **puede** | *you* (form.) *can* | Uds. | **pueden** | *you* (pl.) *can* |

## Para comunicarse

The health professional (A) asks if the patient can do something. The patient (B) answers according to the cued response.

**MODELO**
    A:   ¿Puede Ud. dormir?
    B:   **No, no puedo dormir.**
    A:   **¿Por qué no puede?**
    B:   *I'm nervous*
         **Porque estoy nervioso.**

1. A:  ¿Puede Ud. sentarse?
   B:  *my back hurts*
2. A:  ¿Puedes tú comer?
   B:  *my stomach hurts*
3. A:  ¿Puede Ud. levantar el brazo?
   B:  *it hurts*
4. A:  ¿Puede su padre venir al hospital?
   B:  *he can't walk*
5. A:  ¿Puede el paciente ponerse de pie?
   B:  *his legs hurt*
6. A:  ¿Puede Ud. moverse los dedos?
   B:  *they hurt*

## Notas

### Demonstrative Adjectives

This, That, These, and Those

| | Masculine | Feminine |
|---|---|---|
| *this* | este | esta |
| *that* | ese | esa |
| *these* | estos | estas |
| *those* | esos | esas |

Demonstrative adjectives precede the nouns they modify. They also agree with the noun in gender and number. For example:

Tomo esta medicina.                           *I take this medicine.*
Estos pacientes están enfermos.               *These patients are sick.*

There are two neuter pronoun forms which are used to refer to ideas or situations rather than specific nouns. They are:

esto      *this*
eso       *that*

For example:

¿Qué es esto?                                 *What is this?*
Eso es interesante.                           *That is interesting.*

## Para practicar

Give the italicized words in Spanish.

1. Necesito *these* píldoras.
2. *This* médico es muy agradable.
3. *These* pacientes están muy graves.
4. *These* enfermeras son muy competentes.
5. Necesito leer *that* revista.
6. *This* medicina es buena.
7. *Those* ventanas están limpias.
8. Tengo que comprar *those* píldoras.
9. El médico analiza *these* problemas.
10. Tenemos que abrir *this* puerta.

## RESUMEN Y REPASO

## Gramática

### The Past Participle and the Present Perfect Tense

The present perfect tense is a compound past tense that is used to indicate an action or event that has taken place in the recent past. In Spanish, the present perfect tense is formed by using the present indicative of the irregular verb **haber** (an auxiliary verb meaning *to have*) and the past participle. In English, the past participle usually ends in *-ed* or *-en* (taken, eaten, suffered).

To form the past participle in Spanish of a regular **-ar** verb, drop the final **-ar** and add **-ado** to the stem. To form the past participle of a regular **-er** verb, drop the final **-er** and add **-ido** to the stem. To form the past participle of a regular **-ir** verb, drop the final **-ir** and add **-ido** to the stem. For example:

tomar     tomado          *to take*      *taken*
comer     comido          *to eat*       *eaten*
sufrir    sufrido         *to suffer*    *suffered*

Here is the present perfect tense of the regular verb **hablar:**

| | |
|---|---|
| Yo he hablado. | *I have spoken.* |
| Tú has hablado. | *You* (fam.) *have spoken.* |
| Él ha hablado. | *He has spoken.* |
| Ella ha hablado. | *She has spoken.* |
| Ud. ha hablado. | *You* (form.) *have spoken.* |

| | |
|---|---|
| Nosotros/Nosotras hemos hablado. | *We have spoken.* |
| Ellos/Ellas han hablado. | *They have spoken.* |
| Uds. han hablado. | *You* (pl.) *have spoken.* |

The following are some irregular past participles:

| | |
|---|---|
| abrir *(to open)* | abierto *(opened)* |
| cubrir *(to cover)* | cubierto *(covered)* |
| decir *(to say, tell)* | dicho *(said, told)* |
| escribir *(to write)* | escrito *(written)* |
| hacer *(to make, do)* | hecho *(made, done)* |
| morir *(to die)* | muerto *(died)* |
| poner *(to put)* | puesto *(put, placed)* |
| ver *(to see)* | visto *(seen)* |
| volver *(to return)* | vuelto *(returned)* |

## Los mandatos *(Commands)*

In Spanish, the command form for regular -**ar** verbs is formed by removing the ending of the infinitive and replacing it with -**e** for the singular command and -**en** for the plural forms. The command forms for both -**er** and -**ir** verbs are formed by replacing the infinitive endings with -**a** for the singular command and -**an** for the plural command. For example:

| | | |
|---|---|---|
| hablar | hable Ud. | hablen Uds. |
| comer | coma Ud. | coman Uds. |
| escribir | escriba Ud. | escriban Uds. |

To form a negative command, place the word **no** before the command form:

hable Ud. *(speak)*     no hable Ud. *(don't speak).*

The above are for **Ud.** and **Uds.** For commands in the **tú** form, use the third person singular of the present tense.

| | |
|---|---|
| Habla. | *Speak.* |
| Come. | *Eat.* |

For negative **tú** commands, use -**es** ending for -**ar** verbs, and -**as** for -**er** and -**ir** verbs.

| | |
|---|---|
| No hables. | *Don't speak.* |
| No comas. | *Don't eat.* |

# Vocabulario

| **Los síntomas** | *Symptoms* |
| --- | --- |
| los **cálculos** | *stones* |
| el **dolor** | *pain* |
| el **dolor de cabeza** | *headache* |
| el **dolor de estómago** | *stomachache* |
| el **dolor del oído** | *earache* |
| la **garganta irritada** | *sore throat* |
| la **infección** | *infection* |
| la **irritación** | *irritation* |
| los **problemas con la vista** | *vision problems* |
| la **tos** | *cough* |
| la **visión borrosa** | *blurred vision* |

# Capítulo siete

## En el hospital; los órganos

## 👁 Conversación

| | |
|---|---|
| Doctora: | Buenos días, señora Martínez. ¿Cómo se siente Ud. hoy? |
| Paciente: | No muy bien, doctora. |
| Doctora: | ¿Qué le pasa? ¿Por qué está tan nerviosa? |
| Paciente: | Hace seis meses que tengo un bulto en el seno. Es grande y muy duro, pero no tengo dolor. ¿Puede ser un quiste o un tumor? |
| Doctora: | Trate de calmarse. Vamos a ver lo que tiene. Voy a examinarle el seno. |
| Paciente: | Estoy muy preocupada, doctora. Si es maligno, no quiero una mastectomía. |
| Doctora: | Puedo sentir algo en el seno izquierdo. Puede ser un fibroma, pero no puedo hacer un diagnóstico ahora. Tenemos que hacer una mamografía. |
| Paciente: | ¿Qué es una mamografía? |
| Doctora: | Es una radiografía del seno. |
| Paciente: | ¿Es necesario hacer la mamografía? |
| Doctora: | Sí, y cuanto antes. Si es algo grave, es mejor descubrirlo inmediatamente. |

## Vocabulario

| | |
|---|---|
| un **bulto** | *lump* |
| el **seno** | *breast* |
| **duro, -a** | *hard* |
| un **quiste** | *cyst* |
| un **tumor** | *tumor* |
| **maligno, -a** | *malignant* |
| una **mastectomía** | *mastectomy* |
| un **fibroma** | *fibroid* |
| una **mamografía** | *mammogram* |
| **cuanto antes** | *as soon as possible* |
| **grave** | *serious* |
| **mejor** | *better* |

## Sustituciones

Substitute the underlined words with the cued items. Be sure to make any other necessary changes.

> **MODELO**    Hace <u>seis</u> meses que tengo un bulto en el seno.    dos
> **Hace <u>dos</u> meses que tengo un bulto en el seno.**

1. Hace <u>seis</u> meses que <u>tengo un bulto en el seno</u>.    dos, no puedo dormir
2. Hace <u>seis meses</u> que <u>tengo un bulto en el seno</u>.    dos semanas, fiebre
3. Hace <u>seis meses</u> que <u>tengo un bulto en el seno</u>.    tres días, dolor de cabeza
4. Hace <u>seis meses</u> que <u>tengo un bulto en el seno</u>.    cinco años, fumo
5. Hace <u>seis meses</u> que tengo <u>un bulto en el seno</u>.    dos días, náuseas

## Notas

**Tan, tanto, tantos, tanta, tantas** *and* **tratar de, tratar a**

1. **Tan** is an adverb and it means *so:*

   ¿Por qué está Ud. tan nerviosa?          *Why are you so nervous?*

   **Tanto** is also an adverb and means *so much:*

   ¿Por qué fuma Ud. tanto?                 *Why do you smoke so much?*

   As adjectives, **tantos** and **tantas** mean *so many,* while **tanto** and **tanta** mean *so much.* They must agree with the noun that follows. For example:

   No puedo tomar tantas pastillas.         *I can't take so many pills.*

2. **Tratar** means *to treat* or *to try.* When it means *to treat,* it is followed by **a:**

   Yo trato bien a los pacientes.           *I treat the patients well.*

   However, when it means *to try,* it is followed by **de:**

   Voy a tratar de seguir una dieta.        *I am going to try to follow a diet.*

## Para comunicarse

Practice the following role-playing activity. Student A is the patient, and student B is the health professional.

**MODELO**
    A: **¿Cuándo debo tener la operación?**
    B: esta semana
       **Debe tener la operación esta semana.**
    A: **¿Por cuánto tiempo debo quedarme en el hospital?**
    B: una semana
       **Una semana, por lo menos.**

1. A: _____
   B: mañana

   A: _____
   B: dos semanas

2. A: _____
   B: el lunes

   A: _____
   B: tres días

3. A: _____
   B: pasado mañana

   A: _____
   B: un mes

4. A: _____
   B: la semana que viene *(next week)*

   A: _____
   B: tres semanas

5. A: _____
   B: el miércoles

   A: _____
   B: cinco días

## Vocabulario

**Los órganos *(The organs)***

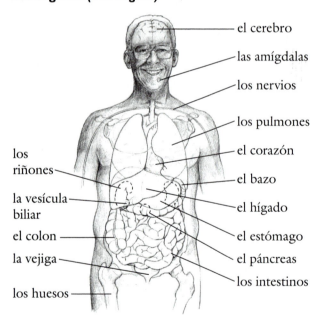

el cerebro
las amígdalas
los nervios
los pulmones
el corazón
los riñones
el bazo
la vesícula biliar
el hígado
el colon
el estómago
la vejiga
el páncreas
los intestinos
los huesos

| | | | |
|---|---|---|---|
| las **amígdalas** | *tonsils* | los **intestinos** | *intestines* |
| el **bazo** | *spleen* | los **nervios** | *nerves* |
| el **cerebro** | *brain* | el **páncreas** | *pancreas* |
| el **colon** | *colon* | los **pulmones** | *lungs* |
| el **corazón** | *heart* | los **riñones** | *kidneys* |
| el **estómago** | *stomach* | la **vejiga** | *bladder* |
| el **hígado** | *liver* | la **vesícula biliar** | *gallbladder* |
| los **huesos** | *bones* | | |

## Para comunicarse

Student A is the patient. Student B, the health professional, tells him or her what operation they are going to do.

> **MODELO**　A:　**¿Qué operación necesito?**
> B:　los pulmones
> **Ud. necesita una operación de los pulmones.**

1. A: _____
   B:　el corazón

2. A: _____
   B:　el estómago

3. A: _____
   B:　el colon

4. A: _____
   B:　el páncreas

5. A: _____
   B:　la vejiga

6. A: _____
   B:　el cerebro

## Conversaciones

A:　Le van a operar a mi hijo mañana.

B:　¿De qué le van a operar?

A:　Le van a operar de las amígdalas.

B:　¿Quién le va a operar?

A:　Le va a operar el Doctor Menéndez, un cirujano muy bueno.

A:　¿De qué le van a operar a Ud.?

B:　Me van a operar de los intestinos.

A:　¿Por qué necesita Ud. la operación?

B:　Porque tengo un tumor maligno.

A:　¿Qué dice la cirujana?

B:　Dice que después de la operación me van a dar la quimioterapia.

A:　¿Tiene Ud. dificultad al respirar?

B:　Sí, de vez en cuando.

A: ¿Sufre Ud. de cansancio?

B: Sí, me canso mucho cuando subo la escalera.

A: ¿Fuma Ud.?

B: Sí, fumo.

A: ¿Cuánto fuma Ud.?

B: Fumo dos paquetes al día.

A: Bueno, tenemos que hacerle algunas radiografías de los pulmones.

## Nota

**¿Cuánto?, ¿cuántos?, ¿cuánta?, ¿cuántas?**

**¿Cuánto?** is an adverb and it means *how much?* For example:

¿Cuánto duerme Ud.?                    *How much do you sleep?*

As an adjective, it has four forms: **¿cuánto?, ¿cuántos?, ¿cuánta?, ¿cuántas?** As an an adjective, it must agree with the noun that follows it. The singular forms mean *How much?* and the plural forms mean *How many?*

¿Cuántos hijos tiene Ud.?                    *How many children do you have?*

 ## Para practicar

You are the health professional. Interview the patients in the following situations.

A. **The patient is suffering from chest pains.**
1. Ask if it hurts all the time.
2. Ask for how long he/she has had the pain.
3. Ask what kind of pain it is.
4. Ask him/her to show you where it hurts.
5. Ask if there are other symptoms.
6. Say that you are going to examine him/her.
7. Say that you are going to take some more tests.

B. **The patient has strong stomach pains.**
1. Find out for how long.
2. Ask what he/she has been taking for the pain.
3. Ask if he/she is constipated or has diarrhea.
4. Ask when it hurts the most.
5. Ask if he/she has an appetite.
6. Say that you need to take some tests.
7. Say that you are going to write a prescription.

## Conversación

Paciente:    ¿Doctora, puede Ud. ayudarme?

Doctora:    Sí, señora, el tumor que Ud. tiene en el seno izquierdo es maligno, pero si le hacemos una operación cuanto antes, creo que va a salir bien.

Paciente:   ¿Qué tipo de operación me va a hacer Ud.?

Doctora:   Vamos a hacerle una lumpectomía. Eso quiere decir que vamos a quitarle el tumor en vez de quitarle el seno entero.

Paciente:   ¿Es un caso muy grave, doctora?

Doctora:   Bueno, con estos casos hay que tener mucho cuidado. Pero el cáncer no está muy avanzado. Por eso, Ud. tiene una posibilidad muy buena de curarse por completo.

Paciente:   ¿Cuándo debo tener la operación?

Doctora:   Esta semana, si es posible.

Paciente:   ¿Por cuánto tiempo tengo que estar en el hospital?

Doctora:   Tiene que quedarse en el hospital por una semana después de la operación.

Paciente:   ¿Van a ser necesarios otros tratamientos?

Doctora:   Sí, Ud. va a tener que tomar tratamientos de radiación y de quimioterapia.

## Vocabulario

| | | | |
|---|---|---|---|
| **creo que** | *I think that* | **curarse** | *to be cured* |
| **quiere decir** | *means* | los **tratamientos** | *treatments* |
| **tener cuidado** | *to be careful* | | |

## Sustituciones

Substitute the underlined words with the cued items. Be sure to make any other necessary changes.

**MODELO**   Tiene que quedarse en el hospital por una o dos semanas.    la clínica
**Tiene que quedarse en la clínica por una o dos semanas.**

1. Tiene que quedarse en el hospital por una o dos semanas.    tomar el antibiótico, diez días
2. Tiene que quedarse en el hospital por una o dos semanas.    descansar en cama, tres días
3. Tiene que quedarse en el hospital por una o dos semanas.    seguir la dieta, dos meses
4. Tiene que quedarse en el hospital por una o dos semanas.    ponerse la crema, una semana

## Continúa la conversación...

### Después de la operación

Enfermera:   Buenos días, señora. ¿Cómo se siente Ud. hoy?

Paciente:   No me siento bien. Quiero hablar con la doctora.

Enfermera:   La doctora llega más tarde, señora. Ahora tengo que tomarle la presión.

Paciente:   ¿Puede Ud. quitarme esta aguja? Me molesta mucho.

Enfermera:   Lo siento, señora. Tiene que quedarse con la intravenosa por dos días más.

Paciente:   ¿Cuándo puedo salir del hospital?

Enfermera:   No sé. Posiblemente en una o dos semanas. Ahora tengo que registrarle el pulso y tomarle la temperatura. ¿Qué quiere Ud. comer esta noche?

Paciente:   No quiero nada. No me gusta la comida del hospital.

Enfermera:   Tiene que comer algo, señora, si quiere salir de aquí y volver a su casa muy pronto.

## Vocabulario

| | |
|---|---|
| más tarde | *later* |
| ahora | *now* |
| quitarme | *take out (of me)* |
| la **aguja** | *needle* |
| molestar | *to bother* |
| **Lo siento.** | *I'm sorry.* |
| la **intravenosa** | *I.V.* |
| **No sé.** | *I don't know.* |
| registrarle el pulso | *take your pulse* |
| tomarle la temperatura | *take your temperature* |
| esta noche | *tonight* |
| no me gusta | *I don't like (it)* |
| algo | *something* |
| aquí | *here* |
| volver | *to return* |

## Nota

### How to Say You Like Something

In Spanish one uses the verb **gustar,** which means *to please* or *to be pleasing to,* to express that one likes something. It is always accompanied by an indirect object pronoun.

| | |
|---|---|
| me gusta | *I like it (it pleases me)* |
| te gusta | *you* (fam.) *like it (it pleases you)* |
| le gusta | *he, she likes it; you* (form.) *like it (it pleases him, her, you)* |
| nos gusta | *we like it (it pleases us)* |
| les gusta | *they, you* (pl.) *like it (it pleases them, you)* |

To form the plural, add **n** to **gusta:**

| | |
|---|---|
| me gustan | *I like them* |
| te gustan | *you* (fam.) *like them* |
| le gustan | *he, she likes them, you* (form.) *like them* |
| nos gustan | *we like them* |
| les gustan | *they, you* (pl.) *like them* |

The prepositional phrases **a mí, a él, a Ud., a nosotros, a ellas,** and **a Uds.** are sometimes added to give emphasis or clarity to the sentence. For example:

| | |
|---|---|
| A él le gusta el libro. | *He likes the book.* |
| A ellas les gusta la ensalada. | *They like the salad.* |
| A mí me gustan las papas fritas. | *I like French fries.* |

## Para practicar

Change the sentences using the cues.

> **MODELO**    A mí me gusta el libro.    a él
> **A él le gusta el libro.**

1. A mí me gusta el cuarto.    a ellos
   a Uds.
   a nosotros
   a ella
2. A él le gustan los regalos.    al paciente
   a las enfermeras
   a la mujer
   a mi padre
3. A mí me gusta trabajar.    al médico
   a los técnicos
   a la asistenta
   a mi hermano

## Para practicar más

Answer the questions first in the affirmative and then in the negative.

> **MODELO**    ¿Le gusta al paciente caminar *(to walk)*?
> **Sí, al paciente le gusta caminar.**
> **No, al paciente no le gusta caminar.**

1. ¿Le gusta a Ud. el hospital?
2. ¿Le gusta a la paciente la comida?
3. ¿Le gustan a la muchacha los regalos?
4. ¿Les gusta a los médicos trabajar?
5. ¿Le gustan a la mujer las revistas?
6. ¿Le gusta al paciente el cuarto?
7. ¿Le gusta a Ud. la comida?

## Para comunicarse

You are the health professional. Interact with a patient and complete the following conversations by using the cued instructions.

1. A:  No puedo dormir.
   B:  *Ask why.*
   A:  Tengo miedo.
   B:  *Say that it is a simple operation.*
   A:  Quiero irme a casa.
   B:  *Say that the operation is very important.*

2. A:  No quiero comer.
   B:  *Ask what is the problem.*
   A:  No me gusta esta comida.
   B:  *Say that he/she should eat.*
   A:  No tengo apetito.
   B:  *Tell him/her to eat a little bit* (un poco).

3. A:  ¿Por qué me molesta Ud. tanto?
   B:  *Say that you have to take the blood pressure.*
   A:  ¿Qué hace Ud. ahora?
   B:  *Say that you are checking his/her pulse.*
   A:  ¿Tengo que tomar una pastilla?
   B:  *Say, yes it is time for your medicine.*

## Vocabulario

**En el hospital** *(In the hospital)*

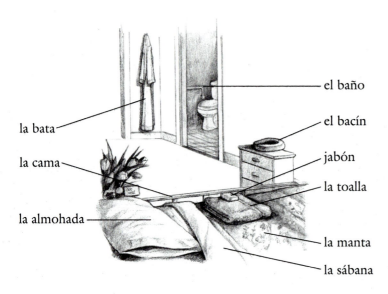

| | |
|---|---|
| el **baño** | *bath, bathroom* |
| el **cuarto** | *room* |
| el **curita** | *small adhesive bandage* |
| **cambiar la venda** | *to change the bandage* |
| **insertar el catéter** | *to insert the catheter* |

# Para practicar

Play the role of the health professional (A) and ask the patient what he/she needs. The patient (B) answers with the cued item.

| **MODELO** | ¿Qué necesita Ud.?    un vaso de agua |
|---|---|
| | **Necesito un vaso de agua.** |

| **A** | **B** |
|---|---|
| 1. ¿Qué necesita Ud.? | una almohada |
| 2. ¿Qué necesita Ud.? | ir al baño |
| 3. ¿Qué necesita el paciente? | una curita |
| 4. ¿Qué necesita la paciente? | el jabón |
| 5. ¿Qué necesitan Uds.? | una manta |
| 6. ¿Qué necesita Ud.? | una toalla |
| 7. ¿Qué necesita hacer el enfermero? | insertar el catéter |
| 8. ¿Qué necesita hacer el médico? | cambiar la venda |

# Recuerde

## The Verb <u>Dormir</u>—to Sleep

Following are the forms of the verb **dormir** *(to sleep):*

**dormir**    *to sleep*

| yo | **duermo** | *I sleep* | nosotros/nosotras | **dormimos** | *we sleep* |
|---|---|---|---|---|---|
| tú | **duermes** | *you* (fam.) *sleep* | | | |
| él/ella | **duerme** | *he/she sleeps* | ellos/ellas | **duermen** | *they sleep* |
| Ud. | **duerme** | *you* (form.) *sleep* | Uds. | **duermen** | *you* (pl.) *sleep* |

# Para practicar

Role-play using the cued responses. Student A asks the questions, and student B responds. Then, change roles.

| | |
|---|---|
| 1. ¿Quién duerme? | el paciente en el cuarto 10 |
| 2. ¿Quién duerme? | todos los pacientes |
| 3. ¿Cuándo duerme el paciente? | por la noche |
| 4. ¿Cómo duerme el paciente? | mal |
| 5. ¿Cómo duermen los pacientes? | demasiado |
| 6. ¿Duermen bien o mal los pacientes? | bien |
| 7. ¿Por qué no duerme la paciente? | está nerviosa |

## Para practicar más

Change the subject of each sentence according to the cues. Make any changes in verb endings where appropriate.

| MODELO | El paciente duerme mucho.    yo |
|---|---|
|  | **Yo duermo mucho.** |

1. El hombre duerme mucho.

    yo
    nosotras
    la niña
    el joven

2. El médico duerme poco.

    las enfermeras
    los pacientes
    tú
    nosotros

3. El paciente duerme mal.

    el enfermo
    la madre
    mi abuela
    Uds.

## Nota

### The Verb <u>Querer</u>—to Want

**Querer** means *to want* or *to love*. The following are its present tense forms:

**querer**    *to want; to love*

| | | | | | |
|---|---|---|---|---|---|
| yo | **quiero** | *I want* | nosotros/nosotras | **queremos** | *we want* |
| tú | **quieres** | *you* (fam.) *want* | | | |
| él/ella | **quiere** | *he/she wants* | ellos/ellas | **quieren** | *they want* |
| Ud. | **quiere** | *you* (form.) *want* | Uds. | **quieren** | *you* (pl.) *want* |

**Querer** can mean *to want something,* as in:

Yo quiero una almohada.          *I want a pillow.*

It can also mean *to want to do something.* In this case, it should be followed by the infinitive of another verb:

Yo quiero dormir.          *I want to sleep.*

## Para practicar

Play the role of the health professional (A) and ask the patient what someone wants. The patient (B) answers with the cued item.

> **MODELO**     ¿Qué quiere el paciente?     las pijamas
> **El paciente quiere las pijamas.**

1. ¿Qué quiere el paciente?     una manta
2. ¿Qué quieren los pacientes?     jabón
3. ¿Qué quiere la señora?     una receta
4. ¿Qué quiere el niño?     un curita
5. ¿Qué quiere Ud.?     una bata
6. ¿Qué quieren ellos?     una toalla
7. ¿Qué quiere hacer la enfermera?     tomarle la temperatura
8. ¿Qué quiere hacer la doctora?     escribir una receta
9. ¿Qué quiere hacer el paciente?     dormir
10. ¿Qué quieres hacer?     comer

## Conversaciones

A: ¿Por qué hace tanto frío aquí?

B: ¿Quiere Ud. una manta?

A: Sí, gracias. Ud. es muy amable.

B: De nada, señor. ¿Necesita Ud. algo más?

A: Sí, por favor. Quiero dormir.

B: Está bien. Llámeme si necesita cualquier otra cosa.

A: ¿Cómo se siente Ud. hoy, señora?

B: Me siento muy débil.

A: ¿Tiene Ud. náuseas?

B: No, pero sí estoy un poco mareada.

A: Después de tomar esta medicina, Ud. va a sentirse mejor. ¿Quiere Ud. algo más?

B: No, doctor, muchas gracias.

## Nota

### Placement of Object Pronouns

Usually, object pronouns precede the verb:

El paciente me llama.        *The patient is calling me.*

However, when one uses the direct command form, pronouns are attached to the end of the verb:

Llámeme.        *Call me.*

---

**NOTA CULTURAL**          **LA MEDICINA FOLKLÓRICA**

Many Hispanic people, especially those from the Caribbean Islands, have strong beliefs in folk remedies for many ailments. These may consist of herbal teas, potions, poultices and other homemade remedies. A patient will often look to a female member of the family for advice concerning these remedies. While these types of treatments may or may not be effective, your patient will probably continue to take them even after he or she has consulted you. It is important to remember that an individual may lose confidence in your treatment if results do not occur quickly enough. In that case, he or she will probably return to some form of folk treatment and will cease to consult with you for that problem.

---

## Lectura:   Los enfermeros en el hospital

Los enfermeros en el hospital tienen muchas responsabilidades. Tienen que cuidar de las necesidades físicas del paciente. Por ejemplo, el enfermero o la enfermera tiene que darle de comer, tomarle la temperatura y la presión, registrarle el pulso, cambiarle las vendas y bañarle.

Tiene otras responsabilidades también. Tiene que ponerle las inyecciones necesarias al paciente y darle el medicamento recetado por el médico. Además, la enfermera o el enfermero tiene que comprender los diagnósticos y los pronósticos y hacer el trabajo del médico o la doctora en su ausencia.

Muchas veces las responsabilidades de los enfermeros dependen de la especialización. En la sala de operaciones la enfermera o el enfermero tiene que conocer bien los instrumentos de la cirugía, pero en la sala de emergencias tiene que estar preparado para cualquier caso.

## Vocabulario

| | |
|---|---|
| cuidar de | *to care for, to look out for (something)* |
| cuidar a | *to take care of (a person)* |
| otras | *other* |
| también | *also* |
| además | *besides; in addition to* |
| comprender | *to understand* |
| la ausencia | *absence* |
| cualquier | *any* |
| conocer | *to know; be acquainted with* |

## Preguntas

1. ¿Cuáles son tres responsabilidades del enfermero o de la enfermera en el hospital?
2. ¿Qué debe comprender el enfermero o la enfermera?
3. ¿Qué deben conocer bien los enfermeros que trabajan en la sala de operaciones?

## RESUMEN Y REPASO

## Gramática

gustar    *to like*

| | | | |
|---|---|---|---|
| me gusta(n) | *I like* | nos gusta(n) | *we like* |
| te gusta(n) | *you* (fam.) *like* | | |
| le gusta(n) | *he/she likes* | les gusta(n) | *they like* |
| le gusta(n) | *you* (form.) *like* | les gusta(n) | *you* (pl.) *like* |

## Vocabulario

| | |
|---|---|
| ¿cuánto? ¿cuánta? | *how much?* |
| ¿cuántos? ¿cuántas? | *how many?* |
| | |
| tan | *so* |
| tanto, -a | *so much* |
| tantos, -as | *so many* |

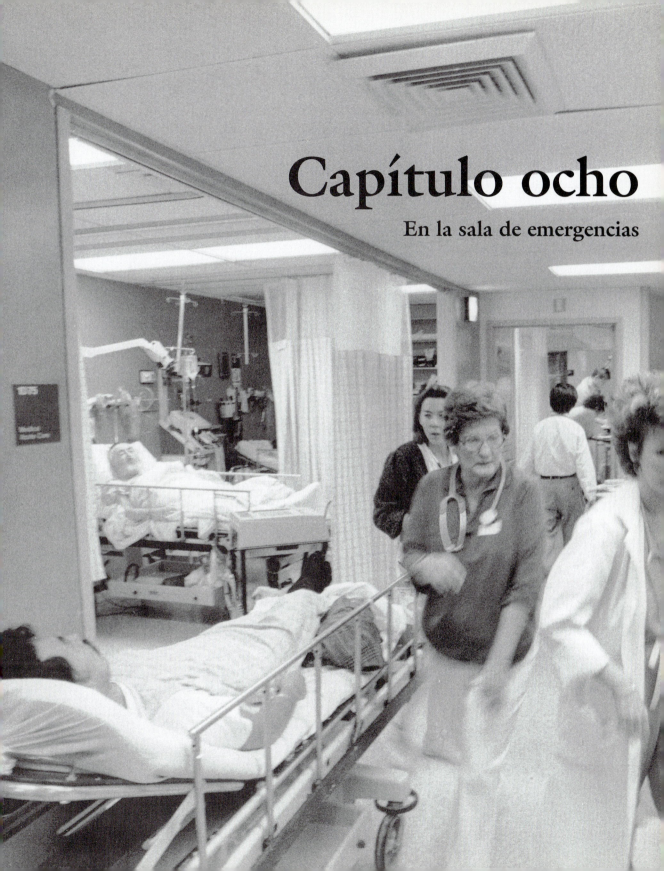

# Capítulo ocho

## En la sala de emergencias

## 👁 Conversación

| | |
|---|---|
| Doctora: | Buenas tardes, señora. ¿Qué le pasó a su hijo? |
| Madre: | Mi hijo se cortó el dedo y no deja de sangrar. |
| Doctora: | ¿Cómo se llama Ud., señora? |
| Madre: | Yo soy la señora Hernández, y mi hijo se llama Felipe. |
| Doctora: | ¿Cuántos años tiene Felipe? |
| Madre: | Tiene ocho años. |
| Doctora: | ¿Cuándo se cortó? |
| Madre: | Hace una hora que se cortó. |
| Doctora: | ¿Cómo lo hizo? |
| Madre: | Se cortó con un cuchillo. |
| Doctora: | Voy a limpiarle la herida a su hijo y aplicarle una solución desinfectante. ¿Ha tenido Felipe una inyección para el tétano recientemente? |
| Madre: | No, doctora. |

## Sustituciones

Substitute the underlined words with the cued items. Be sure to make any other necessary changes.

> **MODELO**     ¿Ha tenido _Felipe_ una inyección contra el tétano?     Ud.
> **¿Ha tenido _Ud._ una inyección contra el tétano?**

1. ¿Ha tenido _Felipe_ una inyección contra el tétano?     el paciente
2. ¿Ha tenido _Felipe_ una inyección contra el tétano?     Uds.
3. ¿Ha tenido _Felipe_ una inyección contra _el tétano_?     la paciente, la hepatitis
4. ¿Ha tenido _Felipe_ _una inyección contra el tétano_?     el señor, un accidente
5. ¿Ha tenido _Felipe_ una inyección contra _el tétano_?     ellos, la viruela

## 👁 Continúa la conversación...

| | |
|---|---|
| Doctora: | Pues, es una cortada bastante profunda. Voy a darle puntadas para controlar la hemorragia. Además, su hijo va a necesitar una inyección contra el tétano. |
| Madre: | ¿Cuántas puntadas se necesitan? |
| Doctora: | Se necesitan doce puntadas. |
| Madre: | ¿Le va a doler mucho? |
| Doctora: | Bueno, señora, un poco. Pero voy a ponerle una anestesia local. Es necesario quitar las puntadas después de cinco días. |
| Madre: | Está bien, doctora, muchas gracias. |

# Vocabulario

| | |
|---|---|
| se cortó | *he cut himself* |
| **dejar de** | *to stop; to cease* |
| **sangrar** | *to bleed* |
| **hizo** | *did; made (preterite tense form of* **hacer***)* |
| un **cuchillo** | *knife* |
| **limpiar** | *to clean* |
| la **herida** | *wound* |
| **aplicar** | *to apply* |
| el **tétano** | *tetanus* |
| una **cortada** | *a cut* |
| **profundo, -a** | *deep* |
| las **puntadas** | *stitches* |
| **dar puntadas** | *to put stitches* |
| la **hemorragia** | *bleeding* |
| **quitar** | *to remove* |

# Preguntas

1. ¿Cómo se llama el hijo de la señora Hernández?
2. ¿Cuántos años tiene?
3. ¿Qué le pasó?
4. ¿Cuántas puntadas se necesitan?

# Notas

### Dejar de and Para as "in Order To"

**Dejar de** means *to stop* or *cease from doing something*. It is followed by the infinitive of another verb. For example:

| | |
|---|---|
| La herida no deja de sangrar. | *The wound does not stop bleeding.* |
| El niño no deja de llorar. | *The child does not stop crying.* |

**Para** before the infinitive verb means *in order to*. For example:

| | |
|---|---|
| El médico da puntadas para controlar el sangramiento. | *The doctor puts in stitches (in order) to control the bleeding.* |
| Voy a la farmacia para comprar la medicina. | *I am going to the pharmacy (in order) to buy the medicine.* |

# Nota

## The Preterite Tense

The following is an example of the preterite tense of regular -**ar** verbs.

**hablar**  *to speak, to talk*

| | | | | | |
|---|---|---|---|---|---|
| yo | **hablé** | *I spoke* | nosotros/nosotras | **hablamos** | *we spoke* |
| tú | **hablaste** | *you* (fam.) *spoke* | | | |
| él/ella | **habló** | *he/she spoke* | ellos/ellas | **hablaron** | *they spoke* |
| Ud. | **habló** | *you* (form.) *spoke* | Uds. | **hablaron** | *you* (pl.) *spoke* |

The following preterite tense endings are the same for both -**er** and -**ir** verb conjugations.

**comer**  *to eat*

| | | | | | |
|---|---|---|---|---|---|
| yo | **comí** | *I ate* | nosotros/nosotras | **comimos** | *we ate* |
| tú | **comiste** | *you* (fam.) *ate* | | | |
| él/ella | **comió** | *he/she ate* | ellos/ellas | **comieron** | *they ate* |
| Ud. | **comió** | *you* (form.) *ate* | Uds. | **comieron** | *you* (pl.) *ate* |

**escribir**  *to write*

| | | | | | |
|---|---|---|---|---|---|
| yo | **escribí** | *I wrote* | nosotros/nosotras | **escribimos** | *we wrote* |
| tú | **escribiste** | *you* (fam.) *wrote* | | | |
| él/ella | **escribió** | *he/she wrote* | ellos/ellas | **escribieron** | *they wrote* |
| Ud. | **escribió** | *you* (form.) *wrote* | Uds. | **escribieron** | *you* (pl.) *wrote* |

The preterite tense is used to indicate a completed past action. For example:

| | |
|---|---|
| Mi mamá se cortó con un cuchillo ayer. | *My mom cut herself with a knife yesterday.* |
| Yo hablé con la doctora la semana pasada. | *I spoke with the doctor last week.* |
| El médico me escribió una receta. | *The doctor wrote me a prescription.* |
| El niño se cortó ayer. | *The child cut himself yesterday.* |
| Yo tomé la medicina. | *I took the medicine.* |
| El paciente llamó a la enfermera. | *The patient called the nurse.* |
| ¿Cuándo pasó el accidente? | *When did the accident happen?* |
| ¿Cuándo ocurrió el accidente? | *When did the accident occur?* |

Note: Please see the Appendix for a list of irregular verbs in the preterite tense.

The following are some more examples of verbs in the preterite or past tense.

corté, cortó          *I cut, he/she/you cut*
tomé, tomó           *I took, he/she/you took*
llamé, llamó         *I called, he/she/you called*
comí, comió          *I ate, he/she/you ate*
compré, compró       *I bought, he/she/you bought*
hablé, habló         *I spoke, he/she/you spoke*
¿Qué pasó?           *What happened?*

## Para practicar

Answer in the preterite tense using the cues.

**MODELO**      ¿Qué tomó el paciente?     la medicina
               **El paciente tomó la medicina.**

1. ¿Qué recetó la doctora?                un antibiótico
2. ¿Quién salió del hospital?             el paciente
3. ¿Quién se fracturó el brazo?           el niño
4. ¿Qué tomó la enfermera?                el pulso
5. ¿Cuándo llamó la señora a la doctora?  ayer
6. ¿Quién llenó los formularios?          mi hermana
7. ¿Quién consultó con el especialista?   ella

## Para practicar más

Student A asks the question. Student B answers with the cued response.

**MODELO**      A:  ¿Quién se cortó ayer?     el niño
               B:  **El niño se cortó ayer.**

1. ¿Qué tomó el paciente?                 un antibiótico
2. ¿Cuándo tomó el antibiótico?           la semana pasada
3. ¿Quién tomó el antibiótico?            yo
4. ¿Qué ocurrió?                          un accidente
5. ¿Cuándo ocurrió el accidente?          ayer
6. ¿Dónde ocurrió el accidente?           en el apartamento
7. ¿Quién llamó a la doctora?             la señora González
8. ¿Cuándo llamó a la doctora?            hace una hora
9. ¿Quién se cortó?                       la paciente
10. ¿Dónde se cortó?                      en la casa
11. ¿Quién no dejó de llorar?            el niño
12. ¿Cuándo dejó de sangrar la herida?   hace cinco minutos

# Nota

## Object Pronouns Attached to Infinitives

When an infinitive is used as part of a verb phrase, you can attach object pronouns to the infinitive. For example:

¿Qué va a darme Ud.?                    *What are you going to give me?*
Voy a darle aspirina.                   *I am going to give you aspirin.*

# Para comunicarse

One student asks the question, and another answers according to the cues.

| MODELO | A: | el médico |
|---|---|---|
|  |  | **¿Qué va a darme el médico?** |
|  | B: | el antibiótico |
|  |  | **El médico va a darle el antibiótico.** |

1.  A:   la doctora
    B:   la receta

2.  A:   la enfermera
    B:   la medicina

3.  A:   el cirujano
    B:   una operación

4.  A:   el terapeuta
    B:   unos ejercicios

5.  A:   el médico
    B:   las pastillas

6.  A:   el recepcionista
    B:   una cita

# Vocabulario

| **Las situaciones de emergencia** | *Emergency Situations* |
|---|---|
| el **accidente** | *accident* |
| la **ambulancia** | *ambulance* |
| el **antídoto** | *antidote* |
| el **ataque al corazón** | *heart attack* |
| la **camilla** | *stretcher* |
| la **dosis excesiva** | *overdose* |
| las **drogas** | *drugs* |
| la **hemorragia** | *hemorrhage* |
| la **herida** | *wound* |
| el **oxígeno** | *oxygen* |
| la **pistola** | *pistol* |
| la **puñalada** | *stabbing* |
| la **quemadura** | *burn* |
| el **veneno** | *poison* |

# Los Primeros Síntomas de un ataque cardíaco.

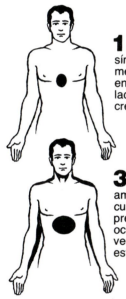

**1.** Uno de los primeros síntomas es presión o dolor en el medio del pecho. Allí es donde se encuentra su corazón, no en el lado izquierdo como muchos creen.

**2.** El dolor puede agravarse y extenderse por todo el pecho así como hacia el brazo izquierdo.

**3.** El dolor puede sentirse en ambos brazos, los hombros, cuello y mandíbula. Sensación de presión, llenura y tensión pueden ocurrir en el estómago, y ésto a veces se confunde con dolor de estómago.

**4.** El dolor puede ocurrir en una o varias de las áreas mencionadas al mismo tiempo. Puede desaparecer y volver más tarde. A veces, sudor, náusea y vómitos, así como dificultad en respirar pueden presentarse con el dolor.

# Qué hacer.

Al primer síntoma, cualquiera de ellos, llame a su médico. Si no puede comunicarse con su médico al instante, vaya a la sala de emergencias del hospital más cercano y pida pronto tratamiento.

**Escuche a su corazón.
Quizás no le avise nuevamente.**

**Por favor, llene éste espacio**

Nombre del médico:

Teléfono del médico:

Dirección del cuarto de emergencias del hospital más cercano:

New York Heart Association. 205 East 42nd Street, New York, NY 10017 Teléfono: (212) 661-5335

| | |
|---|---|
| ahogarse | *to drown; to suffocate* |
| apuñalar | *to stab* |
| asfixiarse | *to smother* |
| atacar | *to attack* |
| atentar el suicidio | *to attempt suicide* |
| atragantarse | *to choke (on something)* |
| caerse | *to fall* |
| cortarse | *to cut (oneself)* |
| desmayarse | *to faint* |
| envenenarse | *to poison (oneself)* |
| enyesar | *to put in a cast* |
| fracturarse | *to break, to fracture* |
| golpear | *to hit* |
| hacerse daño | *to hurt oneself* |
| llevar en camilla | *to carry on a stretcher* |
| perder el conocimiento | *to lose consciousness* |
| quemarse | *to burn (oneself)* |
| atropellado (por un automóvil) | *run over (by a car)* |

## Conversaciones

A:  ¿Dónde ocurrió el accidente?

B:  Ocurrió en la calle.

A:  ¿Qué le pasó a la víctima?

B:  Sufrió un ataque al corazón.

A:  ¿Mandaron por una ambulancia?

B:  Sí, lo llevaron al hospital.

A:  ¿Avisaron a su familia?

B:  Sí, llamaron a su esposa.


A:  ¿Qué le pasó al niño?

B:  Se quemó.

A:  ¿Dónde ocurrió el accidente?

B:  Ocurrió en la cocina.

A:  ¿Es grave su condición?

B:  Sí, está en la sala de cuidado intensivo.


A:  ¿Qué le pasó a Ud., señora?

B:  Creo que me fracturé la muñeca.

A:  ¿Cómo ocurrió?

B:  Me caí en la casa.

A:  Déjeme ver. ¿Le duele mucho aquí?

B:  Sí, doctor, mucho. ¿Está fracturada la muñeca?

A:  Es necesario hacerle radiografías para saber por cierto.

## Para comunicarse

Student A asks the questions, and student B responds according to the cues.

| MODELO | A: | el accidente; ¿dónde ocurrió? |
|---|---|---|
| | | **¿Dónde ocurrió el accidente?** |
| | B: | en la calle |
| | | **El accidente ocurrió en la calle.** |

1. A: el ataque; ¿dónde ocurrió?
   B: en la casa

2. A: el accidente; ¿cuándo ocurrió?
   B: ayer

3. A: la ambulancia; ¿cuándo llegó?
   B: hace una media hora

4. A: la víctima; ¿qué sufrió?
   B: un ataque al corazón

5. A: el accidente; ¿dónde ocurrió?
   B: en la casa

6. A: la pierna; ¿dónde se fracturó?
   B: en la escalera

## Para comunicarse más

Student A asks what happened. Student B answers using the cue. Student A then asks what is needed and student B answers using the cued response.

| MODELO | A: | al paciente |
|---|---|---|
| | | **¿Qué le ocurrió al paciente?** |
| | B: | se fracturó la pierna |
| | | **El paciente se fracturó la pierna.** |
| | A: | **¿Qué es necesario?** |
| | B: | hacer radiografías |
| | | **Es necesario hacer radiografías.** |

1. A: a la víctima
   B: se envenenó

   A: _____
   B: darle el antídoto

2. A: a la señora
   B: se cortó

   A: _____
   B: darle una transfusión de sangre

3. A:  al paciente
   B:  se fracturó el brazo

   A:  _____
   B:  enyesar el brazo

5. A:  al niño
   B:  se cortó

   A:  _____
   B   dar puntadas

4. A:  al hombre
   B:  se desmayó

   A:  _____
   B:  hacer algunas pruebas

6. A:  a la víctima
   B:  se quemó

   A:  _____
   B:  ponerle una venda

---

## NOTA CULTURAL    EL HONOR Y EL ORGULLO

**El honor** is a very important concept for people of Latin descent. It goes beyond the idea of honor and integrity as it includes the concept of personal reputation. Personal insults are taken very seriously, especially if the injured party feels that some damage to his or her reputation in the public eye has occurred.

**El orgullo** *(pride)* is a related concept. People are very proud of their national heritage. Each person has a special feeling for his or her **país** *(country)*, **pueblo** *(town)*, and **nombre de familia** *(family name)*.

---

## Conversación

| | |
|---|---|
| Asistente de ambulancia: | ¿Mandó Ud. por una ambulancia? |
| Vecina: | Sí, señor. |
| Asistente de ambulancia: | ¿Qué pasó? |
| Vecina: | Mi vecino, el señor Moreno, se cayó de la escalera. Creo que se fracturó la pierna. No puede caminar. |
| Asistente de ambulancia: | ¿Dónde está la víctima? |
| Vecina: | Está arriba, en el segundo piso. |
| El señor Moreno: | ¿Ha llegado la ambulancia? |
| Asistente de ambulancia: | Sí, estamos aquí. ¿Cómo se siente Ud.? |
| El señor Moreno: | Me duele mucho la pierna y no puedo caminar. |
| Asistente de ambulancia: | Vamos a llevarle a Ud. al hospital en una camilla. |

## Sustituciones

Substitute the underlined words with the cued items. Be sure to make any other necessary changes.

**MODELO**    Mi <u>vecino</u> se cayó de la escalera.      hijo
**Mi <u>hijo</u> se cayó de la escalera.**

1. Mi <u>vecino</u> se cayó de la escalera.        padre
2. Mi <u>vecino se cayó de la escalera</u>.        abuelo, fracturarse el brazo
3. Mi <u>vecino se cayó de la escalera</u>.        mamá, cortarse con un cuchillo
4. <u>Mi vecino se cayó de la escalera</u>.        el paciente, desmayarse
5. <u>Mi vecino se cayó de la escalera</u>.        los pacientes, quemarse

## Continúa la conversación...

(En el hospital.)

Enfermera:          ¿Cómo se llama?

El señor Moreno:    Me llamo Miguel Moreno.

Enfermera:          ¿Qué le pasó?

El señor Moreno:    Creo que me fracturé la pierna.

Enfermera:          ¿Cuándo ocurrió el accidente?

El señor Moreno:    Ocurrió hace dos horas.

Enfermera:          Vamos a hacer unas radiografías de la pierna.

El señor Moreno:    ¿Me va a doler?

Enfermera:          No, no le va a doler nada en absoluto.

(Un poco más tarde.)

Enfermera:          Ud. se ha fracturado la pierna. El ortopédico va a llegar muy pronto y le va a enyesar la pierna.

El señor Moreno:    ¿Voy a poder caminar?

Enfermera:          Sí, pero será necesario caminar con muletas por seis o siete semanas.

## Vocabulario

| | |
|---|---|
| el **vecino**, la **vecina** | *neighbor* |
| se **cayó** | *fell* |
| de la escalera | *(down) from the stairs* |
| caminar | *to walk* |
| arriba | *up; upstairs* |
| nada en absoluto | *not at all* |
| el **ortopédico** | *the orthopedist* |
| será | *(it) will be* |
| caminar con muletas | *to walk with crutches* |

## Preguntas

1. ¿Qué le pasó al señor Moreno?
2. ¿Quién llamó por la ambulancia?
3. ¿Cómo llevaron al señor Moreno al hospital?
4. ¿Cuándo ocurrió el accidente?
5. ¿Qué hizo la enfermera en el hospital?
6. ¿Quién va a enyesarle la pierna al señor Moreno?

## Recuerde

### Object Pronouns

We saw indirect object pronouns in Chapter 3. Let's review them now and compare them with direct object pronouns.

| Indirect Object Pronouns | | Direct Object Pronouns | |
|---|---|---|---|
| me | *to/for me* | me | *me* |
| te | *to/for you* (fam.) | lo | *it, him, you* (masc.) |
| le | *to/for him, her, you* (form.) | la | *it, her, you* (fem.) |
| nos | *to/for us* | nos | *us* |
| les | *to/for them, you* (pl.) | los | *them, you* (masc.) |
| | | las | *them, you* (fem.) |

Indirect objects are used to take the place of a person who is the object of the verb, while a direct object is usually an inanimate object. The direct object pronoun must agree with the noun that it replaces in gender and number. Often in English one would use a prepositional phrase where in Spanish one would use an indirect object. For example:

Indirect:

El médico **me** prepara la receta.    *The doctor prepares the prescription for me.*

Direct:

El médico la prepara.    *The doctor prepares it.*

Notice that the indirect pronouns precede conjugated verb forms:

Mi vecino **nos** compró la medicina.    *My neighbor bought us the medicine.*

However, indirect object pronouns can be attached to an infinitive:

Mi vecino va a comprar**nos** la medicina.    *My neighbor is going to buy us the medicine.*

When a direct and indirect object pronoun occur together in the same sentence, the indirect object pronoun comes first:

Mi vecino **nos** la compró.    *My neighbor bought it for us.*

If the meanings of **le** and **les** are not clear from the context of the sentence, they can be clarified with the prepositional phrases **a él, a ella, a Ud., a ellos, a ellas, a Uds.** For example:

El farmacéutico le vendió la medicina **a él.**    *The pharmacist sold him the medicine.*

When the indirect object pronouns **le** or **les** appear together with the direct object pronouns **lo, la, los,** or **las,** change the **le** or **les** to **se.**

La doctora **le** da el jarabe.    *The doctor gives him the syrup.*
La doctora **se** lo da.    *The doctor gives it to him.*

## Para comunicarse

Student A plays the role of the patient asking a question. The health professional (B) answers by saying what he or she is going to do.

**MODELO**
A:  dar
   **¿Qué me va a dar?**
B:  **Voy a darle un examen médico.**

1. A:  dar

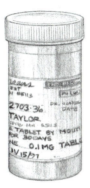

2. A:  poner

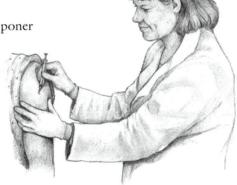

3. A:  hacer

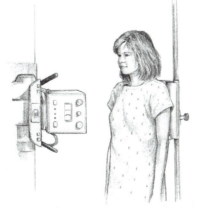

4. A:  preparar

5. A:   tomar

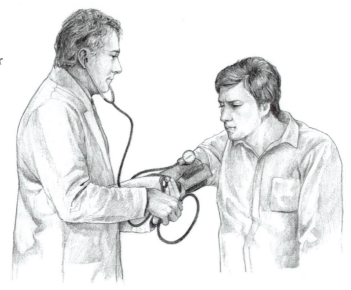

6. A:   dar

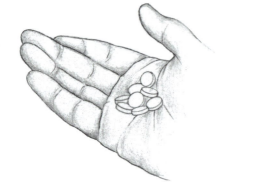

7. A:   tomar

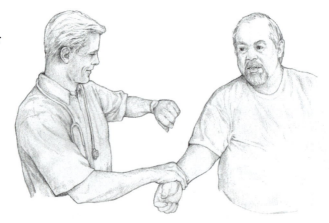

## Para practicar

Replace the underlined direct object nouns with pronouns.

| **MODELO** | La paciente toma <u>las píldoras</u>. | *The patient takes the pills.* |
|---|---|---|
| | **La paciente <u>las</u> toma.** | *The patient takes them.* |

1. El farmacéutico prepara <u>las recetas</u>.
2. La paciente lee <u>la etiqueta</u>.
3. El niño bebe <u>la leche</u>.
4. Ella toma <u>el antibiótico</u>.
5. La doctora analiza <u>las radiografías</u>.

## Conversación

A:    ¿Qué le pasó a su hijo?

B:    Sufrió una concusión.

A:    ¿Cómo ocurrió el accidente?

B:    Se cayó en el parque.

A:    ¿Qué dicen los médicos?

B:    Dicen que va a estar bien pero que tiene que pasar la noche en el hospital.

## Para practicar

One student must find out the following information from the patient. Another student answers with an appropriate response for each question.

1. What happened?
2. Where does it hurt?
3. When did it occur?
4. What is the pain like?
5. Do you take any medicines?
6. Are you allergic to any medicines?

## Lectura:   Los síntomas

La paciente dice que tiene un dolor severo del abdomen. El dolor comenzó una hora después de comer. El dolor está en la parte de arriba del abdomen. Otros síntomas de la paciente son: sudores, náuseas y vómitos. La paciente dice que no toma ningunas medicinas y que nunca ha tenido una operación.

## Preguntas

1. ¿Dónde tiene dolor la paciente?
2. ¿Cómo es el dolor?
3. ¿Cuándo comenzó el dolor?
4. ¿Cuáles son otros síntomas de la paciente?
5. ¿Toma medicinas la paciente?

## RESUMEN Y REPASO

## Vocabulario

| **Verbos útiles para la sala de emergencias** | *Useful Verbs for the Emergency Room* |
|---|---|
| ahogarse | *to drown; to suffocate* |
| apuñalar | *to stab* |
| atragantarse | *to choke (on something)* |
| caerse | *to fall* |
| cortarse | *to cut oneself* |
| desmayarse | *to faint* |
| envenenarse | *to poison oneself, to be poisoned* |
| fracturarse | *to fracture* |
| ocurrir | *to occur* |
| pasar | *to happen* |
| tomar | *to take* |
| tragar | *to swallow* |

| **Más vocabulario para situaciones de emergencia** | *More Vocabulary for Emergency Situations* |
|---|---|
| el camillero | *stretcher bearer* |
| la magulladura, la contusión | *bruise* |
| la mordida | *bite (human)* |
| la picadura | *bite (insect)* |
| la respiración | *respiration* |
| la sala de cuidado intensivo | *intensive care* |
| el salpullido | *rash* |
| escupir sangre | *to spit up blood* |
| estar sangrando | *to be bleeding* |
| lesionarse | *to injure oneself* |
| magullado, -a | *bruised* |

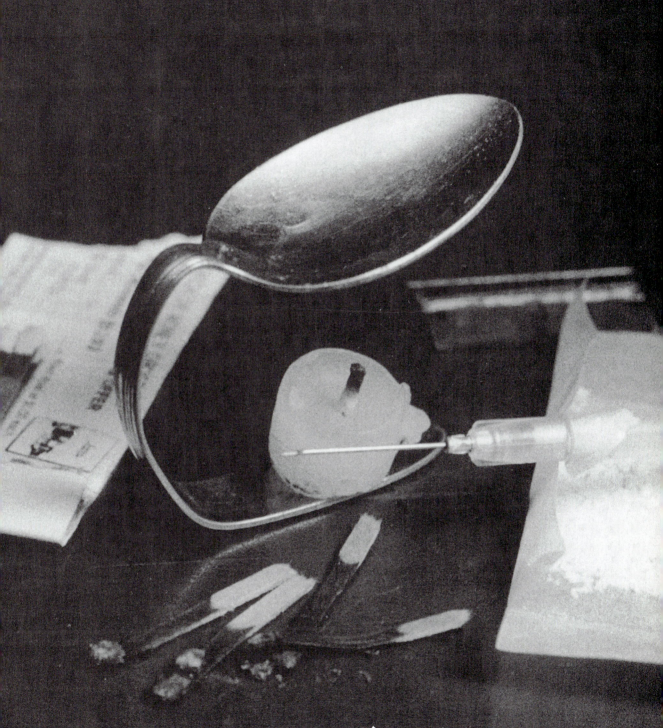

# Capítulo nueve

Las drogas y el alcoholismo

## Conversación

| | |
|---|---|
| Señora: | Perdone, doctora, ¿puedo hablar con Ud.? |
| Doctora: | Sí, por supuesto. ¿Cuál es su problema, señora? |
| Señora: | Creo que mi hijo toma drogas. |
| Doctora: | ¿Por qué cree Ud. eso? |
| Señora: | Pues, anoche volvió a casa muy tarde, hablaba tonterías, y no sabía donde estaba. |
| Doctora: | Posiblemente estaba borracho. |
| Señora: | No, a veces mi marido viene a casa borracho y no es lo mismo. |

## Sustituciones

Substitute the underlined words with the cued items. Be sure to make any other necessary changes.

| MODELO | Creo que mi hijo toma drogas.    hija |
|---|---|
| | **Creo que mi hija toma drogas.** |

1. Creo que mi hijo toma drogas.       esposa
2. Creo que mi hijo toma drogas.       marido, fuma marihuana
3. Creo que mi hijo toma drogas.       padre, está borracho
4. Creo que mi hijo toma drogas.       mamá, toma cocaína
5. Creo que mi hijo toma drogas.       hijos, anfetaminas

## Continúa la conversación...

| | |
|---|---|
| Doctora: | ¿Cuántos años tiene su hijo? |
| Señora: | Tiene solamente catorce años. |
| Doctora: | ¿Sabe Ud. qué drogas toma? |
| Señora: | Creo que fuma la marihuana. Quizás toma cocaína o crack también, pero espero que no. |
| Doctora: | ¿Ha encontrado alguna vez píldoras en el dormitorio de su hijo? |
| Señora: | No. ¿Por qué? |
| Doctora: | Porque las píldoras como los barbitúricos, las anfetaminas y otras son muy dañinas. Ud. debe traer a su hijo aquí para un examen médico. |
| Señora: | Sí, creo que Ud. tiene razón, doctora. Muchas gracias por su ayuda. |

## Vocabulario

| | | | |
|---|---|---|---|
| **por supuesto** | *of course* | **lo mismo** | *the same* |
| **pues** | *well, then* | **quizás** | *maybe* |
| **anoche** | *last night* | **el dormitorio** | *bedroom* |
| **hablaba tonterías** | *was talking nonsense* | **los barbitúricos** | *barbiturates* |
| **sabía** | *knew* | **las anfetaminas** | *amphetamines* |
| **estaba** | *was (located)* | **dañino, -a** | *harmful* |
| **borracho, -a** | *drunk* | | |

## Preguntas

1. ¿Cuál es el problema de la señora?
2. ¿Por qué cree que su hijo toma drogas?
3. ¿Cuántos años tiene su hijo?
4. ¿Qué debe hacer la señora?

## Recuerde

The interrogative **¿por qué?** means *why?*, and the response is **porque...** *(because...)*:

| | |
|---|---|
| ¿Por qué usa Ud. drogas? | *Why do you use drugs?* |
| Porque la vida es muy dura. | *Because life is very hard.* |

The neuter form **eso** means *that* and is used when referring to a general idea rather than a specific noun. Also, **esto,** meaning *this,* is used in the same way. For example:

| | |
|---|---|
| ¿Por qué cree Ud. eso? | *Why do you think that?* |
| Esto es muy interesante. | *This is very interesting.* |

Remember that **aquí** means *here* and **allí** means *there*. However, to say *come here*, use the expression **Venga acá** (pronounced **vengacá**).

## Notas

### The Verb <u>Creer</u>—to Believe or Think—and <u>Tener</u> with <u>Razón</u>

The verb **creer** *(to think; to believe)* is used to talk about a person's feelings, beliefs, or opinions. Look at the following examples:

| | |
|---|---|
| ¿Qué cree Ud.? | *What do you think?* |
| Creo que mi hijo toma drogas. | *I think that my son takes drugs.* |
| ¿Qué creen Uds.? | *What do you* (pl.) *think?* |
| Creemos que este médico es muy bueno. | *We think that this doctor is very good.* |
| Creo que sí. | *I think so.* |
| Creo que no. | *I don't think so.* |

The verb **tener** is used with **razón** to say that someone is right. For example:

| | |
|---|---|
| El médico tiene razón. | *The doctor is right.* |
| Nosotros tenemos razón. | *We are right.* |

Also:

| | |
|---|---|
| Mi marido no tiene razón. | *My husband is wrong.* |

## Para practicar

Answer the question, **¿Qué cree Ud.?** using the cues provided.

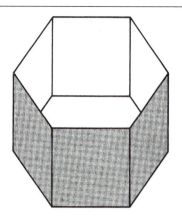

**MODELO**    ¿Qué cree Ud.?    mi hijo toma drogas
**Creo que mi hijo toma drogas.**

1. ¿Qué cree Ud.?    mi hijo fuma marihuana
2. ¿Qué cree Ud.?    mi marido toma cocaína
3. ¿Qué cree Ud.?    mi esposa bebe demasiado
4. ¿Qué cree Ud.?    mi vecino vende drogas
5. ¿Qué cree Ud.?    la doctora tiene razón
6. ¿Qué cree Ud.?    mi hijo no tiene razón

Now use the same cues to answer the question, **¿Qué creen Uds.?** Be sure to change **mi** to **nuestro** (*mas.*) or **nuestra** (*fem.*).

**MODELO**    ¿Qué creen Uds.?    What do you (pl.) think?

**Creemos que nuestro hijo fuma marihuana.**    We think that our son smokes marijuana.

 **Vocabulario**

| Las drogas y el alcohol | *Drugs and Alcohol* |
| --- | --- |
| el **adicto** | *addict* |
| el **alcohólico** | *alcoholic* |
| el **alcoholismo** | *alcoholism* |
| las **anfetaminas** | *amphetamines* |
| los **barbitúricos** | *barbiturates* |
| la **codeína** | *codeine* |
| la **desintoxicación** | *detoxification* |
| la **dosis excesiva** | *overdose* |
| la **drogadicción** | *drug addiction* |
| la **heroína** | *heroin* |
| la **inyección** | *injection* |
| el **joven**, la **joven** | *young person* |
| el **jovencito**, la **jovencita** | *teenager* |
| la **metadona** | *methadone* |
| el **narcómano**, la **narcómana** | *narcotics addict* |
| los **narcóticos** | *narcotics* |
| la **sobredosis** | *overdose* |
| la **suspensión del uso** | *withdrawal* |

## Si toma bebidas alcohólicas, hágalo con moderación

Las bebidas alcohólicas tienden a ser altas en calorías y poco nutritivas. Aún cuando tome moderadamente, tal vez necesite disminuir la cantidad si desea reducir a un peso "ideal".

Los que beben en exceso suelen desarrollar deficiencias nutritivas y otras enfermedades más graves, tales como cirrosis del hígado y ciertos tipos de cáncer, especialmente los que fuman cigarrillos. En parte, esto se debe a la pérdida de apetito, menor consumo de alimentos y absorción desigual de nutrientes.

El consumo excesivo de bebidas alcohólicas en mujeres embarazadas ha causado defectos de nacimiento u otros problemas durante el embarazo. No se ha establecido el nivel de consumo alcohólico bajo el cual se presentan problemas para el bebé por nacer. Por ello, el Instituto Nacional Sobre Abuso de Alcohol y Alcoholismo advierte que las mujeres embarazadas no deben consumir alcohol.

Una o dos bebidas alcohólicas al día parece no causar daño en personas adultas con buena salud y en mujeres no embarazadas. Doce onzas de cerveza regular, 5 onzas de vino y 1,5 onzas de espíritus destilados, tienen el mismo contenido de alcohol.

**Si bebe, hágalo con moderación y ¡NO CONDUZCA!**

| | |
|---|---|
| **beber** | *to drink* |
| **tomar** | *to take; to drink (alcohol)* |
| **usar drogas** | *to take drugs* |
| **borracho, -a** | *drunk* |

la aguja hipodérmica

la cocaína

el alcohol

el crack

la marihuana

# Recuerde

Remember that the letter **h** is silent in Spanish. **El alcohol** is pronounced **el alco'ol.**

# Nota

### How to Say "Used to..." or "Was..."—Expressing Continuing Past Action with the Imperfect Tense

The following are some examples of imperfect tense verb forms:

| | | | | |
|---|---|---|---|---|
| bebía | *was drinking, drank, used to drink* | | iba | *was going, went, used to go* |
| era | *was* | | podía | *was able to, could* |
| estaba | *was (in or at)* | | sufría | *was suffering, suffered, used to suffer* |
| fumaba | *was smoking, smoked, used to smoke* | | tenía | *had, used to have* |
| hablaba | *was talking, talked, used to talk* | | tomaba | *was taking, took, used to take* |
| hacía | *was doing/making, used to do/make* | | usaba | *was using, used, used to use* |

For more complete verb forms and examples, see **Gramática** in the **Resumen y repaso** section on pages 152–55.

The imperfect tense is used to indicate something habitual or customary, a repeated action that took place in the past. The most common English equivalents are *used to, would,* and past progressive compound verb forms (*I was speaking, you were eating, etc.*).

## Para practicar

Answer using the cues provided.

**MODELO**    ¿Quién usaba drogas?    el joven
**El joven usaba drogas.**

1. ¿Quién fumaba marihuana?    la joven
2. ¿Quién usaba crack?    el padre
3. ¿Quién usaba heroína?    el jovencito
4. ¿Quién usaba narcóticos?    el paciente
5. ¿Quién tomaba alcohol?    la madre
6. ¿Quién estaba borracho?    el hijo
7. ¿Quién era un drogadicto?    la víctima
8. ¿Quién tomaba píldoras?    la hija

## Conversaciones

A:    ¿Por qué usaba drogas Ud.?
B:    Tenía muchos problemas.
A:    ¿Qué problemas tenía Ud.?
B:    Mi marido no tenía trabajo y tomaba demasiado.
A:    ¿Qué drogas usaba Ud.?
B:    Yo usaba crack pero ahora no.

A:    ¿Por qué tomó Ud. las anfetaminas?
B:    Estaba muy deprimido.
A:    ¿Dónde las compró?
B:    En la escuela.
A:    ¿Tomó algunas píldoras anoche?
B:    No, anoche no tomé nada.

## Para practicar

**Sentence build-up.** Form sentences from individual words and fragments.

**MODELO**    no tenía    mi marido, trabajo
**Mi marido no tenía trabajo.**

1. no tenía    mi esposa, dinero
2. no tenía    el paciente, seguro
3. no tenía    la señora, síntomas
4. no usaba    el joven, drogas
5. no usaban    los jóvenes, drogas

6.  usaba        la chica, heroína
7.  tomaba       el hombre, demasiado
8.  no tomaban   los hombres, demasiado
9.  tenía        el paciente, dolor
10. tenía        la paciente, dolor de cabeza
11. fumaba       la jovencita, marihuana, en la escuela
12. fumaban      las jovencitas, cigarrillos, en la casa
13. vendía       ese hombre, drogas, en la calle
14. estaba       la madre, nerviosa
15. visitaba     la madre, a su hijo, en el hospital
16. era          mi padre, un alcohólico
17. no usaba     yo, drogas

---

## Nota cultural   La jerga de las drogas

Some of the drug slang **(la jerga de las drogas)** used on the street is derived from or borrowed from English, and, like all forms of slang, is constantly changing. Also, there are many words that have regional uses, with some being common to the Caribbean, others to Mexico and the southwestern United States, and still other areas having their own words. However, there is some terminology with which you should be familiar.

A very common word for cocaine is **nieve** *(snow)*, with **polvito** *(little dust)* being more common in Puerto Rico. In Mexico, *heroin* is **tecata,** and *an addict* is **un tecato,** while *marijuana* is called **tacote.** However, a much more common slang word for marijuana is **hierba** (also spelled **yerba**). In Puerto Rico *heroin* might be called **estofa** *(stuff?)*. *Needle tracks* are **traques,** while *a pusher* might be called **un traquetero. Filerearse** and **picarse** can both mean *to shoot up,* while **kikear** is *to go cold turkey,* and **puchar** could be used to mean *to push drugs.*

---

## Más vocabulario

| | |
|---|---|
| la **aguja sucia** | *dirty needle* |
| la **depresión** | *depression* |
| las **huellas** | *tracks* |
| las **pupilas dilatadas** | *dilated pupils* |
| los **somníferos** | *sleeping pills* |
| **envenenarse, se envenenó** | *to poison oneself, poisoned oneself* |
| **morir, murió** | *to die, died* |
| **deprimido, -a** | *depressed* |
| **desorientado, -a** | *disoriented* |
| **anoche** | *last night* |
| **ayer** | *yesterday* |

**Para practicar**

Answer the questions that correspond to the following statements.

1. El adicto se envenenó ayer con una aguja sucia.
   ¿Quién se envenenó?
   ¿Cómo se envenenó?
   ¿Cuándo se envenenó?

2. El hombre sufrió una sobredosis de heroína y murió anoche.
   ¿Quién sufrió una sobredosis?
   ¿Qué le pasó al hombre?
   ¿Cuándo murió el hombre?

3. El paciente tenía huellas de aguja hipodérmica en ambos brazos.
   ¿Quién tenía huellas?
   ¿Qué tenía el paciente?
   ¿En qué parte del cuerpo tenía huellas?

## Para practicar más

A child has come into the emergency room accompanied by her mother. She is semiconscious. The mother tells the doctor that her daughter took her sleeping pills. Find out or explain the following information.

1. How many pills were taken?
2. When did she take them?
3. How old is the child?
4. Does she have any special medical conditions?
5. Does the child take any other medications, or did she take any other pills?
6. Explain to the mother what you are going to do for her child, and what she can expect.

## Nota

### The Verb <u>Poder</u>—to Be Able, Can

You have seen the verb **poder** in Chapter 6. Let's review its present tense forms and compare those with the imperfect tense.

**Present Tense**

| | | | | | |
|---|---|---|---|---|---|
| yo | **puedo** | *I can* | nosotros/nosotras | **podemos** | *we can* |
| tú | **puedes** | *you* (fam.) *can* | | | |
| él/ella | **puede** | *he/she can* | ellos/ellas | **pueden** | *they can* |
| Ud. | **puede** | *you* (form.) *can* | Uds. | **pueden** | *you* (pl.) *can* |

**Past (Imperfect) Tense**

| | | | | | |
|---|---|---|---|---|---|
| yo | **podía** | *I could* | nosotros/nosotras | **podíamos** | *we could* |
| tú | **podías** | *you* (fam.) *could* | | | |
| él/ella | **podía** | *he/she could* | ellos/ellas | **podían** | *they could* |
| Ud. | **podía** | *you* (form.) *could* | Uds. | **podían** | *you* (pl.) *could* |

This verb is usually followed by the infinitive of another verb. For example:

El paciente no podía dormir.                    *The patient could not sleep.*

## Para practicar

Make up sentences using the verb **poder** and the cues.

 **MODELO**    el paciente, caminar
**El paciente puede caminar.** *or* **El paciente no puede caminar.**
**El paciente podía caminar.** *or* **El paciente no podía caminar.**

1. el joven, dejar de usar drogas
2. el paciente, levantarse
3. la madre, tomar la medicina
4. el papá, dejar de tomar
5. los pacientes, venir a la clínica hoy
6. los jóvenes, dormir ocho horas
7. la doctora, decirme cómo está mi padre
8. el adicto, abrir los ojos
9. el padre, encontrar trabajo
10. la jovencita, visitar a su abuela

## Lectura:   Las drogas y la sala de emergencias

El profesional médico que trabaja en la sala de emergencias puede encontrar una gran variedad de casos. Por eso es un trabajo muy difícil, con muchas responsabilidades. Un caso que se encuentra a menudo es el de un individuo que tomó una dosis excesiva de drogas. Es importante saber qué drogas tomó esa persona para que se pueda darle el tratamiento adecuado. Otros datos sobre el individuo también son de mucha importancia. Por ejemplo, es necesario saber cuántos años tiene, si tiene otras enfermedades y si tomó otras medicinas, píldoras o drogas. Es por estas razones que es tan importante la comunicación entre los profesionales médicos y el paciente o su familia y amigos.

## Vocabulario

| | |
|---|---|
| el **profesional médico** | *health professional* |
| **encontrar** | *to find* |
| una **gran variedad** | *large variety* |
| **por eso** | *for that reason* |
| **se encuentra** | *one finds* |
| **a menudo** | *often* |
| **otros datos** | *other facts* |

## Preguntas

1. ¿Qué tipo de caso se encuentra a menudo en la sala de emergencias?
2. ¿Cuáles son algunos datos que uno debe saber sobre un paciente?
3. ¿Qué es importante tener entre el profesional médico y el paciente?
4. ¿Qué otros casos ha encontrado Ud. en la sala de emergencias?

## Nota

### Otro and Otra

**Otro** *(mas.)* or **otra** *(fem.)* by itself means *another.* A common mistake is placing the indefinite article **un** (or **una**) in front of it to make it sound more like the word in English. Be sure to use it correctly, as in the following example:

Hay **otro** paciente en la sala de espera.    *There is **another** patient in the waiting room.*

## Recuerde

### The Impersonal <u>Se</u> before Verbs

Remember that you can place **se** before a verb to show that the subject is nonspecific. For example:

A menudo **se encuentra** un caso difícil.    *One often finds a difficult case.*
No **se puede** hacer nada para ese individuo.    *You (one) cannot do anything for that individual.*

## RESUMEN Y REPASO

## Gramática

### The Imperfect Tense, Formation and Usage

The imperfect tense is used to indicate a repeated, customary, or habitual past action. The most common English equivalents are *used to, would,* and the past progressive tense *(I was speaking, you were eating, etc.).*

The following are regular imperfect tense forms:

**hablar** *to speak*

| | | | | | |
|---|---|---|---|---|---|
| yo | **hablaba** | *I used to speak,*<br>*I was speaking* | nosotros/nosotras | **hablábamos** | *we used to speak,*<br>*we were speaking* |
| tú | **hablabas** | *you* (fam.) *used to speak,*<br>*you were speaking* | | | |
| él/ella | **hablaba** | *he/she used to speak,*<br>*he/she were speaking* | ellos/ellas | **hablaban** | *they used to speak,*<br>*they were speaking* |
| Ud. | **hablaba** | *you* (form.) *used to speak,*<br>*you were speaking* | Uds. | **hablaban** | *you* (pl.) *used to speak,*<br>*you were speaking* |

**comer** *to eat*

| | | | | | |
|---|---|---|---|---|---|
| yo | **comía** | *I used to eat,*<br>*I was eating* | nosotros/nosotras | **comíamos** | *we used to eat,*<br>*we were eating* |
| tú | **comías** | *you* (fam.) *used to eat,*<br>*you were eating* | | | |
| él/ella | **comía** | *he/she used to eat,*<br>*he/she was eating* | ellos/ellas | **comían** | *they used to eat,*<br>*they were eating* |
| Ud. | **comía** | *you* (form.) *used to eat,*<br>*you were eating* | Uds. | **comían** | *you* (pl.) *used to eat,*<br>*you were eating* |

**escribir** *to write*

| | | | | | |
|---|---|---|---|---|---|
| yo | **escribía** | *I used to write,*<br>*I was writing* | nosotros/nosotras | **escribíamos** | *we used to write,*<br>*we were writing* |
| tú | **escribías** | *you* (fam.) *used to write,*<br>*you were writing* | | | |
| él/ella | **escribía** | *he/she used to write,*<br>*he/she was writing* | ellos/ellas | **escribían** | *they used to write,*<br>*they were writing* |
| Ud. | **escribía** | *you* (form.) *used to*<br>*write, you were writing* | Uds. | **escribían** | *you* (pl.) *used to write,*<br>*you were writing* |

The following verbs are irregular in the imperfect tense:

**ir**    *to go*

| | | | | | |
|---|---|---|---|---|---|
| yo | **iba** | *I used to go, I was going* | nosotros/nosotras | **íbamos** | *we used to go, we were going* |
| tú | **ibas** | *you* (fam.) *used to go, you were going* | | | |
| él/ella | **iba** | *he/she used to go, he/she was going* | ellos/ellas | **iban** | *they used to go, they were going* |
| Ud. | **iba** | *you* (form.) *used to go, you were going* | Uds. | **iban** | *you* (pl.) *used to go, you were going* |

**ser**    *to be*

| | | | | | |
|---|---|---|---|---|---|
| yo | **era** | *I used to be, I was* | nosotros/nosotras | **éramos** | *we used to be, we were* |
| tú | **eras** | *you* (fam.) *used to be, you were* | | | |
| él/ella | **era** | *he/she used to be, he/she was* | ellos/ellas | **eran** | *they used to be, they were* |
| Ud. | **era** | *you* (form.) *used to be, you were* | Uds. | **eran** | *you* (pl.) *used to be, you were* |

**ver**    *to see*

| | | | | | |
|---|---|---|---|---|---|
| yo | **veía** | *I used to see, I was seeing* | nosotros/nosotras | **veíamos** | *we used to see, we were seeing* |
| tú | **veías** | *you* (fam.) *used to see, you were seeing* | | | |
| él/ella | **veía** | *he/she used to see, he/she was seeing* | ellos/ellas | **veían** | *they used to see, they were seeing* |
| Ud. | **veía** | *you* (form.) *used to see, you were seeing* | Uds. | **veían** | *you* (pl.) *used to see, you were seeing* |

## Uses of the Imperfect Tense

1. To talk about repeated past actions:

Íbamos a su casa todos los días.                *We would go to his house every day.*
Consultaba con el médico cada semana.           *He consulted the doctor every week.*

2. To describe feelings, desires, emotions, and state of mind in the past:

| | |
|---|---|
| La paciente quería ir a casa. | *The patient wanted to go home.* |
| El paciente tenía miedo. | *The patient was scared.* |
| Ella no sabía que su hijo estaba enfermo. | *She didn't know that her son was sick.* |

3. To describe a person, place, situation, or thing in the past:

| | |
|---|---|
| La enfermera era muy simpática. | *The nurse was very nice.* |
| El hospital era muy grande. | *The hospital was very big.* |
| Era una muchacha bonita. | *She was a pretty girl.* |

4. To indicate time in the past:

| | |
|---|---|
| Eran las dos cuando el médico llegó. | *It was two o'clock when the doctor arrived.* |

### Contrasting Preterite and Imperfect Tenses

The preterite tense is used to tell what happened; the imperfect tense tells what was happening. For example:

| | |
|---|---|
| El joven fumó marihuana ayer. | *The young man smoked marijuana yesterday.* |
| El joven fumaba marihuana con frecuencia. | *The young man smoked marijuana frequently.* |

The preterite and imperfect tenses are often used in the same sentence. The imperfect might be used to describe what was happening or to describe a scene in the past, while the preterite is used to tell what happened to interrupt that scene. For example:

| | |
|---|---|
| El paciente dormía cuando la enfermera entró en el cuarto. | *The patient was sleeping when the nurse entered the room.* |

Because of the nature of each tense, some verbs will change meaning depending on whether they are used in the imperfect or preterite tense. For example:

| Infinitive | | Imperfect | | Preterite | |
|---|---|---|---|---|---|
| saber | *to know* | sabía | *knew* | supo | *found out* |
| tener | *to have* | tenía | *had* | tuvo | *got* |
| poder | *to be able* | podía | *was able* | pudo | *managed to* |
| querer | *to want* | no quería | *didn't want* | no quiso | *refused to* |

## Vocabulario

| Las drogas | Drugs |
|---|---|
| el **ácido** | *acid* |
| las **anfetaminas** | *amphetamines* |
| los **barbitúricos**, los **barbituratos** | *barbiturates* |
| la **cocaína** | *cocaine* |
| la **codeína** | *codeine* |
| el **crack** | *crack* |
| la **heroína** | *heroin* |
| **LSD**, la **dietilamida del ácido lisérgico** | *LSD* |

| | |
|---|---|
| la marihuana | *marijuana* |
| la mescalina | *mescaline* |
| la metadona | *methadone* |
| la metedrina | *methedrine* |
| el opio | *opium* |
| PCP, la fencicladina | *PCP* |

**Síntomas del abuso de las drogas** — ***Symptoms of Drug Abuse***

| | |
|---|---|
| la ansiedad | *anxiety* |
| los cambios en la personalidad | *personality changes* |
| el cansancio | *fatigue* |
| el comportamiento insociable | *antisocial behavior* |
| las convulsiones | *convulsions* |
| la depresión | *depression* |
| la desorientación | *disorientation* |
| la diarrea | *diarrhea* |
| la esquizofrenia | *schizophrenia* |
| el exceso de secreciones nasales | *excessive nasal secretions* |
| la falta de apetito | *lack of appetite* |
| la falta de coordinación | *lack of coordination* |
| las huellas de aguja hipodérmica | *needle tracks* |
| la irritabilidad | *irritability* |
| la locuacidad | *talkativeness* |
| la nariz enrojecida | *red nose* |
| la nerviosidad | *nervousness* |
| los ojos aguados | *watery eyes* |
| los ojos enrojecidos | *red eyes* |
| la paranoia | *paranoia* |
| la pérdida de la memoria | *memory loss* |
| la pérdida de peso | *weight loss* |
| las pupilas dilatadas | *dilated pupils* |
| la somnolencia | *drowsiness* |
| los temblores | *tremors* |

**Vocabulario adicional sobre las drogas** — ***Additional Vocabulary about Drugs***

| | |
|---|---|
| las alucinaciones | *hallucinations* |
| la cantidad | *quantity, amount* |
| las cicatrices | *scars* |
| el coma | *coma* |
| la dependencia | *dependency* |
| los estimulantes | *stimulants* |
| los síntomas del retiro | *symptoms of withdrawal* |
| | |
| de larga duración | *of long duration* |
| desnutrido, -a | *undernourished* |

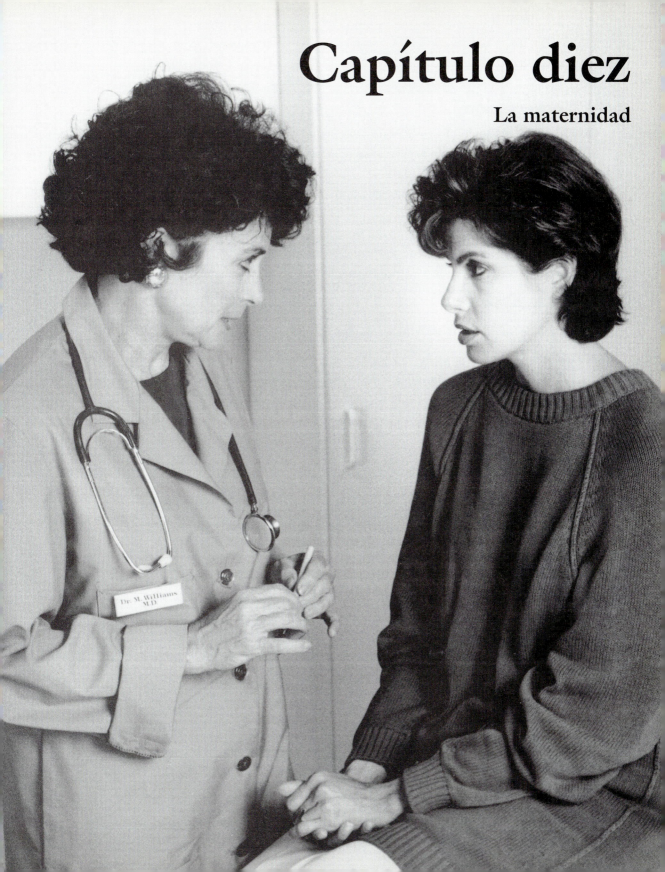

# Capítulo diez

## La maternidad

## Conversación

Doctora:   Los resultados del laboratorio indican que Ud. está encinta.

Señorita:  ¡No es posible! No puedo cuidar a un niño.

Doctora:   ¿Cuántos años tiene Ud.?

Señorita:  Tengo solamente dieciocho años y no tengo dinero.

Doctora:   ¿Tiene Ud. marido?

Señorita:  No, doctora. Tengo un novio, pero él no tiene trabajo.

Doctora:   ¿Entonces, vive Ud. con sus padres?

Señorita:  Sí, pero no me van a ayudar porque no quieren problemas en su casa.

## Sustituciones

Substitute the underlined words with the cued items.

> **MODELO**    ¿Tiene Ud. marido?    familia
> **¿Tiene Ud. familia?**

1. trabajo
2. dinero
3. seguro
4. hermanos
5. cita

## Continúa la conversación...

Doctora:   Pues, si Ud. quiere, el niño o la niña puede ser adoptado fácilmente.

Señorita:  No, doctora. La verdad es que no quiero seguir con el embarazo. ¿Puede recomendarme la mejor clínica para tener un aborto?

Doctora:   Por supuesto. Pero también le voy a dar información sobre algunos servicios sociales que le pueden ayudar con el cuidado del niño, si Ud. decide no tener el aborto.

Señorita:  Muchas gracias por toda su ayuda, doctora.

Doctora:   De nada, señorita.

## Vocabulario

| | | | |
|---|---|---|---|
| los **resultados** | *results* | la **verdad** | *truth* |
| **encinta** | *pregnant* | el **embarazo** | *pregnancy* |
| **cuidar a** | *to take care of* | el **aborto** | *abortion* |
| un **niño**, una **niña** | *child* | **por supuesto** | *of course* |
| el **novio** | *boyfriend* | el **cuidado** | *care* |
| la **novia** | *girlfriend* | | |

## Preguntas

1. ¿Qué indican los resultados del laboratorio?
2. ¿Cuántos años tiene la señorita?
3. ¿Tiene trabajo su novio?
4. ¿Qué quiere la señorita?

# Notas

## Mejor and Peor

**Mejor** means *better*. Its opposite is **peor** *(worse)*. When used in a comparison, *than* is translated **que.** For example:

El doctor Gómez es mejor que el doctor
  Rodríguez.

*Doctor Gómez is better than Doctor Rodríguez.*

*The best* is **el mejor, la mejor, los mejores,** or **las mejores.** *The worst* is **el peor, la peor, los peores,** or **las peores.** Choose a form to agree with the noun that it is describing. For example.

El doctor Gómez es el mejor.
Éstas son las mejores medicinas de todas.

*Doctor Gómez is the best.*
*These are the best medicines of all.*

**Recomendar** means *to recommend*. Here are its present tense forms:

**recomendar**    *to recommend*

| | | | | | |
|---|---|---|---|---|---|
| yo | **recomiendo** | *I recommend* | nosotros/nosotras | **recomendamos** | *we recommend* |
| tú | **recomiendas** | *you* (fam.) *recommend* | | | |
| él/ella | **recomienda** | *he/she recommends* | ellos/ellas | **recomiendan** | *they recommend* |
| Ud. | **recomienda** | *you* (form.) *recommend* | Uds. | **recomiendan** | *you* (pl.) *recommend* |

Some examples are:

¿Recomienda Ud. una clínica?
Yo recomiendo los servicios sociales.
¿Puede Ud. recomendarme una clínica?

*Do you recommend a clinic?*
*I recommend social services.*
*Can you recommend a clinic for me?*

# Para comunicarse

Practice each short conversation with your partner, using the cues provided, as in the example below. Be sure to reverse roles so that each partner can practice as much as possible.

**MODELO**    A:  clínica / el médico
            **¿Qué clínica recomienda el médico?**
         B:  esta clínica
            **Recomienda esta clínica.**
         A:  ¿Por qué?
         B:  **Porque es la mejor clínica de todas.**

1.  A:  hospital / la doctora
    B:  esta clínica
    A:  ¿Por qué?

    B:  _____

2.  A:  método / el ginecólogo
    B:  la píldora
    A:  ¿Por qué?

    B:  _____

3. A:    medicina / el doctor García
   B     el antibiótico
   A:    ¿Por qué?

   B:    _____

4. A:    terapeuta / el médico
   B:    la terapeuta física
   A:    ¿Por qué?

   B:    _____

## Para practicar

Answer the questions using the cues provided.

1. ¿Qué recomienda Ud.?            el aborto
2. ¿Qué recomienda el médico?      la adopción
3. ¿Qué recomienda la doctora?     el uso del profiláctico
4. ¿Qué recomiendan los padres?    el descanso
5. ¿Qué recomienda la enfermera?   las vitaminas

## Vocabulario

| El embarazo | The Pregnancy |
|---|---|
| el **bebé** | *baby, infant* |
| la **bolsa de aguas** | *bag of waters (amniotic sac)* |
| los **calambres** | *cramps* |
| la **comadrona** | *midwife* |
| las **contracciones** | *contractions* |
| el **cordón umbilical** | *umbilical cord* |
| el **cuello uterino** | *cervix* |
| la **dilatación** | *dilation* |
| el **feto** | *fetus* |
| la **maternidad** | *maternity* |
| el **obstétrico**, la **obstétrica** | *obstetrician* |
| la **partera** | *midwife* |
| el **parto** | *childbirth* |
| la **sala de partos** | *delivery room* |
| | |
| **empujar** | *to push* |
| **estar embarazada** | *to be pregnant* |
| **estar encinta** | *to be pregnant* |
| **nacer** | *to be born* |
| **pesar** | *to weigh* |

## ...para prevenir el cáncer de cuello del útero.

Cada año mueren en los Estados Unidos unas 7.000 mujeres a causa del cáncer de cuello del útero. La mayoría de esas mujeres estarían vivas si se hubieran sometido periódicamente a la prueba de Papanicolaou (frotis de Pap). Esta prueba ayuda a los médicos a detectar el cáncer de cuello del útero en una etapa precoz cuando casi siempre es 100% curable. Todas las mujeres deberían someterse regularmente a la prueba de Papanicolaou desde el momento en que empiezan a tener relaciones sexuales (o cumplen 18 años), y seguir haciéndolo durante toda su vida.

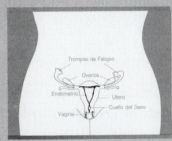

Hay muchos casos de cáncer de cuello del útero entre las mujeres negras, hispanas y nativas americanas. Cuando se lo realiza periódicamente, el frotis de Pap es para esas, y para *todas* las mujeres, el mejor medio de protección contra esta enfermedad.

### ¿Quiénes contraen cáncer de cuello del útero?

Cualquier mujer puede contraer cáncer de cuello del útero, pero según los estudios efectuados, hay varios factores que, al parecer, colocan a algunas mujeres en una situación de mayor riesgo:

- Las relaciones sexuales antes de los 18 años de edad.
- Las relaciones sexuales con varias parejas sexuales. Cuanto mayor sea el número de parejas sexuales que tiene una mujer, mayores serán las posibilidades de que contraiga una enfermedad venérea. Se ha comprobado que muchas mujeres que padecen de cáncer de cuello del útero o que presentan síntomas preliminares tienen ciertos tipos de enfermedades venéreas, especialmente verrugas genitales.

Si usted está en una de esas situaciones de riesgo, es importante que se someta a la prueba de Papanicolaou por lo menos una vez al año. En realidad, lo mejor sería que la mayoría de las mujeres se sometieran a esta prueba una vez al año. Siga el calendario de exámenes ginecológicos que su médico le indique.

### ¿Cómo se hace el frotis de Pap?

Generalmente, el frotis de Pap forma parte del examen rutinario de la pelvis que el médico hace en su consultorio o en la clínica. Puede causar cierta incomodidad, pero la mayoría de las mujeres no lo consideran doloroso. Durante el examen, el médico o la enfermera introduce un tapón de algodón en la vagina y toca suavemente el cuello del útero para recoger algunas células. Esta parte del examen no tarda ni un minuto. Las células se envían a un laboratorio para su estudio.

### ¿Qué pasa después?

Si todas las células enviadas al laboratorio tienen un aspecto sano, usted puede seguir con su calendario corriente de exámenes ginecológicos. Si hay algunas células que están comenzando a presentar signos de anormalidad, usted tendrá que volver al consultorio para que le hagan más pruebas o la sometan a tratamiento.

**Conversaciones**

A:  ¿Es éste su primer embarazo?

B:  No, es mi segundo.

A:  ¿Ha tenido Ud. alguna vez un aborto?

B:  No, no he tenido nunca un aborto.

A:  ¿Tuvo Ud. problemas con su primer embarazo?

B:  Sí, fue necesario hacer una operación cesárea.

A:  ¿Tuvo la paciente problemas con su primer embarazo?

B:  Sí, su bebé nació con defectos de nacimiento.

A:  ¿Por qué ocurrió eso?

B:  No sé por cierto. Creo que fue porque tuvo rubéola *(measles)* durante el embarazo.

## Para practicar

Answer each question in a complete sentence using the cues provided.

> **MODELO**      ¿Qué tuvo que usar el obstétrico?      fórceps
> **El obstétrico tuvo que usar fórceps.**

1. ¿Cuál fue el problema de su primer embarazo?      tuvo rubéola
2. ¿Cómo nació el niño?      con defectos de nacimiento
3. ¿Qué recomendó la obstétrica?      una operación cesárea
4. ¿Qué tuvo la mujer?      un aborto espontáneo
5. ¿Qué le dieron a la mujer?      la anestesia general
6. ¿Cómo nació el niño?      prematuro
7. ¿Qué le dio a la mujer el anestesiólogo?      una inyección

## Recuerde

### Saber and Conocer

These two verbs both mean *to know*. However, **saber** is used when talking about knowing *a fact*, while **conocer** means *to be acquainted with* and is usually used to say that one knows *a person*.

In the present tense both verbs are irregular in the **yo** form only:

yo sé          *I know*
yo conozco     *I am acquainted with*

For example:

No sabemos dónde está el hospital.      *We don't know where the hospital is.*
Yo no sé qué hora es.      *I don't know what time it is.*
Yo conozco bien a la doctora.      *I know the doctor well.*

But:

Yo sé que la doctora es muy lista.      *I know that the doctor is very smart.*

Notice also that you must use the personal **a** after the verb **conocer** when its object is a person. For example:

¿A quién conoce Ud.?                             *Whom do you know?*
Conozco al padre.                                *I know the father.*

## Para practicar

Answer according to the model.

MODELO       ¿Qué sabe Ud.?              *What do you know?*
             qué hora es                 *what time it is*
             **Yo sé qué hora es.**      *I know what time it is.*
             *or* **Yo no sé nada.**     *I don't know anything.*

1. ¿Qué sabe la mujer?        que está encinta
2. ¿Qué sabe Ud.?             dónde está el hospital
3. ¿Qué sabe la abuela?       el nombre del bebé
4. ¿Qué saben Uds.?           cuánto pesa el bebé
5. ¿Qué sabe la madre?        que no debe usar drogas

## Para practicar más

MODELO       ¿A quién conoce Ud.?               *Whom do you know?*
             a la doctora                       *the doctor*
             **Yo conozco a la doctora.**       *I know the doctor.*
             *or* **Yo no conozco a nadie.**    *I don't know anybody.*

1. ¿A quién conoce Ud.?           a la madre
2. ¿A quién conoce la doctora?    al padre
3. ¿A quién conocen ellos?        a la doctora
4. ¿A quién conoce el obstétrico? a la paciente
5. ¿A quién conoce la madre?      a los otros pacientes

## Conversaciones

A:   ¿Cómo se siente Ud.?

B:   Tengo mucho dolor. Me duele la espalda y tengo calambres muy fuertes también.

A:   ¿Quiere una inyección para aliviar el dolor?

B:   No sé. ¿Qué droga me va a dar?

A:   Puedo darle a Ud. un calmante, o quizás le puedo anestesiar.

A:   ¿Se ha preparado para el parto natural?

B:   Sí, doctora.

A:   Entonces, trate de calmarse con los ejercicios de respiración. Tanto su marido como las enfermeras están aquí para ayudarle a Ud.

B:   Gracias, doctora. Si tengo mucho dolor, ¿puede darme algo para aliviarlo?

A:   Sí, señora. Si es necesario, podemos ponerle una inyección.

## Recuerde

**Si and Sí**

**Sí** (with accent mark) means *yes,* while **si** (without accent mark) means *if.*

## Más vocabulario

| **La contracepción** | **Contraception** |
|---|---|
| los **aparatos intrauterinos** | *intrauterine devices* |
| el **condón** | *condom* |
| el **diafragma** | *diaphragm* |
| la **ducha** | *douche* |
| la **esperma** | *sperm* |
| la **espuma** | *foam* |
| la **ligadura de los tubos** | *tubal ligation* |
| el **método anticonceptivo** | *method of contraception* |
| el **método de ritmo** | *rhythm method* |
| la **píldora** | *the pill* |
| el **profiláctico** | *prophylactic* |
| las **relaciones sexuales** | *sexual relations* |
| la **retirada** | *withdrawal* |
| la **vasectomía** | *vasectomy* |

## NOTA CULTURAL                LA PARTERA

The **partera** or *midwife* has traditionally performed a very important role in childbirth in many Spanish-speaking countries. The woman feels more comfortable with another woman to assist her in labor and often fears the hospital as a place where sickness and death occur. **La partería,** or *midwifery,* is becoming more popular in the United States, and as a result, the woman is more likely now to have her child born with the help of a **partera,** even though it might take place in a hospital setting.

## Conversación

Señora:   Quiero usar la píldora como método anticonceptivo. ¿Puede Ud. darme alguna información?

Doctora:   ¿Qué quiere saber Ud.?

Señora:   ¿Es un método eficaz?

Doctora:   Sí, es un método anticonceptivo muy eficaz.

Señora:   ¿Puede causar efectos secundarios?

Doctora:   Sí, puede causar algunos efectos secundarios. Depende del individuo.

| Señora: | ¿Cuándo se toman las píldoras? |
|---|---|
| Doctora: | Se toma una píldora cada día. |
| Señora: | ¿Se necesita una receta para comprarlas? |
| Doctora: | Claro que sí. |

## Sustituciones

Substitute the underlined word with the cued items.

> **MODELO**    ¿Puede Ud. darme <u>información</u>?    una receta
> **¿Puede Ud. darme <u>una receta</u>?**

1. un antibiótico
2. medicina
3. una cita
4. una operación
5. ayuda

## Notas

### Se necesita *(You need, one needs, it is needed)*

Remember, the impersonal expression **se** is used in many places where one would use the passive voice in English, especially where a doer of the action is not stated or strongly implied. Some examples:

| | |
|---|---|
| Se habla español en este hospital. | *Spanish is spoken in this hospital.* |
| Se escribe una receta cada día. | *A prescription is written every day.* |
| Aquí se venden vitaminas. | *Vitamins are sold here.* |
| No se quiere su ayuda. | *His help is not wanted.* |
| Se toman antibióticos para una infección. | *Antibiotics are taken for an infection.* |
| Se necesita una receta para comprarlas. | *A prescription is needed to buy them.* |

### Direct Object Pronouns

Direct object pronouns are similar to indirect object pronouns (see Chapter 3) except that a direct object is usually a thing. The direct object pronouns that take the place of things are:

| | | | |
|---|---|---|---|
| lo | *it* | los | *them* |
| la | *it* | las | *them* |

Like indirect object pronouns, they precede the verb but can be attached to an infinitive. For example:

| | |
|---|---|
| El médico prepara **la receta.** | *The doctor prepares **the prescription.*** |
| El médico **la** prepara. | *The doctor prepares **it.*** |
| El paciente tomó **las píldoras.** | *The patient took **the pills.*** |
| El paciente **las** tomó. | *The patient took **them.*** |
| El paciente no quiere tomar **las píldoras.** | *The patient doesn't want to take **the pills.*** |
| El paciente no quiere tomar**las.** | *The patient doesn't want to take **them.*** |

# Para comunicarse

Complete each conversation by using the cues provided.

> **MODELO**
>
> A:  ¿Qué preparó el médico?
> B:  la receta
> **El médico preparó la receta.**
> A:  ¿La preparó el médico?
> B:  **Sí, el médico la preparó.**

A:  ¿Qué tomó el paciente?
B:  el antibiótico
A:  ¿Lo tomó el paciente?

B:  _____


A:  ¿Qué usaba la mujer?
B:  la píldora
A:  ¿La usaba la mujer?

B:  _____


A:  ¿Quién recomendó la operación?
B:  el cirujano
A:  ¿La recomendó el cirujano?

B:  _____


A:  ¿Quién tuvo un aborto?
B:  la señora Salazar
A:  ¿Lo tuvo la señora Salazar?

B:  _____


# Conversaciones

A:  Doctora, quiero usar un método para el control de la natalidad. ¿Qué recomienda Ud.?
B:  Se puede usar el método del diafragma.
A:  ¿Es un método bueno?
B:  Sí, es fácil de usar y es bastante eficaz.
A:  ¿Qué debo hacer para usar este método?
B:  Yo tengo que determinar la medida correcta para Ud. Después voy a mostrarle a Ud. cómo usarlo correctamente.
A:  Muchas gracias, doctora.

...

A:  Doctor, quiero escoger el mejor método de parto.

B:  ¿Quiere Ud. usar el método natural?

A:  ¿Qué es eso?

B:  No se usan drogas y el padre está presente durante el parto natural.

A:  ¿Qué ventaja tiene este método?

B:  Bueno, es más difícil para Ud., pero es mejor para el bebé, porque no sufre los efectos secundarios de las drogas.

# Notas

## Bastante

**Bastante** means *quite, rather,* or, with **ya,** *enough:*

| | |
|---|---|
| Es un método bastante eficaz. | *It is a rather efficient method.* |
| La madre está bastante nerviosa. | *The mother is quite nervous.* |
| Estamos bastante interesados en el parto natural. | *We are quite interested in natural childbirth.* |
| Ella ya ha sufrido bastante. | *She has suffered enough.* |

## Comparisons

Place the word **más** *(more)* in front of an adjective to form a comparison:

| | |
|---|---|
| Este método es más difícil. | *This method is more difficult (harder).* |
| Ese método es más fácil. | *That method is easier.* |
| Estos niños son más listos. | *These children are smarter.* |

For the opposite, use **menos** *(less):*

| | |
|---|---|
| Este método es menos difícil. | *This method is less difficult.* |
| Ese método es menos fácil. | *That method is not as easy (less easy).* |
| Estos niños son menos listos. | *These children are not as smart (less smart).* |

Exceptions to the above comparisons are:

| | |
|---|---|
| mejor | *better* |
| peor | *worse* |

To express *than,* use **que:**

| | |
|---|---|
| La doctora Salazar es más inteligente **que** la doctora Gómez. | *Doctor Salazar is more intelligent **than** Doctor Gómez.* |

To compare two nouns that are equal, use **tan... como:**

| | |
|---|---|
| La doctora Salazar es **tan** inteligente **como** la doctora Gómez. | *Doctor Salazar is **as** intelligent **as** Doctor Gómez.* |
| Él es **tan** alto **como** yo. | *He is **as** tall **as** I.* |

## Para practicar

Form comparison sentences using the fragments.

> **MODELO**    el jarabe / eficaz / la pastilla
> **El jarabe es más eficaz que la pastilla.**
> *or*
> **El jarabe es menos eficaz que la pastilla.**

1. la píldora / eficaz / el ritmo
2. el parto natural / difícil / el parto con anestesia
3. el primer niño / grande / el segundo
4. la anestesia / peligrosa / el parto natural

Now give the same sentences using the comparison of equality, **tan... como.**

> **MODELO**    el jarabe / eficaz / la pastilla
> **El jarabe es tan eficaz como la pastilla.**

## Lectura: El embarazo

Hay varios métodos que una mujer puede usar para determinar si de veras está encinta. Hoy día puede darse a sí misma una prueba del embarazo en su propio hogar. Estas pruebas se pueden comprar en cualquier farmacia. Sin embargo, una mujer que sospecha que puede estar encinta debe visitarle al médico. De esta manera puede saber por cierto si está encinta o no. Y al mismo tiempo puede tener la oportunidad de recibir el consejo del médico o de la doctora sobre lo que debe hacer para tener un embarazo saludable.

## Vocabulario

| | |
|---|---|
| de veras | *really* |
| hoy día | *nowadays* |
| su propio hogar | *her own home* |
| sin embargo | *nevertheless* |
| sospechar | *to suspect* |
| el consejo | *advice* |
| saludable | *healthy* |

## Preguntas

1. ¿Dónde se puede comprar una prueba del embarazo?
2. ¿Por qué debe visitar a su médico o doctora la mujer embarazada?
3. ¿Qué consejos puede recibir de su médico o doctora?

# RESUMEN Y REPASO

## Vocabulario

| | |
|---|---|
| el **aborto terapéutico** | *therapeutic abortion* |
| la **anestesia caudal** | *caudal anesthesia* |
| la **anestesia general** | *general anesthesia* |
| la **anestesia local** | *local anesthesia* |
| el **anestesiólogo**, la **anestesióloga** | *anesthesiologist* |
| el **anillo** | *ring* |
| las **cremas vaginales** | *vaginal creams* |
| la **criatura** | *infant* |
| los **dolores del parto** | *labor pains* |
| el **escudo** | *shield* |
| el **flujo de sangre** | *discharge of blood* |
| los **gemelos** | *twins* |
| el **gorro cervical** | *cervical cap* |
| la **hemorragia** | *hemorrhage* |
| el **huevo** | *egg* |
| la **incubadora** | *incubator* |
| la **jalea** | *jelly* |
| los **lavados vaginales** | *douches* |
| el **lazo** | *loop* |
| el **mareo** | *dizziness* |
| la **menopausia** | *menopause* |
| la **menstruación** | *menstruation* |
| el **nacimiento** | *birth* |
| las **náuseas del embarazo** | *morning sickness* |
| la **nena**, el **nene** | *baby* |
| el **obstétrico**, la **obstétrica** | *obstetrician* |
| la **operación cesárea** | *caesarean operation* |
| el **parto múltiple** | *multiple birth* |
| el **parto prematuro** | *premature birth* |
| el **pene** | *penis* |
| el **pentotal sódico** | *sodium pentothal* |
| el **período** | *menstrual period* |
| la **regla** | *menstrual period* |
| la **vagina** | *vagina* |
| los **vómitos del embarazo** | *morning sickness* |
| | |
| **anestesiar** | *to anesthetize* |
| **dar a luz** | *to give birth* |
| **dar el seno** | *to breastfeed* |
| **estar de parto** | *to be in labor* |
| **estar en estado** | *to be pregnant* |
| **estar preñada** | *to be pregnant* |
| **pesar** | *to weigh* |

# Capítulo once

El cuidado postnatal y la pediatría

## Conversación

| | |
|---|---|
| Señora: | Estoy muy preocupada, doctor. |
| Doctor: | ¿Qué pasa? |
| Señora: | Hace dos días que mi bebé llora todito el tiempo, y además creo que tiene fiebre. |
| Doctor: | ¿Cuántos años tiene la criatura? |
| Señora: | Tiene dieciséis meses de edad. |
| Doctor: | ¿Tose mucho el niño? |
| Señora: | Sí, tiene tos y tiene la garganta irritada también. |
| Doctor: | ¿Tiene diarrea? |
| Señora: | No, no tiene diarrea pero no quiere comer nada. |
| Doctor: | Voy a examinarle al niño ahora. |

## Sustituciones

Substitute the underlined words with the cued items. Be sure to make any other necessary changes.

**MODELO**     Voy a examinarle al <u>niño</u> ahora.     su hijo
**Voy a examinarle a <u>su hijo</u> ahora.**

1. Voy a examinarle al <u>niño</u> ahora.          Ud.
2. Voy a <u>examinarle</u> al niño ahora.          operar
3. Voy a <u>examinarle</u> al niño <u>ahora</u>.          operar, mañana
4. Voy a <u>examinarle al niño</u> ahora.          darle a Ud. la receta
5. Voy a <u>examinarle al niño</u> <u>ahora</u>.          darle a Ud. la receta, más tarde

## Continúa la conversación...

(Un poco más tarde.)

| | |
|---|---|
| Doctor: | Acabo de examinar a su bebé, señora. |
| Señora: | ¿Y qué le pasa? |
| Doctor: | Tiene la temperatura en cien grados, y tiene una infección de la garganta que le ha llegado hasta los oídos. |
| Señora: | ¿Es esto muy grave, doctor? |
| Doctor: | Es bastante común en la niñez, pero si se deja sin tratar puede ser peligroso para el niño. |
| Señora: | ¿Estará bien mi hijo? |
| Doctor: | Sí, señora, no se preocupe. Le voy a dar un antibiótico para la infección y algo para aliviar el dolor de oído que sufre. |
| Señora: | Muchas gracias, doctor. |

## Vocabulario

| | |
|---|---|
| preocupado, -a | *worried* |
| todito el tiempo | *all the time* |
| acabo de | *I have just* |
| hasta | *until, up to, as far as* |
| grave | *serious* |
| común | *common* |
| peligroso, -a | *dangerous* |
| no se preocupe | *don't worry* |

## Notas

### «Todito el tiempo» and Diminutives

The endings -**ito** or -**ita** can be added to a word to show that it is smaller or to indicate familiarity or affection. Such endings are often considered very colloquial and might be used when referring to children and babies, as in the sentence below:

Mi bebé llora todito el tiempo.   *My baby cries all the time (poor thing).*
  (*instead of* **todo el tiempo**)

Some other examples:

| | |
|---|---|
| Vamos a tomar un cafecito (café). | *Let's have a (nice) cup of coffee.* |
| El niño está dormidito (dormido). | *The child is asleep.* |
| Cómete un poquito (un poco) más. | *Eat a little bit more.* |

### Acabo de (*I have just*)

Use a form of **acabar** (*to finish*) with **de** to show that an action has just been completed. For example:

| | |
|---|---|
| El paciente acaba de comer. | *The patient has just eaten.* |
| Acabo de examinarle al niño. | *I have just examined the child.* |

### «Estará bien» and the Future Tense

Add the following endings to the verb to form the future tense: -**é**, -**ás**, -**á**, -**emos**, and -**án**. The endings are the same for all classes of verbs; -**ar**, -**er**, and -**ir** verbs. (For irregular future tense verbs, see **Resumen y repaso** at the end of the chapter.) For example:

| | | | | | |
|---|---|---|---|---|---|
| yo | **hablaré** | *I will talk* | nosotros/nosotras | **hablaremos** | *we will talk* |
| tú | **hablarás** | *you* (fam.) *will talk* | | | |
| él/ella | **hablará** | *he/she will talk* | ellos/ellas | **hablarán** | *they will talk* |
| Ud. | **hablará** | *you* (form.) *will talk* | Uds. | **hablarán** | *you* (pl.) *will talk* |

## Para practicar

Add the correct form of **acabar** to these fragments to show that an action has just been completed.

> **MODELO**    la paciente / tomar la medicina
> **La paciente acaba de tomar la medicina.**

1. la doctora / llegar al hospital
2. la enfermera / hablar con la familia.
3. la paciente / tomar el antibiótico.
4. yo / despertarme
5. nosotros / hablar con la doctora
6. el médico / examinarle al niño
7. el farmacéutico / preparar la receta
8. la niña / acostarse

## Vocabulario

### El cuidado postnatal (*Postnatal care*)

el biberón

bañar

el pezón del biberón

cambiar el pañal

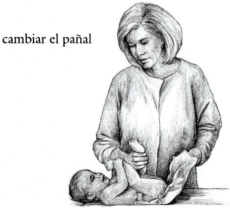

alimentar

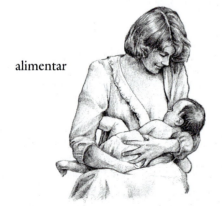

esterilizar

probar la leche

## Recuerde

Remember to use a form of the verb **ir,** followed by the preposition **a,** and the infinitive of another verb to express an action that will take place in the immediate future. For example:

La doctora va a escribir una receta. *The doctor is going to write a prescription.*

## Para practicar

Tell who will do something using the cues provided and the future tense.

**MODELO** ¿Quién va a preparar la fórmula para el bebé? el padre
**El padre preparará la fórmula para el bebé.**

1. ¿Quién va a limpiar el cuarto? los padres
2. ¿Quién va a esterilizar los biberones? la madre
3. ¿Quién va a usar pañales? el bebé
4. ¿Quién le va a examinar al niño? la pediatra
5. ¿Quién va a comprar el talco? yo
6. ¿Quién va a llevar a la niña a la pediatra? los abuelos
7. ¿Quién va a cambiar los pañales? nosotros

## Conversaciones

A: Mi bebé y yo vamos a salir del hospital hoy.

B: ¿Cuándo tiene Ud. que llevarlo al pediatra para su primer chequeo?

A: Dentro de seis semanas vamos para nuestra primera visita. A partir del primer chequeo, tengo que visitar al pediatra una vez al mes durante los primeros seis meses.

B: ¿Por qué es necesario visitarle al médico con tanta frecuencia?

A: Para asegurar la buena salud del bebé.

...

A:     Llamé hoy a la pediatra porque el bebé sufre de irritación de la piel.

B:     ¿Qué dijo la doctora?

A:     Me dijo que es una condición que sufren muchos bebés. Tengo que tratar de mantenerle la piel muy seca.

B:     Entonces, ¿no tiene que llevar al bebé a su consultorio?

A:     Por ahora no, pero tengo que visitar a la pediatra si el problema persiste por más de unos días seguidos.

## Más vocabulario

| **La pediatría** | *Pediatrics* |
|---|---|
| la **anemia** | *anemia* |
| el **cereal enriquecido** | *enriched cereal* |
| la **digestión** | *digestion* |
| la **escaldadura** | *diaper rash* |
| el **hierro** | *iron* |
| el **impétigo** | *impetigo* |
| la **proteína** | *protein* |
| | |
| **digerir** | *to digest* |
| **eructar** | *to belch* |
| **llorar** | *to cry* |
| **vomitar** | *to vomit* |
| | |
| **cólico, -a** | *colicky* |

## Para comunicarse

Practice with a partner talking about past actions using the cues.

 **MODELO**      A:   llamar / hoy
**¿A quién llamaste hoy?**
B:   a la pediatra
**Hoy llamé a la pediatra.**

1. A:   bañar / ayer
   B:   a la niña

2. A:   visitar / la semana pasada
   B:   a mi madre

3. A:   consultar / el otro día
   B:   al médico

4. A:   llamar / anteayer
   B:   a la doctora

## Para comunicarse más

Now talk about future actions using the cues.

| MODELO | A: | tomar / el paciente / mañana |
| --- | --- | --- |
| | | **¿Qué tomará el paciente mañana?** |
| | B: | la medicina |
| | | **Mañana el paciente tomará la medicina.** |

1. A:  recomendar / la pediatra / mañana
   B:  el cereal enriquecido

2. A:  beber / el niño / más tarde
   B:  la leche

3. A:  esterilizar / la madre / pasado mañana
   B:  los biberones

4. A:  preparar / el padre / la semana que viene
   B:  el cuarto del bebé

## Conversaciones

A:  ¿Cuántos años tiene su hija?

B:  Tiene cinco años.

A:  ¿Cuántas veces al año tiene Ud. que llevarla a la pediatra?

B:  Dos veces al año.

A:  ¿Por qué tiene que llevarla hoy?

B:  Porque el médico va a ponerle unas inyecciones.

A:  Hola, doctora. ¿Puede Ud. ayudarme?

B:  Por supuesto. ¿En qué puedo servirle?

A:  Hace una semana que mi hija no quiere comer.

B:  ¿Cuántos años tiene?

A:  Tiene dos años.

B:  Voy a darle un examen médico, y después voy a recomendar algunas pruebas.

## Para practicar

You are a pediatrician giving instructions to a new mother. Using the vocabulary you have already learned and with the help of the vocabulary below, tell her that in her visits the following will be necessary.

1. The child must be immunized against the illnesses and diseases that can occur during childhood. Mention these illnesses and diseases and explain what must be done to prevent them.
2. She must bring the child in for regular physical examinations in order to check the following:

| weight | general health | behavior |
| --- | --- | --- |
| height | development | |

## Vocabulario

### Childhood Diseases and Vaccinations

| | |
|---|---|
| la **bronquitis** | *bronchitis* |
| el **comportamiento** | *behavior* |
| las **convulsiones** | *convulsions* |
| la **difteria** | *diphtheria* |
| las **enfermedades transmisibles** | *communicable diseases* |
| las **paperas** | *mumps* |
| la **poliomielitis** | *polio* |
| la **rubéola** | *rubella* |
| el **sarampión** | *measles* |
| la **tos ferina** | *whooping cough* |
| la **tuberculosis** | *tuberculosis* |
| las **viruelas locas** | *chicken pox* |
| | |
| **inmunizar** | *to immunize* |
| **medir** | *to measure (height)* |
| **pesar** | *to weigh* |
| **vacunar** | *to vaccinate* |

Las vacunas... no son sólo para los niños

| **NOTA CULTURAL** | **LOS NOMBRES** |
|---|---|

Do not be confused when you meet a person of Latin descent who has several names. It is really very simple. A person will have a first and last name: **Carlos González,** and will often add the mother's maiden name as a means of further identification and as an indication of family descent: **Carlos González (y) Juárez.** When a woman marries she may keep her maiden name or she may add **de** with the husband's last name to her own: **Ana Pérez (y) Márquez de González.**

Their child will carry the last names of both father and mother: **Benito González (y) Pérez.**

## Conversación

Médico:    Acabo de examinar a su hijo, señora, y está bien de salud. No hay ningún problema.

Señora:    Me alegro de eso doctor. Pero hay un problema que quisiera discutir con Ud.

Médico:    Dígame.

Señora:    Trato de alimentar bien a mi hijo pero él no quiere comer las comidas saludables.

Médico:    ¿Qué come su hijo?

Señora:    Come muchos bocadillos, dulces y pasteles. No quiere comer ni los vegetales ni la leche.

## Sustituciones

| **MODELO** | Quisiera <u>discutir un problema</u> con Ud. | consultar | I would like to discuss a problem with you. | to consult |
|---|---|---|---|---|
| | **Quisiera <u>consultar</u> con Ud.** | | I would like to consult with you. | |

1. Quisiera <u>discutir un problema con Ud.</u>    pedirle un favor
2. Quisiera <u>discutir un problema con Ud.</u>    darle las gracias
3. Quisiera <u>discutir un problema</u> con Ud.    tener una cita
4. Quisiera <u>discutir un problema</u> con Ud.    hablar
5. Quisiera <u>discutir un problema con Ud.</u>    venir más temprano

## Continúa la conversación...

Médico:    Eso es muy malo, señora. Un niño debe acostumbrarse a comer toda clase de comidas. Si no, no va a desarrollarse bien. Debe beber mucha leche para obtener la proteína y el calcio, comer vegetales y frutas para las vitaminas y el hierro, y comer mucha carne también.

Señora:    ¿Pero si él no quiere comer?

Médico:    Ud. tiene que mantenerse firme, señora. El niño debe comer las comidas buenas antes que los dulces. Es para la salud de su hijo. Recomiendo también una vitamina diaria.

Señora:    Muchas gracias, doctor. Trataré de hacer lo que Ud. recomienda.

## Vocabulario

| | |
|---|---|
| **alimentar** | *to feed* |
| los **bocadillos** | *snacks* |
| los **dulces** | *sweets* |
| los **pasteles** | *cakes* |
| **ni... ni** | *neither...nor* |
| **acostumbrarse** | *to become accustomed to* |
| **desarrollarse** | *to develop* |
| **obtener** | *to obtain* |
| el **calcio** | *calcium* |
| el **hierro** | *iron* |
| **mantenerse firme** | *to be firm* |

## Preguntas

1. ¿Cuál es el problema de la señora?
2. ¿Qué come su hijo?
3. ¿Qué comidas no le gustan?
4. ¿Qué comidas son las más saludables para un niño?
5. Según el médico, ¿que debe hacer la señora?

## Notas

### Ninguno, -a

Use **ninguno** or **ninguna** to express *none, no,* or *any*. **Ninguno** is shortened to **ningún** when it comes directly before a masculine noun.

The double negative is perfectly correct in Spanish, so put **no** before the verb. For example:

| | |
|---|---|
| No hay **ningún** problema. | *There is no problem.* |
| ¿Hay pacientes en la oficina? | *Are there any patients in the office?* |
| No, no hay **ninguno.** | *No, there are none.* |

To express *any* in the plural, no adjective is necessary. For example:

| | |
|---|---|
| La señora no tiene hijos. | *The lady doesn't have (any) children.* |

### Quisiera (I would like)

**Quisiera** is often used instead of **quiero** *(I want)* as a polite way of asking for something. For example:

| | |
|---|---|
| **Quisiera** hablar con la doctora. | *I would like to speak with the doctor.* |
| **Quisiera** examinarle al paciente. | *I would like to examine the patient.* |

### Lo que (What, that which)

Use **lo que** to express *what* in a noninterrogative sentence. For example:

| | |
|---|---|
| El niño no hace **lo que** le digo. | *The child doesn't do what I tell him.* |
| El niño come **lo que** quiere. | *The child eats what he wants.* |
| Quiero hacer **lo que** recomienda el médico. | *I want to do what the doctor recommends.* |

## Para practicar

Use the polite form to ask for something in each of these sentences.

 Quiero hablar con el pediatra.
**Quisiera hablar con el pediatra.**

1. Quiero hacer una cita para el miércoles.
2. Quiero discutir el caso con la doctora.
3. Quiero visitar a mi amigo en el hospital.
4. Quiero cambiar la cita para la próxima semana.
5. Quiero consultar con el médico.
6. Quiero comprar una medicina para la tos.

## Para practicar más

Practice with a partner using the sentence fragments and **ningún** or **ninguna**.

**MODELO**　　síntomas / tiene / el paciente
A:　**¿Tiene síntomas el paciente?**
B:　**No, el paciente no tiene ningún síntoma.**

1. hijos / tiene / la señora
2. pacientes / tiene / la pediatra
3. dinero / tiene / Ud.
4. medicina / toma / su hijo
5. cita / tiene / el paciente

## RESUMEN Y REPASO

## Gramática

### Irregular Future Tense Verbs

The following verbs are irregular in the future tense.

**decir**　　*to say, tell*

| yo | **diré** | *I will say/tell* | nosotros/nosotras | **diremos** | *we will say/tell* |
|---|---|---|---|---|---|
| tú | **dirás** | *you* (fam.) *will say/tell* | | | |
| él/ella | **dirá** | *he/she will say/tell* | ellos/ellas | **dirán** | *they will say/tell* |
| Ud. | **dirá** | *you* (form.) *will say/tell* | Uds. | **dirán** | *you* (pl.) *will say/tell* |

**haber    auxiliary verb, meaning *to have (done something)***

| | | | | | | |
|---|---|---|---|---|---|---|
| yo | **habré** | *I will have* | nosotros/nosotras | **habremos** | *we will have* | |
| tú | **habrás** | *you* (fam.) *will have* | | | | |
| él/ella | **habrá** | *he/she will have* | ellos/ellas | **habrán** | *they will have* | |
| Ud. | **habrá** | *you* (form.) *will have* | Uds. | **habrán** | *you* (pl.) *will have* | |

**hacer    *to make, to do***

| | | | | | |
|---|---|---|---|---|---|
| yo | **haré** | *I will make/do* | nosotros/nosotras | **haremos** | *we will make/do* |
| tú | **harás** | *you* (fam.) *will make/do* | | | |
| él/ella | **hará** | *he/she will make/do* | ellos/ellas | **harán** | *they will make/do* |
| Ud. | **hará** | *you* (form.) *will make/do* | Uds. | **harán** | *you* (pl.) *will make/do* |

**poder    *to be able***

| | | | | | |
|---|---|---|---|---|---|
| yo | **podré** | *I will be able* | nosotros/nosotras | **podremos** | *we will be able* |
| tú | **podrás** | *you* (fam.) *will be able* | | | |
| él/ella | **podrá** | *he/she will be able* | ellos/ellas | **podrán** | *they will be able* |
| Ud. | **podrá** | *you* (form.) *will be able* | Uds. | **podrán** | *you* (pl.) *will be able* |

**poner    *to put***

| | | | | | |
|---|---|---|---|---|---|
| yo | **pondré** | *I will put* | nosotros/nosotras | **pondremos** | *we will put* |
| tú | **pondrás** | *you* (fam.) *will put* | | | |
| él/ella | **pondrá** | *he/she will put* | ellos/ellas | **pondrán** | *they will put* |
| Ud. | **pondrá** | *you* (form.) *will put* | Uds. | **pondrán** | *you* (pl.) *will put* |

**querer    *to want***

| | | | | | |
|---|---|---|---|---|---|
| yo | **querré** | *I will want* | nosotros/nosotras | **querremos** | *we will want* |
| tú | **querrás** | *you* (fam.) *will want* | | | |
| él/ella | **querrá** | *he/she will want* | ellos/ellas | **querrán** | *they will want* |
| Ud. | **querrá** | *you* (form.) *will want* | Uds. | **querrán** | *you* (pl.) *will want* |

**saber**   *to know*

| | | | | | | |
|---|---|---|---|---|---|---|
| yo | **sabré** | *I will know* | nosotros/nosotras | **sabremos** | *we will know* |
| tú | **sabrás** | *you* (fam.) *will know* | | | |
| él/ella | **sabrá** | *he/she will know* | ellos/ellas | **sabrán** | *they will know* |
| Ud. | **sabrá** | *you* (form.) *will know* | Uds. | **sabrán** | *you* (pl.) *will know* |

**salir**   *to leave*

| | | | | | | |
|---|---|---|---|---|---|---|
| yo | **saldré** | *I will leave* | nosotros/nosotras | **saldremos** | *we will leave* |
| tú | **saldrás** | *you* (fam.) *will leave* | | | |
| él/ella | **saldrá** | *he/she will leave* | ellos/ellas | **saldrán** | *they will leave* |
| Ud. | **saldrá** | *you* (form.) *will leave* | Uds. | **saldrán** | *you* (pl.) *will leave* |

**tener**   *to have*

| | | | | | | |
|---|---|---|---|---|---|---|
| yo | **tendré** | *I will have* | nosotros/nosotras | **tendremos** | *we will have* |
| tú | **tendrás** | *you* (fam.) *will have* | | | |
| él/ella | **tendrá** | *he/she will have* | ellos/ellas | **tendrán** | *they will have* |
| Ud. | **tendrá** | *you* (form.) *will have* | Uds. | **tendrán** | *you* (pl.) *will have* |

**venir**   *to come*

| | | | | | | |
|---|---|---|---|---|---|---|
| yo | **vendré** | *I will come* | nosotros/nosotras | **vendremos** | *we will come* |
| tú | **vendrás** | *you* (fam.) *will come* | | | |
| él/ella | **vendrá** | *he/she will come* | ellos/ellas | **vendrán** | *they will come* |
| Ud. | **vendrá** | *you* (form.) *will come* | Uds. | **vendrán** | *you* (pl.) *will come* |

# Vocabulario

| | |
|---|---|
| el **agua hirviente** | *boiling water* |
| el **defecto congénito** | *congential defect* |
| el **desarrollo** | *development* |
| la **dislexia** | *dyslexia* |
| el **eczema** | *eczema* |
| el **pañal desechable** | *disposable diaper* |
| el **pañal de tela** | *cloth diaper* |
| la **parálisis cerebral** | *cerebral palsy* |
| la **raquitis** | *rickets* |
| los **sólidos** | *solids* |
| la **tos** | *cough* |

| | |
|---|---|
| atragantarse | *to choke (on)* |
| desarrollarse | *to develop* |
| eliminar | *to defecate* |
| eructar | *to belch* |
| lavar | *to wash* |
| limpiar | *to clean* |
| llorar | *to cry* |
| mimar | *to spoil (a child)* |
| molestar | *to bother* |
| rascarse | *to scratch oneself* |
| toser | *to cough* |
| | |
| atrasado, -a mentalmente | *mentally retarded* |
| ciego, -a | *blind* |
| estreñido, -a | *constipated* |
| hiperactivo, -a | *hyperactive* |
| sordo, -a | *deaf* |

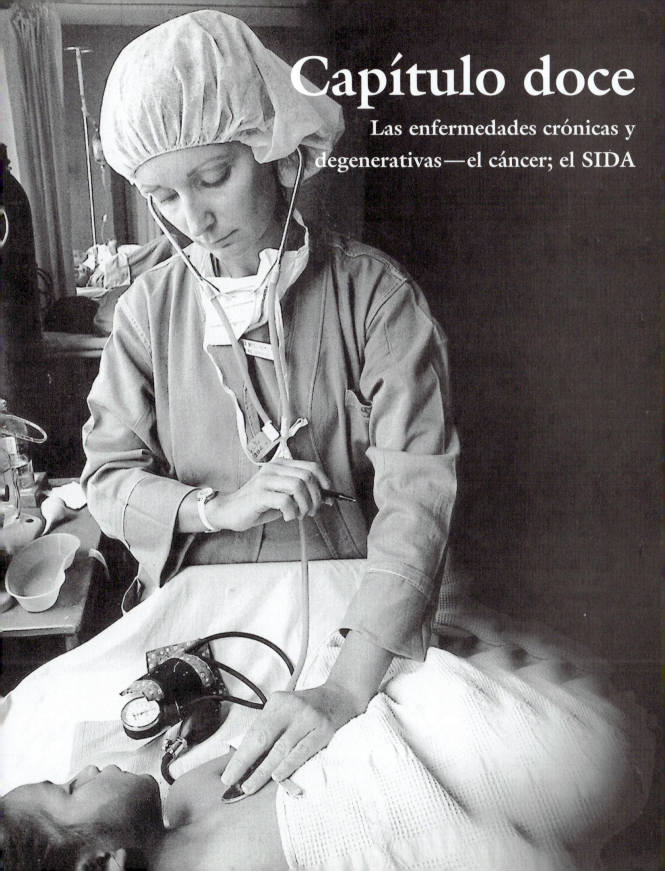

# Capítulo doce

Las enfermedades crónicas y
degenerativas—el cáncer; el SIDA

## 👁 Conversación

Médico:     Buenos días, señor. ¿Qué tiene Ud.?

Paciente:   Doctor, tengo mucha tos.

Médico:     ¿Desde cuándo tiene tos?

Paciente:   Hace tres meses. Y es una tos muy dolorosa.

Médico:     ¿Fuma Ud.?

Paciente:   Sí, doctor, fumo como un paquete diario.

Médico:     ¿Desde cuándo fuma Ud.?

Paciente:   Desde los dieciocho años de edad. Ya hace tiempo que mi esposa me pide que deje el hábito, pero no lo he podido hacer.

## Vocabulario

| | | | |
|---|---|---|---|
| **doloroso, -a** | *painful* | **años de edad** | *years of age* |
| **fumar** | *to smoke* | **pedir** | *to ask (for), to request* |

## Notas

### Como *(About, around, approximately)*

**Como** can be used somewhat colloquially with the above meanings. For example:

Fumo como un paquete al día.              *I smoke about a pack a day.*
Hace como cinco años que no fumo.         *I haven't been smoking for about five years.*

## Sustituciones

Substitute the underlined word with the cued items. Be sure to make any other necessary changes.

**MODELO**      ¿Desde cuándo tiene Ud. tos?      flema
                **¿Desde cuándo tiene Ud. flema?**

1. ¿Desde cuándo tiene Ud. tos?        irritación
2. ¿Desde cuándo tiene Ud. tos?        escalofríos
3. ¿Desde cuándo tiene Ud. tos?        el niño, fiebre
4. ¿Desde cuándo tiene Ud. tos?        su abuelo, náuseas
5. ¿Desde cuándo tiene Ud. tos?        el paciente, debilidad
6. ¿Desde cuándo tiene Ud. tos?        tú, dolor de cabeza

## Nota

### The Subjunctive

Mi esposa me pide que deje.            *My wife asks me to stop. (My wife asks that I stop.)*

This is an example of the subjunctive mood in Spanish. It is used in sentences that have two clauses separated by **que** *(that)* with a different subject in each clause and that also express emotion, desire, wanting, asking, needing, and so forth.

The subjunctive is formed in the same way as formal commands. That is, end -**ar** verbs with -**e,** and -**er** and -**ir** verbs with -**a.** For example:

**hablar**    *to speak*

| | |
|---|---|
| yo/él/ella/Ud. | **hable** |
| tú | **hables** |
| nosotros | **hablemos** |
| Uds./ellos/ellas | **hablen** |

**comer**    *to eat*

| | |
|---|---|
| yo/él/ella/Ud. | **coma** |
| tú | **comas** |
| nosotros | **comamos** |
| Uds./ellos/ellas | **coman** |

**vivir**    *to live*

| | |
|---|---|
| yo/él/ella/Ud. | **viva** |
| tú | **vivas** |
| nosotros | **vivamos** |
| Uds./ellos/ellas | **vivan** |

While we will not go into too much detail here, it might be useful to see some more examples of how it is used:

| | |
|---|---|
| Quiero que mi marido deje de fumar. | *I want my husband to stop smoking.* |
| Espero que el médico me examine. | *I hope that the doctor examines me.* |
| Es necesario que Ud. tome la medicina. | *It is necessary that you take the medicine.* |
| Me alegro que mi hijo esté mejor. | *I am glad that my son is better.* |

## Para practicar

Answer the question using the subjunctive mood and the cues provided.

> **MODELO**    ¿Qué quiere la señora?    su marido, dejar de fumar
> **La señora quiere que su marido deje de fumar.**

1. ¿Qué quiere la doctora?      el paciente, tomar los antibióticos
2. ¿Qué espera la madre?        su hijo, mejorar pronto
3. ¿Qué pide la esposa?         su marido, dejar de tomar drogas
4. ¿Qué quiere el médico?       el paciente, aceptar su consejo
5. ¿Qué necesita el paciente?   la doctora, preparar la receta

## Continúa la conversación...

Médico:    ¿Cuántos años tiene Ud.?

Paciente:    Tengo cincuenta y cuatro años.

Médico:    ¿Hay otros síntomas además de la tos?

Paciente:    A veces escupo sangre. ¿Qué puede ser, doctor?

Médico:    Bueno, primero es necesario hacer algunas pruebas para saber qué le pasa.

(Dos semanas después.)

Paciente:    ¿Qué me pasa, doctor?

Médico:    Hay un tumor maligno en el pulmón izquierdo.

Paciente:    ¿Qué voy a hacer?

Médico:    Afortunadamente, el cáncer no ha llegado a ninguna otra parte. Pero es necesario hacer una operación lo más pronto posible.

## Vocabulario

| | |
|---|---|
| además de | *besides, in addition to* |
| a veces | *sometimes* |
| lo más pronto posible | *as soon as possible* |

## Sustituciones

Substitute the underlined word for the cued items. Be sure to make any other necessary changes.

**MODELO**    Es necesario hacer <u>algunas pruebas</u>.    un examen completo
**Es necesario hacer <u>un examen completo</u>.**

1. Es necesario <u>hacer algunas pruebas</u>.    tomarle la temperatura
2. Es necesario <u>hacer algunas pruebas</u>.    tomar un antibiótico
3. Es <u>necesario</u> <u>hacer algunas pruebas</u>.    importante, comer bien
4. Es <u>necesario</u> <u>hacer algunas pruebas</u>.    importante, tomar la medicina
5. Es <u>necesario</u> <u>hacer algunas pruebas</u>.    mejor, consultar con un especialista

## Vocabulario

| | |
|---|---|
| **El cáncer** | *Cancer* |
| la **biopsia** | *biopsy* |
| el **bulto** | *lump* |
| el **cáncer** | *cancer* |
| el **cáncer de la próstata** | *prostate cancer* |
| el **cáncer del cerebro** | *brain cancer* |
| el **cáncer del pulmón** | *lung cancer* |
| el **cáncer del seno** | *breast cancer* |
| los **ganglios linfáticos** | *lymph nodes* |

En los últimos años los hombres de ciencia han logrado identificar muchas de las causas del cáncer. Se sabe hoy día que aproximadamente el 80 por ciento de los casos de cáncer están relacionados con el estilo de vida de las personas. Por ejemplo, los alimentos que consumen, el trabajo que realizan y el hábito de fumar son factores que influyen en la probabilidad de contraer cáncer.

Cuando usted conoce algunos de los factores que aumentan la posibilidad de contraer cáncer, usted puede hacer algo para controlarlos. Algunos, como su lugar de trabajo, son difíciles de controlar, pero otros pueden controlarse fácilmente, por ejemplo, consumiendo alimentos sanos. A continuación se menciona una serie de medidas que usted puede tomar a diario para protegerse del cáncer.

**NO** fume ni consuma tabaco en ninguna forma.

**NO** use estrógenos por más tiempo del que sea necesario.

**SÍ,** consuma alimentos con mucha fibra y poca grasa; coma mucha fruta fresca, verduras y cereales integrales.

**SÍ,** evite las radiografías innecesarias.

**NO** se exponga excesivamente a los rayos solares; use ropa y cremas protectoras.

**NO** tome bebidas alcohólicas o hágalo con moderación.

**SÍ,** observe las normas de salud y seguridad en su trabajo.

| | |
|---|---|
| las **glándulas linfáticas** | *lymph glands* |
| la **leucemia** | *leukemia* |
| el **linfoma** | *lymphoma* |
| la **lumpectomía** | *lumpectomy* |
| el **mamograma** | *mammogram* |
| la **mastectomía** | *mastectomy* |
| la **prueba de Pap (Papanicolaou)** | *Pap smear* |
| la **quimioterapia** | *chemotherapy* |
| la **radiación** | *radiation* |
| la **radioterapia** | *radiation therapy* |
| el **tumor** | *tumor* |
| **benigno, -a** | *benign* |
| **maligno, -a** | *malignant* |

# Conversación

Doctora:    Señorita, lamento decirle que su mamá tiene un tumor maligno en el seno.

Señorita:    Esto es terrible. ¿Puede hacer algo para ayudarle?

Doctora:    Vamos a hacer una mastectomía.

Señorita:    ¿Cuándo se va a hacer la operación?

Doctora:    Debemos hacer la operación lo más pronto posible.

Señorita:    ¿Y qué va a pasar después?

Doctora:    Su mamá va a tener un período de recuperación. Despúes vamos a hacer la radioterapia y la quimioterapia para eliminar el cáncer por completo.

Señorita:    ¿Causan efectos secundarios estos tratamientos?

Doctora:    Sí, muchas veces las pacientes sufren de efectos secundarios. Por ejemplo, puede sufrir de vómitos, náuseas y posiblemente la pérdida temporal del pelo.

# Vocabulario

| | |
|---|---|
| lamento decirle | *I am sorry to tell you* |
| de una vez | *all at once; at one time* |
| por completo | *completely* |
| la pérdida temporal del pelo | *temporary hair loss* |

# Más vocabulario

| **Palabras contrarias** | | **Opposites** | |
|---|---|---|---|
| afortunadamente | *fortunately* | desafortunadamente; por desgracia | *unfortunately* |
| alguien | *somebody* | nadie | *nobody* |
| antes | *before* | después | *after* |
| de una vez | *all at once* | poco a poco | *little by little* |
| maligno, -a | *malignant* | benigno, -a | *benign* |
| nunca | *never* | siempre | *always* |
| poco | *little* | mucho | *much* |
| tener | *to have* | faltar | *to lack; to be lacking in* |
| todo | *everything* | nada | *nothing* |

# Sustituciones

Substitute the underlined words with the cued items. Be sure to make any other necessary changes.

**MODELO**    Nosotros vamos a hacer <u>una operación</u>.    algunas pruebas
**Nosotros vamos a hacer <u>algunas pruebas</u>.**

1. <u>Nosotros</u> vamos a hacer una operación.    la doctora
2. <u>Nosotros</u> vamos a hacer una operación.    el cirujano

3. <u>Nosotros</u> vamos a hacer una operación.        yo
4. <u>Nosotros</u> vamos a <u>hacer una operación</u>.        ella, darle una receta
5. <u>Nosotros</u> vamos a <u>hacer una operación</u>.        él, darle una cita

## Para practicar

Change these sentences to make them opposites.

| MODELO | El médico me dice todo. |
|---|---|
| | **El médico no me dice nada.** |

1. El paciente habla poco.
2. El tumor es benigno.
3. Ud. debe descansar antes de la operación.
4. El médico siempre hace una mastectomía.
5. Nadie sabe que tengo un tumor.

## Vocabulario

| **El SIDA y otras enfermedades pasadas sexualmente** | *AIDS and Other Sexually Transmitted Diseases* |
|---|---|
| las **causas** | *causes* |
| el **condón** | *condom* |
| el **contacto casual** | *casual contact* |
| el **contacto sexual** | *sexual contact* |
| las **enfermedades venéreas** | *venereal diseases* |
| la **gonorrea** | *gonorrhea* |
| el **herpes genital** | *genital herpes* |
| la **infección oportunística** | *opportunistic infection* |
| el **medicamento antiviral; antivirósico** | *antiviral medication* |
| el **peligro** | *danger* |
| la **pulmonía** | *pneumonia* |
| el **síndrome de inmunodeficiencia adquirida (SIDA)** | *acquired immune deficiency syndrome (AIDS)* |
| el **sistema inmunológico** | *immune system* |
| la **transmisión sexual** | *sexual transmission* |
| el **virus de inmunodeficiencia humana (VIH-1)** | *human immunodeficiency virus (HIV)* |
| **compartir agujas hipodérmicas** | *to share needles* |
| **infectado, -a** | *infected* |

## Conversación

Joven:      Señora, ¿puede Ud. darme alguna información sobre el SIDA?

Enfermera:  Sí, claro. ¿Qué quieres saber?

Joven:      Muchos de mis compañeros de clase hablan del peligro del SIDA, y tengo miedo. ¿Qué debo hacer para no infectarme?

Enfermera:  Bueno, primero debes tener mucho cuidado en tus relaciones sexuales. Debes conocer bien a la persona con quien vas a tener relaciones, y es muy importante siempre usar un condón.

## Vocabulario

| | |
|---|---|
| **tengo miedo** | *I am afraid* |
| **los compañeros de clase** | *classmates* |
| **tener mucho cuidado** | *to be very careful* |

## Nota

### Claro (*Of course*)

Some more expressions having the same meaning as *of course* include:

por supuesto

desde luego

naturalmente

claro que sí

## Sustituciones

Substitute with the cued word.

> **MODELO**    ¿Qué debo hacer para no <u>infectarme</u>?    caerme
> **¿Qué debo hacer para no <u>caerme</u>?**

1. enfermarme
2. tener un accidente
3. tener miedo
4. sufrir
5. lastimarme

## Más sustituciones

> **MODELO**    Es muy importante siempre <u>usar un condón</u>.    tener cuidado
> **Es muy importante siempre <u>tener cuidado</u>.**

1. conocer a la persona
2. estar bien informado
3. protegerse
4. descansar mucho
5. consultar con el especialista

### Continúa la conversación...

Joven:      ¿Cómo puede saber una persona si tiene VIH-1?

Enfermera:  La única manera de saber por cierto es con una prueba de sangre.

Joven:      ¿No hay síntomas?

Enfermera:  Un individuo que tiene VIH no sufrirá de ningún síntoma. Pero el individuo que tiene SIDA puede manifestar muchos síntomas.

Joven:      ¿Cómo es eso?

Enfermera:  El SIDA es un virus que reduce la habilidad del sistema inmunológico para proteger el cuerpo de cualquier enfermedad. Por eso, un individuo que tiene SIDA puede tener muchos otros síntomas y enfermedades. Una de las enfermedades más comunes de la víctima del SIDA es la pulmonía.

## Vocabulario

| | |
|---|---|
| la **única manera** | *the only way* |
| **por cierto** | *for sure* |
| **proteger** | *to protect* |

## Recuerde

**Eso** means *that* when referring to a general idea or situation, rather than modifying a specific noun.

Eso no es cierto.                    *That is not true.*

# Notas

### Some and None

| | |
|---|---|
| *some, a few* | algún, alguno, algunos, alguna, algunas |
| *none, no* | ningún, ninguno, ninguna |

The preceding words agree with the noun in gender and number. **Algún** and **ningún** are used when *directly* followed by a masculine singular noun. For example:

| | |
|---|---|
| Hay algunos pacientes en la oficina. | *There are some patients in the office.* |
| No hay ningún médico aquí. | *There is no doctor here.* |

# Para practicar

Student A asks the question using **algún, alguno, algunos, alguna,** or **algunas.** Student B answers using **ningún, ninguno,** or **ninguna.**

**MODELO**    paciente / aquí

A:  **¿Hay algún paciente aquí?**
B:  **No, no hay ningún paciente aquí.**

1. doctora / en la oficina
2. médico / en el hospital
3. pacientes / en la sala de espera
4. joven / en la clínica
5. libro / junto a la cama
6. enfermeras / en el tercer piso
7. cirujano / en la sala de emergencias

## Continúa la conversación...

| | |
|---|---|
| Joven: | ¿Es cierto que solamente los homosexuales pueden tener el SIDA? |
| Enfermera: | No, eso no es cierto. Si una persona tiene relaciones sexuales con otro individuo, sea hombre o mujer, puede infectarse. Y hay otras causas del SIDA además de las relaciones sexuales. |
| Joven: | ¿De veras? |
| Enfermera: | Sí, claro. Por ejemplo, es posible infectarse si se comparte una aguja hipodérmica con otro individuo infectado. |
| Joven: | ¿Es posible infectarse de otra manera? |
| Enfermera: | Hay casos de personas que se infectaron con una transfusión de sangre, pero se ha reducido este peligro con nuevos métodos sanitarios. |

# Vocabulario

| | | | |
|---|---|---|---|
| **cierto, -a** | *true; certain* | **se comparte** | *share* |
| **cualquier** | *any* | **de otra manera** | *in another way* |

# Nota

### Sea hombre o mujer *(Whether it be man or woman)*

**Sea** (subjunctive of **ser**) can be used in this way to express *either of two* or *both*. For example:

sea el cáncer o el SIDA    *whether it be cancer or AIDS*

# Sustituciones

Substitute according to the model.

> **MODELO**    ¿Es posible <u>infectarse</u> de otra manera?    protegerse
> **¿Es posible <u>protegerse</u> de otra manera?**

1. curarse
2. expresarse
3. mejorarse
4. explicarse

## Continúa la conversación...

Joven:        ¿Hay algún remedio para la víctima del SIDA?

Enfermera:    Por desgracia, no hay una cura para la víctima del SIDA, pero sí hay varios tratamientos que se utilizan para demorar el progreso de la infección.

Joven:        Señora, le agradezco mucho la información y los consejos que me ha dado. Me siento mucho más tranquilo ahora que estoy bien informado.

# Vocabulario

| | | | |
|---|---|---|---|
| **por desgracia** | *unfortunately* | **demorar** | *to delay* |

# Notas

### La víctima *(The victim)*

Notice that the word **víctima** is always female, regardless of whether it refers to a man or a woman. Other such words include:

la persona *(always feminine)*        *person*
el individuo *(always masculine)*     *individual*
el sujeto *(always masculine)*        *person (in question)*

### Sí *(Indeed)*

**Sí** *(yes)* can mean *indeed* in some situations. For example:

No hay una cura, pero sí hay varios        *There is no cure, but there are indeed a*
tratamientos.                              *variety of treatments.*

### Le agradezco mucho

**Le agradezco mucho** means *I am very grateful (to you)*. One can also say: **Se lo agradezco.**

## Para practicar

**Le agradezco mucho por... Muchas gracias por...** Thank someone two ways according to the cues.

> **MODELO**    su ayuda
> **Le agradezco mucho por su ayuda.**
> **Muchas gracias por su ayuda.**

1. la información
2. el consejo
3. su tiempo
4. la medicina
5. su apoyo *(your support)*

## Sustituciones

Substitute according to the model.

> **MODELO**    ¿Hay algún remedio para la víctima del <u>SIDA</u>?    el cáncer
> **¿Hay algún remedio para la víctima del <u>cáncer</u>?**

1. la leucemia
2. la diabetis
3. un accidente
4. la depresión
5. la artritis

---

**NOTA CULTURAL**    **ARABIC INFLUENCE IN THE SPANISH LANGUAGE**

There is considerable Arabic influence in both Spanish culture and language as the Arabs, or Moors, as they were called, occupied Spain from the eighth to the fifteenth centuries. One expression that comes directly from Arabic is **ojalá** *(O Allah)* and means *I wish, I hope,* or *If only it were so.* It can stand alone or be used in a sentence with the subjunctive. For example:

| | |
|---|---|
| Ojalá que mi madre mejore pronto. | *I hope that my mother will get better soon.* |
| Ojalá (que) el médico la ayude. | *Hopefully, the doctor can help her.* |

Also, many words that begin with the letters **al-** are of Arabic origin. For example:

| | |
|---|---|
| el **alcalde** | *mayor* |
| la **alcántara** | *jug* |
| el **alcohol** | *alcohol* |
| la **alfombra** | *carpet* |
| la **almohada** | *pillow* |
| las **almorranas** | *piles; hemorrhoids* |
| el **almuerzo** | *lunch* |

# RESUMEN Y REPASO

## Gramática

### Más sobre el subjuntivo

Verbos regulares

Conjugate **-ar** verbs as follows:

**examinar**    *to examine*

| | | | | | |
|---|---|---|---|---|---|
| (que) yo | **examine** | *(that) I examine* | (que) nosotros/nosotras | **examinemos** | *(that) we examine* |
| (que) tú | **examines** | *(that) you* (fam.) *examine* | | | |
| (que) él/ella | **examine** | *(that) he/she examine* | (que) ellos/ellas | **examinen** | *(that) they examine* |
| (que) Ud. | **examine** | *(that) you* (form.) *examine* | (que) Uds. | **examinen** | *(that) you* (pl.) *examine* |

Conjugate **-er** verbs as follows:

**comer**    *to eat*

| | | | | | |
|---|---|---|---|---|---|
| (que) yo | **coma** | *(that) I eat* | (que) nosotros/nosotras | **comamos** | *(that) we eat* |
| (que) tú | **comas** | *(that) you* (fam.) *eat* | | | |
| (que) él/ella | **coma** | *(that) he/she eat* | (que) ellos/ellas | **coman** | *(that) they eat* |
| (que) Ud. | **coma** | *(that) you* (form.) *eat* | (que) Uds. | **coman** | *(that) you* (pl.) *eat* |

Conjugate **-ir** verbs as follows:

**escribir**    *to write*

| | | | | | |
|---|---|---|---|---|---|
| (que) yo | **escriba** | *(that) I write* | (que) nosotros/nosotras | **escribamos** | *(that) we write* |
| (que) tú | **escribas** | *(that) you* (fam.) *write* | | | |
| (que) él/ella | **escriba** | *(that) he/she write* | (que) ellos/ellas | **escriban** | *(that) they write* |
| (que) Ud. | **escriba** | *(that) you* (form.) *write* | (que) Uds. | **escriban** | *(that) you* (pl.) *write* |

## Verbos irregulares

Verbs that are irregular in the **yo** form of the present tense usually have the same irregularity in the subjunctive. Remember to adjust the ending for the subjunctive mood. For example:

**tener** *to have*

| | |
|---|---|
| present tense: | yo **tengo** |
| subjunctive: | **tenga, tengas, tenga, tengamos, tengan** |

**poner** *to put*

| | |
|---|---|
| present tense: | yo **pongo** |
| subjunctive: | **ponga, pongas, ponga, pongamos, pongan** |

**conocer** *to know, to be acquainted with*

| | |
|---|---|
| present tense: | yo **conozco** |
| subjunctive: | **conozca, conozcas, conozca, conozcamos, conozcan** |

## Usos del subjuntivo

Use the subjunctive in many sentences that have two clauses separated by **que** with two different subjects. It is used in situations that show emotion, surprise, doubt, uncertainty, desire, wanting, requesting, and so forth. For example:

| | |
|---|---|
| Quiero que mi hijo mejore pronto. | *I want my son to get better soon.* |
| Deseamos que todos salgan de la oficina. | *We want everyone to leave the office.* |
| Dudo que el médico me ayude. | *I doubt that the doctor will help me.* |
| Me sorprendo que el niño coma los vegetales. | *I am surprised that the child is eating the vegetables.* |
| Pido a mi marido que tome las vitaminas. | *I ask my husband to take the vitamins.* |

# Capítulo trece

Pruebas y procedimientos

# Conversación

**La colonoscopia**

| | |
|---|---|
| Anestesiólogo: | Buenos días, señora García. Yo soy el anestesiólogo, el doctor Ramírez. Como Ud. ya sabe, Ud. va a tener la colonoscopia mañana. Yo le voy a dar la anestesia. |
| Paciente: | ¿A qué hora me van a hacer el procedimiento? |
| Anestesiólogo: | Vamos a hacerlo a las nueve de la mañana. No se preocupe. Todo va bien. Ahora tengo que hacerle algunas preguntas importantes. ¿Está bien? |
| Paciente: | Sí, por supuesto, doctor. |

# Nota

**Ya** *(Already, now)*

**Ya** is often used in idiomatic expressions referring to time. For example:

| | |
|---|---|
| Ya es hora de empezar. | *It's time to begin.* |
| Ya es hora de irnos. | *It's time for us to go.* |
| Ya basta. | *It's enough already.* |
| Ya lo sé. | *I know it already.* |
| Ya voy. | *I'm coming (right now).* |
| Ya no. | *No longer; not any more.* |

# Vocabulario

| **La anestesiología** | *Anesthesiology* |
|---|---|
| la **alergia** | *allergy* |
| la **anestesia** | *anesthesia* |
| el **anestesiólogo**, la **anestesióloga** | *anesthesiologist* |
| el **anestético** | *anesthetic* |
| el **asma** | *asthma* |
| la **cirugía** | *surgery* |
| la **fiebre de heno** | *hay fever* |
| la **máscara de oxígeno** | *oxygen mask* |
| la **sala de recuperación** | *recovery room* |
| | |
| **preocuparse** | *to worry* |

# Sustituciones

Substitute the underlined words for the cued item. Be sure to make any other necessary changes.

> **MODELO**     Yo le voy a dar <u>la anestesia</u>.     la información.
> **Yo le voy a dar <u>la información</u>.**

1. Yo le voy a dar <u>la anestesia</u>.     la receta
2. Yo le voy a dar <u>la anestesia</u>.     la medicina
3. Yo le voy a dar <u>la anestesia</u>.     el antibiótico
4. Yo le voy a dar <u>la anestesia</u>.     la inyección

5. <u>Yo</u> le voy a dar la anestesia.   la doctora
6. <u>Yo</u> le voy a dar la anestesia.   el anestesiólogo
7. <u>Yo</u> le voy a dar la anestesia.   nosotros
8. <u>Yo</u> le voy a dar la anestesia.   te

## Recuerde

**¿Ha tenido Ud.?** means *Have you had?* Use it to ask a patient if he/she has had a particular disease in the past. The response is **Sí, he tenido...** or **No, no he tenido.**

## Para practicar

Practice with a partner following the model.

> **MODELO**   fiebre de heno
>   A:   **¿Ha tenido fiebre de heno?**
>   B:   **Sí, he tenido fiebre de heno, pero ya no.**
>   *or*
>   B:   **No, no he tenido nunca fiebre de heno.**

1. gripe
2. alergias
3. úlceras
4. dolor de espalda
5. diarrea
6. náuseas
7. la pulmonía

 **Continúa la conversación...**

| | |
|---|---|
| Anestesiólogo: | ¿Sufre Ud. de asma? |
| Paciente: | No, no sufro de asma. |
| Anestesiólogo: | ¿Sufre Ud. de fiebre de heno o de alergias? |
| Paciente: | No, no sufro de ninguna alergia. |
| Anestesiólogo: | ¿Ha tenido Ud. problemas del corazón, de los pulmones o de los riñones? |
| Paciente: | Creo que no. |
| Anestesiólogo: | ¿Ha tenido alguna vez Ud. alta presión? |
| Paciente: | No, doctor. |
| Anestesiólogo: | ¿Tiene Ud. catarro o dolor de garganta? |
| Paciente: | No, no tengo catarro y no me duele la garganta. |
| Anestesiólogo: | ¿Tiene Ud. tos? |
| Paciente: | Tengo un poco de tos ahora pero creo que es a causa de los nervios. |
| Anestesiólogo: | Entonces, eso es todo. Le vamos a poner una inyección mañana y Ud. se va a dormir. Después de la prueba le vamos a llevar a la sala de recuperación, donde Ud. va a descansar. Hasta mañana, señora. |
| Paciente: | Hasta mañana, doctor. |

# Nota

**A causa de** *(Because of)*

Remember that **¿por qué?** means *why?* and **porque** means *because.* However, to say *because of,* use the expression **a causa de.** For example:

Él no puede dormir a causa de sus problemas.     *He can't sleep because of his problems.*

# Preguntas

1. ¿Quién es el doctor Ramírez?
2. ¿Cuándo le van a operar a la señora García?
3. ¿Qué le van a hacer a la señora?
4. ¿Sufre ella del corazón, de los pulmones o de los riñones?
5. ¿Tiene la señora tos?
6. ¿Adónde van a llevar a la señora después de la operación?

# Vocabulario

**Pruebas y procedimientos** *(Tests and procedures)*

| **Pruebas generales** | **General Tests** |
|---|---|
| el análisis de orina | *urine test* |
| el análisis de sangre | *blood test* |
| la biopsia | *byopsy* |
| la citología | *cytology* |
| el frotis de Pap | *Pap smear* |
| la gammagrafía | *radionuclide scanning* |
| la imagen por resonancia magnética | *MRI* |
| la radiografía | *X ray* |
| los rayos X (equis) | *X rays* |
| el sonograma | *sonogram* |
| la tomografía computada (TAC) | *CT scan* |

| **Pruebas del sistema cardiovascular** | **Tests of the Cardiovascular System** |
|---|---|
| el electrocardiograma | *electrocardiogram* |
| la prueba de esfuerzo | *stress test* |
| la prueba de Holter | *Holter monitor* |

| **Pruebas del sistema digestivo** | **Tests of the Digestive System** |
|---|---|
| la colonoscopia | *colonoscopy* |
| la enema de bario | *barium enema* |
| la gastroscopia | *gastroscopy* |
| la proctoscopia | *proctoscopy* |
| la sigmoidoscopia | *sigmoidoscopy* |

| **Pruebas del sistema respiratorio** | **Tests of the Respiratory System** |
|---|---|
| el angiograma pulmonar | *angiogram* |
| la broncoscopia | *bronchoscopy* |
| la prueba de la tuberculina | *tuberculin test* |
| la radiografía de tórax | *chest x-ray* |

## Que Puede Hacer Usted:

- Debe someterse a la prueba de Papanicolaou por lo menos una vez al año si en su caso existen factores de riesgo para el desarrollo del cáncer de cuello del útero. Si no existen factores de riesgo, pregúntele a su médico con cuánta frecuencia debe someterse al frotis de Pap.

- Hágase curar cualquier infección vaginal o enfermedad venérea tan pronto se dé cuenta que la tiene. Si su pareja sexual le dice que tiene una enfermedad venérea, consulte a su médico inmediatamente, aunque no tenga ningún síntoma.

- Hable con su compañero sobre la posibilidad de usar condones. Los condones contribuirán a protegerla de los virus que causan las verrugas genitales que podrían tener relación con el cáncer cervical. Los condones también contribuyen a protergerla contra otras enfermedades venéreas, contra embarazos no deseados y contra el SIDA.

- No fume. Al parecer, con el cigarrillo aumentan las probabilidades de contraer cáncer cervical, aunque nadie sabe con seguridad por qué.

- Si usted nota que:
  - sangra después de las relaciones sexuales
  - pierde sangre entre sus períodos
  - tiene flujo vaginal

acuda inmediatamente a su médico o a una clínica para que la examinen.

## Para Obtener Más Información

Si desea obtener más información sobre cualquier tipo de cáncer, llame gratuitamente al 1-800-462-1884. También puede llamar al número (518) 474-1222 del Departamento de Salud del Estado de Nueva York.

*Ilustracíon de la tapa:*
*"Moça Pensando"*
*por Emiliano Di Cavalcanti*

Estado de Nueva York
Mario M. Cuomo, Gobernador

David Axelrod, M.D.
Comisionado de Salud

0417

5/89

Lo que usted debe saber...

# Conversación

### El angiograma

Técnico:    Le voy a hacer una radiografía del pecho.

Paciente:   ¿Para qué se necesita la radiografía?

Técnico:    Para saber si Ud. tiene alguna enfermedad de los pulmones.

Paciente:   ¿Qué tengo que hacer?

Técnico:    Tiene que quitarse la camisa y pararse enfrente de este aparato.

Paciente:   ¿Va a durar mucho tiempo?

Técnico:    No. Sólo va a durar quince minutos.

Paciente:   ¿Me va a doler?

Técnico:    No. Ud. no va a sentir ningún dolor en absoluto.

Paciente:   ¿Cuándo voy a saber los resultados?

Técnico:    Después de la prueba el médico discutirá los resultados con Ud.

## Vocabulario

| | | | |
|---|---|---|---|
| **quitarse** | *to take off; remove* | **durar** | *to last* |
| **pararse** | *to stand* | **en absoluto** | *at all* |
| **enfrente de** | *in front of* | los **resultados** | *results* |
| el **aparato** | *device* | | |

## Preguntas

1. ¿Qué prueba va a hacer el técnico?
2. ¿Qué indicará la prueba?
3. ¿Qué tiene que hacer el paciente?
4. ¿Cuánto tiempo durará la prueba?
5. ¿Le va a doler al paciente?

## Notas

### Prepositions

We have been using prepositions throughout this text in a variety of situations. Here now is a list of prepositions and some notes on how they are used:

| | |
|---|---|
| a | *to* |
| antes de | *before* |
| después de | *after* |
| con | *with* |
| sin | *without* |
| de | *of; from* |
| debajo de | *underneath* |
| encima de | *on top of* |
| sobre | *over* |

| desde | *since* |
|---|---|
| detrás de | *behind* |
| en | *in; at* |
| entre | *among; between* |
| hasta | *until; up to* |
| junto a | *next to* |
| para | *for (the use of); in order to* |
| por | *for (the sake of); by; through* |

## Prepositional Pronouns

Here are the pronouns that are used after prepositions:

| mí | *me* |
|---|---|
| ti | *you* (fam.) |
| él | *him* |
| ella | *her* |
| Ud. | *you* (form.) |
| nosotros/nosotras | *us* |
| ellos/ellas | *them* |
| Uds. | *you* (pl.) |

Exceptions to the above include:

| conmigo | *with me* |
|---|---|
| contigo | *with you* |

**a** followed by **el** becomes **al**

**de** followed by **el** becomes **del**

For example:

| Esta receta es para mí. | *This prescription is for me.* |
|---|---|
| Hay un secreto entre nosotros. | *There is a secret between us.* |
| El médico habla conmigo. | *The doctor is speaking with me.* |
| El paciente va al hospital. | *The patient is going to the hospital.* |
| La doctora sale del hospital. | *The doctor is leaving (from) the hospital.* |

# Para practicar

Answer using the cues.

> **MODELO**    ¿Con quién habla el médico?    *with me*
> **El médico habla conmigo.**

1. ¿Dónde está la doctora?            *in her office*
2. ¿Con quién habla el cirujano?      *with me*
3. ¿Dónde está la enfermera?          *in the emergency room*
4. ¿Dónde está la intravenosa?        *next to the bed*
5. ¿Con quién va Ud. al hospital?     *with my father*

## NOTA CULTURAL — LA SUPERSTICIÓN

Many Latino superstitions originated in popular rural folk culture. Among these superstitions are **mal aire, mal de ojo,** and **envidia.**

It is considered unhealthy to sleep with an open window as this might cause **mal aire** *(bad air; evil air)* to enter and cause illness.

**Mal de ojo** *(evil eye)* occurs when one is looked upon by another with intense admiration. The person who is the focus of this "excessive" emotion falls ill as a result.

**Envidia** *(envy)* can cause illness. When one is prosperous he or she brings the «**envidia**» of others upon him- or herself, causing bad fortune and illness.

## Conversación

### Las radiografías de bario

| | |
|---|---|
| Doctora: | Tenemos que hacerle unas radiografías. Vamos a tratar de determinar si Ud. tiene úlceras o un tumor en el sistema digestivo. |
| Paciente: | ¿Que me van a hacer? |
| Doctora: | Primero Ud. tiene que tomar este líquido. Se llama el sulfato de bario. Tiene mal sabor pero no le va a hacer ningún daño. Después le voy a apretar el estómago. |
| Paciente: | ¿Me va a causar mucho dolor? |
| Doctora: | Posiblemente Ud. va a tener calambres. |
| Paciente: | ¿Va a durar mucho tiempo? |
| Doctora: | Solamente va a durar cuarenta y cinco minutos más o menos. |

## Vocabulario

| | | | |
|---|---|---|---|
| el **sulfato de bario** | *barium sulfate* | **apretar** | *to press* |
| **tiene mal sabor** | *it tastes bad* | **más o menos** | *more or less* |

## Recuerde

### Sólo, solamente

**Sólo** and **solamente** mean *only* or *just.* **Solo, sola, solos,** and **solas** are adjectives and they mean *alone.*

## Preguntas

1. ¿Qué prueba le van a hacer al paciente?
2. ¿Qué quiere saber la doctora?
3. ¿Qué tiene que tomar el paciente?
4. ¿Qué efecto secundario va a sufrir el paciente?
5. ¿Cuánto tiempo va a durar la prueba?

## Conversación

### Las radiografías con enema bariado

Doctora:    Vamos a hacerle unas radiografías, pero primero tenemos que ponerle un enema. Este enema contiene una solución de sulfato de bario.

Paciente:   ¿Para qué tiene que hacer esta prueba?

Doctora:    Tenemos que saber si tiene úlceras del colon.

Paciente:   ¿Habrá efectos secundarios?

Doctora:    Es posible que Ud. sufra algunos calambres, pero no durará mucho tiempo.

## Vocabulario

| | |
|---|---|
| contiene | *it contains* |
| ¿Para qué? | *Why?; For what purpose?* |
| ¿Habrá...? | *Will there be...?* |

### Preguntas

1. ¿Qué prueba va a hacer la doctora?
2. ¿Qué van a ponerle al paciente?
3. ¿Para qué tienen que hacer esta prueba?
4. ¿Va a sufrir efectos secundarios el paciente?

## Conversación

### La tomografía

Paciente:   ¿Qué me pasa, doctor? Todavía con los dolores de cabeza.

Médico:     Vamos a hacer una tomografía computada de la cabeza, o prueba de TAC.

Paciente:   ¿Qué es eso?

Médico:     Es un procedimiento que nos permite verle cabeza adentro. De esa forma podemos saber si hay tumores u otras anormalidades.

Paciente:   ¿Qué tengo que hacer?

Médico:     Ud. no más tiene que quedarse acostado y quieto durante la prueba.

Paciente:   Voy a tener dolor?

Médico:     No, Ud. no va a tener ningún dolor.

Paciente:   ¿Cuándo voy a saber los resultados?

Médico:     Vamos a saber los resultados casi inmediatamente. Después de la prueba los técnicos me darán los resultados, y entonces hablaré con Ud.

## Vocabulario

| | |
|---|---|
| de esa forma | *in that way* |
| quedarse acostado, -a | *to remain lying down* |
| quieto, -a | *still; quiet* |

# Preguntas

1. ¿Qué síntomas tiene el paciente?
2. ¿Qué prueba le va a dar el médico?
3. ¿Qué tiene que hacer el paciente durante la prueba?

# Notas

### Todavía con, cabeza adentro

In colloquial speech, both verb and subject are omitted with **todavía.** For example:

| | |
|---|---|
| Todavía con los mismos dolores de cabeza. | *Still with the same headaches.* |
| Todavía con los mismos problemas. | *I still have the same problems.* |
| Todavía con el carro viejo. | *I still have the same old car.* |

Notice how the preposition can come after the following kind of construction.

| | |
|---|---|
| cabeza adentro | *inside the head* |
| calle abajo | *down the street* |

# Conversación

### La exploración nuclear: El hígado y la vesícula biliar

Paciente:   ¿Qué me va a hacer?

Doctora:   Vamos a inyectar una materia radioactiva en el brazo. Después, vamos a usar un aparato que saca fotos del hígado y de la vesícula biliar. De esa forma podemos examinar estos órganos para saber si hay anormalidades.

Paciente:   ¿Me va a doler?

Doctora:   No, pero tiene que quedarse acostada por mucho tiempo. La máquina no le va a hacer ningún daño. No más va a registrar la señal de la materia radioactiva.

# Vocabulario

| | |
|---|---|
| la **materia radioactiva** | *radioactive material* |
| sacar fotos | *to take photos* |
| la **señal** | *signal* |

# Preguntas

1. ¿Qué le van a inyectar al paciente?
2. ¿Qué va a hacer el aparato?
3. ¿Qué quiere saber la doctora?
4. ¿Qué tiene que hacer el paciente durante la prueba?

# Nota

### No más

**No más** is often used colloquially instead of **solamente** to express the meaning *just* or *only*. For example:

| | |
|---|---|
| No más va a registrar la señal. | *It is just going to pick up the signal.* |
| No más quería hablar. | *I just wanted to talk.* |
| No más vamos a echar una siestecita. | *We are just going to take a little nap.* |

Remember that the subject pronoun is often omitted and is understood by the context.

# Conversación

### El sonograma

| | |
|---|---|
| Doctora: | Tenemos que hacerle una prueba del hígado. |
| Paciente: | ¿Por qué? ¿Cuál es el problema? |
| Doctora: | Queremos determinar si hay tumores en este órgano. |
| Paciente: | ¿Cuál es la prueba que va a hacer? |
| Doctora: | Vamos a hacer un sonograma. Para esta prueba se usa un aparato que transmite sonidos producidos por el órgano. Se llama un transmisor ultrasonido. De esa forma, podemos estudiar el órgano con mucho detalle y hacer un diagnóstico correcto. |
| Paciente: | ¿Qué tengo que hacer? |
| Doctora: | Ud. tiene que quedarse acostada durante la prueba. |

# Vocabulario

| | |
|---|---|
| los **sonidos** | *sounds* |
| un **transmisor ultrasonido** | *ultrasound transmitter* |
| el **detalle** | *detail* |

# Preguntas

1. ¿Cuál es el órgano que van a examinar?
2. ¿Qué quiere determinar la doctora?
3. ¿Cómo se llama la prueba?
4. ¿Qué tiene que hacer la paciente durante la prueba?

# Recuerde

### Se usa *(It is used)*

Remember to use the impersonal expression with **se** in most passive voice situations. For example:

| | |
|---|---|
| Aquí se habla español. | *Spanish is spoken here.* |
| No se sabe la razón. | *The reason is not known.* |
| No se come nada en la sala de emergencias. | *Nothing is eaten in the emergency room.* |

# RESUMEN Y REPASO

## Vocabulario

| | |
|---|---|
| el **catéter** | *catheter* |
| la **dilatación y legrado** | *dilatation and curettage* |
| el **examen de las heces** | *examination of the feces* |
| el **examen parasitológico** | *parasitological exam* |
| el **hemograma completo** | *full blood count* |
| las **piedras biliares** | *gall stones* |
| las **piedras nefríticas** | *kidney stones* |
| el **pielograma intravenoso** | *intravenous pielogram* |
| la **prueba del embarazo** | *pregnancy test* |
| la **reacción alérgica** | *allergic reaction* |
| la **sangre oculta** | *occult blood* |
| la **sonda** | *catheter* |
| la **tinta** | *dye* |
| el **tubo** | *tube* |
| el **yodo** | *iodine* |
| | |
| **insertar** | *to insert* |
| | |
| **con contraste** | *with contrast* |
| **sin contraste** | *without contrast* |

# Capítulo catorce

El dentista, el terapeuta físico
y el optometrista

# EL DENTISTA, LA DENTISTA

## Conversación

| | |
|---|---|
| Dentista: | Buenos días, señor. ¿Cómo está Ud.? |
| Paciente: | Buenos días, doctor. Me duele mucho un diente. |
| Dentista: | Indique dónde le duele. |
| Paciente: | Aquí atrás a la izquierda. |
| Dentista: | ¿Cuánto tiempo hace que visitó al dentista? |
| Paciente: | Hace tres años. |
| Dentista: | Es mucho tiempo. |
| Paciente: | Ya lo sé. Pero no he tenido tiempo. Y además no me gusta ir al dentista. |
| Dentista: | Bueno. Tengo que hacer radiografías. Abra. Diga, «ah». |

(Un poco más tarde.)

| | |
|---|---|
| Dentista: | El diente está muy mal. Para salvarlo será necesario hacer canal radicular. |

## Vocabulario

### El dentista, la dentista *(The dentist)*

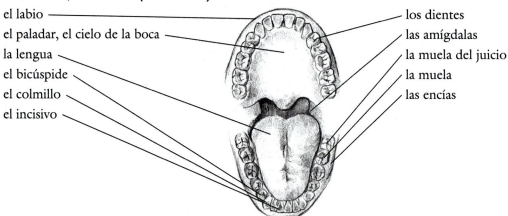

el labio

el paladar, el cielo de la boca

la lengua

el bicúspide

el colmillo

el incisivo

los dientes

las amígdalas

la muela del juicio

la muela

las encías

| | |
|---|---|
| el **absceso** | *abscess* |
| las **amígdalas** | *tonsils* |
| el **bicúspide** | *bicuspid* |
| el **canal radicular** | *root canal* |
| la **caries** (*pl.* las **caries**) | *cavity* |
| el **cepillo de dientes** | *toothbrush* |
| el **colmillo** | *eyetooth* |
| la **crema dental** | *toothpaste* |

| | |
|---|---|
| la **dentadura** | *denture* |
| los **dientes** | *teeth* |
| el **dolor de muelas** | *toothache* |
| el **empaste** | *filling* |
| las **encías** | *gums* |
| la **extracción** | *extraction* |
| el **higienista dental**, la **higienista dental** | *dental hygienist* |
| el **incisivo** | *incisor* |
| el **labio** | *lip* |
| la **lengua** | *tongue* |
| la **limpieza** | *cleaning* |
| la **muela** | *tooth* |
| la **muela del juicio** | *wisdom tooth* |
| el **paladar** | *palate* |
| el **taladro** | *drill* |
| | |
| **Abra.** | *Open.* |
| **cepillarse los dientes** | *to brush one's teeth* |
| **empastar** | *to fill* |
| **enjuagarse** | *to rinse* |
| **escupir** | *to spit* |
| **extraer** | *to extract* |
| **masticar** | *to chew* |
| **sacar** | *to take out, remove* |
| **taladrar** | *to drill* |
| | |
| **a la izquierda** | *on the left* |
| **a la derecha** | *on the right* |
| **atrás** | *in the back* |
| **de abajo** | *lower* |
| **de arriba** | *upper* |

# Nota

## «Los dientes» and «las muelas»

**Los dientes** and **las muelas** both mean *teeth*. **Dientes** is a more general term. **Muelas** is usually used to refer to a toothache or other problems with the teeth.

# Recuerde

**Tener que** means *to have to*. Use a form of **tener** and the infinitive of another verb. For example:

El dentista tiene que sacar la muela.     *The dentist has to take out the tooth.*

## Para practicar

Form sentences using the cues.

 **MODELO**    el dentista / sacar la muela
**El dentista tiene que sacar la muela.**

1. yo / cepillarme los dientes
2. el paciente / abrir la boca
3. los pacientes / escupir en la taza
4. Ud. / cerrar la boca
5. nosotros / visitar al dentista
6. el higienista dental / hacer la limpieza

### Continúa la conversación...

Paciente:    ¿Qué va a hacer, doctor?

Dentista:    Creo que tengo que extraer la muela.

Paciente:    ¿Me va a doler mucho?

Dentista:    Le voy a dar un anestético. Ud. no tendrá ningún dolor en absoluto.

Paciente:    Bueno. Entonces creo que es mejor sacar la muela.

## Sustituciones

Substitute the underlined word with the cued items. Be sure to make any other necessary changes.

**MODELO**    Creo que es mejor sacarle <u>la muela</u>.    el tumor
**Creo que es mejor sacarle <u>el tumor</u>.**

1. Creo que es mejor sacarle <u>la muela</u>.    el diente
2. Creo que es mejor <u>sacarle la muela</u>.    tomar el antibiótico
3. Creo que es mejor <u>sacarle la muela</u>.    hacer la operación
4. Creo que es <u>mejor</u> sacarle la muela.    más fácil
5. Creo que es <u>mejor</u> sacarle la muela.    peor

## Más sustituciones

Change the sentence using the cues.

**MODELO**    Tengo que visitar a la dentista porque <u>me duele una muela</u>.    necesito un examen
**Tengo que visitar a la dentista porque <u>necesito un examen</u>.**

1. me duelen las encías
2. necesito una limpieza

3. tengo una muela impactada
4. tengo una infección
5. tengo un absceso
6. necesito una dentadura
7. tengo mucha caries

## LA TERAPIA FÍSICA

## Conversación

Terapeuta: Buenos días, señor Gómez. ¿Cómo se siente Ud. hoy?

Paciente: Me siento mucho mejor, gracias. Pero todavía me duele la muñeca.

Terapeuta: Sí, por supuesto. Hace sólo una semana que Ud. viene aquí. Ahora, agárrese de la barra y tire.

Paciente: Eso duele mucho.

Terapeuta: No tire tan fuertemente. Ahora, haga un puño.

Paciente: Eso es un poco más fácil.

Terapeuta: Ahora, muévase los dedos, uno a uno. Primero el pulgar, luego el índice y después el meñique.

Paciente: Eso es muy difícil.

Terapeuta: Sin duda. Eso ya basta. No se olvide de la próxima cita, el martes a las dos y media. Practique los ejercicios en casa y pronto se sentirá mejor.

Paciente: Espero que sí. Muchas gracias. Hasta la próxima cita.

## Vocabulario

| | |
|---|---|
| la **muñeca** | *wrist* |
| la **barra** | *bar* |
| los **dedos** | *fingers* |
| el **pulgar** | *thumb* |
| el **índice** | *index finger* |
| el **meñique** | *little finger* |
| **Sin duda.** | *Without a doubt.* |

## Preguntas

1. ¿Cómo se siente el señor Gómez?
2. ¿Qué le duele?
3. ¿Por qué tiene que hacer tantas visitas a la terapeuta?
4. ¿Qué ejercicios hace?
5. ¿Cuándo es su próxima cita con la terapeuta?

# Vocabulario

| | |
|---|---|
| **Los mandatos** | *More Command Forms* |
| agárrese | *grab* |
| haga | *make; do* |
| muévase | *move* |
| no se olvide | *don't forget* |
| practique | *practice* |
| tire | *pull* |

| | |
|---|---|
| **Frases útiles con <u>que sí</u>** | *Useful Phrases with «que sí»* |
| Creo que sí. | *I believe so.* |
| Creo que no. | *I believe not.* |
| Espero que sí. | *I hope so.* |
| Espero que no. | *I hope not.* |
| Pienso que sí. | *I think so.* |
| Pienso que no. | *I think not.* |

# Sustituciones

Substitute the underlined words with the cued items. Be sure to make any other necessary changes.

> **MODELO**    Ud. se ha fracturado <u>la muñeca</u>.    el brazo
> **Ud. se ha fracturado <u>el brazo</u>.**

1. Ud. se ha fracturado <u>la muñeca</u>.    la pierna
2. Ud. se ha fracturado <u>la muñeca</u>.    la mano
3. <u>Ud.</u> se ha fracturado la muñeca.    tú
4. <u>Ud.</u> se ha fracturado la muñeca.    ellos
5. Ud. se ha <u>fracturado</u> la muñeca.    roto

# Para practicar

Review the parts of the body listed in Chapter 3. Then answer the question using the verb **moverse** and the cued responses. Remember to use the definite article (**el** or **la**) with parts of the body.

> **MODELO**    ¿Qué se mueve el paciente?
> **El paciente se mueve la cabeza.**

**moverse**    *to move*

| yo | **me muevo** | *I move* | nosotros/nosotras | **nos movemos** | *we move* |
| tú | **te mueves** | *you* (fam.) *move* | | | |
| él/ella | **se mueve** | *he/she moves* | ellos/ellas | **se mueven** | *they move* |
| Ud. | **se mueve** | *you* (form.) *move* | Uds. | **se mueven** | *you* (pl.) *move* |

1. ¿Qué se mueve el niño?

2. ¿Qué se mueve la muchacha?

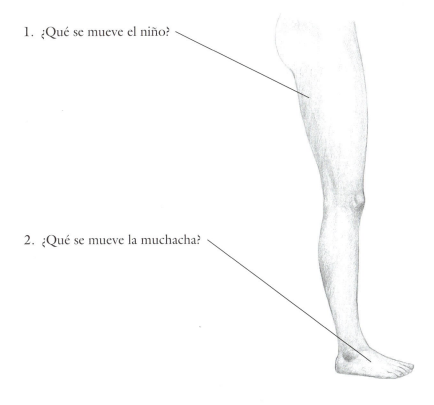

3. ¿Qué se mueve Ud.?

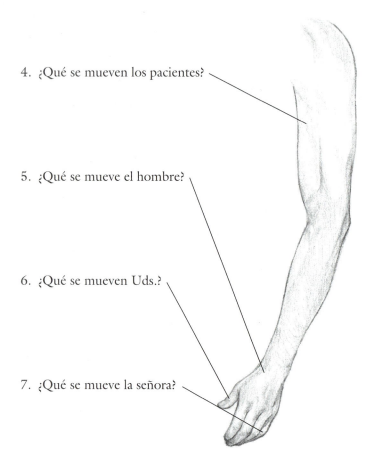

4. ¿Qué se mueven los pacientes?

5. ¿Qué se mueve el hombre?

6. ¿Qué se mueven Uds.?

7. ¿Qué se mueve la señora?

# Para practicar más

Change the following alternative commands to direct commands.

**MODELO**    Favor de empujar.
**Empuje.**

1. Favor de hacer un puño.
2. Favor de moverse los pies.
3. Favor de sentarse.
4. Favor de practicar los ejercicios.
5. Favor de agarrarse de la barra.
6. Favor de tirar de la barra.
7. Favor de moverse la muñeca.
8. Favor de usar las muletas.

# CUIDE SUS OJOS

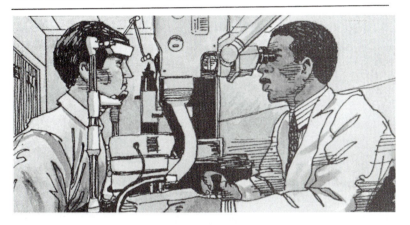

La diabetes es una de las principales causas de ceguera. Pero si usted controla debidamente el contenido de azúcar de su sangre y su presión arterial, reduce el riesgo de sufrir trastornos de la vista. Si se producen cambios en sus ojos, el tratamiento oportuno disminuye las posibilidades de que vaya perdiendo la visión.

Recuerde que:

- Aproximadamente 8 de cada 10 personas que han tenido diabetes durante 15 años sufren alteraciones en la parte posterior del ojo (la retina).

- La mayoría de esas personas no notan ningún cambio a medida que la afección avanza.

- Aunque no todas las alteraciones de la retina son graves, en algunos casos empeoran y pueden provocar disminución de la vista o inclusive ceguera.

- En consecuencia, se DEBE conceder atención especial al cuidado de los ojos de TODOS los enfermos de diabetes para descubrir a tiempo cualquier alteración.

## EL OPTOMETRISTA, LA OPTOMETRISTA

### Conversación

| | |
|---|---|
| Paciente: | ¿Va a examinarme los ojos ahora? |
| Optometrista: | Sí, pase por favor. Mire esta carta y dígame lo que ve. Ahora lea la segunda línea, por favor. |
| Paciente: | La segunda línea dice, O, F, D, P, R. |
| Optometrista: | Lea la tercera línea, por favor. |
| Paciente: | E, C, U, B, F. |
| Optometrista: | Y ahora la cuarta línea. |
| Paciente: | No puedo ver bien la cuarta línea. Está muy borrosa. |
| Optometrista: | ¿No puede ver ninguna letra en la cuarta línea? |
| Paciente: | No, todo se vuelve borroso después de la tercera línea. ¿Necesito usar lentes? |
| Optometrista: | Sí, señorita. Le voy a preparar una receta ahora. |
| Paciente: | ¿Cuándo estarán listos los lentes? |
| Optometrista: | Estarán listos dentro de una hora. |

## Vocabulario

| | |
|---|---|
| **borroso, -a** | *blurred* |
| **se vuelve** | *becomes* |
| los **lentes** | *eyeglasses* |
| **listos** | *ready* |

## Preguntas

1. ¿Qué línea no puede ver bien la señorita?
2. ¿Qué necesita la señorita?
3. ¿Cuándo estarán preparados los lentes?

## Sustituciones

Substitute the underlined words with the cued items. Be sure to make any other necessary changes.

| MODELO | ¿Va a examinarme Ud. los ojos ahora?     el estómago |
|---|---|
| | **¿Va a examinarme Ud. el estómago ahora?** |

1. ¿Va a examinarme Ud. los ojos ahora?     los pies
2. ¿Va a examinarme Ud. los ojos ahora?     la cabeza

3. ¿Va a examinarme <u>Ud.</u> los ojos ahora?     Uds.
4. ¿Va a examinarme <u>Ud.</u> los ojos ahora?     la doctora
5. ¿Va a examinar<u>me</u> Ud. los ojos ahora?     le

## Vocabulario

| Los mandatos | The Commands |
|---|---|
| dígame | *tell me* |
| lea | *read* |
| mire | *look at* |
| pase | *come in* |

## Más Vocabulario

| El optometrista, la optometrista | The Optometrist |
|---|---|
| los **anteojos** | *eyeglasses* |
| las **armaduras** | *frames* |
| el **astigmatismo** | *astigmatism* |
| los **bifocales** | *bifocals* |
| las **cataratas** | *cataracts* |
| los **espejuelos** | *eyeglasses* |
| las **gafas** | *eyeglasses* |
| las **gafas de sol** | *sunglasses* |
| el **glaucoma** | *glaucoma* |
| los **lentes de contacto** | *contact lenses* |
| la **miopia** | *myopia; nearsightedness* |
| la **vista** | *vision; sight* |

## Para practicar

Answer using the cues.

> **MODELO**    ¿Qué quiere el paciente?    bifocales
> **El paciente quiere bifocales.**

1. ¿Qué necesita la señorita?        lentes
2. ¿Qué quiere la paciente?          lentes de contacto
3. ¿Qué mira la señora?              la carta
4. ¿Qué lee el hombre?               las letras
5. ¿Qué prepara el optometrista?     la receta
6. ¿Qué quiere Ud.?                  gafas de sol
7. ¿Qué necesita Ud.?                lentes más fuertes

## Para practicar más

Answer each question using a direct object pronoun.

| MODELO | ¿Puede Ud. leer la primera línea de la carta? |
|---|---|

**Sí, la puedo leer.**

*or*

**No, no la puedo leer.**

1. ¿Quiere Ud. usar los bifocales?
2. ¿Quiere Ud. lentes de contacto?
3. ¿Prepara Ud. la receta ahora?
4. ¿Usa Ud. las gafas de sol todo el tiempo?
5. ¿Prepara la optometrista los lentes?
6. ¿Puede Ud. ver las letras?
7. ¿Lee el paciente la carta?
8. ¿Tiene Ud. una cita?

## NOTA CULTURAL — LATINOS IN THE HOSPITAL SETTING

Latinos newly arrived in the northern United States are often susceptible to illnesses which require hospitalization due to radical differences in living conditions and climates. Unfortunately, many Latinos resist hospitalization due to a fear of the unknown and the desire to cure themselves by using folk remedies or by gaining the assistance of a **curandero** *(folk healer)*. The delay often causes exacerbation of existing medical problems. Therefore, the patient and family members may benefit from encouragement and reassurance regarding the hospital setting.

 ## RESUMEN Y REPASO

## Vocabulario

| **El dentista, la dentista** | *The Dentist* |
|---|---|
| el **anestético local** | *local anesthetic* |
| el **bicúspide** | *bicuspid* |
| el **cielo de la boca** | *roof of the mouth* |
| el **colmillo** | *eyetooth* |
| la **corona** | *crown* |
| la **dentadura completa** | *complete denture* |
| la **dentadura parcial** | *partial denture* |
| el **esmalte** | *enamel* |
| los **incisivos** | *incisors* |
| la **lengua** | *tongue* |
| el **paladar** | *palate* |

| | |
|---|---|
| la **piorrea** | *pyhorrea* |
| el **puente** | *bridge* |
| la **raíz** | *root* |
| | |
| adormecer el nervio | *to deaden the nerve* |

**El terapeuta, la terapeuta**  *The Therapist*

| | |
|---|---|
| la **almohadilla eléctrica** | *electric heating pad* |
| las **aplicaciones calientes** | *hot compresses* |
| el **bastón** | *cane* |
| el **masaje** | *massage* |
| las **muletas** | *crutches* |
| la **parálisis** | *paralysis* |
| la **silla de ruedas** | *wheelchair* |
| el **soporte** | *brace* |
| el **torniquete** | *tourniquet* |
| | |
| empujar | *to push* |
| hacer un puño | *to make a fist* |
| poner en cabestrillo | *to put in a sling* |
| poner en yeso | *to put in a cast* |

**El optometrista, la optemtrista**  *The Optometrist*

| | |
|---|---|
| el **daltonismo** | *colorblindness* |
| la **hipermetropía** | *farsightedness* |
| la **retina** | *retina* |
| | |
| arreglar | *to adjust* |
| leer | *to read* |
| tener buena vista | *to have good vision* |
| usar | *to wear* |
| ver | *to see* |
| | |
| claro, -a | *clear* |

# Appendix A

## Everyday Greetings and Expressions of Courtesy

| | |
|---|---|
| ¡Hola! | *Hello!* |
| Buenos días. | *Good morning.* |
| Buenas tardes. | *Good afternoon.* |
| Buenas noches. | *Good night.* |
| Perdón; Perdóneme. | *Pardon; Pardon me.* |
| Con su permiso. | *Excuse me.* |
| Pase Ud. — adelante (same thing) | *Come in.* |
| Permítame presentarme. | *Allow me to introduce myself.* |
| Encantado,-a. | *Pleased (to meet you).* |
| Mucho gusto. | *It's a pleasure.* |
| Siéntese, por favor. | *Sit down, please.* |
| ¿Habla Ud. inglés? | *Do you speak English?* |
| ¿Me entiende? | *Do you understand me?* |
| ¿Cuál es su problema? Cuál es el problema | *What is your problem?* – what is the problem |
| ¿En qué puedo servirle? | *How can I help you?* |
| Lo siento mucho. | *I'm very sorry.* |
| ¿Cómo está Ud. hoy? | *How are you today?* |
| ¿Cómo se siente hoy? | *How do you feel today?* |
| ¿Cómo le va? | *How are you doing?* |
| ¿Qué le pasa? | *What's happening to you?* |
| ¿Qué tal? | *How are you?* |
| ¿Qué tal está su familia? | *How is your family?* |
| Bien, gracias, ¿y Ud.? | *Fine, thanks, and you?* |
| Hasta luego. | *See you later.* |
| Hasta mañana. | *See you tomorrow.* |
| Hasta la vista. | *See you later.* |
| Hasta la próxima cita. | *Until the next appointment.* |
| Adiós | *Good-bye.* |
| Gracias. | *Thank you.* |
| De nada; No hay de qué. por nada | *You're welcome.* |

## Admissions and General Information

| | |
|---|---|
| ¿Cómo se llama Ud.? | *What is your name?* |
| ¿Cuál es su dirección? | *What is your address?* |

| | |
|---|---|
| ¿Dónde vive Ud.? | *Where do you live?* |
| ¿Cuál es la zona postal? | *What is the zip code?* |
| ¿Cuál es su número de teléfono? | *What is your telephone number?* |
| ¿Dónde nació Ud.? | *Where were you born?* |
| ¿Es Ud. ciudadano americano? | *Are you an American citizen?* |
| ¿Cuándo nació Ud.? | *When were you born?* |
| ¿Qué edad tiene Ud.? | *What is your age?* |
| ¿Cuántos años tiene Ud.? | *How old are you?* |
| ¿Es Ud. soltero, -a? | *Are you single?* |
| ¿Es Ud. casado, -a? | *Are you married?* |
| ¿Es Ud. divorciado, -a? | *Are you divorced?* |
| ¿Es Ud. separado, -a? | *Are you separated?* |
| ¿Es Ud. viudo? | *Are you a widower?* |
| ¿Es Ud. viuda? | *Are you a widow?* |
| ¿Cuál es su religión? | *What is your religion?* |
| ¿Tiene Ud. trabajo? | *Do you have a job?* |
| ¿Cuál es su trabajo? | *What is your job?* |
| ¿Qué trabajo hace Ud.? | *What work do you do?* |
| ¿En qué trabaja Ud.? | *What work do you do?* |
| ¿Quién es su pariente (familiar) más cercano? | *Who is your nearest relative?* |
| ¿Tiene Ud. seguro? | *Do you have insurance?* |
| ¿Cuál es su compañía de seguro? | *What is your insurance company?* |
| ¿Tiene Ud. Medicare? | *Do you have Medicare?* |
| ¿Tiene Ud. Medicaid? | *Do you have Medicaid?* |
| ¿Tiene Ud. un médico de familia? | *Do you have a family doctor?* |
| ¿Están vivos sus padres? | *Are your parents living?* |
| ¿Están muertos sus padres? | *Are your parents deceased?* |
| ¿Cómo murió su madre? | *How did your mother die?* |
| ¿Cómo murió su padre? | *How did your father die?* |
| ¿Tiene Ud. hermanos? | *Do you have any brothers or sisters?* |
| ¿Cuántos años tiene su esposo (esposa)? | *How old is your husband (wife)?* |
| ¿Tiene Ud. hijos? | *Do you have any children?* |
| ¿Cuántos años tienen sus hijos? | *How old are your children?* |
| ¿Ha asistido Ud. a la escuela primaria, secundaria, a la universidad? | *Have you attended elementary school, high school, college?* |

*[handwritten annotations: "which" next to "¿Cuál es la zona postal?"; "Norte (NorthAmerican)" next to "americano"; "(niños)" next to "hijos"]*

## Commands

| | |
|---|---|
| Abra la boca. | *Open your mouth.* |
| Acérquese a la máquina. | *Go up to the machine.* |
| Acuéstese boca abajo (arriba). | *Lie face down (up).* |
| Agárrese de la barra. | *Hold on to the bar.* |
| Aplíquese esto. | *Apply this.* |
| Beba esto. | *Drink this.* |
| Cálmese. | *Calm down.* |
| Cambie el vendaje. | *Change the dressing.* |
| Camine despacio. | *Walk slowly.* |

| | |
|---|---|
| Colóquese aquí. | *Stand here.* |
| Coma ahora. | *Eat now.* |
| Consulte con el especialista. | *Consult with the specialist.* |
| Deje de fumar. | *Stop smoking.* |
| Déjeme registrarle el pulso | *Let me take your pulse* |
| (tomarle la temperatura, la presión). | *(take your temperature, your blood pressure).* |
| Desnúdese (Desvístase), por favor. | *Please undress.* |
| Diga, «Ah». | *Say, "Ah."* |
| Dígame... | *Tell me . . .* |
| Dóblese hacia adelante (hacia atrás). | *Bend forward (backward).* |
| Doble la cabeza a la derecha (a la izquierda). | *Bend your head to the right (to the left).* |
| Duerma más. | *Sleep more.* |
| Enséñeme dónde le duele. | *Show me where it hurts.* |
| Escriba su dirección. | *Write your address.* |
| Espere aquí (en la sala de espera, etc.). | *Wait here (in the waiting room, etc.).* |
| Firme la autorización (para la cirugía). | *Sign the authorization (for the surgery).* |
| Haga un puño. | *Make a fist.* |
| Indíqueme dónde le duele. | *Show me where it hurts.* |
| Llámeme por teléfono. | *Phone me.* |
| Llene los formularios (las recetas). | *Fill out the forms (Fill the prescriptions).* |
| Levántese. | *Get up.* |
| Levante los brazos (las piernas, etc.). | *Raise your arms (legs, etc.).* |
| Mantenga la respiración. | *Hold your breath.* |
| Mastique las píldoras. | *Chew the pills.* |
| Mire hacia arriba (abajo). | *Look up (down).* |
| Muéstreme dónde le duele. | *Show me where it hurts.* |
| Mueva los pies (los dedos de los pies). | *Move your feet (toes, etc.).* |
| No se mueva. | *Don't move.* |
| No se preocupe. | *Don't worry.* |
| No se queje tanto. | *Don't complain so much.* |
| No tenga miedo. | *Don't be afraid.* |
| Pague ahora (en la oficina, etc.). | *Pay now (in the office, etc.).* |
| Párese (Póngase de pie). | *Stand up.* |
| Póngase la ropa (la blusa, la camisa, etc.). | *Put on your clothes (blouse, shirt, etc.).* |
| Quítese la ropa. | *Take off your clothes.* |
| Respire profundamente. | *Breathe deeply.* |
| Salga temprano. | *Leave early.* |
| Saque la lengua. | *Stick out your tongue.* |
| Señáleme dónde le duele. | *Show me where it hurts.* |
| Siéntese. | *Sit down.* |
| Siga la dieta (las instrucciones). | *Follow the diet (the instructions).* |
| Súbase a la mesa (en la balanza). | *Get on the table (the scale).* |
| Tenga cuidado. | *Be careful.* |
| Tome esta medicina. | *Take this medicine.* |
| Toque el timbre. | *Ring the bell.* |
| Tosa. | *Cough.* |
| Trague esto. | *Swallow this.* |

| | |
|---|---|
| Trate de moverse las piernas (los brazos, etc.). | *Try to move your legs (arms, etc.).* |
| Vaya a la clínica, (a la farmacia, etc.). | *Go to the clinic, (to the pharmacy, etc.).* |
| Venga mañana (pasado mañana, etc.). | *Come tomorrow (the day after tomorrow, etc.).* |
| Vuelva en una semana (en un mes, etc.). | *Return in a week (in a month, etc.).* |
| Vuélvase a la derecha (a la izquierda). | *Turn to the right (left).* |

## General Questions about Health: Present Illness, Past Illness, Accidents, Diseases

| | |
|---|---|
| ¿Tiene dolor? | *Are you in pain?* |
| ¿Dónde tiene dolor? | *Where do you have pain?* |
| ¿Qué le duele? | *What is hurting you?* |
| ¿Qué le pasó? | *What happened to you?* |
| ¿Tuvo un accidente? | *Did you have an accident?* |
| ¿Se desmayó? | *Did you faint?* |
| ¿Perdió el conocimiento? | *Did you lose consciousness?* |
| ¿Se cayó? | *Did you fall?* |
| ¿Cómo se cayó? | *How did you fall?* |
| ¿Dónde se cayó? | *Where did you fall?* |
| ¿Está bajo tratamiento de un médico? | *Are you under doctor's care?* |
| ¿Duerme bien? | *Do you sleep well?* |
| ¿Fuma mucho? | *Do you smoke a lot?* |
| ¿Toma medicina? | *Are you taking medicine?* |
| ¿Toma bebidas alcohólicas? | *Do you drink alcoholic beverages?* |
| ¿Toma drogas? | *Are you on drugs?* |
| ¿Se cansa fácilmente? | *Do you tire easily?* |
| ¿Tiene calor? | *Are you warm?* |
| ¿Tiene catarro? | *Do you have a cold?* |
| ¿Tiene fiebre (calentura)? | *Do you have a fever?* |
| ¿Tiene frío? | *Are you cold?* |
| ¿Tiene hambre? | *Are you hungry?* |
| ¿Tiene hinchazón en las piernas (en los tobillos, etc.)? | *Do you have swelling in your legs (ankles, etc.)?* |
| ¿Tiene irritación de la piel? | *Do you have skin irritation?* |
| ¿Tiene mareos? | *Are you dizzy?* |
| ¿Tiene náuseas? | *Are you nauseous?* |
| ¿Tiene nerviosidad? | *Are you nervous?* |
| ¿Tiene sangre en la expectoración (en la orina)? | *Do you have blood in your expectoration (in your urine)?* |
| ¿Tiene sed? | *Are you thirsty?* |
| ¿Tiene tos? | *Do you have a cough?* |
| ¿Tiene tos con flema? | *Do you have a cough with phlegm?* |
| ¿Tiene diarrea? | *Do you have diarrhea?* |
| ¿Está estreñido,-a? | *Are you constipated?* |
| ¿Tiene problemas con la digestión (la respiración)? | *Do you have digestive (respiratory) problems?* |

| | |
|---|---|
| ¿Sufre de enfermedades del corazón (de los pulmones, de los riñones)? | *Do you suffer from heart (lung, kidney) disease?* |
| ¿Sufre de enfermedades venéreas? | *Do you suffer from venereal diseases?* |
| ¿Sufre de catarros frecuentes? | *Do you suffer from frequent colds?* |
| ¿Sufre de bronquitis? | *Do you suffer from bronchitis?* |
| ¿Sufre de laringitis? | *Do you suffer from laryngitis?* |
| ¿Sufre de cáncer? | *Are you suffering from cancer?* |
| ¿Sufre de leucemia? | *Are you suffering from leukemia?* |
| ¿Sufre de los nervios? | *Are you suffering from nervousness?* |
| ¿Sufre de la alta (baja) presión? | *Are you suffering from high blood pressure (low blood pressure)?* |
| ¿Sufre de úlceras? | *Are you suffering from ulcers?* |
| ¿Sufrió un ataque al corazón? | *Did you have a heart attack?* |
| ¿Ha tenido (padecido de, sufrido de) | *Have you had (suffered from)* |
| alergias? | *allergies?* |
| anemia? | *anemia?* |
| apendicitis? | *appendicitis?* |
| artritis? | *arthritis?* |
| asma? | *asthma?* |
| bursitis? | *bursitis?* |
| cólera? | *cholera?* |
| colitis? | *colitis?* |
| diabetis? | *diabetes?* |
| difteria? | *diphtheria?* |
| disentería? | *dysentery?* |
| epilepsia? | *epilepsy?* |
| fiebre amarilla? | *yellow fever?* |
| fiebre de heno? | *hay fever?* |
| fiebre reumática? | *rheumatic fever?* |
| gonorrea? | *gonorrhea?* |
| hepatitis? | *hepatitis?* |
| ictericia? | *jaundice?* |
| malaria? | *malaria?* |
| meningitis? | *meningitis?* |
| paperas? | *mumps?* |
| pleuresía? | *pleurisy?* |
| pulmonía? | *pneumonia?* |
| rubéola? | *rubella, German measles?* |
| sarampión? | *measles?* |
| sífilis? | *syphilis?* |
| tifoidea? | *typhoid fever?* |
| tos ferina? | *whooping cough?* |
| tuberculosis? | *tuberculosis?* |
| viruela? | *smallpox?* |
| viruelas locas (varicela)? | *chicken pox?* |

# Appendix B
## Verbs and Tenses

## Present Indicative Tense

### Regular -ar Verbs

**hablar**, *to speak:* **hablo**, *I speak, I am speaking, I do speak*

| | | | | | | |
|---|---|---|---|---|---|---|
| yo | **hablo** | *I speak* | | nosotros/nosotras | **hablamos** | *we speak* |
| tú | **hablas** | *you* (fam.) *speak* | | | | |
| él/ella | **habla** | *he/she speaks* | | ellos/ellas | **hablan** | *they speak* |
| Ud. | **habla** | *you* (form.) *speak* | | Uds. | **hablan** | *you* (pl.) *speak* |

### Regular -er Verbs

**comer**, *to eat:* **como**, *I eat, I am eating, I do eat*

| | | | | | | |
|---|---|---|---|---|---|---|
| yo | **como** | *I eat* | | nosotros/nosotras | **comemos** | *we eat* |
| tú | **comes** | *you* (fam.) *eat* | | | | |
| él/ella | **come** | *he/she eats* | | ellos/ellas | **comen** | *they eat* |
| Ud. | **come** | *you* (form.) *eat* | | Uds. | **comen** | *you* (pl.) *eat* |

### Regular -ir Verbs

**vivir**, *to live:* **vivo**, *I live, I do live, I am living*

| | | | | | | |
|---|---|---|---|---|---|---|
| yo | **vivo** | *I live* | | nosotros/nosotras | **vivimos** | *we live* |
| tú | **vives** | *you* (fam.) *live* | | | | |
| él/ella | **vive** | *he/she lives* | | ellos/ellas | **viven** | *they live* |
| Ud. | **vive** | *you* (form.) *live* | | Uds. | **viven** | *you* (pl.) *live* |

## Verbs Irregular Only in the First Person Singular

| caer | to fall | caigo | caes | cae | caemos | caen |
|------|---------|-------|------|-----|--------|------|
| conocer | to know | conozco | conoces | conoce | conocemos | conocen |
| dar | to give | doy | das | da | damos | dan |
| hacer | to do, make | hago | haces | hace | hacemos | hacen |
| ofrecer | to offer | ofrezco | ofreces | ofrece | ofrecemos | ofrecen |
| padecer | to suffer | padezco | padeces | padece | padecemos | padecen |
| poner | to put, place | pongo | pones | pone | ponemos | ponen |
| saber | to know | sé | sabes | sabe | sabemos | saben |
| salir | to leave | salgo | sales | sale | salimos | salen |
| ver | to see | veo | ves | ve | vemos | ven |

## Other Irregular Verbs

| acostar | to put to bed | acuesto | acuestas | acuesta | acostamos | acuestan |
|---------|---------------|---------|----------|---------|-----------|----------|
| almorzar | to have lunch | almuerzo | almuerzas | almuerza | almorzamos | almuerzan |
| cerrar | to close | cierro | cierras | cierra | cerramos | cierran |
| contar | to count | cuento | cuentas | cuenta | contamos | cuentan |
| costar | to cost | — | — | cuesta | — | cuestan |
| decir | to say, tell | digo | dices | dice | decimos | dicen |
| despertar | to awaken | despierto | despiertas | despierta | despertamos | despiertan |
| doler | to hurt | — | — | duele | — | duelen |
| dormir | to sleep | duermo | duermes | duerme | dormimos | duermen |
| encender | to light | enciendo | enciendes | enciende | encendemos | encienden |
| entender | to understand | entiendo | entiendes | entiende | entendemos | entienden |
| estar | to be | estoy | estás | está | estamos | están |
| ir | to go | voy | vas | va | vamos | van |
| morir | to die | muero | mueres | muere | morimos | mueren |
| mostrar | to show | muestro | muestras | muestra | mostramos | muestran |
| mover | to move | muevo | mueves | mueve | movemos | mueven |
| pensar | to think | pienso | piensas | piensa | pensamos | piensan |
| perder | to lose | pierdo | pierdes | pierde | perdemos | pierden |
| poder | to be able | puedo | puedes | puede | podemos | pueden |
| preferir | to prefer | prefiero | prefieres | prefiere | preferimos | prefieren |
| querer | to wish, want | quiero | quieres | quiere | queremos | quieren |
| seguir | to follow | sigo | sigues | sigue | seguimos | siguen |
| sentir | to feel | siento | sientes | siente | sentimos | sienten |
| ser | to be | soy | eres | es | somos | son |
| tener | to have | tengo | tienes | tiene | tenemos | tienen |
| venir | to come | vengo | vienes | viene | venimos | vienen |
| volver | to return | vuelvo | vuelves | vuelve | volvemos | vuelven |

# Preterite Tense

## Regular -ar Verbs

hablar, *to speak:* hablé, *I spoke*

| | | | | | |
|---|---|---|---|---|---|
| yo | **hablé** | *I spoke* | nosotros/nosotras | **hablamos** | *we spoke* |
| tú | **hablaste** | *you* (fam.) *spoke* | | | |
| él/ella | **habló** | *he/she spoke* | ellos/ellas | **hablaron** | *they spoke* |
| Ud. | **habló** | *you* (form.) *spoke* | Uds. | **hablaron** | *you* (pl.) *spoke* |

## Regular -er Verbs

comer, *to eat:* comí, *I ate*

| | | | | | |
|---|---|---|---|---|---|
| yo | **comí** | *I ate* | nosotros/nosotras | **comimos** | *we ate* |
| tú | **comiste** | *you* (fam.) *ate* | | | |
| él/ella | **comió** | *he/she ate* | ellos/ellas | **comieron** | *they ate* |
| Ud. | **comió** | *you* (form.) *ate* | Uds. | **comieron** | *you* (pl.) *ate* |

## Regular -ir Verbs

vivir, *to live:* viví, *I lived*

| | | | | | |
|---|---|---|---|---|---|
| yo | **viví** | *I lived* | nosotros/nosotras | **vivimos** | *we lived* |
| tú | **viviste** | *you* (fam.) *lived* | | | |
| él/ella | **vivió** | *he/she lived* | ellos/ellas | **vivieron** | *they lived* |
| Ud. | **vivió** | *you* (form.) *lived* | Uds. | **vivieron** | *you* (pl.) *lived* |

## Verbs Irregular Only in the First Person Singular

| | | | | | | |
|---|---|---|---|---|---|---|
| **aplicar** | *to apply* | apliqué | aplicaste | aplicó | aplicamos | aplicaron |
| **buscar** | *to look for* | busqué | buscaste | buscó | buscamos | buscaron |
| **explicar** | *to explain* | expliqué | explicaste | explicó | explicamos | explicaron |
| **indicar** | *to indicate* | indiqué | indicaste | indicó | indicamos | indicaron |
| **llegar** | *to arrive* | llegué | llegaste | llegó | llegamos | llegaron |
| **masticar** | *to chew* | mastiqué | masticaste | masticó | masticamos | masticaron |
| **pagar** | *to pay* | pagué | pagaste | pagó | pagamos | pagaron |
| **sacar** | *to take out* | saqué | sacaste | sacó | sacamos | sacaron |
| **tocar** | *to touch* | toqué | tocaste | tocó | tocamos | tocaron |
| **tragar** | *to swallow* | tragué | tragaste | tragó | tragamos | tragaron |

## Other Irregular Verbs

| | | | | | |
|---|---|---|---|---|---|
| **caer** | *to fall* | caí | caíste | cayó | caímos | cayeron |
| **creer** | *to believe* | creí | creíste | creyó | creímos | creyeron |
| **dar** | *to give* | di | diste | dio | dimos | dieron |
| **decir** | *to say, tell* | dije | dijiste | dijo | dijimos | dijeron |
| **estar** | *to be* | estuve | estuviste | estuvo | estuvimos | estuvieron |
| **hacer** | *to do, make* | hice | hiciste | hizo | hicimos | hicieron |
| **ir** | *to go* | fui | fuiste | fue | fuimos | fueron |
| **leer** | *to read* | leí | leíste | leyó | leímos | leyeron |
| **morir** | *to die* | morí | moriste | murió | morimos | murieron |
| **poder** | *to be able* | pude | pudiste | pudo | pudimos | pudieron |
| **poner** | *to put* | puse | pusiste | puso | pusimos | pusieron |
| **querer** | *to wish, want* | quise | quisiste | quiso | quisimos | quisieron |
| **saber** | *to know* | supe | supiste | supo | supimos | supieron |
| **seguir** | *to follow* | seguí | seguiste | siguió | seguimos | siguieron |
| **ser** | *to be* | fui | fuiste | fue | fuimos | fueron |
| **tener** | *to have* | tuve | tuviste | tuvo | tuvimos | tuvieron |
| **venir** | *to come* | vine | viniste | vino | vinimos | vinieron |
| **ver** | *to see* | vi | viste | vio | vimos | vieron |

# Imperfect Tense

## Regular -ar Verbs

**hablar**, *to speak:* **hablaba**, *I was speaking, I used to speak*

| | | | | | |
|---|---|---|---|---|---|
| yo | **hablaba** | *I was speaking* | nosotros/nosotras | **hablábamos** | *we were speaking* |
| tú | **hablabas** | *you* (fam.) *were speaking* | | | |
| él/ella | **hablaba** | *he/she was speaking* | ellos/ellas | **hablaban** | *they were speaking* |
| Ud. | **hablaba** | *you* (form.) *were speaking* | Uds. | **hablaban** | *you* (pl.) *were speaking* |

## Regular -er Verbs

**comer**, *to eat:* **comía**, *I was eating, I used to eat*

| | | | | | |
|---|---|---|---|---|---|
| yo | **comía** | *I was eating* | nosotros/nosotras | **comíamos** | *we were eating* |
| tú | **comías** | *you* (fam.) *were eating* | | | |
| él/ella | **comía** | *he/she was eating* | ellos/ellas | **comían** | *they were eating* |
| Ud. | **comía** | *you* (form.) *were eating* | Uds. | **comían** | *you* (pl.) *were eating* |

## Regular -ir Verbs

**vivir,** *to live:* **vivía,** *I was living, I used to live*

| | | | | | |
|---|---|---|---|---|---|
| yo | **vivía** | *I was living* | nosotros/nosotras | **vivíamos** | *we were living* |
| tú | **vivías** | *you* (fam.) *were living* | | | |
| él/ella | **vivía** | *he/she was living* | ellos/ellas | **vivían** | *they were living* |
| Ud. | **vivía** | *you* (form.) *were living* | Uds. | **vivían** | *you* (pl.) *were living* |

## Irregular Verbs

| | | | | | | |
|---|---|---|---|---|---|---|
| **ir** | *to go* | iba | ibas | iba | íbamos | iban |
| **ser** | *to be* | era | eras | era | éramos | eran |
| **ver** | *to see* | veía | veías | veía | veíamos | veían |

# Future Tense

## Regular -ar Verbs

**hablar,** *to speak:* **hablaré,** *I will speak*

| | | | | | |
|---|---|---|---|---|---|
| yo | **hablaré** | *I will speak* | nosotros/nosotras | **hablaremos** | *we will speak* |
| tú | **hablarás** | *you* (fam.) *will speak* | | | |
| él/ella | **hablará** | *he/she will speak* | ellos/ellas | **hablarán** | *they will speak* |
| Ud. | **hablará** | *you* (form.) *will speak* | Uds. | **hablarán** | *you* (pl.) *will speak* |

## Regular -er Verbs

**comer,** *to eat:* **comeré,** *I will eat*

| | | | | | |
|---|---|---|---|---|---|
| yo | **comeré** | *I will eat* | nosotros/nosotras | **comeremos** | *we will eat* |
| tú | **comerás** | *you* (fam.) *will eat* | | | |
| él/ella | **comerá** | *he/she will eat* | ellos/ellas | **comerán** | *they will eat* |
| Ud. | **comerá** | *you* (form.) *will eat* | Uds. | **comerán** | *you* (pl.) *will eat* |

## Regular -ir Verbs

**vivir,** *to live:* **viviré,** *I will live*

| | | | | | |
|---|---|---|---|---|---|
| yo | **viviré** | *I will live* | nosotros/nosotras | **viviremos** | *we will live* |
| tú | **vivirás** | *you* (fam.) *will live* | | | |
| él/ella | **vivirá** | *he/she will live* | ellos/ellas | **vivirán** | *they will live* |
| Ud. | **vivirá** | *you* (form.) *will live* | Uds. | **vivirán** | *you* (pl.) *will live* |

## Irregular Verbs

| | | | | | | |
|---|---|---|---|---|---|---|
| **decir** | *to say, tell* | diré | dirás | dirá | diremos | dirán |
| **haber** | *to have* (aux.) | habré | habrás | habrá | habremos | habrán |
| **hacer** | *to do, make* | haré | harás | hará | haremos | harán |
| **poder** | *to be able* | podré | podrás | podrá | podremos | podrán |
| **poner** | *to put, place* | pondré | pondrás | pondrá | pondremos | pondrán |
| **querer** | *to wish, want* | querré | querrás | querrá | querremos | querrán |
| **saber** | *to know* | sabré | sabrás | sabrá | sabremos | sabrán |
| **salir** | *to leave* | saldré | saldrás | saldrá | saldremos | saldrán |
| **tener** | *to have* | tendré | tendrás | tendrá | tendremos | tendrán |
| **venir** | *to come* | vendré | vendrás | vendrá | vendremos | vendrán |

# Present Progressive Tense

## Regular -ar Verbs

**hablar,** *to speak:* **estoy hablando,** *I am speaking*

| | | | | | |
|---|---|---|---|---|---|
| yo | **estoy hablando** | *I am speaking* | nosotros/nosotras | **estamos hablando** | *we are speaking* |
| tú | **estás hablando** | *you* (fam.) *are speaking* | | | |
| él/ella | **está hablando** | *he/she is speaking* | ellos/ellas | **están hablando** | *they are speaking* |
| Ud. | **está hablando** | *you* (form.) *are speaking* | Uds. | **están hablando** | *you* (pl.) *are speaking* |

## Regular -er Verbs

**comer,** *to eat:* **estoy comiendo,** *I am eating*

| | | | | | |
|---|---|---|---|---|---|
| yo | **estoy comiendo** | *I am eating* | nosotros/nosotras | **estamos comiendo** | *we are eating* |
| tú | **estás comiendo** | *you* (fam.) *are eating* | | | |
| él/ella | **está comiendo** | *he/she is eating* | ellos/ellas | **están comiendo** | *they are eating* |
| Ud. | **está comiendo** | *you* (form.) *are eating* | Uds. | **están comiendo** | *you* (pl.) *are eating* |

## Regular -ir Verbs

**vivir,** *to live:* **estoy viviendo,** *I am living*

| | | | | | |
|---|---|---|---|---|---|
| yo | **estoy viviendo** | *I am living* | nosotros/nosotras | **estamos viviendo** | *we are living* |
| tú | **estás viviendo** | *you* (fam.) *are living* | | | |
| él/ella | **está viviendo** | *he/she is living* | ellos/ellas | **están viviendo** | *they are living* |
| Ud. | **está viviendo** | *you* (form.) *are living* | Uds. | **están viviendo** | *you* (pl.) *are living* |

## Irregular Gerunds

| | | | |
|---|---|---|---|
| caer | *to fall* | **cayendo** | *falling* |
| creer | *to believe* | **creyendo** | *believing* |
| decir | *to say, tell* | **diciendo** | *saying, telling* |
| leer | *to read* | **leyendo** | *reading* |
| morir | *to die* | **muriendo** | *dying* |
| seguir | *to follow* | **siguiendo** | *following* |
| sentir | *to feel* | **sintiendo** | *feeling* |
| venir | *to come* | **viniendo** | *coming* |

# Present Perfect Tense

## Regular -ar Verbs

**hablar,** *to speak:* **he hablado,** *I have spoken*

| | | | | | |
|---|---|---|---|---|---|
| yo | **he hablado** | *I have spoken* | nosotros/nosotras | **hemos hablado** | *we have spoken* |
| tú | **has hablado** | *you* (fam.) *have spoken* | | | |
| él/ella | **ha hablado** | *he/she has spoken* | ellos/ellas | **han hablado** | *they have spoken* |
| Ud. | **ha hablado** | *you* (form.) *have spoken* | Uds. | **han hablado** | *you* (pl.) *have spoken* |

## Regular -er Verbs

**comer,** *to eat:* **he comido,** *I have eaten*

| yo | he comido | I have eaten | nosotros/nosotras | hemos comido | we have eaten |
|---|---|---|---|---|---|
| tú | has comido | you (fam.) have eaten | | | |
| él/ella | ha comido | he/she has eaten | ellos/ellas | han comido | they have eaten |
| Ud. | ha comido | you (form.) have eaten | Uds. | han comido | you (pl.) have eaten |

## Regular -ir Verbs

**vivir,** *to live:* **he vivido,** *I have lived*

| yo | he vivido | I have lived | nosotros/nosotras | hemos vivido | we have lived |
|---|---|---|---|---|---|
| tú | has vivido | you (fam.) have lived | | | |
| él/ella | ha vivido | he/she has lived | ellos/ellas | han vivido | they have lived |
| Ud. | ha vivido | you (form.) have lived | Uds. | han vivido | you (pl.) have lived |

## Irregular Past Participles

| abrir | to open | abierto | opened |
|---|---|---|---|
| cubrir | to cover | cubierto | covered |
| decir | to say, tell | dicho | said, told |
| escribir | to write | escrito | written |
| hacer | to do, make | hecho | done, made |
| morir | to die | muerto | died |
| poner | to put, place | puesto | put, placed |
| ver | to see | visto | seen |

# Subjunctive

## Regular -ar Verbs

**examinar,** *to examine:* (**que**) **examine,** *(that) I examine*

| | | | | | |
|---|---|---|---|---|---|
| (que) yo | **examine** | *(that) I examine* | (que) nosotros/nosotras | **examinemos** | *(that) we examine* |
| (que) tú | **examines** | *(that) you* (fam.) *examine* | | | |
| (que) él/ella | **examine** | *(that) he/she examine* | (que) ellos/ellas | **examinen** | *(that) they examine* |
| (que) Ud. | **examine** | *(that) you* (form.) *examine* | (que) Uds. | **examinen** | *(that) you* (pl.) *examine* |

## Regular -er Verbs

**comer,** *to eat:* (**que**) **coma,** *(that) I eat*

| | | | | | |
|---|---|---|---|---|---|
| (que) yo | **coma** | *(that) I eat* | (que) nosotros/nosotras | **comamos** | *(that) we eat* |
| (que) tú | **comas** | *(that) you* (fam.) *eat* | | | |
| (que) él/ella | **coma** | *(that) he/she eat* | (que) ellos/ellas | **coman** | *(that) they eat* |
| (que) Ud. | **coma** | *(that) you* (form.) *eat* | (que) Uds. | **coman** | *(that) you* (pl.) *eat* |

## Regular -ir Verbs

**escribir,** *to write:* (**que**) **escriba,** *(that) I write*

| | | | | | |
|---|---|---|---|---|---|
| (que) yo | **escriba** | *(that) I write* | (que) nosotros/nosotras | **escribamos** | *(that) we write* |
| (que) tú | **escribas** | *(that) you* (fam.) *write* | | | |
| (que) él/ella | **escriba** | *(that) he/she write* | (que) ellos/ellas | **escriban** | *(that) they write* |
| (que) Ud. | **escriba** | *(that) you* (form.) *write* | (que) Uds. | **escriban** | *(that) you* (pl.) *write* |

## Irregular Verbs

Verbs that are irregular in the **yo** form of the present tense usually have the same irregularity in the subjunctive. Remember to adjust the ending for the subjunctive mood.

**tener,** *to have*

> *present tense:* yo **tengo**
> *subjunctive:* **tenga, tengas, tenga, tengamos, tengan**

**poner,** *to put*

> *present tense:* yo **pongo**
> *subjunctive:* **ponga, pongas, ponga, pongamos, pongan**

**conocer,** *to know, to be acquainted with*

> *present tense:* yo **conozco**
> *subjunctive:* **conozca, conozcas, conozca, conozcamos, conozcan**

# Appendix C

## Parts of the Body

### La cabeza *(The head)*

(1) scalp
(2) hair
(3) forehead
(4) eyebrow
(5) eye
(6) temple
(7) (outer) ear
(8) (inner) ear
(9) cheek
(10) nose
(11) nostrils
(12) jaw
(13) mouth
(14) chin
(15) neck
(16) Adam's apple

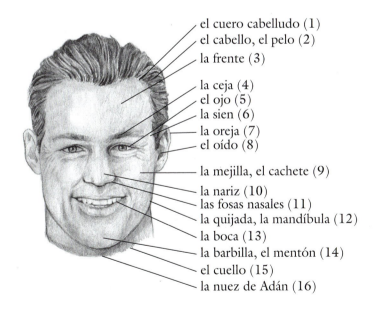

el cuero cabelludo (1)
el cabello, el pelo (2)
la frente (3)
la ceja (4)
el ojo (5)
la sien (6)
la oreja (7)
el oído (8)
la mejilla, el cachete (9)
la nariz (10)
las fosas nasales (11)
la quijada, la mandíbula (12)
la boca (13)
la barbilla, el mentón (14)
el cuello (15)
la nuez de Adán (16)

Also:

| | |
|---|---|
| el **cerebro** | *brain* |
| la **nuca** | *nape of the neck* |
| los **párpados** | *eyelids* |
| las **pestañas** | *eyelashes* |

# La boca *(The mouth)* ✓

(1)  lip
(2)  gums
(3)  palate
(4)  tonsils
(5)  tongue
(6)  teeth
(7)  wisdom tooth
(8)  molar
(9)  bicuspid
(10) eyetooth
(11) incisor

Also:

| la **corona** | *crown* |
| la **dentadura postiza** | *false teeth* (dentures) |
| el **diente de leche** | *milk tooth* (Canine) |
| el **puente** | *bridge* |

el labio (1)
las encías (2)
el paladar, el cielo — { The Sky or Ceiling of the mouth }
de la boca (3)
las amígdalas (4)
la lengua (5)
los dientes (6)   el diente
la muela del juicio (7)
la muela (8)
el bicúspide (9)
el colmillo (10)
el incisivo (11)

# El brazo *(The arm)* ✓

(1)  elbow
(2)  forearm
(3)  wrist
(4)  hand
(5)  thumb
(6)  index finger
(7)  middle finger
(8)  ring finger
(9)  little finger

Also:

| el **dorso de la mano** | *the back of the hand* |
| la **palma de la mano** | *palm* |
| el **puño** | *fist* |
| el **nudillo** | *knuckle* |
| la **uña** | *fingernail* → Toenail |

las palmas de las manos

el codo (1)

el antebrazo (2)

la muñeca (3)

la mano (4)

el dedo pulgar (5)
los dedos pulgares
el dedo índice (6)
los dedos índices
el dedo medio (7)
los dedos medios
el dedo anular (8)

el dedo meñique (9)

# La pierna *(The leg)* ✓

(1) thigh
(2) kneecap
(3) knee
(4) shin
(5) calf
(6) ankle
(7) foot
(8) heel
(9) sole
(10) instep
(11) toes

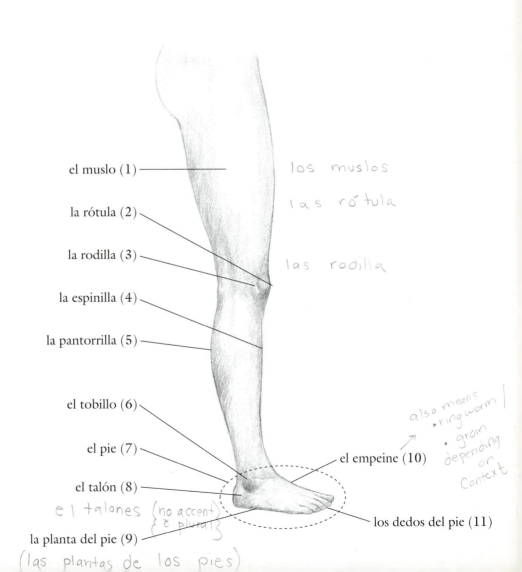

el muslo (1) ——————

*los muslos*

*las rótula*

la rótula (2)

la rodilla (3)

*las rodilla*

la espinilla (4)

la pantorrilla (5)

el tobillo (6)

el pie (7)

*also means*
*• ringworm*
*↗     • groin*
*depending*
*on*
*context*

el empeine (10)

el talón (8)

*el talones (no accent)*
*{ ? plural}*

la planta del pie (9)

los dedos del pie (11)

*(las plantas de los pies)*

# El tronco (*The trunk*) ✓

(1) shoulder
(2) breast/chest
(3) armpit
(4) nipple
(5) abdomen
(6) waist
(7) navel
(8) crotch
(9) back
(10) hip
(11) buttock

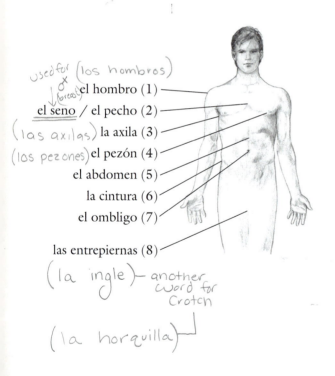

used for (los hombros)
♂
(breast)
el hombro (1)
el seno / el pecho (2)
(las axilas) la axila (3)
(los pezones) el pezón (4)
el abdomen (5)
la cintura (6)
el ombligo (7)
las entrepiernas (8)

(la ingle) – another word for Crotch

(la horquilla)

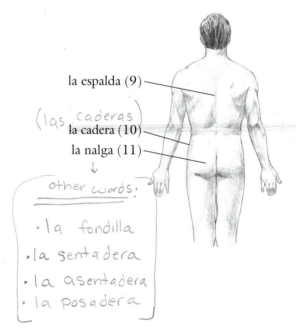

la espalda (9)
(las caderas)
la cadera (10)
la nalga (11)
↓
other words:
• la fondilla
• la sentadera
• la asentadera
• la posadera

Also:

| | |
|---|---|
| la **barriga** | *belly* → also la panza (think of Sancho Panza) of Don Quixote |
| el **diafragma** | *diaphragm* |
| el **tórax** | *thorax* |
| el **vientre** | *womb, abdomen* |

# El sistema digestivo *(The digestive system)* ✓

(1) throat
(2) liver
(3) stomach
(4) gallbladder —— or la bilis (used by natives) { the word is bile }
(5) pancreas
(6) intestine
(7) colon
(8) rectum
(9) anus
(10) appendix

large intestine
(el intestino grueso) —— thick  ✻ on test

Small intestine   ✻ on test
(el intestino delgado) ← Small or Slender

esophagus = el esófago ✻ on test

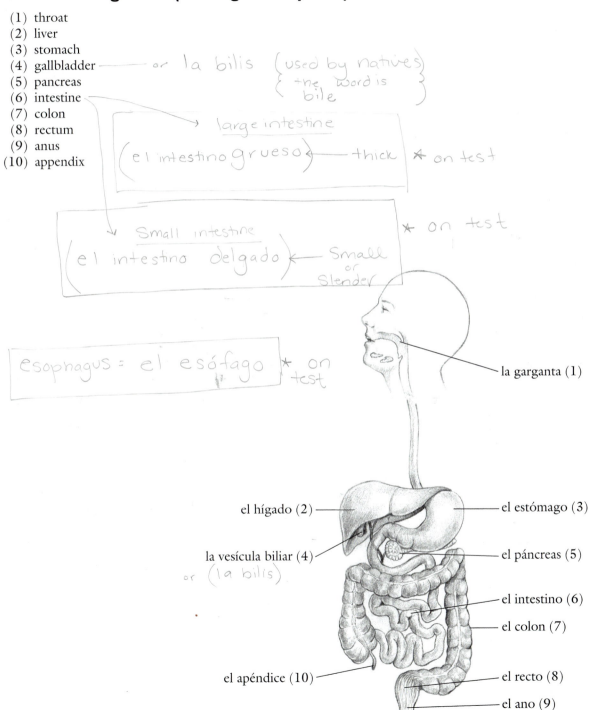

la garganta (1)

el hígado (2)

la vesícula biliar (4)
or (la bilis)

el apéndice (10)

el estómago (3)

el páncreas (5)

el intestino (6)

el colon (7)

el recto (8)

el ano (9)

## El esqueleto (The skeleton) ✓

(1) skull
(2) collar bone
(3) shoulder blade
(4) rib
(5) breastbone
(6) spinal column
(7) pelvis

el cráneo (1)
la clavícula (2)
la escápula, el omóplato (3)
la costilla (4)
las costillas
el esternón (5)
la columna vertebral (6)
la pelvis (7)

next
Test

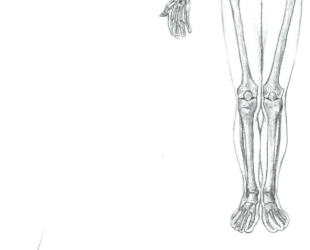

## Otros órganos (Other organs) ✓

- el **bazo** — *spleen* ——→ Slang: el esplín
- los **bronquios** — *bronchial tubes*
- el **corazón** — *heart*
- el **cuello uterino,** la **cerviz** — *cervix*

|  |  |
|---|---|
| los **órganos genitales** | *genital organs* ← or los órganos ocultos (hidden organs) |
| el **ovario**, los ovarios | *ovary* |
| el **pene,** el **miembro** | *penis* |
| la **piel** | *skin* |
| el **pulmón**, los pulmones | *lung* |
| el **riñón**, los riñones | *kidney* |
| la **sangre** | *blood* |
| los **testículos** | *testicles* |
| el **útero,** la **matriz** | *uterus* |
| la **vagina** | *vagina* |
| la **vejiga** | *urinary bladder* |

last test

# Appendix D
## Pronunciation

## Syllabification and Diphthongs

There are definite rules in Spanish about dividing words into syllables:

1. A word has as many syllables as it has vowels or diphthongs.

2. Each syllable begins with a consonant. For example:

   | | | | |
   |---|---|---|---|
   | beso | be-so | tomate | to-ma-te |
   | vida | vi-da | lazo | la-zo |

3. When there are two consonants together, they are usually separated. For example:

   | | | | |
   |---|---|---|---|
   | puerta | puer-ta | adelante | a-de-lan-te |
   | perdón | per-dón | excepto | ex-cep-to |

   EXCEPTIONS: The following combinations of consonants cannot be broken up: **bl, cl, fl, gl, pl, cr, fr, gr, br, dr,** and **tr.** For example:

   | | | | |
   |---|---|---|---|
   | madre | ma-dre | palabra | pa-la-bra |
   | mueble | mue-ble | negro | ne-gro |

4. An **s** combined with another consonant can never begin a syllable. It must go with the preceding syllable. For example:

   | | | | |
   |---|---|---|---|
   | especial | es-pe-cial | estúpido | es-tú-pi-do |

5. When there are three consonants in a row, generally, the word is divided after the first consonant (except when the second consonant is an **s**). For example:

   | | | | |
   |---|---|---|---|
   | hombre | hom-bre | entrar | en-trar |
   | ingle | in-gle | comprendo | com-pren-do |

6. In Spanish vowels are considered either strong or weak. the strong vowels are **a, e,** and **o**. The weak vowels are **i** and **u**. When two strong vowels occur together in a word they form two separate syllables. For example:

   | | | | |
   |---|---|---|---|
   | canoa | ca-no-a | mareado | ma-re-a-do |

7. A strong vowel combined with a weak vowel (or two weak vowels together) form only one syllable. For example:

| viejo | vie-jo | cuidado | cui-da-do |
|-------|--------|---------|-----------|
| ejercicio | e-jer-ci-cio | ciudad | ciu-dad |

An accent mark indicates that the sound should be broken into two syllables. For example:

| tío | tí-o | farmacéutico | far-ma-cé-u-ti-co |
|-----|------|--------------|-------------------|

8. When two vowels come together in a syllable to form one sound, it is called a diphthong. The following are the diphthongs in Spanish:

**ia** sounds like *yah* in English: famil**ia**r, f**ia**do, malar**ia**.
**ua** sounds like *wa* in *wander:* ag**ua**, estat**ua**, enj**ua**gar.
**ai** sounds like *ie* in *pie:* c**ai**go, p**ai**saje, s**ai**nete.
**au** sounds like *ou* in *house:* **au**nque, g**au**cho, p**au**sa.
**ie** sounds like *ye* in *yellow:* c**ie**go, p**ie**l, n**ie**bla.
**ue** sounds like the word *way:* b**ue**no, d**ue**le, m**ue**la.
**ei, ey** sounds like the *ay* in *hay:* p**ei**ne, r**ey**, s**ei**s.
**eu** has no real equivalent in English. Combine Spanish **e** with **u**: terap**eu**ta, s**eu**dónimo, n**eu**rólogo.
**io** sounds like the *yo* in *yoga:* rad**io**, secundar**io**, m**io**pe.
**uo** sounds like *uo* in *quota:* d**uo**décimo, c**uo**ta.
**oi, oy** sounds like the *oy* in *boy:* b**oi**na, c**oi**to, **oi**go.
**ui, uy** sounds like the word *we:* c**ui**dado, m**uy**, s**ui**zo.
**iu, yu** sounds like the word *you:* c**iu**dad, d**iu**rético.

## Consonants

| | | |
|---|---|---|
| **b, v** | [b] | occurs at the beginning of a breath group or after an **m** or **n**. It sounds like the *b* in *baby:* **b**eso, **v**aso, hom**b**re. |
| **b, v** | [b̶] | occurs in all places except after **m, n,** or at the beginning of a breath group. It is similar to [b] except that the lips do not close completely as the sound is made: bo**b**o, to**b**illo, Cu**b**a. |
| **c** | [k] | occurs before the vowels **a, o, u,** and all consonants. It is like the *c* in *cat:* **c**omer, **c**asa, se**cc**ión, a**c**tual. |
| **c** | [s] | occurs before the vowels **e** and **i**. It is like the *s* in *soap:* **c**eja, **c**ine, **c**ocina. |
| **ch** | [ĉ] | sounds like *ch* in *choice* in all places: o**ch**o, ha**ch**a, **ch**aqueta. |
| **d** | [d] | occurs after an **n, l,** or at the beginning of a breath group. It is like the *d* in *dark:* **d**iente, an**d**o, fal**d**a. |
| **d** | [d̶] | occurs in all places except after **n** or **l** or at the beginning of a breath group. It is similar to the *th* in the word *then:* to**d**o, co**d**o, de**d**o. |
| **f** | [f] | is identical to the *f* in *fact, effort:* e**f**icaz, **f**laco, **f**rente. |
| **g** | [g] | occurs after **n** or at the beginning of a breath group before the letters **a, o,** and **u**. It sounds like the *g* in *gap, globe,* and *angry:* **g**oma, **g**ato, án**g**ulo, **g**uisante, **g**uante. |
| | | NOTE: When **gu** is followed by **e** or **i**, the **u** is not pronounced—unless a diaeresis is placed over the **u** (**güe** or **güi**) to indicate that it is pronounced. |
| **g** | [g̶] | occurs before **a, o,** and **u** in all places except after **n** or at the beginning of an utterance. This sound is similar to [g] except that a small amount of air is permitted |

to pass through the roof of the mouth and the palate, thereby producing a softer sound: a**g**ua, lle**g**a, a**g**otar.

| | | |
|---|---|---|
| **g** | [x] | occurs before **e** or **i** and is like the *h* in *hat,* but more guttural: **g**ente, **g**esto, **g**itano. |
| **h** | | represents no sound in Spanish. It is *always* silent. |
| **j** | [x] | is similar to the English *h,* as in *he,* or *wh,* as in *who,* in all places: **j**íbaro, **j**ugo, **j**abón, **j**ota. |
| **l** | [l] | similar to the *ll* in *sill* in all places, except that the tongue strikes farther back on the roof of the mouth, producing a more liquid sound: **l**uz, ca**l**ambre, seña**l.** |
| **ll** | [ɏ] | sounds similar to the *y* in *yes* in all places, but the tongue touches the roof of the mouth slightly so that it sounds almost like the *j* in *jelly:* ca**ll**e, meji**ll**a, **ll**evar. |
| **m** | [m] | sounds identical to the *m* in *mother* in all places: **m**adre, ca**m**a, enfer**m**o. |
| **n** | [n] | sounds the same as the *n* in *noon* in all places: **n**ada, e**n**tre, espi**n**aca. |
| **ñ** | [ñ] | sounds like the *ni* in *onion* in all places: se**ñ**or, pu**ñ**o, u**ñ**a, ri**ñ**on. |
| **p** | [p] | sounds like the *p* in *paper* in all places, but it is unaspirated, that is, less air is allowed to escape from the lips when the sound is made: **p**apá, **p**luma, **p**lato. |
| **q** | [k] | is like the *k* in *kite* in all places. Notice that the **q** is always followed by a **u,** which is not pronounced: **q**ueso, **q**uien, por**q**ue. |
| **r** | [r] | occurs in all places except at the beginning of a word, or after **l, n,** or **s.** This sound is called a flap and it is like the *d* in the word *ready* when pronounced rapidly: ca**r**a, na**r**iz, gene**r**al. |
| **rr, r** | [r̃] | occurs where the letter **r** follows **n, l,** or **s,** or is at the beginning of a word, and in all places where the letter **rr** occurs. This sound is called a multiple flap or a trill and has no equivalent in the English language: **r**oto, ca**rr**o, en**r**iquecer, al**r**ededor, es **r**ico. |
| **s** | [s] | is like the *s* in *stop* or *kiss* in all places: to**s**er, **s**en**s**ación, tri**s**te. |
| **t** | [t] | sounds in all places like the *t* in *tip* but it is unaspirated: **t**orta, pa**t**ata, es**t**e. |
| **v** | | represents the same sound as the letter **b** in all places. |
| **x** | [ɡs] | occurs between vowels. It is like the *ggs* in *eggs:* e**x**aminar, e**x**agerar, e**x**asperar, e**x**acto. |
| | | EXCEPTIONS: Mé**x**ico, me**x**icano, are pronounced Mé**j**ico, me**j**icano. |
| **x** | [s] | occurs before a consonant. It is the same as the *s* in *stop:* e**x**periencia, e**x**tremo, e**x**ceso. |
| **y** | [ɏ] | sounds the same as the letter **ll** in all places: **y**eso, **y**odo, apo**y**ar. |
| **z** | [s] | is the same as the *s* in *soap* in all places. It is *never* like the *z* in *zebra:* **z**apato, ta**z**a, **z**ona, feli**z**. |

# Linking

In a sentence, the final vowel of one word will join with the initial vowel of the next word. Look at the following examples:

Tome⌣esta medicina.

Mira‿hacia⌣arriba.

Como⌣ahora.

Llego⌣a las dos.

Como⌣en la cafetería

# Dialectal Variations

Many variations occur in the pronunciation of Spanish. These dialectal differences may be confusing to students who are not familiar with them. The following are guides to variations that may occur in speakers of three major Hispanic groups: Puerto Rican, Mexican, and Cuban. It must be kept in mind that these guides are general and that the variations will not be heard in all speakers from these regions. Also, the same variations may be heard from Spanish-speaking peoples of other geographical areas.

### Puerto Rican

| | |
|---|---|
| d | is often eliminated at the end of a word: ciudad → ciudá, mitad → mitá. It is eliminated when intervocalic: hablado → hablao, cuidado → cuidao. |
| ll | is pronounced like the English *j:* inyección → injección, llegar → jegar. |
| n | when it occurs at the end of a word, is pronounced like the *ng* in *singing:* muy bien → muy bieng. |
| r | is pronounced like **l** when it precedes a consonant: verdad → beldá, puerta → puelta. When it is at the end of a word, it is also pronounced like **l**: hablar → hablal, por favor → pol favol. It is sometimes pronounced like the English *shr* when it is at the beginning of a word: Puerto Rico → Puelto Shrico. |
| s | is eliminated when it precedes a consonant: respirar → repiral, está → etá |
| | NOTE: Sometimes the entire syllable is eliminated: está bien → tá bieng. |
| | It is eliminated when it comes at the end of a word: ojos azules → ojo azule, los dos → lo dó. And sometimes it is pronounced like the aspirated *h:* los dos → loh doh. |
| y | is pronounced like the English *j:* yo → jo, yeso → jeso. |

Final syllables of words are often eliminated: todo → to, nada → na, para → pa.

In some cases, syllables may merge together: para abajo → pabajo, para atrás → patrá, para adelante → palante.

### Mexican

| | |
|---|---|
| bue, vue | is sometimes pronounced as **güe:** bueno → güeno, vuelvo → güelvo. |
| d | is eliminated at the end of a word: usted → usté, pared → paré |
| f | when followed by **u** sounds like the English *h:* fuerte → huerte, fue → hue. |
| gua | sounds like the English *wa:* agua → awa, igual → iwal. |
| gn | often loses the **g:** ignorar → inorar, repugnante → repunante. |
| ll | sounds like the English **y:** calle → caye, gallina → gayina. |
| r | before a consonant or at the end of a word often has the sound of **l**: pardo → paldo, hablar → hablal. |

### Cuban

| | |
|---|---|
| c | a hard *c* sound is often eliminated at the end of a syllable: actor → ator, conductor → condutor. |
| ch | is pronounced like the English *sh* in *shop:* chico → shico, pecho → pesho. |
| d | is often eliminated in the combination -**ado:** cerrado → cerrao, cuñado → cuñao. |
| n | when it occurs at the end of a word, is pronounced like the *ng* in *singing:* saben → sabeng, estación → estación. |
| o | when it occurs at the end of a word, sounds like the English *u* in *lure:* chico → chicu, cuarto → cuartu. |
| s | often has the sound of the English aspirated *h:* especial → ehpecial, estos → ehtoh. **x** before a consonant has the same sound: extracción → ehtracción. |

# Vocabulary

These vocabularies are not intended to serve as a dictionary but merely as a guide. They include all of the words identified in the text plus a number of other important medical terms that were not in any of the lessons. The gender of Spanish nouns is indicated only when they do not end in the masculine -o or the feminine -a. Adjectives ending in -o and -a are only given in the masculine form.

## Abbreviations

| | | | |
|---|---|---|---|
| *a* | adjective | *mf* | common gender |
| *f* | feminine | *n* | noun |
| *m* | masculine | *pl* | plural |

# Spanish to English

## A

**a** at; to
**abajo** down; underneath
**abandonar** to abandon
**abdomen** *m* abdomen
**abierto** open
**abogado** attorney
**aborto** abortion; —
  **espontáneo** miscarriage; —
  **provocado** abortion; —
  **terapéutico** therapeutic
  abortion
**abril** *m* April
**abrir** to open
**absceso** abscess
**abstenerse** to abstain
**abuela** grandmother
**abuelo** grandfather; —s
  grandparents
**aburrido** bored; boring
**acabar** to end, finish; — **de**
  to have just
**accidente** *m* accident
**aceite** *m* oil
**aceptar** to accept
**acercarse (a)** to approach
**ácido** acid
**aconsejar** to advise
**acordarse de** to remember
**acostado** lying down
**acostarse** to lie down; go to
  bed
**acostumbrarse** to become
  accustomed to
**actitud** *f* attitude
**actividad** *f* activity

**actor** *m* actor
**actriz** *f* actress
**adelante** ahead
**adelgazar** to lose weight
**además** furthermore; — **de**
  besides, in addition to
**adentro** inside
**adicional** additional
**adicto** addict
**adiós** goodbye
**adoptar** to adopt
**adormecer el nervio** to
  deaden the nerve
**adquirido** acquired
**adulto** adult
**agarrarse (de)** to grab; hold
  on to
**agitado** to become agitated,
  excited, nervous
**agosto** August
**agotado** exhausted
**agradable** pleasant
**agradecer** to thank
**agresivo** aggressive
**agrio** bitter
**agua** water; — **mineral**
  mineral water
**aguado** watery
**agudo** sharp
**aguja hipodérmica**
  hypodermic needle
**ahijada** goddaughter
**ahijado** godson
**ahogarse** to drown, suffocate
**ahora** now; — **mismo** right
  now

**aire** *m* air; — **acondicionado**
  air conditioning
**ajo** garlic
**al (a + el)** to the
**albaricoque** *m* apricot
**alcohol** *m* alcohol
**alcohólico** alcoholic
**alcoholismo** alcoholism
**alegre** happy
**alergia** allergy
**alérgico** allergic
**algo** something
**alguno** some, any; —**s**
  some, a few
**alimentar** to feed
**alimento** food
**aliviar** to relieve
**allí** there
**almeja** clam
**almohada** pillow
**almohadilla eléctrica** heating
  pad
**almorranas** *f pl* hemorrhoids,
  piles
**almorzar** to have lunch
**almuerzo** lunch; **tomar el**
  — to have lunch
**alternativa** alternative
**alto** tall; high
**alucinación** *f* hallucination
**alucinar** to hallucinate
**amable** kind, friendly
**ama de casa** housewife
**ambiente** *m* environment
**ambulancia** ambulance
**amígdalas** *f pl* tonsils

**amigdalitis** *f* tonsilitis
**amigo, -a** friend
**amputar** to amputate
**analgésico** analgesic
**análisis** *m* analysis; **hacer el — ** to do the analysis
**analizar** to analyze
**anatomía** anatomy
**anciano, -a** *n* elderly person; *a* elderly, old
**anemia** anemia
**anestesia** anesthesia; — **caudal** caudal anesthesia; — **general** general anesthesia; — **local** local anesthesia
**anestesiar** to anesthetize
**anestesiólogo, -a** anesthesiologist
**anestético** anesthetic
**anfetamina** amphetamine
**angiograma pulmonar** *m* pulmonary angiogram
**anillo** ring
**ano** anus
**anoche** last night
**anormalidad** *f* abnormality
**ansiedad** *f* anxiety
**ansioso** anxious
**anteayer** the day before yesterday
**anteojos** *m pl* eyeglasses
**antes (de)** before
**antiácido** antacid
**antibiótico** antibiotic
**anticonceptivo** contraceptive
**antídoto** antidote
**antihistamina** antihistamine
**antihistamínico** antihistaminic
**antipático** unpleasant, disagreeable
**antiviral** antiviral
**antivirosico** antiviral
**año** year; **el — pasado** last year; **tener... —s** to be . . . years old

**apagar la luz** to turn off the light
**aparato** device, appliance, machine; — **intrauterino** intrauterine device
**apariencia** appearance
**apartamento** apartment
**apéndice** *m* appendix
**apetito** appetite
**apio** celery
**aplicaciones calientes** *f pl* hot compresses
**aplicar** to apply
**apoyo** support
**aprender (a)** to learn (to)
**apretar** to press, squeeze
**apropiado** appropriate
**apuñalar** to knife, stab
**aquí** here; **por — ** around here
**ardor** *m* burning
**argentino, -a** Argentine
**armaduras** *f pl* eyeglass frames
**arreglarse** to arrange, work out, fix
**arriba** above, up
**arroz** *m* rice
**articulación** *f* joint
**artista** *mf* artist
**artritis** *f* arthritis
**ascensor** *m* elevator
**asegurar** to assure
**asfixiarse** to asphyxiate
**así** so, thus, like this; **así así** so-so
**asignado** assigned
**asistenta** assistant, attendant, aide
**asistente** *m* assistant, attendant, orderly
**asma** asthma
**aspecto** aspect, appearance
**aspirar** to inhale
**aspirina** aspirin
**astigmatismo** astigmatism
**asumir** to assume, take on
**asustado** frightened

**atacar** to attack
**ataque** *m* attack; — **al corazón** heart attack
**atentar** to attempt; — **el suicidio** to attempt suicide
**atento** attentive
**atleta** *mf* athlete
**atontado** bewildered, stupified
**atragantarse** to choke (on)
**atrás** behind, back
**atrasado mentalmente** mentally retarded
**atribuirse (a)** to be attributed to
**atropellado** run over
**atún** *m* tuna
**aturdido** dazed
**auscultar** to listen with a stethoscope
**ausencia** absence
**autor, -a** author
**autorización** *f* authorization
**avanzado** advanced
**averiguar** to find out
**avisar** to notify, warn, advise
**ayer** yesterday
**ayuda** help; enema
**ayudar** to help
**azúcar** *m* sugar

## B

**bacín** *m* bedpan
**bajarse (de)** to go down, to come down from
**bajo** short, low
**balanceado** balanced
**banco** bank
**bañar** to bathe someone; **—se** to take a bath
**baño** bath
**barbero** barber
**barbilla** chin
**barbiturato** barbiturate
**barbitúrico** barbiturate
**bario** barium

**barras paralelas** *f pl*   parallel bars
**barriga**   belly
**bastante**   enough, sufficient
**bastón** *m*   cane, walking stick
**bata**   bathrobe
**bazo**   spleen
**bebé** *mf*   baby
**beber**   to drink
**bebida alcohólica**   alcoholic drink
**beneficioso**   beneficial
**benigno**   benign
**biberón** *m*   baby's bottle
**bicúspide** *m*   bicuspid
**bien**   well
**bienestar** *m*   well-being
**bifocales** *m pl*   bifocals
**biología**   biology
**biopsia**   biopsy
**bistec** *m*   beefsteak
**bizcocho**   biscuit
**blanco**   white
**blando**   bland
**boca**   mouth; **— abajo**   on one's stomach; **— arriba** on one's back
**bocadillo**   snack; sandwich
**bolsa de aguas**   bag of waters, amniotic sac
**bonito**   pretty
**borracho** *n*   drunkard; *a*   drunk
**borroso**   blurred
**botar**   to throw away
**botella**   bottle
**brazo**   arm
**bróculi** *m*   broccoli
**broncoscopia**   bronchoscopy
**bronquios** *m pl*   bronchial tubes
**bronquitis** *f*   bronchitis
**bueno**   good
**bulto**   lump
**buscar**   to look for

## C

**cabello**   hair
**cabestrillo**   sling
**cabeza**   head
**cachete** *m*   cheek
**cada**   each, every
**cadera**   hip
**caer**   to fall; **—se**   to fall down, slip
**café** *m*   coffee
**cafetería**   cafeteria
**cajero**   cashier
**calabaza**   squash; pumpkin
**calambre** *m*   cramp
**calcio**   calcium
**cálculo biliar**   gallstone
**cálculo renal**   kidney stone
**calentura**   fever
**caliente**   warm, hot
**calmante** *m*   tranquilizer
**calmarse**   to calm down
**calor** *m*   heat; **tener —**   to be warm
**caloría**   calorie
**calle** *f*   street
**cama**   bed
**cámara**   cavity, chamber
**camarera**   waitress
**camarero**   waiter
**camarones** *m pl*   shrimp
**cambiar**   to change
**cambio**   change; **en —**   on the other hand
**camilla**   stretcher; **llevar en —** to carry on a stretcher
**camillero**   stretcher-bearer
**caminar**   to walk
**camisa**   shirt
**canal radicular** *m*   root canal
**cáncer** *m*   cancer
**cangrejo**   crab
**cansado**   tired
**cansancio**   tiredness
**cansarse**   to become tired
**cantidad** *f*   quantity
**cápsula**   capsule

**cara**   face
**cardiólogo, -a**   cardiologist
**cariado**   decayed
**caries** *f*   tooth decay, cavity
**carne** *f*   meat; **— de res**   beef
**carnicero**   butcher
**carpintero**   carpenter
**carta**   letter
**cartero**   mailman
**casa**   house; **en —**   at home
**casado**   married
**caso**   case; **en todo —**   in any case
**cataratas** *f pl*   cataracts
**catarro**   head cold; **tener —** to have a cold
**catéter** *m*   catheter
**causa**   cause; **a — de**   because of
**cebolla**   onion
**ceja**   eyebrow
**cena**   dinner
**cenar**   to eat dinner
**cepillarse los dientes**   to brush one's teeth
**cepillo**   brush; **— de dientes** toothbrush
**cereal** *m*   cereal
**cerebro**   brain
**cereza**   cherry
**cerrado**   closed
**cerrar**   to close
**cerveza**   beer
**cerviz** *f*   cervix
**cheque** *m*   check
**chequeo**   check-up
**chica**   girl
**chico**   boy
**chocolate**   chocolate
**cicatriz** *f*   scar
**ciego**   blind
**cielo de la boca**   roof of the mouth
**cierto**   certain; **es —**   it is certain; **por —**   as a matter of fact, in fact

**cigarrillo**  cigarette
**cintura**  waist
**ciruela**  plum; **— pasa**  prune
**cirugía**  surgery
**cirujano, -a**  surgeon
**cita**  appointment, date
**citología**  cytology
**ciudad** *f*  city
**claro**  clear; of course
**clavícula**  collar bone
**clínica**  clinic
**cocaína**  cocaine
**cocer**  to cook
**cocina**  kitchen
**cocinar**  to cook
**coco**  coconut
**codeína**  codeine
**codo**  elbow
**coito**  coitus
**cojo**  lame
**colado**  strained
**colesterol** *m*  cholesterol
**cólico**  colic
**coliflor** *f*  cauliflower
**colmillo**  eyetooth
**colombiano**  Colombian
**colon** *m*  colon
**colonoscopia**  colonoscopy
**columna vertebral**  vertebral
  column
**coma** *m*  coma
**comadrona**  midwife
**comer**  to eat; **dar de —**  to
  feed
**comida**  food
**como**  as, like
**¿cómo?**  how?; **¿cómo no?**  of
  course
**cómodo**  comfortable
**compañía**  company; **— de
  seguro**  insurance company
**compartir**  to share
**competente**  competent
**complicación** *f*  complication
**comportamiento**  behavior,
  bearing

**comprender**  to understand
**común**  common
**comunicación** *f*
  communication
**con**  with; **— respecto a**  with
  respect to, regarding
**condición** *f*  condition
**condón** *m*  condom
**conducto biliar**  bile duct
**conductor** *m*  driver
**confinar en una institución**
  to confine in an institution
**confundido**  confused
**confuso**  confused, confusing
**conjunto**  set, group,
  ensemble
**conmigo**  with me
**conocer**  to know
**conocimiento**  knowledge
**consecuencia**  consequence
**conseguir**  to obtain
**consejero**  counselor
**consejo**  advice, counsel
**constante**  constant
**consulta**  consultation, advice
**consultar**  to consult
**consultorio**  doctor's office
**contacto**  contact
**contagioso**  contagious
**contaminación** *f*
  contamination
**contento**  content
**contracción** *f*  contraction
**contracepción** *f*  contraception
**contraste** *m*  contrast
**control** *m*  control
**conveniente**  convenient
**convulsión** *f*  convulsion
**corazón** *m*  heart
**cordero**  lamb
**cordón umbilical** *m*  umbilical
  cord
**corea**  chorea
**corona**  crown
**correctamente**  correctly
**correcto**  correct

**correr**  to run; **— el riesgo**
  to run the risk
**cortada**  cut
**cortar**  to cut; **—se**  to cut
  oneself
**cosa**  thing
**costar**  to cost
**costilla**  rib
**crack** *m*  crack
**cráneo**  skull
**creer**  to believe
**crema**  cream; **— de cacahuete**
  peanut butter; **— vaginal**
  vaginal cream
**criatura**  infant; child
**criminal** *m*  criminal
**crónico**  chronic
**¿cuál?**  which?; what?
**cualquier**  any
**cuando**  when
**¿cuándo?**  when?
**¿cuánto?**  how much?; **¿—s?**
  how many?
**cuanto antes**  as soon as
  possible, quickly
**cuarto**  room; **— doble**
  double room; **— múltiple**
  ward; **— privado**  private
  room
**cubano, -a**  Cuban
**cubrir**  to cover
**cuchara**  spoon
**cucharada**  spoonful
**cuchillo**  knife
**cuello**  neck
**cuello uterino**  cervix
**cuero cabelludo**  scalp
**cuerpo**  body
**cuidado**  care; **con —**
  carefully; **— intensivo**
  intensive care; **cuidado
  postnatal**  postnatal care; **—
  prenatal**  prenatal care;
  **tener —**  to be careful
**cuidar a**  to care for (a person)
**cuidar de**  to take care of

**cuñada**   sister-in-law
**cuñado**   brother-in-law
**cura** *m*   priest; *f*   cure
**curar**   to cure
**curarse**   to be cured
**curita**   small adhesive bandage

# D

**daltonismo**   colorblindness
**dañino**   harmful
**daño**   to hurt, harm; **hacerse
  —**   to hurt oneself
**dar**   to give; **— a luz**   to give
  birth;   **dar el seno** to
  breastfeed; **dar puntadas**
  to give stitches
**dato**   fact
**de**   of from; **— veras, —
  verdad**   truly, really, indeed
**debajo de**   underneath, below
**deber** *m*   duty
**deber**   to owe, must, should
**débil**   weak
**decidir**   to decide
**decir**   to say, tell
**decisión** *f*   decision; **tomar
  una —**   to make a decision
**dedo**   finger; **— anular**   ring
  finger; **— del pie**   toe;
  **— índice**   index finger;
  **— medio**   middle finger;
  **— meñique**   little finger;
  **— pulgar**   thumb
**defecto congénito**   congenital
  defect
**defecto de nacimiento**   birth
  defect
**defender**   to defend
**deficiencia**   deficiency
**degenerativo**   degenerative
**dejar**   to leave; **— de**   to stop,
  cease; **— en paz**   to leave
  (one) alone
**del (de + el)**   of the
**delgado**   thin, slender
**delicioso**   delicious

**demasiado**   too much; **—s**
  too many
**demorar**   to delay
**dentadura**   denture;
  **— completa**   full denture;
  **— parcial**   partial denture;
  **— postiza**   false teeth
**dental**   dental
**dentista** *mf*   dentist
**dentro de**   inside of; **por —**
  within
**Departamento de Seguridad
  Social**   Department of
  Social Security
**dependencia**   dependency
**dependiente, -a** *n*   clerk; *a*
  dependent
**depresión** *f*   depression
**deprimido**   depressed
**derecho**   right, right side; **a la
  derecha**   to the right
**desarrollarse**   to develop
**desarrollo**   development
**desayunarse**   to have breakfast
**desayuno**   breakfast; **tomar el
  —**   to have breakfast
**descansar**   to rest
**descanso**   rest
**descubrir**   to discover
**desde**   from, since
**desear**   to desire, want
**desinfectante** *m*   disinfectant
**desintoxicación** *f*
  detoxification
**desintoxicar**   to detoxicate
**desmayarse**   to faint
**desnutrición** *f*   malnutrition
**desnutrido**   malnourished
**desorientado**   disoriented
**despacio**   slowly
**despertar**   to wake someone
  up; **— se**   to awaken
**despierto**   awake
**después de**   after
**detalle** *m*   detail
**determinar**   to determine
**detrás de**   behind

**día** *m*   day; **al —**   per day
**diabético**   diabetic
**diabetis** *f*   diabetes
**diafragma** *m*   diaphragm
**diagnóstico**   diagnosis
**diarrea**   diarrhea
**diciembre** *m*   December
**diente** *m*   tooth; **— cariado**
  decayed tooth; **— de leche**
  milk tooth
**dieta**   diet; **seguir una —**   to
  follow a diet
**dietista** *mf*   dietitian
**difícil**   difficult
**dificultad** *f*   difficulty
**difteria**   diphtheria
**digerido**   digested
**digerir**   to digest
**digestión** *f*   digestion
**digestivo**   digestive; **sistema
  —** *m*   digestive system
**dilatación** *f*   dilation; **— del
  cuello de la matriz**
  dilation of the cervix; **— y
  legrado**   dilation and
  curettage
**dilatado**   dilated
**diligente**   diligent
**dinero**   money
**dirección** *f*   direction; address
**dirigir**   direct; **— se (a)**   to
  go toward, direct oneself to
**discutir**   to discuss
**disentería**   dysentery
**dislexia**   dyslexia
**divertirse**   to have fun, enjoy
  oneself
**divorciado**   divorced
**doblar**   to bend, turn
**doctor, -a**   doctor
**doler**   to hurt
**dolor** *m*   pain; **— de cabeza**
  headache; **— de oído**
  earache; **—es del parto**
  labor pains; **tener —**   to be
  in pain
**domingo**   Sunday

**dominicano, -a** Dominican

**donde** where

**¿dónde?** where?; **¿a —?** to where?; **¿de —?** from where?

**dormido** asleep, sleeping

**dormir** to sleep; **—se** to fall asleep

**dorso** spine, back; **— de la mano** back of the hand

**dosis excesiva** *f* overdose

**droga** drug

**drogadicción** *f* drug addiction

**ducha** shower, douche

**duda** doubt; **sin —** without a doubt, undoubtedly

**dudar** to doubt

**dudoso** doubtful

**dulce** *a* sweet; *n m* candy

**duración** duration

**durante** during

**durar** to last

**duro** hard

# E

**ecografía** sonogram

**eczema** eczema

**echar** to throw

**ecuatoriano, -a** Ecuadoran

**edad** *f* age

**efecto secundario** side effect

**eficaz** (*pl* **eficaces**) efficient

**ejercer** to exercise

**ejercicio** exercise; **hacer —** to exercise

**electricista** *mf* electrician

**electrocardiograma** *m* electrocardiogram

**eliminar** to eliminate

**embarazada** pregnant

**embarazarse** to become pregnant

**embarazo** pregnancy

**emergencia** emergency

**emocional** emotional

**empastar** to fill a tooth, do a filling

**empaste** *m* filling

**empeine** *m* instep

**empeorar** to worsen, become worse

**empleo** employment, work, job

**empujar** to push

**en** in, on; **— cuanto a** as for, concerning; **— seguida** right away

**encargarse (de)** to take charge of

**encender la luz** to turn on the light

**encía** gum

**encima de** on top of

**encinta** pregnant

**encontrar** to find, meet

**enema** *mf* enema

**enero** January

**enfermarse** to become sick

**enfermedad** *f* sickness; **— contagiosa** contagious disease; **— transmisible** communicable disease; **— venérea** venereal disease

**enfermero, -a** nurse

**enfermo** sick

**enfrentarse (con)** to face, confront

**enfrente (de)** in front of

**enjuagarse** to rinse

**enojado** angry

**enriquecido** enriched

**enrojecido** flushed

**ensuciar** to dirty, to soil

**entero** whole

**entonces** then

**entrar** to enter

**entre** among, between

**entrepiernas** *f pl* crotch

**envenenarse** to be poisoned

**enyesar** to put in a cast

**epilepsia** epilepsy

**equilibrado** balanced

**eructar** to belch

**eructo** belch; **tener —s** to have gas, to belch

**escaldadura** diaper rash

**escalera** stairs, staircase; **— abajo** downstairs; **— arriba** upstairs

**escalofrío** chill

**escaparse** to escape

**escápula** shoulder blade

**escarlatina** scarlet fever

**escoger** to choose

**escribir** to write

**escuchar** to listen

**escudo** shield

**escuela** school

**escupir** to spit

**esencial** essential

**esmalte** *m* polish; enamel

**eso** that

**espalda** back

**español** *n m* Spanish (language); Spaniard; *a* Spanish

**espárrago** asparagus

**especia** spice

**especial** special

**especialista** *mf* specialist

**especializarse** to specialize

**específico** specific

**espejuelos** *m pl* eyeglasses

**esperar** to wait, to hope

**esperma** sperm, semen

**espinaca** spinach

**espinilla** shin

**espiral** *f* spiral

**esposa** wife

**esposo** husband

**espuma** foam

**esqueleto** skeleton

**esquizofrenia** schizophrenia

**estado** state; **— civil** marital status; **— de salud** state of health

**estar** to be; **— a favor de** to be in favor of; **— de acuerdo con** to agree with; **— de**

**pie**  to be standing; **—en estado**  to be pregnant; **— seguro de**  to be sure of
**esterilización** *f*  sterilization
**esterilizar**  to sterilize
**esternón** *m*  breastbone
**estimulante** *m*  stimulant
**estómago**  stomach
**estornudar**  to sneeze
**estrenuo**  strenuous
**estreñido**  constipated
**estreñimiento**  constipation
**estricto**  strict
**estudiar**  to study
**etiqueta**  label
**evitar**  to avoid
**examen** *m*  exam, test
**examinar**  to examine
**excepción** *f*  exception; **con — de**  except for
**exceso**  excess
**exigente**  demanding
**existir**  to exist
**experimentar**  to experience
**explicación** *f*  explanation
**explicar**  to explain
**exploración nuclear** *f*  nuclear scanning
**expresar**  to express
**extracción** *f*  extraction
**extraer**  to extract
**extraño**  strange
**extremidad** *f*  extremity

**F**
**fábrica**  factory
**fácil**  easy
**fácilmente**  easily
**factor** *m*  factor
**falta**  lack
**familia**  family
**familiar** *n mf*  relative, family member; *a*  familiar
**familiarizarse con**  to become familiar with
**farmacéutico**  pharmacist

**farmacia**  pharmacy
**favor** *m*  favor; **— de** + *inf* please; **por —**  please
**febrero**  February
**fencicladina**  fencyclidine; PCP
**feo**  ugly
**fértil**  fertile
**feto**  fetus
**fibra**  fiber
**fibroma** *m*  fibroma
**fiebre** *f*  fever; **— amarilla** yellow fever; **— de heno** hay fever; **— reumática** rheumatic fever
**fin** *m*  end; **por —**  finally
**firmar**  to sign
**firme** *a*  firm
**físico** *a*  physical
**fisioterapeuta** *mf*  physical therapist
**fisioterapia**  physical therapy
**flaco**  thin, slender, skinny
**flema**  phlegm
**flexible**  flexible
**fluido** *a n*  fluid
**flujo de sangre**  discharge of blood
**forceps** *m*  forceps
**forma**  form
**fórmula**  formula
**formulario**  form, application
**fosas nasales** *f pl*  nostrils
**foto** *f*  photograph; **sacar —s** to take pictures
**fracturarse**  to break; to fracture
**frecuencia**  frequency; **con —** frequently
**frecuentemente**  frequently
**frente** *f*  forehead
**fresa**  strawberry
**frijol** *m*  bean
**frío**  cold; **tener —**  to be cold
**frito**  fried

**frotis de PAP** *m*  PAP smear
**fruta**  fruit
**fuerte**  strong
**fumar**  to smoke
**función** *f*  function
**funcionar**  to function, work; **— mal**  to malfunction

**G**
**gafas** *f pl*  eyeglasses; **— de sol** sunglasses
**galleta**  cracker, biscuit
**gambas** *f pl*  shrimp
**gammagrafía**  nuclear scan
**ganar**  to win
**ganglio linfático**  lymph node
**gangrena**  gangrene
**garganta**  throat
**gárgara**  gargling; **hacer —s** to gargle
**gas** *m*  gas
**gasto**  expense, cost
**gastritis** *m*  gastritis
**gastrointestinal** gastrointestinal
**gastroscopia**  gastroscopy
**gelatina**  gelatin
**gemelo**  twin
**generalmente**  generally
**genital**  genital
**ginecólogo, -a**  gynecologist
**glándula linfática**  lymph gland
**glaucoma** *m*  glaucoma
**globo del ojo**  eyeball
**golpear**  to hit
**gonorrea**  gonorrhea
**gordo**  fat
**gorro cervical**  cervical cap
**gota**  drop
**gracias**  thank you; **¡— a Dios!** thank God!
**gradual**  gradual
**grande**  large, big; great
**grasa**  grease, fat
**grasiento**  greasy

**grasoso** greasy, fatty
**gratis** free, gratis
**grave** serious, grave
**gripe** *f* flu
**guapo** handsome, pretty
**guatemalteco, -a** Guatemalan
**guayaba** guava
**guineo** banana
**guisante** *m* pea
**gustar** to like, please; to be pleasing to
**mucho gusto** it's a pleasure

## H

**habichuela verde** green bean
**habilidad** *f* ability
**hábito** habit
**hablar** to speak, talk
**hacer** to make, do
**hacerse daño** to hurt oneself
**hacia** toward
**hambre** *f* hunger; **tener —** to be hungry; **tener mucha —** to be very hungry
**hamburguesa** hamburger
**hasta** until
**hay** there is, there are
**heces** *f pl* feces
**helado** ice cream
**hembra** female
**hemograma** *m* blood count
**hemorragia** hemorrhage
**hemorroides** *m pl* hemorrhoids
**hepatitis** *f* hepatitis
**herida** wound
**hermana** sister
**hermano** brother
**hermoso** beautiful
**heroína** heroin
**herpes** *mf* herpes
**hierba** grass; marijuana
**hierro** iron
**hígado** liver
**higienista dental** *mf* dental hygienist

**hija** daughter
**hijo** son; **—s** children
**hinchazón** *m* swelling
**hiperactivo** hyperactive
**hipermetropía** farsightedness
**hirviente** boiling
**histerectomía** hysterectomy
**historia clínica** clinical history
**hogar** *m* home
**hombre** *m* man
**hombro** shoulder
**homosexual** homosexual
**hondureño, -a** Honduran
**hongo** mushroom
**hora** hour; time; **¿qué — es?** what time is it?
**hospital** *m* hospital
**hospitalizar** to hospitalize
**hoy** today
**huellas** tracks
**hueso** bone
**huevo** egg; **— duro** hard boiled egg; **— frito** fried egg; **— pasado por agua** soft-boiled egg; **— revuelto, — batido** scrambled egg
**humano** human
**húmedo** moist, damp, wet

## I

**idea** idea
**idioma** *m* language
**imagen por resonancia magnética** *f* MRI
**impaciente** impatient
**impactado** impacted
**impedimento** impediment
**impertinente** impertinent
**impétigo** impetigo
**importante** important
**impulsar** to impel
**incisivo** incisor
**incluir** to include; **—se** to be included
**incómodo** uncomfortable
**incompetente** incompetent

**incomprensible** incomprehensible
**incubadora** incubator
**indicar** to indicate
**indigestión** indigestion
**individuo** individual
**infección** *f* infection
**infectarse** to become infected
**inferior** inferior
**inflamación** *f* inflammation
**inflamado** inflamed
**inflexible** inflexible
**influenza** influenza, flu
**información** *f* information
**ingeniero, -a** engineer
**ingle** *f* groin
**inglés** *n m* English (language); *a* English
**ingresos** *m pl* admissions
**inhalar** to inhale
**inmunización** *f* immunization
**inmunizar** to immunize
**inmunología** immunology
**inocular** to inoculate
**inquieto** restless
**insertar** to insert
**insociable** antisocial
**institución** *f* institution
**instrucción** *f* instruction
**insulina** insulin
**inteligente** intelligent
**interesado** interested; **estar — en** to be interested in
**intestino** intestine
**intravenoso** intravenous
**inútil** useless
**investigar** to investigate
**inyección** *f* injection; **— intravenosa** intravenous injection
**inyectar** to inject
**ir** to go; **— a + *inf*** to be going to; **—se** to leave
**irregular** irregular
**irresponsable** irresponsible
**irritabilidad** *f* irritability

**irritación** *f*  irritation
**irritado**  irritated
**irritar**  to irritate
**izquierdo**  left, left side; **a la izquierda**  to the left

## J

**jabón** *m*  soap
**jalea**  jelly
**jamón** *m*  ham
**jaqueca**  headache
**jarabe** *m*  syrup
**joven** *n mf*  youth; *a*  young
**jovencito, -a**  teenager
**jueves** *m*  Thursday
**jugo**  juice; **— de china, — de naranja**  orange juice; **— de tomate**  tomato juice; **— de toronja**  grapefruit juice
**julio**  July
**junio**  June
**junto a**  next to

## L

**labio**  lip
**labor** *f*  labor
**laboratorio**  laboratory
**lado**  side
**lamentar**  to be sorry
**langosta**  lobster
**lápiz** (*pl* **lápices**) *m*  pencil
**largo**  long
**laringitis** *f*  laryngitis
**lástima**  pity; **¡qué —!**  what a pity!
**lavabo**  washbasin
**lavado**  enema; **— vaginal** douche
**lavaplatos** *m*  dishwasher
**lavar**  to wash; **—se**  to wash oneself
**lavativa**  enema
**lazo**  loop
**lección** *f*  lesson
**lectura**  reading
**leche** *f*  milk; **— de magnesia** milk of magnesia

**lechuga**  lettuce
**leer**  to read
**legumbre** *f*  vegetable
**lejos**  far
**lengua**  tongue; language
**lente** *m*  lens; **— de contacto** contact lens
**lesión** *f*  lesion, injury
**lesionarse**  to be injured
**letra**  letter
**leucemia**  leukemia
**levantar**  to raise, lift; **—se** to get up, arise
**leve**  light, slight
**ley** *f*  law
**libro**  book
**ligadura de los tubos**  tubal ligation
**limitación** *f*  limitation
**limitado**  limited
**limón** *m*  lemon
**limpiar**  to clean
**limpieza**  cleaning
**limpio**  clean
**línea**  line
**linfoma** *m*  lymphoma
**linimento**  liniment
**líquido**  liquid
**listo**  ready; **estar —**  to be ready; **ser —**  to be clever
**llamada telefónica**  telephone call
**llamar**  to call
**llegar**  to arrive
**llenar**  to fill
**lleno**  full
**llevar**  to carry; **— en camilla**  to carry on a stretcher
**llorar**  to cry
**loco**  insane, crazy
**locuacidad** *f*  talkativeness
**lo mismo**  the same
**lo que**  that which
**luego**  then, later
**lumpectomía**  lumpectomy
**lunes** *m*  Monday

**luz** (*pl* **luces**) *f*  light; **encender la —**  to turn on the light

## M

**macho**  male
**madre** *f*  mother
**madrina**  godmother
**madrugada**  dawn
**maestro, -a**  teacher
**magullado**  bruised
**magulladura**  bruise
**maíz** *m*  corn
**mal**  badly
**malaria**  malaria
**malestar** *m*  ailment
**maleta**  suitcase
**maligno**  malignant
**malo**  bad
**maltrato de los niños**  child abuse
**mamá**  mother, mommy
**mamar**  to breast-feed
**mamografía**  mammography
**mandar**  to order, command
**mandíbula**  jaw
**manera**  way, manner; **de esta —**  in this manner; **de ninguna —**  in no way
**mano** *f*  hand
**manta**  blanket
**mantenerse**  to remain
**mantequilla**  butter
**manzana**  apple
**mañana**  morning; tomorrow; **de la —**  AM; **por la —**  in the morning
**máquina**  machine; **— ultrasónica**  ultrasonic machine
**mareado**  dizzy, seasick
**mareo**  dizziness, seasickness; **tener —**  to be dizzy, seasick
**margarina**  margarine
**marido**  husband
**marihuana**  marijuana

**mariscos** *m pl* shellfish
**martes** *m* Tuesday
**marzo** March
**más** more; **— o menos** more or less
**masaje** *m* massage
**máscara** mask
**mastectomía** mastectomy
**masticar** to chew
**materia radioactiva** radioactive material
**maternidad** *f* maternity
**matriz** *f* womb, matrix
**mayo** May
**mayonesa** mayonnaise
**mayor** older; **el/la —** the oldest
**mecánico** mechanic
**medianoche** *f* midnight
**medicamento** medicine, medication
**médico** physician, doctor
**medida** size
**medio** half; middle; **por — de** by means of
**mediodía** *m* noon; **al —** at noon
**medir** to measure
**mejilla** cheek
**mejor** better; **a lo —** maybe, perhaps; **es —** it is better
**mejorarse** to improve, get better
**melocotón** *m* peach
**memoria** memory
**meningitis** *f* meningitis
**menopausia** menopause
**menor** younger; **el/la menor** the youngest
**menos** less, least; **por lo —** at least
**menstruación** *f* menstruation
**mentir** to lie
**mentón** *m* chin
**(a) menudo** often
**mes** *m* month

**mesa** table
**mescalina** mescaline
**metadona** methadone
**metedrina** methedrine
**meter** to put in, to insert
**método** method; **— anticonceptivo** birth control method; **— de ritmo** rhythm method
**miedo** fear; **tener —** to be afraid
**miembro** member; penis
**mientras** while; **— tanto** in the meantime
**miércoles** *m* Wednesday
**migraña** migraine
**mimar** to spoil (a child)
**minuto** minute
**miopía** myopia
**mirar** to look at
**mismo** same; **ahora —** right now
**molestar** to bother
**molestia** bother
**molesto** bothersome, bothered
**momento** moment
**morder** to bite (human)
**mordida** *n* bite (human)
**morir** to die
**mostrar** to show
**moverse** to move
**muchacha** girl
**muchacho** boy; **—s** children, boys
**mucho** much; **—s** *pl* many; **muchas veces** often
**muela** molar; **— del juicio impactado** impacted wisdom tooth
**muerto** dead
**muestra** sample; **— de sangre** blood sample; **— de la orina** urine sample
**mujer** *f* woman
**muleta** crutch
**muñeca** wrist

**muslo** thigh
**muy** very

# N

**nacer** to be born
**nacimiento** birth
**nada** nothing; **de —** you're welcome
**nadie** no one
**nalga** buttock
**naranja** orange
**narcómano** drug addict
**narcótico** narcotic
**nariz** *f* nose; **— tupida, — tapada** stuffy nose
**natalidad** *f* birth
**náuseas** *f pl* nausea; **— del embarazo** morning sickness
**necesario** necessary
**necesidad** *f* necessity
**necesitar** to need
**negativo** negative
**negocio** business
**nene, -a** baby, infant
**nervio** nerve
**nervioso** nervous
**neurólogo, -a** neurologist
**neutralizar** to neutralize
**nieta** granddaughter
**nieto** grandson
**ningún, ninguna, ninguno** none, not any
**niña** girl
**niño** boy; **—s** children, boys
**no** no, not; **— hay de qué** you're welcome
**noche** *f* night; **de la —** PM; **por la —** in the evening; at night
**nombre** *m* name
**normal** normal
**notar** to note, notice
**noticia** news; notice
**notificar** to notify
**noviembre** *m* November
**novia** girlfriend

**novio** boyfriend
**nuca** nape
**nudillo** knuckle
**nuera** daughter-in-law
**nuez de Adán** *f* Adam's apple
**número** number
**nunca** never
**nutrición** *f* nutrition

## O

**obstetra** *mf* obstetrician
**obstetricia** obstetrics
**obstétrico, -a** obstetrician
**obstruir el nervio** to obstruct the nerve
**obtener** to obtain
**obvio** obvious
**octubre** *m* October
**oculto** hidden
**ocupado** busy, occupied
**ocurrir** to occur, happen
**oficial** *m* official
**oficina** office
**ofrecer** to offer
**oftalmólogo, -a** ophthalmologist
**oído** ear, hearing
**ojo** eye
**olvidar** to forget, leave behind; **—se (de)** to forget (about)
**ombligo** navel
**omóplato** shoulder blade
**operación** *f* operation
**operar** to operate
**opinión** *f* opinion
**opio** opium
**oportunidad** *f* opportunity
**oportunística** opportunistic
**óptico** optician
**optometrista** *mf* optometrist
**oral** oral; **por vía —** to be taken orally
**orden** *m* order, harmony; *f* order, command
**oreja** ear, outer ear

**órgano** organ; **—s genitales** genital organs
**orina** urine
**orinar** to urinate
**ortopédico, -a** orthopedist
**ortopedista** *mf* orthopedist
**ostra** oyster (in shell)
**otro** other, another; **otra vez** again
**ovario** ovary
**oxígeno** oxygen

## P

**paciencia** patience
**paciente** *mf* patient
**padecer** to suffer, be afflicted with
**padre** *m* father; **—s** parents
**padrino** godfather
**pagar** to pay
**palabra** word
**paladar** *m* palate
**pálido** pale
**palma de la mano** palm of the hand
**palpitación** *f* palpitation
**paludismo** malaria
**pan** *m* bread; **— blanco** white bread; **— de centeno** rye bread; **— de trigo entero** whole wheat bread
**panameño, -a** Panamanian
**páncreas** *m* pancreas
**pantorrilla** calf
**pañal** *m* diaper; **— desechable** disposable diaper; **— de tela** cloth diaper
**papa** potato; **— al horno** baked potato; **— frita** fried potato
**papá** *m* father, daddy
**paperas** *f pl* mumps
**paquete** *m* package
**par** *m* pair, couple; **un — de** a couple of

**para** for; **— que** so that; **¿— qué?** what for?
**parado** standing
**parálisis** *f* paralysis; **— cerebral** cerebral palsy
**paralizado** paralyzed
**pararse** to stop; to stand up
**parasitológico** parasitological
**parecer** to seem
**pariente, -a** *n* relative
**párpado** eyelid
**parte** *f* part
**partera** midwife
**participar** to participate
**particular** particular
**partir** to split, divide; depart; **a — de** from, starting from
**parto** childbirth; **— múltiple** multiple childbirth; **— natural** natural childbirth; **— prematuro** premature childbirth
**pasado** past; **el año —** last year; **— mañana** the day after tomorrow
**pasar** to happen; to pass; to enter; **¿Qué pasa?** What's the matter?
**pasillo** hallway
**paso preparativo** preparatory step
**pastel** *m* pie, cake
**pastilla** pill; **— para dormir** sleeping pill
**pavo** turkey
**pecho** breast, chest; **dar el —** to breast-feed
**pediatra** *mf* pediatrician
**pediatría** pediatry
**pedir** to ask for
**peligroso** dangerous
**pelo** hair
**pelvis** *f* pelvis
**pene** *m* penis
**penetrante** *a* penetrating
**penetrar** to penetrate

**penicilina** penicillin
**pensar** to think; — + *inf* to intend to; — **de** to think about
**pentotal sódico** *m* sodium pentothal
**peor** worse
**pepinillo** pickle
**pepino** cucumber
**pera** pear
**perder** to lose; — **el conocimiento** to lose consciousness
**pérdida** loss
**perdonar** to pardon
**periódico** newspaper
**período** period
**permiso** permission; **con su —** with your permission, excuse me
**permitir** to permit
**pero** but
**persona** person
**personal** personal
**personalidad** *f* personality
**peruano, -a** Peruvian
**pesadilla** nightmare
**pesar** to weigh
**pescado** fish
**peso** weight; **aumentar de —** to gain weight; **perder —** to lose weight
**pestaña** eyelash
**pezón** *m* nipple; — **de biberón** nipple on baby's bottle
**picadura** *n* bite (insect)
**picante** spicy
**picar** to bite (insect)
**pie** *m* foot; **al — de la letra** to the letter, verbatim
**piedra** stone; — **biliar** gallstone; — **nefrítica** kidney stone
**piel** *f* skin

**pielograma intravenoso** *m* intravenous pyelogram
**pierna** leg
**pijamas** *f pl* pajamas
**píldora** pill; — **para dormir** sleeping pill
**pimienta** pepper
**piña** pineapple
**piorrea** pyorrhea
**piso** floor
**pistola** pistol
**planta baja** first floor
**planta del pie** sole of the foot
**plátano** plantain, banana
**pluma** pen, feather
**poco** little; — **a —** little by little; —**s** few; **un —** a little
**poder** to be able; **puede ser** it may be
**policía** *f* police; *m* policeman; **mujer —** *f* policewoman
**poliomielitis** *f* poliomyelitis
**pollo** chicken
**poner** to put; — **en cabestrillo** to put in a sling; — **en yeso** to put in a cast; — **una inyección** to give an injection; —**se** + *adj* to become; —**se borroso** to become blurred; —**se de pie** to stand; —**se la ropa** to put on one's clothing
**por** for; by; because of; **por desgracia** unfortunately; — **sí mismo** by oneself; —**supuesto** of course
**porque** because
**¿por qué?** why?
**posibilidad** *f* possibility
**posible** possible
**posiblemente** possibly
**postre** *m* dessert
**práctica** practice
**precaucionarse** to take precautions

**preferible** preferable
**preferiblemente** preferably
**preferir** to prefer
**pregunta** *n* question; **hacer una —** to ask a question
**preguntar** to ask, question
**prematuro** premature
**preñada** pregnant
**preocupado** worried
**preocuparse** to worry
**preparar** to prepare
**presión** *f* pressure; **alta —** high blood pressure; — **baja** low blood pressure; — **sanguínea** *f* blood pressure; **tomar la —** to take the blood pressure
**prestar** to lend
**primero** first
**primo, -a** cousin
**prisa** *f* hurry; **tener —** to be in a hurry
**privado** *a* private
**probar** to test, try, prove
**problema** *m* problem
**procedimiento** procedure
**proctoscopia** proctoscopy
**producido (por)** produced by
**producir** to produce
**profesión** *f* profession
**profesor, -a** professor
**profiláctico** prophylactic
**profundamente** deeply, profoundly
**profundo** deep
**progreso** progress
**pronóstico** prognosis, forecast
**pronto** soon; **lo más — posible** as soon as possible
**propio** *a* own
**propósito** purpose; **a —** by the way; on purpose
**protección** *f* protection
**proteger(se)** to protect (oneself)
**proteína** protein

**próximo** next

**prueba** test; — **de esfuerzo** stress test; — **del embarazo** pregnancy test; — **de Holter** Holter test; — **de PAP** PAP test; — **de tuberculina** tuberculin test

**psicólogo, -a** psychologist

**psiquíatra** *mf* psychiatrist

**psiquiatría** psychiatry

**público** public

**pudín** pudding

**puente** *m* bridge

**puerco** pork

**puerta** door

**puertorriqueño, -a** Puerto Rican

**pues** well, then

**pulgar** *m* thumb

**pulmón** *m* lung

**pulmonía** pneumonia

**pulso** pulse; **registrar el —** to take the pulse

**puñalada** stab wound

**puntadas** *f pl* stitches; **puntos** *m pl* stitches

**puño** fist; **hacer un —** to make a fist

**pupila** pupil

## Q

**que** that; **hay —** it is necessary; **tener —** to have to

**¿qué?** what?

**quedar** to have left over; to remain; **—se** to stay, remain; **—se con** to keep

**quejarse (de)** to complain (about)

**quemadura** burn

**quemante** burning

**quemar** to burn; **—se** burn oneself

**querer** to want, wish; love

**queso** cheese; — **crema** cream cheese

**quien** who, whom

**¿quién?** who?, whom?; **¿de —?** whose?

**quieto** still, quiet

**quijada** jaw

**quimioterapia** chemotherapy

**quiste** *m* cyst

**quitar** to take away; **—se** to remove, take off

**quizá(s)** maybe, perhaps

## R

**rábano** radish

**radiación** *f* radiation

**radioactivo** radioactive

**radiografía** X ray; **hacer una —** to take an X ray

**radiólogo** radiologist

**radioterapia** radiation therapy

**raíz** (*pl* **raíces**) *f* root

**rápidamente** quickly

**rápido** fast

**raquitis** *m* rickets

**rascarse** to scratch oneself

**rayos X** *m pl* X rays

**razón** *f* reason; **tener —** to be right

**reacción** *f* reaction; — **alérgica** allergic reaction

**realidad** *f* reality; **en —** in reality

**recepcionista** *mf* receptionist

**receta** prescription

**recetar** to prescribe

**recibir** to receive

**recoger** to pick up

**recomendar** to recommend

**reconocimiento médico** physical exam

**recordar** to remember

**recto** straight

**recuperación** *f* recuperation

**recuperar** to recuperate

**recurrir (a)** to resort to

**referirse (a)** to refer to

**regalo** gift

**régimen** *m* diet

**registrar(le) el pulso** to take the pulse

**regla** rule; menstrual period

**regresar** to return

**reírse (de)** to laugh (at)

**relaciones sexuales** *f pl* sexual relations

**relajarse** to relax

**relativamente** relatively

**remedio** remedy

**remojar** to soak

**remolacha** beet

**repetir** to repeat

**requerir** to require

**requesón** *m* cottage cheese

**(carne de) res** *f* beef

**resfriado** *n* cold

**resistencia** resistance

**respiración** *f* respiration; — **artificial** artificial respiration; — **boca a boca** mouth-to-mouth resuscitation

**respirar** to breathe

**respiratorio** respiratory

**responder** to respond, answer

**responsabilidad** *f* responsibility

**responsable** responsible

**resucitar** to resuscitate

**resultado** result

**retina** retina

**retirada** withdrawal

**retiro** withdrawal

**rico** rich

**riesgo** risk

**riñón** *m* kidney

**rodilla** knee

**romper** to break

**ronquera** hoarseness

**ropa** clothing; — **interior** underwear

**rosbif** *m* roast beef

**rótula** patella

**rubéola** German measles

**ruido** noise

# S

**sábado**  Saturday
**sábana**  sheet
**sabor** *m*  taste
**sacar**  to remove, take out; —
  **fotos**  to take pictures
**sacarina**  saccharin
**sal** *f*  salt
**sala**  room; — **de emergencias**
  emergency room; — **de**
  **espera**  waiting room; — **de**
  **operaciones**  operating
  room; — **de partos**
  delivery room; — **de**
  **recuperación**  recovery
  room
**salchicha**  sausage, bologna
**salir**  to leave; — **bien**  to
  turn out well; — **mal**  to
  turn out badly
**saliva**  saliva
**salmón** *m*  salmon
**salpullido**  rash
**salud** *f*  health
**saludable**  healthy
**salvadoreño, -a**  Salvadoran
**sangramiento**  bleeding
**sangrar**  to bleed
**sangre** *f*  blood
**sanitario**  sanitary
**sarampión** *m*  measles
**sardina**  sardine
**sección cesárea** *f*  caesarean
  section
**seco**  dry
**secreción** *f*  secretion
**sed** *f*  thirst
**seguido**  continuously
**según**  according to
**seguridad** *f*  safety; **con —**
  safely
**seguro** *a*  sure; *n*  insurance
**semana**  week; — **pasada**  last
  week; — **que viene**  next
  week
**sencillo**  simple
**seno**  breast

**sensación** *f*  sensation
**sentado**  seated
**sentarse**  to sit down
**sentirse**  to feel
**señal** *f*  sign, signal
**señalar**  to signal
**señor** *m*  Mr.
**señora**  Mrs.
**señorita**  Miss
**separado**  separated
**septiembre**  September
**ser**  to be; — **cuestión de**  to
  be a question of; — **humano**
  human being
**serio**  serious
**servicio**  service
**servicios sociales**  social
  services
**servir**  to serve
**severo**  severe
**sexual**  sexual
**si**  if; — **no**  if not
**sí**  yes
**SIDA** *m*  AIDS
**siempre**  always
**sigmoidoscopia**
  sigmoidoscopy
**silla de ruedas**  wheelchair
**simpático**  likable, nice
**sin**  without; — **duda**
  undoubtedly; — **embargo**
  nevertheless, however
**síndrome** *m*  syndrome
**sino**  but instead
**síntoma** *m*  symptom
**sinusitis** *f*  sinusitis
**sistema** *m*  system; —
  **circulatorio**  circulatory
  system; — **digestivo**
  digestive system; — **nervioso**
  nervous system; —
  **respiratorio**  respiratory
  system
**sobre**  over, above, on top of;
  — **todo**  above all
**sobredosis** *f*  overdose
**sobrina**  niece

**sobrino**  nephew
**sobrio**  sober
**soda**  soda
**solamente**  only
**solicitar**  to solicit, ask for
**sólido**  solid
**solo**  alone
**sólo**  only
**soltero**  single, unmarried
**solución** *f*  solution
**somnífero**  sleeping pill
**somnolencia**  sleepiness
**sonda**  catheter
**sonido**  sound
**sonograma** *m*  sonogram
**sopa**  soup
**soporte** *m*  support
**sordo**  deaf
**sospechar**  to suspect
**sótano**  basement
**subir(se)**  to go up; to raise
**substancia radioactiva**
  radioactive substance
**suceder**  to happen
**sucio**  dirty
**sudores** *m pl*  sweating
**suegra**  mother-in-law
**suegro**  father-in-law
**sueño**  dream; **tener —**  to be
  sleepy
**suficiente**  sufficient
**sufrir (de)**  to suffer (from)
**suicidio**  suicide; **atentar el —**
  to attempt suicide
**sulfato de bario**  barium
  sulfate

# T

**tableta**  tablet
**TAC** *f*  CAT scan
**tal**  such, such as
**taladrar**  to drill
**taladro**  drill
**talco**  talcum
**talón** *m*  heel
**tamaño**  size
**tambalear**  to stagger

**también** also, too

**tampoco** not . . . either, neither

**tan** so, as

**tanto** as much, so much; —s as many

**tapado** covered

**tapar** to cover

**tarde** *f* afternoon; *a* late; **de la** — PM; **por la** — in the afternoon

**taza** cup

**té** *m* tea

**técnico** technician

**telefónico** *a* telephone, phone

**teléfono** telephone

**televisión** *f* television

**temblores** *m pl* tremors

**temperatura** temperature

**temprano** early

**tener** to have

**terapeuta** *mf* therapist; — **físico** physical therapist

**terapéutico** therapeutic

**terapia física** physical therapy

**terminar** to finish, end

**ternera** veal

**testículo** testicle

**tétano** tetanus

**tía** aunt

**tiempo** time; weather; **al mismo** — at the same time; **¿cuanto — hace?** how long has it been?; **hace buen** — the weather is good; **hace mucho** — it has been a long time; **¿que — hace?** what is the weather like?

**tienda** store

**tifoidea** typhoid

**timbre** *m* bell

**tinta** ink; — **de yodo** tincture of iodine

**tío** uncle

**tipo** type, kind

**tirar (de)** to pull

**toalla** towel

**tobillo** ankle

**tocar** to touch

**tocino** bacon

**todavía** still, yet

**todo** every; —s all; —s los días every day

**tolerante** tolerant

**tomar** to take; — **medidas** to take measures

**tomate** *m* tomato

**tomografía axial computarizada** CAT scan

**tontería** foolishness

**tórax** *m* thorax

**torcedura** sprain

**torcer** to twist, turn, sprain

**torniquete** *m* tourniquet

**toronja** grapefruit

**torta** cake

**tortilla** omelette, flat bread

**tos** *f* cough; — **ferina** whooping cough

**toser** to cough

**toxemia** toxemia

**trabajador** *m* worker

**trabajar** to work

**trabajo** work

**tradicional** traditional

**traer** to bring

**tragar** to swallow

**tranquilizante** *m* tranquilizer

**tranquilo** calm, tranquil

**transmisible** communicable

**transmisor ultrasonido** *m* ultrasound transmitter

**transmitir** to transmit

**tratamiento** treatment

**tratar (a)** to treat

**tratar (de)** to try to

**través: a — de** through; by means of

**triste** sad

**tuberculosis** *f* tuberculosis

**tubo** pipe; tube

**tumor** *m* tumor

**turno** turn

**U**

**úlcera** ulcer

**último** last

**ungüento** ointment

**único** only, unique

**unidad** *f* unit, unity

**uña** nail

**urinálisis** *m* urinalysis

**urólogo** urologist

**usar** to use

**útero** uterus

**utilizar** to utilize

**uva** grape

**V**

**vacío** empty

**vacuna** vaccination

**vacunar** to vaccinate

**vagina** vagina

**valiente** brave

**variado** varied

**varicela** chicken pox

**variedad** *f* variety

**vasectomía** vasectomy

**vasija** receptacle, container

**vaso** drinking glass

**vecino** *n* neighbor; *a* neighboring

**vegetal** *m* vegetable

**vejiga** bladder

**velar** to watch over

**venda** bandage

**vendaje** *m* bandages, dressing

**vender** to sell

**veneno** poison

**venezolano, -a** Venezuelan

**venir** to come

**ventaja** advantage

**ventana** window

**ver** to see

**verdad** *f* truth; **de** — really, truly, indeed

**verduras** *f pl* greens

**vértigo**  dizziness
**vesícula biliar**  gallbladder
**vestirse**  to dress oneself, to get dressed
**vez** (*pl* **veces**) *f*  time; **a —s**  at times; sometimes; **muchas —s**  many times; **pocas —s**  few times, seldom; **una —**  one time, once
**víctima**  victim
**vientre** *m*  womb, abdomen
**viernes** *m*  Friday
**vinagre** *m*  vinegar
**vínculo**  link, bond, tie
**vino**  wine
**violación** *f*  rape; violation
**violar**  to rape, violate
**viral**  viral

**viruela**  smallpox; **—s locas**  chicken pox
**virus** *m*  virus
**visión** *f*  vision
**visita**  visit
**visitar**  to visit
**vista**  sight, vision; **tener buena —**  to have good vision
**vitamina**  vitamin
**viudo, -a**  widower, widow
**vivir**  to live
**volar**  to fly
**volver**  to return
**vomitar**  to vomit
**vómito**  vomit, vomiting; **—s del embarazo**  morning sickness

**Y**

**y**  and
**ya**  already; **— no**  no longer; **— que**  since, inasmuch as
**yema del huevo**  egg yolk
**yerba**  grass; marijuana
**yerno**  son-in-law
**yeso**  plaster cast; **poner en —**  to put in a cast
**yodo**  iodine

**Z**

**zanahoria**  carrot
**zapatilla**  slipper, pumps (women's shoes)
**zapato**  shoe

# English to Spanish

## A

**to abandon** abandonar
**abdomen** abdomen *m*
**ability** habilidad *f*
**to be able** poder
**abnormality** anormalidad *f*
**abortion** aborto, aborto provocado; **therapeutic —** aborto terapéutico
**above** arriba; sobre, encima de
**abscess** absceso
**absence** ausencia
**to abstain** abstener(se)
**to accept** aceptar
**accident** accidente *m*
**according to** según
**acid** ácido
**acidity** acidez *f*
**acquired** adquirido
**activity** actividad *f*
**actor** actor *m*
**actress** actriz *f*
**Adam's apple** nuez de Adán *f*
**addict** adicto; **addicted to** adicto a
**additional** adicional
**admissions** ingresos *m pl*
**to adopt** adoptar
**adult** adulto
**advanced** avanzado
**advantage** ventaja
**advice** consejo
**to advise** aconsejar
**after** después (de)
**afternoon** tarde *f*

**age** edad *f*
**aggressive** agresivo
**to agree (with)** estar de acuerdo (con)
**ahead** adelante
**AIDS** SIDA *m*
**ailment** malestar *m*
**air** aire *m;* **— conditioning** aire acondicionado
**alcohol** alcohol *m*
**alcoholic** alcohólico; **— drink** bebida alcohólica
**alcoholism** alcoholismo
**all** todos
**allergic** alérgico; **— reaction** reacción alérgica
**allergy** alergia
**alone** solo
**already** ya
**also** también
**alternative** alternativa
**always** siempre
**ambulance** ambulancia
**amniotic sac** bolsa de aguas
**among** entre
**amphetamine** anfetamina
**to amputate** amputar
**analgesic** analgésico
**analysis** análisis *m;* **to do an —** hacer un análisis
**to analyze** analizar
**anatomy** anatomía
**and** y
**anemia** anemia
**anesthesia** anestesia; **caudal —** anestesia caudal; **general**

**—** anestesia general; **local —** anestesia local
**anesthesiologist** anestesiólogo, -a
**anesthetic** anestético
**to anesthetize** anestesiar
**angry** enojado
**ankle** tobillo
**another** otro
**antacid** antiácido
**antibiotic** antibiótico
**antidote** antídoto
**antihistamine** antihistamina
**antihistaminic** antihistamínico
**antisocial** insociable
**antiviral** antiviral; antivirósico
**anus** ano
**anxiety** ansiedad *f*
**anxious** ansioso
**any** alguno, cualquier
**apartment** apartamento
**appearance** apariencia, aspecto
**appendix** apéndice *m*
**appetite** apetito
**apple** manzana
**appliance** aparato
**to apply (to oneself)** aplicar(se)
**appointment** cita
**to approach** acercar(se) a
**appropriate** apropiado
**apricot** albaricoque *m*
**April** abril *m*
**Argentine** argentino, -a

**arm** brazo
**to arrange** arreglar
**to arrive** llegar
**arthritis** artritis *f*
**artist** artista *mf*
**as** tan, como; — **for** en
   cuanto a
**to ask** preguntar; — **for**
   pedir, solicitar
**asleep** dormido
**asparagus** espárrago
**aspect** aspecto
**asphyxiate** asfixiarse
**aspirin** aspirina
**assigned** asignado
**assistant** asistente, -a
**to assume** asumir
**to assure** asegurar
**asthma** asma
**astigmatism** astigmatismo
**at** a, en
**athlete** atleta *mf*
**attack** ataque *m;* **heart** —
   ataque al corazón
**to attack** atacar
**attendant** asistente, -a
**attentive** atento
**attitude** actitud *f*
**attorney** abogado
**August** agosto
**aunt** tía
**author** autor, -a
**authorization** autorización *f*
**to avoid** evitar
**awake** despierto
**to awaken someone**
   despertar; **to wake up**
   despertarse

## B

**baby** nene, -a; niño, -a
**back (behind)** *prep* atrás; *n*
   espalda; **on one's** — boca
   arriba
**bacon** tocino
**bad** malo
**badly** mal

**baked potato** papa al horno
**balanced** equilibrado
**banana** guineo, plátano
**bandage** venda
**bank** banco
**barber** barbero, peluquero
**barbiturate** barbiturato,
   barbitúrico
**barium sulfate** sulfato de
   bario
**basement** sótano
**bath** baño
**to bathe** bañar; **to take a**
   **bath** bañarse
**bathrobe** bata
**to be** estar; ser
**bean** frijol *m;* **green** —
   habichuela verde
**beautiful** hermoso
**because** porque; — **of** a
   causa de
**to become** ponerse; —
   **accustomed to**
   acostumbrarse (a); —
   **infected** infectarse
**bed** cama; **to go to** —
   acostarse; **to put to** —
   acostar
**bedpan** bacín *m*
**beef** carne de res *f*
**beefsteak** bistec *m*
**beer** cerveza
**beet** remolacha
**before** antes (de)
**to begin** comenzar, empezar
**behavior** comportamiento
**behind** atrás, detrás de
**belch** eructo
**to belch** eructar, tener
   eructos
**to believe** creer, pensar
**bell** timbre *m*
**belly** barriga
**to bend** doblar
**beneficial** beneficioso
**benign** benigno
**besides** además de

**better** mejor; **to get** —
   mejorar(se)
**between** entre
**bewildered** atontado
**bicuspid** bicúspide *m*
**bifocals** bifocales *m pl*
**big** grande
**bile duct** conducto biliar
**biology** biología
**biopsy** biopsia
**birth** nacimiento, natalidad;
   **to give** — dar a luz
**biscuit** bizcocho, galleta
**to bite (human)** morder
**bite (human)** mordida
**bite (insect)** picadura
**to bite (insect)** picar
**bitter** agrio
**bladder** vejiga
**bland** blando
**blanket** manta
**to bleed** sangrar
**bleeding** sangramiento
**blind** ciego
**blood** sangre *f;* — **count**
   hemograma *m;* — **pressure**
   presión sanguínea *f;* —
   **sample** muestra de sangre
**blurred** borroso; **to become**
   — ponerse borroso
**body** cuerpo
**boiling** hirviente
**bone** hueso
**book** libro
**bored, boring** aburrido
**to be born** nacer
**bother** molestia
**to bother** molestar
**bothersome** molesto
**bottle** botella; **baby's** —
   biberón *m*
**boy** muchacho, chico
**boyfriend** novio
**brain** cerebro
**brave** valiente
**bread** pan *m;* **rye** — pan de
   centeno; **white** — pan

blanco; **whole wheat —** pan de trigo entero

**to break**   romper, fracturarse, quebrar

**breakfast**   desayuno; **to have — ** tomar el desayuno, desayunar(se)

**breast**   seno, pecho

**breastbone**   esternón *m*

**to breast-feed**   dar el pecho, mamar

**to breathe**   respirar

**bridge**   puente *m*

**to bring**   traer

**broccoli**   bróculi *m*

**bronchial tubes**   bronquios *m pl*

**bronchitis**   bronquitis *f*

**bronchoscopy**   broncoscopia

**brother**   hermano

**brother-in-law**   cuñado

**bruise**   magulladura

**bruised**   magullado

**brush**   cepillo; **toothbrush** cepillo de dientes

**to brush**   cepillar(se)

**burn**   quemadura

**to burn**   quemar; **— oneself** quemarse

**burning**   quemante

**business**   negocio

**busy**   ocupado

**but**   pero; sino

**butcher**   carnicero

**butter**   mantequilla

**buttock**   nalga

## C

**caesarean section**   sección cesárea *f*

**cafeteria**   cafetería

**cake**   torta, pastel

**calcium**   calcio

**calf**   pantorrilla

**to call**   llamar; **to be called** llamarse

**calm**   tranquilo

**to calm down**   calmar(se)

**calorie**   caloría

**cancer**   cáncer *m*

**cane**   bastón *m*

**capsule**   cápsula

**cardiologist**   cardiólogo, -a

**care**   cuidado; **intensive —** cuidado intensivo; **prenatal —**   cuidado prenatal

**to care for**   cuidar (a)

**carefully**   con cuidado, cuidadosamente

**carpenter**   carpintero

**carrot**   zanahoria

**to carry**   llevar; **— on a stretcher**   llevar en camilla

**case**   caso; **in any —**   en todo caso

**cashier**   cajero

**cast**   yeso; **to put in a —** enyesar, poner en yeso

**CAT scan**   TAC *f*

**cataracts**   cataratas

**catheter**   catéter *m;* sonda

**cauliflower**   coliflor *f*

**cause**   causa

**cavity**   caries *f;* cavidad *f*

**celery**   apio

**cereal**   cereal *m*

**cerebral palsy**   parálisis cerebral *m*

**certain**   cierto

**cervical cap**   gorro cervical

**cervix**   cerviz *f;* cuello uterino

**change**   cambio

**to change**   cambiar

**check**   cheque *m*

**checkup**   chequeo

**cheek**   cachete *m;* mejilla

**cheese**   queso; **cream —** queso crema

**chemotherapy**   quimioterapia

**cherry**   cereza

**to chew**   masticar

**chicken**   pollo

**chicken pox**   varicela; viruelas locas

**child**   niño, -a; **child abuse** maltrato de los niños

**childbirth**   parto; **multiple —** parto múltiple; **natural —** parto natural; **premature —** parto prematuro

**chill**   escalofrío

**chin**   barbilla; mentón *m*

**chocolate**   chocolate *m*

**to choke**   atragantar(se)

**cholesterol**   colesterol *m*

**to choose**   escoger

**chorea**   corea

**chronic**   crónico

**cigarette**   cigarrillo

**city**   ciudad *f*

**clam**   almeja

**clean**   limpio

**to clean**   limpiar

**cleaning**   limpieza

**clear**   claro

**clerk**   dependiente, -a

**clinic**   clínica

**clinical history**   historia clínica

**closed**   cerrado

**clothing**   ropa

**cocaine**   cocaína

**coconut**   coco

**codeine**   codeína

**coffee**   café *m*

**coitus**   coito

**cold**   frío; catarro, resfriado; **to be —**   tener frío; **to have a —**   tener catarro, tener resfriado

**colic**   cólico

**collar bone**   clavícula

**Colombian**   colombiano, -a

**colon**   colon *m*

**colonoscopy**   colonoscopia

**colorblindness**   daltonismo

**coma**   coma *m*

**to come**   venir

**comfortable**   cómodo

**common**   común

communicable   transmisible

communication   comunicación *f*

company   compañía;
insurance —   compañía de seguro

competent   competente

to complain   quejar(se)

complication   complicación *f*

(hot) compresses   aplicaciones calientes *f pl*

condition   condición *f*

condom   condón *m*

to confine in an institution   confinar en una institución

to confront   enfrentar(se) con

confused, confusing   confuso

consequence   consecuencia

constant   constante

constipated   estreñido

constipation   estreñimiento

to consult   consultar

consultation   consulta

contact   contacto

contagious   contagioso

contamination   contaminación *f*

content   contento

continuously   continuamente, seguido

contraception   contracepción *f*

contraceptive   anticonceptivo

contraction   contracción *f*

contrast   contraste *m*

control   control *m*

convenient   conveniente

convulsion   convulsión *f*

to cook   cocer, cocinar

corn   maíz *m*

correct   correcto

correctly   correctamente

cost   gasto

to cost   costar

cough   tos *f*

to cough   toser

counselor   consejero

couple   par *m;* a — of   un par de

(of) course   por supuesto

cousin   primo, -a

to cover   cubrir, tapar

covered   tapado

crab   cangrejo

crack   crack *m*

cracker   galleta

cramp   calambre *m*

crazy   loco

criminal   criminal

crotch   entrepiernas *f pl*

crown   corona

crutch   muleta

to cry   llorar

Cuban   cubano, -a

cucumber   pepino

cup   taza

cure   cura *f*

to cure   curar

to be cured   curarse

cut   cortada

to cut   cortar; — oneself   cortarse

cyst   quiste *m*

cytology   citología

## D

damp   húmedo

dangerous   peligroso

daughter   hija

daughter-in-law   nuera

dawn   madrugada

day   día *m;* the — after tomorrow   pasado mañana; the — before yesterday   anteayer

dazed   aturdido

dead   muerto

deaf   sordo

(tooth) decay   caries *f*

decayed   cariado

December   diciembre *m*

to decide   decidir

decision   decisión *f;* to make a — tomar una decisión

deep   profundo

defect   defecto; birth — defecto de nacimiento; congenital — defecto congénito

to defend   defender

deficiency   deficiencia

degenerative   degenerativo

to delay   demorar

delicious   delicioso

delivery room   sala de partos

demanding   exigente

dental   dental; — hygienist   higienista dental *mf*

denture   dentadura; full — dentadura completa; partial — dentadura parcial

Department of Social Security   Departamento de Seguridad Social

dependency   dependencia

dependent   dependiente

depressed   deprimido

depression   depresión *f*

to desire   desear, querer

dessert   postre *m*

detail   detalle *m*

to determine   determinar

to detoxicate   desintoxicar

detoxification   desintoxicación *f*

to develop   desarrollarse

development   desarrollo

device   aparato; intrauterine — aparato intrauterino

diabetes   diabetis *f*

diabetic   diabético

diagnosis   diagnóstico

diaper   pañal *m;* cloth — pañal de tela; — rash   escaldadura; disposable — pañal desechable

diaphragm   diafragma *m*

diarrhea   diarrea

to die   morir

diet   dieta; to follow a — seguir una dieta

**dietitian**   dietista *mf*
**different**   diferente
**difficult**   difícil
**difficulty**   dificultad *f*
**to digest**   digerir
**digested**   digerido
**digestion**   digestión *f;*
   **digestive**   digestivo; —
   **system**   sistema digestivo *m*
**dilated**   dilatado
**dilation and curettage**
   dilatación y legrado *f*
**dilation of the cervix**
   dilatación del cuello de la
   matriz *f*
**diligent**   diligente
**dinner**   cena
**diphtheria**   difteria
**to direct oneself to**   dirigirse a
**direction**   dirección *f*
**dirty**   sucio
**to dirty**   ensuciar
**discharge**   flujo
**to discover**   descubrir
**to discuss**   discutir
**disease**   enfermedad *f;*
   **communicable** —
   enfermedad transmisible;
   **contagious** — enfermedad
   contagiosa; **venereal** —
   enfermedad venérea
**dishwasher**   lavaplatos *m*
**disinfectant**   desinfectante *m*
**disoriented**   desorientado
**divorced**   divorciado
**dizziness**   mareo, vértigo
**dizzy**   mareado; **to be** —
   tener mareo, estar mareado
**to do**   hacer
**doctor**   doctor, -a
**Dominican**   dominicano, -a
**door**   puerta
**doubt**   duda; **without a** —
   sin duda
**to doubt**   dudar
**doubtful**   dudoso

**douche**   ducha, lavado vaginal
**down**   abajo; **to go** —
   bajar(se)
**dream**   sueño
**to dress (someone)**   vestir; **to
   get dressed**   vestirse
**dressing**   vendaje *m*
**drill**   taladro
**to drill**   taladrar
**to drink**   beber
**driver**   conductor *m*
**drop**   gota
**to drown**   ahogar(se)
**drug**   droga; — **addict**
   drogadicto, narcómano; —
   **addiction**   drogadicción
**drunk**   borracho
**dry**   seco
**duration**   duración
**during**   durante
**duty**   deber *m*
**dysentery**   disentería
**dyslexia**   dislexia

**E**

**each**   cada
**ear**   oído, oreja
**earache**   dolor de oído *m*
**early**   temprano
**easily**   fácilmente
**easy**   fácil
**to eat**   comer; — **dinner**
   cenar
**Ecuadoran**   ecuatoriano, -a
**eczema**   eczema
**efficient**   eficaz
**egg**   huevo; **fried** —   huevo
   frito; **hard-boiled** —   huevo
   duro; **soft-boiled** —   huevo
   pasado por agua; **scrambled**
   —   huevo revuelto, huevo
   batido
**egg yolk**   yema del huevo
**elbow**   codo
**elderly**   anciano, viejo
**electrician**   electricista *mf*

**electrocardiogram**
   electrocardiograma *m*
**elevator**   ascensor *m*
**to eliminate**   eliminar
**emergency**   emergencia; —
   **room**   sala de emergencias
**emotional**   emocional
**employment**   empleo, trabajo
**empty**   vacío
**enamel**   esmalte *m*
**end**   fin *m*
**enema**   ayuda, enema, lavado,
   lavativa
**engineer**   ingeniero, -a
**English**   inglés
**to enjoy oneself**   divertirse
**enough**   bastante
**enriched**   enriquecido
**to enter**   entrar, pasar
**environment**   ambiente *m*
**epilepsy**   epilepsia
**to escape**   escapar(se)
**essential**   esencial
**every**   cada; todo
**exam**   examen *m*
**to examine**   examinar
**except for**   con excepción de
**exception**   excepción *f*
**excess**   exceso
**excited**   agitado
**exercise**   ejercicio
**to exercise**   ejercer, hacer
   ejercicio
**exhausted**   agotado
**to exist**   existir
**expense**   gasto
**to experience**   experimentar
**to explain**   explicar
**explanation**   explicación
**to express**   expresar
**to extract**   extraer
**extraction**   extracción *f*
**extremity**   extremidad *f*
**eye**   ojo
**eyeball**   globo del ojo
**eyebrow**   ceja

**eyeglasses** anteojos *m pl;* espejuelos *m pl;* gafas *f pl*
**eyelash** pestaña
**eyelid** párpado
**eyetooth** colmillo

## F

**face** cara
**to face** enfrentar(se) con
**fact** dato
**factor** factor *m*
**factory** fábrica
**to faint** desmayarse
**to fall** caer(se); — **asleep** dormirse
**false teeth** dentadura postiza
**familiar** *a* familiar
**family** familia
**far** lejos
**farsightedness** hipermetropía
**fat** gordo
**father** padre *m;* papá *m*
**father-in-law** suegro
**favor** favor *m*
**fear** miedo
**February** febrero
**feces** heces *f pl*
**to feed** alimentar, dar de comer
**to feel** sentirse
**female** hembra
**fertile** fértil
**fetus** feto
**fever** calentura, fiebre *f;* **hay** — fiebre de heno; **rheumatic** — fiebre reumática; **scarlet** — escarlatina; **yellow** — fiebre amarilla
**few** pocos, -as
**fiber** fibra
**fibroma** fibroma *m*
**to fill** llenar
**filling** empaste *m;* **to do a** — empastar
**finally** por fin

**to find** encontrar, hallar; — **out** averiguar
**finger** dedo; **index** — dedo índice; **little** — dedo meñique; **middle** — dedo medio; **ring** — dedo anular
**to finish** acabar, terminar
**firm** firme
**first** primero, — **floor** planta baja
**fish** pescado
**fist** puño; **to make a** — hacer un puño
**to fix** arreglar
**flexible** flexible
**floor** piso
**flu** gripe *f*
**fluid** fluido
**flushed** enrojecido
**to fly** volar
**foam** espuma
**food** alimento, comida
**foolishness** tontería
**foot** pie
**for** para; por
**forceps** forceps *m*
**forehead** frente *f*
**to forget** olvidar(se) de
**form** forma, formulario
**formula** fórmula
**to fracture** fracturarse
**frames (eyeglasses)** armaduras *f pl*
**free** gratis
**frequency** frecuencia
**frequently** con frecuencia, frecuentemente
**Friday** viernes *m*
**fried** frito
**friend** amigo, -a
**frightened** asustado
**from** de; desde
**in front of** enfrente de
**fruit** fruta
**full** lleno
**to have fun** divertirse

**function** función *f*

## G

**gallbladder** vesícula biliar
**gallstone** cálculo biliar, piedra biliar
**gangrene** gangrena
**to gargle** hacer gárgaras
**gargling** gárgara
**garlic** ajo
**gas** gas *m*
**gastritis** gastritis *m*
**gastrointestinal** gastrointestinal
**gastroscopy** gastroscopia
**gelatin** gelatina
**generally** generalmente
**genital herpes** herpes genital *m*
**genital organs** órganos genitales *m pl*
**to get up** levantarse
**gift** regalo
**girl** muchacha; chica
**girlfriend** novia
**to give** dar; — **an injection** poner una inyección
**glass** vaso
**glaucoma** glaucoma *m*
**to go** ir; — **up** subir
**goddaughter** ahijada
**godfather** padrino
**godmother** madrina
**godson** ahijado
**gonorrhea** gonorrea
**good** bueno
**good-bye** adiós
**to grab** agarrar(se) de
**gradual** gradual
**granddaughter** nieta
**grandfather** abuelo
**grandmother** abuela
**grandson** nieto
**grape** uva
**grass** hierba, yerba
**grapefruit** toronja

**grease**  grasa
**greasy**  grasoso, grasiento
**greens**  verduras *f pl*
**groin**  empeine *m;* ingle *f*
**Guatemalan**  guatemalteco, -a
**guava**  guayaba
**gums**  encías
**gynecologist**  ginecólogo, -a

## H

**habit**  hábito
**hair**  cabello, pelo
**half**  medio
**to hallucinate**  alucinar
**hallucination**  alucinación *f*
**hallway**  pasillo
**ham**  jamón *m*
**hamburger**  hamburguesa
**hand**  mano *f;* **back of the —**
   dorso de la mano
**handsome**  guapo
**to happen**  pasar, suceder
**happy**  alegre
**hard**  duro
**harm**  daño; **to — oneself**
   hacerse daño, dañarse
**harmful**  dañino
**to have**  tener
**head**  cabeza
**headache**  dolor de cabeza *m;*
   jaqueca
**health**  salud *f*
**healthy**  saludable
**hearing**  oído
**heart**  corazón *m*
**heat**  calor *m*
**heating pad**  almohadilla
   eléctrica
**heel**  talón *m*
**help**  ayuda
**to help**  ayudar
**hemorrhage**  hemorragia
**hemorrhoids**  almorranas;
   hemorroides *m pl*
**hepatitis**  hepatitis *f*
**here**  aquí
**heroin**  heroína

**herpes**  herpes *mf*
**hidden**  oculto
**high**  alto
**hip**  cadera
**to hit**  golpear
**hoarseness**  ronquera
**to hold onto**  agarrar(se) de
**Holter test**  prueba de Holter
**home**  hogar *m*
**homosexual**  homosexual
**Honduran**  hondureño, -a
**to hope**  esperar
**to hurt**  doler
**hospital**  hospital *m*
**to hospitalize**  hospitalizar
**hot**  caliente; **to be —**  tener
   calor
**hour**  hora
**house**  casa
**housewife**  ama de casa
**how?**  ¿cómo?; **how many?**
   ¿cuántos, -as?; **how much?**
   ¿cuánto?
**hunger**  hambre *f*
**to be hungry**  tener hambre
**to hurt oneself**  dañarse,
   hacerse daño
**husband**  esposo, marido
**hyperactive**  hiperactivo
**hypodermic needle**  aguja
   hipodérmica
**hysterectomy**  histerectomía

## I

**ice cream**  helado
**idea**  idea
**immunization**  inmunización *f*
**to immunize**  inmunizar
**immunology**  inmunología
**impacted**  impactado
**impatient**  impaciente
**impediment**  impedimento
**to impel**  impulsar
**impertinent**  impertinente
**impetigo**  impétigo
**important**  importante
**in**  en; dentro, dentro de

**incisive**  incisivo
**incisor**  incisivo
**to include**  incluir
**incompetent**  incompetente
**incomprehensible**
   incomprensible
**incubator**  incubadora
**to indicate**  indicar
**indigestion**  indigestión *f*
**individual**  individuo
**infant**  criatura; nene, nena;
   bebé
**infection**  infección
**inferior**  inferior
**inflamed**  inflamado
**inflammation**  inflamación *f*
**inflexible**  inflexible
**influenza**  influenza
**information**  información *f*
**to inhale**  aspirar, inhalar
**to inject**  inyectar
**injection**  inyección *f*
**to be injured**  lesionarse
**injury**  herida; lesión *f*
**ink**  tinta
**to inoculate**  inocular
**insane**  loco
**to insert**  insertar, meter
**inside**  adentro; **— of**  dentro
   de
**instep**  empeine *m*
**institution**  institución *f*
**instruction**  instrucción *f*
**insulin**  insulina
**insurance**  seguro
**intelligent**  inteligente
**to intend to**  pensar + *inf.*
**interested**  interesado; **to be**
   **— in**  estar interesado en
**intestine**  intestino
**intravenous**  intravenoso; **—**
   **injection**  inyección
   intravenosa *f*
**to investigate**  investigar
**iodine**  yodo
**iron**  hierro
**irregular**  irregular

**irresponsible**  irresponsable
**irritability**  irritabilidad
**to irritate**  irritar
**irritated**  irritado
**irritation**  irritación *f*

## J

**January**  enero
**jaw**  mandíbula, quijada
**jelly**  jalea
**joint**  articulación *f*
**juice**  jugo; **grapefruit —**
    jugo de toronja; **orange —**
    jugo de china, jugo de
    naranja; **tomato —**  jugo de
    tomate
**July**  julio
**June**  junio

## K

**kidney**  riñón *m;* **— stone**
    piedra nefrítica
**kind** *a*  amable; *n*  tipo, clase
    de
**kitchen**  cocina
**knee**  rodilla
**knife**  cuchillo
**to know**  conocer; saber
**knowledge**  conocimiento
**knuckle**  nudillo

## L

**label**  etiqueta
**labor**  labor *f;* parto
**laboratory**  laboratorio
**lack**  falta
**lamb**  cordero
**lame**  cojo
**language**  idioma *m;* lengua
**large**  grande
**laryngitis**  laringitis *f*
**last**  último
**to last**  durar
**late**  tarde
**later**  después, luego, más
    tarde
**to laugh (at)**  reírse (de)

**law**  ley *f*
**laxative**  laxante *m*
**to learn**  aprender; **— to**
    aprender a
**least**  menos; **at —**  por lo
    menos
**to leave**  dejar, salir
**left**  izquierdo; **to the —**  a la
    izquierda
**leg**  pierna
**lemon**  limón *m*
**to lend**  prestar
**lens**  lente *m;* **contact —**
    lente de contacto
**lesion**  lesión *f*
**less**  menos
**lesson**  lección *f*
**letter**  carta
**lettuce**  lechuga
**leukemia**  leucemia
**to lie**  mentir
**to lie down**  acostar(se); **lying
    down**  acostado
**light**  luz *f;* **to turn off the —**
    apagar la luz; **to turn on the
    —** encender la luz
**likable**  simpático
**like**  como
**to like (to be pleasing to)**
    gustar
**limitation**  limitación *f*
**limited**  limitado
**line**  línea
**liniment**  linimento
**link**  vínculo
**lip**  labio
**liquid**  líquido
**to listen**  escuchar
**to listen with a stethoscope**
    auscultar
**to live**  vivir
**liver**  hígado
**lobster**  langosta
**long**  largo
**to look at**  mirar
**to look for**  buscar
**loop**  lazo

**to lose**  perder; **—
    consciousness**  perder el
    conocimiento; **— weight**
    adelgazar
**loss**  pérdida
**lump**  bulto
**lumpectomy**  lumpectomía
**lunch**  almuerzo; **to have —**
    almorzar
**lung**  pulmón *m*
**lymph gland**  glándula
    linfática
**lymph node**  ganglio linfático
**lymphoma**  linfoma *m*

## M

**machine**  máquina; **ultrasonic
    —** máquina ultrasónica
**mailcarrier**  cartero, -a
**to make**  hacer
**malaria**  malaria, paludismo
**male** *a*  macho; *n*  varón
**to malfunction**  funcionar mal
**malignant**  maligno
**malnourished**  desnutrido
**malnutrition**  desnutrición *f*
**mammography**  mamografía
**man**  hombre *m*
**manner**  manera; **in this —**
    de esta manera
**many**  muchos
**March**  marzo
**margarine**  margarina
**marijuana**  marihuana
**married**  casado
**mask**  máscara
**massage**  masaje *m*
**mastectomy**  mastectomía
**material**  material *m*
**maternity**  maternidad *f*
**May**  mayo
**maybe**  quizá, quizás
**mayonnaise**  mayonesa
**measles**  sarampión *m;*
    **German —**  rubéola
**to measure**  medir
**meat**  carne *f*

**mechanic** mecánico
**medication** medicamento
**medicine** medicina
**member** miembro
**memory** memoria
**meningitis** meningitis *f*
**menopause** menopausia
**menstruation** menstruación *f*
**method** método; **birth control —** método anticonceptivo; **rhythm —** método de ritmo
**mescaline** mescalina
**methadone** metadona
**methedrine** metedrina
**middle** medio
**midnight** medianoche *f*
**midwife** comadrona; partera
**migraine** migraña
**milk** leche; **— of magnesia** leche de magnesia
**minute** minuto
**miscarriage** aborto espontáneo
**Miss** señorita
**moist** húmedo
**molar** muela
**moment** momento
**Monday** lunes *m*
**money** dinero
**month** mes *m*
**more** más; **— or less** más o menos
**morning** mañana; **— sickness** náuseas del embarazo, vómitos del embarazo
**mother** madre *f*; mamá
**mother-in-law** suegra
**mouth** boca; **roof of the —** cielo de la boca
**to move** moverse
**Mr.** señor
**MRI** imagen por resonancia magnética *f*
**Mrs.** señora
**much** mucho; **as —, so —** tanto
**mumps** paperas *f pl*

**mushroom** hongo
**myopia** miopia

## N

**nail** uña
**name** nombre *m*
**to be named** llamarse
**nape** nuca
**narcotic** narcótico
**nausea** náuseas *f pl*
**navel** ombligo
**necessary** necesario
**necessity** necesidad *f*
**neck** cuello
**to need** necesitar
**needle** aguja
**negative** negativo
**neighbor** vecino
**neither** tampoco
**nephew** sobrino
**nerve** nervio; **to deaden the —** adormecer el nervio
**nervous** agitado, nervioso; **— shock** choque nervioso *m*
**neurologist** neurólogo, -a
**to neutralize** neutralizar
**never** nunca
**nevertheless** sin embargo
**newspaper** periódico
**next** próximo, siguiente
**next to** junto (a)
**niece** sobrina
**night** noche *f*; **last —** anoche
**nightmare** pesadilla
**nipple** pezón *m*; **(on baby's bottle)** pezón de biberón *m*
**no** no
**no one** nadie
**noise** ruido
**none** ninguno, -a
**noon** mediodía *m*; **at —** al mediodía
**normal** normal
**nose** nariz *f*; **stuffed —** nariz tupida, nariz tapada
**nostrils** fosas nasales *f pl*
**not** no

**nothing** nada
**to notice** notar
**to notify** avisar; notificar
**November** noviembre *m*
**now** ahora; **right —** ahora mismo
**nuclear scan** gammagrafía
**nuclear scanning** exploración nuclear *f*
**number** número
**nurse** enfermero, -a
**nutrition** nutrición *f*

## O

**obstetrician** obstétrico, -a
**obstetrics** obstetricia
**to obtain** conseguir, obtener
**obvious** obvio
**occupied** ocupado
**to occur** occurrir
**October** octubre *m*
**of** de
**of course** claro
**to offer** ofrecer
**office** consultorio, oficina
**official** oficial
**often** a menudo
**oil** aceite *m*
**ointment** ungüento
**old** anciano, viejo
**older** mayor; **oldest** el/la mayor
**omelette** tortilla
**on** en, encima de, sobre
**on top of** encima de, sobre
**onion** cebolla
**only** sólo; solamente
**open** abierto
**to open** abrir
**to operate** operar
**operating room** sala de operaciones
**operation** operación *f*
**ophthalmologist** oftalmólogo, -a
**opinion** opinión *f*
**opium** opio

**opportunistic**  oportunístico
**opportunity**  oportunidad *f*
**optician**  óptico
**optometrist**  optometrista *mf*
**oral**  oral
**orange**  naranja
**order** *(harmony)*  orden *m;*
   **order** *(command)*  orden *f*
**to order**  mandar
**orderly**  asistente *m*
**organ**  órgano
**orthopedist**  ortopédico, -a;
   ortopedista *mf*
**other**  otro
**ovary**  ovario
**over**  sobre
**overdose**  dosis excesiva *f;*
   sobredosis *f*
**to owe**  deber
**own**  propio
**oxygen**  oxígeno
**oyster**  ostra

**P**

**package**  paquete *m*
**pain**  dolor *m;* **to be in —**
   tener dolor; **labor —s**
   dolores del parto
**pair**  par *m;* **a — of**  un par
   de
**pajamas**  pijamas *f pl*
**palate**  paladar *m*
**pale**  pálido
**palm of the hand**  palma de la
   mano
**palpitation**  palpitación *f*
**Panamanian**  panameño, -a
**pancreas**  páncreas *m*
**PAP smear**  frotis de PAP *m*
**PAP test**  prueba de PAP
**parallel bars**  barras paralelas
   *f pl*
**paralysis**  parálisis *f*
**paralyzed**  paralizado
**parasitological**  parasitológico
**to pardon**  perdonar
**parents**  padres *m pl*

**part**  parte *f*
**to participate**  participar
**particular**  particular
**to pass**  pasar
**patella**  rótula
**patience**  paciencia *f*
**patient**  paciente *mf*
**to pay**  pagar
**PCP**  fenancicladina
**pea**  guisante *m*
**peach**  melocotón *m*
**peanut butter**  crema de
   cacahuete
**pear**  pera
**pediatrician**  pediatra *mf*
**pediatry**  pediatría
**pelvis**  pelvis *f*
**pen**  pluma; **ballpoint —**
   bolígrafo
**pencil**  lápiz *m*
**to penetrate**  penetrar
**penetrating**  penetrante
**penicillin**  penicilina
**penis**  pene *m*
**pepper**  pimienta
**period**  período; **menstrual —**
   regla
**permission**  permiso
**to permit**  permitir
**person**  persona
**personal**  personal
**personality**  personalidad *f*
**Peruvian**  peruano, -a
**pharmacist**  farmacéutico
**pharmacy**  farmacia
**phlegm**  flema
**physical**  físico; **— exam**
   examen físico; **— therapist**
   fisioterapeuta *mf;* **— therapy**
   fisioterapia, terapia física
**physician**  doctora; médico
**to pick up**  recoger
**pickle**  pepinillo
**picture**  foto *f;* **to take —s**
   sacar fotos
**pie**  pastel *m*
**piles**  almorranas *f pl*

**pill**  pastilla, píldora; **sleeping**
   **—**  píldora para dormir
**pillow**  almohada
**pineapple**  piña
**pipe**  tubo
**pistol**  pistola
**pity**  lástima
**pleasant**  agradable
**plum**  ciruela
**pneumonia**  pulmonía
**point**  punto
**poison**  veneno
**to be poisoned**  envenenarse
**police**  policía
**policeman**  policía *m*
**policewoman**  mujer policía
**poliomyelitis**  poliomielitis
**pork**  puerco
**possible**  posible
**possibility**  posibilidad *f*
**possibly**  posiblemente
**postnatal care**  cuidado
   postnatal
**potato**  papa; **baked —**  papa
   al horno; **fried —**  papa frita
**practice**  práctica
**to prefer**  preferir
**preferable**  preferible
**preferably**  preferiblemente
**pregnancy**  embarazo
**pregnancy test**  prueba del
   embarazo
**pregnant**  embarazada,
   encinta, preñada; **to become**
   **—**  embarazarse
**premature**  prematuro
**to prepare**  preparar
**to prescribe**  recetar
**prescription**  receta
**to press**  apretar, oprimir
**pressure**  presión *f;* **blood —**
   presión arterial, presión
   sanguínea; **high blood —**
   alta presión; **low blood —**
   baja presión; **to take the**
   **blood —**  tomar la presión
**pretty**  lindo; bonito

**priest**   cura *m*
**private**   privado
**problem**   problema *m*
**procedure**   procedimiento
**proctoscopy**   proctoscopia
**to produce**   producir
**profession**   profesión *f*
**professor**   profesor, -a
**profoundly**   profundamente
**prognosis**   pronóstico
**progress**   progreso
**prophylatic**   profiláctico
**to protect oneself**   protegerse
**protection**   protección *f*
**protein**   proteína
**prune**   ciruela pasa
**psychiatrist**   psiquiatra *mf*
**psychiatry**   psiquiatría
**psychologist**   psicólogo, -a
**public**   público
**pudding**   pudín *m*
**Puerto Rican**
   puertorriqueño, -a
**to pull**   tirar (de)
**pulmonary angiogram**
   angiograma pulmonar *m*
**pulse**   pulso; **to take the —**
   registrar el pulso
**pumpkin**   calabaza
**pupil**   pupila
**to push**   empujar
**to put**   poner; **— in a cast**
   enyesar; poner en yeso
**(intravenous) pyelogram**
   pielograma intravenoso *m*
**pyorrhea**   piorrea

## Q

**quantity**   cantidad *f*
**quarter**   cuarto
**question**   pregunta; **to ask a
   —**   hacer una pregunta
**quickly**   rápidamente
**quiet**   quieto

## R

**radiation therapy**
   radioterapia

**radioactive**   radioactivo; **—
   material**   materia
   radioactiva; **— substance**
   substancia radioactiva
**radiologist**   radiólogo
**radish**   rábano
**to raise**   levantar; **— oneself,
   to get up**   levantarse
**rape**   violación *f*
**to rape**   violar
**rash**   salpullido
**to read**   leer
**reading**   lectura
**ready**   listo
**reality**   realidad *f*; **in —**   en
   realidad
**really**   de veras, realmente
**reason**   razón *f*
**to receive**   recibir
**receptacle**   vasija
**receptionist**   recepcionista *mf*
**to recommend**   recomendar
**to recuperate**   recuperar
**recuperation**   recuperación *f*
**to register**   registrar
**relative**   familiar *mf*;
   pariente, -a
**relatively**   relativamente
**to relax**   relajar(se)
**to relieve**   aliviar
**to remain**   quedar(se)
**remedy**   remedio
**to remember**   recordar,
   acordarse (de)
**to remove**   quitar(se)
**to repeat**   repetir
**to require**   requerir
**resistance**   resistencia
**to resort to**   recurrir (a)
**respiration**   respiración *f*;
   **artificial —**   respiración
   artificial
**respiratory**   respiratorio
**to respond**   responder
**responsibility**
   responsabilidad *f*
**responsible**   responsable
**rest**   descanso

**to rest**   descansar
**restless**   inquieto
**result**   resultado
**to resuscitate**   resucitar;
   **(mouth-to-mouth)
   resuscitation**   respiración
   boca a boca
**(mentally) retarded**   atrasado
   mentalmente
**retina**   retina
**to return**   regresar; volver
**rib**   costilla
**rice**   arroz *m*
**rich**   rico
**rickets**   raquitis *m*
**right**   derecho; **to the —**   a la
   derecha; **to be —**   tener
   razón; **— away**   en seguida
**ring**   anillo
**to rinse**   enjuagar(se)
**risk**   riesgo
**roast beef**   rosbif *m*
**room**   cuarto, sala; **double —**
   cuarto doble; **private —**
   cuarto privado; **recovery —**
   sala de recuperación
**root**   raíz *f*; **— canal**   canal
   radicular *m*
**to run**   correr
**run over**   atropellado

## S

**saccharin**   sacarina
**sad**   triste
**safely**   con seguridad
**safety**   seguridad *f*
**saliva**   saliva
**salmon**   salmón *m*
**salt**   sal *f*
**Salvadoran**   salvadoreño, -a
**same**   mismo; **the —**   lo
   mismo
**sample**   muestra
**sandwich**   bocadillo
**sanitary**   sanitario
**sardine**   sardina
**Saturday**   sábado
**sausage**   salchicha

**to say** decir
**scalp** cuero cabelludo
**scar** cicatriz *f*
**schizophrenia** esquizofrenia
**school** escuela
**to scratch (oneself)** rascar(se)
**seasick** mareado
**seated** sentado
**secretion** secreción
**to see** ver
**seldom** pocas veces
**to sell** vender
**sensation** sensación *f*
**separated** separado
**September** septiembre
**serious** grave, serio
**to serve** servir
**service** servicio
**set** conjunto
**severe** severo
**sexual** sexual; **— relations**
  relaciones sexuales *f pl*
**to share** compartir
**sharp** agudo
**sheet** sábana
**shellfish** mariscos *m pl*
**shield** escudo
**shin** espinilla
**shirt** camisa
**shoe** zapato
**shopkeeper** dependiente, -a
**short** bajo
**should** deber
**shoulder** hombro; **— blade**
  escápula, omóplato
**to show** mostrar
**shower** ducha
**shrimp** camarones *m pl;*
  gambas *f pl*
**sick** enfermo; **to become —**
  enfermarse
**sickness** enfermedad *f*
**side** lado
**side effects** efectos
  secundarios
**sight** vista
**sigmoidoscopy**
  sigmoidoscopia

**sign** señal *f*
**to sign** firmar
**signal** señal *f*
**to signal** señalar
**simple** sencillo
**since** desde; ya que
**single** soltero
**sinusitis** sinusitis *f*
**sister** hermana
**sister-in-law** cuñada
**to sit down** sentarse
**size** tamaño, medida
**skeleton** esqueleto
**skin** piel *f*
**skinny** flaco, delgado
**skull** cráneo
**to sleep** dormir; **to fall —**
  dormirse
**sleepiness** somnolencia
**sleeping** durmiendo; **— pill**
  somnífero
**to be sleepy** tener sueño
**slender** delgado, flaco
**slight** leve
**sling** cabestrillo; **to put in a**
  **—** poner en cabestrillo
**slipper** zapatilla
**slowly** despacio
**smallpox** viruela
**smart** listo
**to smoke** fumar
**snack** bocadillo
**to sneeze** estornudar
**so** así
**to soak** remojar
**soap** jabón *m*
**sober** sobrio
**social services** servicios
  sociales
**soda** soda
**sodium pentothal** pentotal
  sódico
**sole of the foot** planta del pie
**solid** sólido
**solution** solución *f*
**some** algunos, -as
**something** algo
**son** hijo

**son-in-law** yerno
**sonogram** ecografía;
  sonograma *m*
**soon** pronto; **as — as**
  **possible** lo más pronto
  posible
**to be sorry** lamentar
**sound** sonido
**Spanish** español
**to speak** hablar
**special** especial
**specialist** especialista *mf*
**to specialize** especializar(se)
**specific** específico
**sperm** esperma
**spice** especia
**spicy** picante
**spinach** espinaca
**spiral** espiral *f*
**to spit** escupir
**spleen** bazo
**to spoil (a child)** mimar
**spoon** cuchara
**spoonful** cucharada
**sprain** torcedura
**to sprain** torcer
**squash** calabaza
**to squeeze** apretar
**to stab** apuñalar
**stab wound** puñalada
**to stagger** tambalear
**stairs** escalera; **downstairs**
  escalera abajo; **upstairs**
  escalera arriba
**to stand** parar(se), poner(se)
  de pie
**standing** parado, de pie
**state** estado; **— of health**
  estado de salud
**to stay** quedar(se)
**sterilization** esterilización *f*
**to sterilize** esterilizar
**still** todavía; *a* quieto
**stimulant** estimulante *m*
**to stitch** dar puntadas
**stitches** puntadas *f pl*
**stomach** estómago; **(to lie)**
  **on one's —** boca abajo

**stone**    cálculo, piedra
**to stop**    dejar
**store**    tienda
**straight**    recto
**strained**    colado
**strange**    extraño
**strawberry**    fresa
**street**    calle *f*
**strenuous**    estrenuo
**stress test**    prueba de esfuerzo
**stretcher**    camilla; **to carry on
     a —**    llevar en camilla;
     **stretcher-bearer**    camillero
**strict**    estricto
**strong**    fuerte
**to study**    estudiar
**such**    tal
**to suffer from**    padecer
**sufficient**    bastante, suficiente
**to suffocate**    ahogar(se)
**sugar**    azúcar *m*
**suicide**    suicidio; **to attempt
     —**    atentar el suicidio
**suitcase**    maleta
**Sunday**    domingo
**sunglassess**    gafas de sol *f pl*
**sure**    cierto, seguro
**surgeon**    cirujano, -a
**surgery**    cirugía
**to suspect**    sospechar
**to swallow**    tragar
**sweat**    sudor *m*
**swelling**    hinchazón *m*
**sweet**    dulce
**symptom**    síntoma *m*
**syndrome**    síndrome *m*
**syrup**    jarabe *m*
**system**    sistema *m;* **circulatory
     —**    sistema circulatorio;
     **digestive —**    sistema
     digestivo; **nervous —**
     sistema nervioso; **respiratory
     —**    sistema respiratorio

**T**

**table**    mesa
**tablet**    tableta

**to take**    tomar; **— care of**
     cuidar de; **— charge of**
     encargarse de; **— pictures**
     sacar fotos; **— precautions**
     precaucionar(se); **— the
     pulse**    registrar el pulso
**talcum**    talco
**to talk**    hablar
**talkativeness**    locuacidad *f*
**tall**    alto
**taste**    sabor *m;* gusto
**tea**    té *m*
**teacher**    maestro, -a
**technician**    técnico
**teenager**    jovencito, -a
**telephone**    teléfono; **— call**
     llamada telefónica
**television**    televisión *f*
**to tell**    decir
**temperature**    temperatura
**test**    examen *m;* prueba
**to test**    probar
**testicle**    testículo
**tetanus**    tétano
**to thank**    agradecer
**thank you**    gracias
**that**    que
**then**    entonces, luego
**therapeutic**    terapéutico
**therapist**    terapeuta *mf*
**therapy**    terapia
**there**    allí
**there is, there are**    hay
**thigh**    muslo
**thin**    delgado, flaco
**thing**    cosa
**to think**    pensar; **— about**
     pensar en
**thirst**    sed *f*
**thorax**    tórax *m*
**throat**    garganta
**to throw**    echar; **to — away**
     botar
**thumb**    pulgar *m;* dedo pulgar
**Thursday**    jueves *m*
**time**    hora; tiempo, vez; **at the
     same —**    al mismo tiempo;

**at —s**    a veces; **for a long
     —**    por mucho tiempo;
**many —s**    muchas veces;
**one —**    una vez; **sometimes**
     a veces
**tincture of iodine**    tinta de
     yodo
**tired**    cansado; **to become —**
     cansarse
**tiredness**    cansancio
**to**    a
**today**    hoy
**toe**    dedo del pie
**tolerant**    tolerante
**tomato**    tomate *m*
**tomorrow**    mañana; **the day
     after —**    pasado mañana
**tongue**    lengua
**tonsilitis**    amigdalitis *f*
**tonsils**    amígdalas *f pl*
**too**    también; **— many**
     demasiados, -as; **— much**
     demasiado, -a
**tooth**    diente *m;* **decayed —**
     diente cariado; **false teeth**
     dentadura postiza; **milk —**
     diente de leche; **to fill a —**
     empastar
**toothbrush**    cepillo de
     dientes
**to touch**    tocar
**tourniquet**    torniquete *m*
**toward**    hacia
**towel**    toalla
**toxemia**    toxemia
**tracks**    huellas
**traditional**    tradicional
**tranquilizer**    calmante *m;*
     tranquilizante *m*
**to transmit**    transmitir
**to treat**    tratar (a)
**treatment**    tratamiento
**tremors**    temblores *m pl*
**truly**    de veras
**truth**    verdad *f*
**to try**    probar; **— to**    tratar
     de

**tubal ligation**   ligadura de los tubos
**tube**   tubo
**tuberculin test**   prueba de tuberculina
**tuberculosis**   tuberculosis *f*
**Tuesday**   martes *m*
**tumor**   tumor *m*
**tuna**   atún *m*
**turkey**   pavo
**turn**   turno
**to turn**   doblar, torcer
**twin**   gemelo
**to twist**   torcer
**type**   tipo; clase de *f*
**typhoid**   tifoidea

## U

**ugly**   feo
**ulcer**   úlcera
**ultrasound transmitter**   transmisor ultrasonido *m*
**umbilical cord**   cordón umbilical *m*
**uncle**   tío
**uncomfortable**   incómodo
**underneath**   abajo, debajo de
**to understand**   comprender
**underwear**   ropa interior
**unfortunately**   por desgracia; desafortunadamente
**unit**   unidad *f*
**unguent**   ungüento
**unmarried**   soltero
**unpleasant**   antipático
**until**   hasta
**up**   arriba
**upstairs**   escalera arriba
**urinalysis**   urinálisis *m;* análisis de la orina *m*
**to urinate**   orinar
**urine**   orina; — **sample** muestra de la orina
**urologist**   urólogo
**to use**   usar
**useless**   inútil
**uterus**   útero

**to utilize**   utilizar

## V

**to vaccinate**   vacunar
**vaccination**   vacuna
**vagina**   vagina
**vaginal cream**   crema vaginal
**varied**   variado
**variety**   variedad *f*
**vasectomy**   vasectomía
**veal**   ternera
**vegetable**   legumbre *f;* vegetal *m*
**veneral disease**   enfermedad venérea *f*
**Venezuelan**   venezolano, -a
**vertebral column**   columna vertebral
**very**   muy
**victim**   víctima
**vinegar**   vinagre *m*
**to violate**   violar
**viral**   viral
**virus**   virus *m*
**vision**   visión *f;* vista; **to have good —**   tener buena vista
**visit**   visita
**to visit**   visitar
**vitamin**   vitamina
**vomit**   vómito
**to vomit**   vomitar

## W

**waist**   cintura
**to wait**   esperar
**waiter**   camarero
**waiting room**   sala de espera
**waitress**   camarera
**to wake up**   despertar(se)
**to walk**   caminar
**to want**   desear, querer
**ward**   cuarto múltiple
**warm**   caliente
**to warn**   avisar
**to wash (oneself)**   lavar(se)
**washbasin**   lavabo
**to watch over**   velar

**water**   agua; **bag of —s** bolsa de aguas; **mineral —** agua mineral
**watery**   aguado
**weak**   débil
**Wednesday**   miércoles *m*
**to weigh**   pesar
**weight**   peso; **to gain —** aumentar de peso; **to lose —** perder peso
**(you're) welcome**   de nada, no hay de qué
**well**   bien
**well-being**   bienestar *m*
**wet**   mojado
**what**   que; **what?** ¿que?, ¿cuál?
**wheelchair**   silla de ruedas
**when**   cuando; **when?** ¿cuándo?
**where**   donde; **where?** ¿dónde?; **to where?** ¿a dónde?
**which?**   ¿cuál?
**while**   mientras
**white**   blanco
**who, whom**   quien, quienes; **who?, whom?** ¿quién?, ¿quiénes?
**whole**   entero
**whooping cough**   tos ferina *f*
**why?**   ¿por qué?
**widow**   viuda
**widower**   viudo
**wife**   esposa, mujer
**to win**   ganar
**window**   ventana
**wine**   vino
**wisdom tooth**   muela del juicio
**to wish**   querer
**with**   con
**withdrawal**   retiro; retirada
**within**   por dentro
**woman**   mujer
**womb**   matriz *f;* vientre *m*
**work**   empleo, trabajo

to work    trabajar
worker    trabajador, -a
worried    preocupado
to worry    preocupar(se)
worse    peor
to worsen    empeorar
wound    herida
wrist    muñeca
to write    escribir

# X

X ray    radiografía, rayo X; **to take an —**    hacer una radiografía

# Y

year    año; **last —**    el año pasado

yesterday    ayer; **the day before —**    anteayer
yet    todavía, aún
yolk    yema (del huevo)
young    joven *mf;* **younger** menor; **youngest**    el/la menor
youth    juventud *f*

# Photo Credits

# Index of Medical Vocabulary

# Index of Grammatical and Structural Items